The Triple Thinkers
&
The Wound and the Bow

D1560164

EDMUND WILSON

The Triple Thinkers

&

The Wound and the Bow

A COMBINED VOLUME

With a new foreword by
FRANK KERMODE

NORTHEASTERN UNIVERSITY PRESS
Boston

Northeastern University Press edition 1984

Reprinted 1984 by arrangement with Farrar, Straus and Giroux

Library of Congress Cataloging in Publication Data

Wilson, Edmund, 1895–1972.
The triple thinkers; & The wound and the bow.
Reprint (1st work). Originally published: New York:
Harcourt, Brace, c1938.
Reprint (2nd work). Originally published: New York:
Oxford University Press, 1947.
1. Literature — History and criticism — Addresses,
essays, lectures.   I. Wilson, Edmund. Wound and the
bow. 1984.   II. Title: Triple thinkers.   III. Title:
Wound and the bow.
PN511.W632   1984   809'.03   84-10201
ISBN 0-930350-67-7 (pbk.: alk. paper)

Printed and bound by the Alpine Press, Stoughton,
Massachusetts. The paper is Warren's 1854, an
acid-free sheet.

MANUFACTURED IN THE UNITED STATES OF AMERICA
89   88   87   86   85   84   5   4   3   2   1

Cover photo courtesy of Culver Pictures

ACKNOWLEDGMENTS

Some of the material in *The Triple Thinkers* first appeared in the *Atlantic Monthly*, the *Hound & Horn*, the *New Republic*, the *New Yorker*, and *Partisan Review*. "The Historical Interpretation of Literature" was published by the Princeton University Press in a volume called *The Intent of the Critic*.

A large part of the material in *The Wound and the Bow* appeared in a different form in the *Atlantic Monthly* and the *New Republic*.

CONTENTS

CONTENTS

FOREWORD

THERE WAS a time when literary criticism—with a reasonably secure foundation in high-level journalism—was a possible, though rarely a secure, career for American and English writers. At its best the work of such critics was scholarly but not academic. Now that scholarship finds its only home in the academy, and is not invariably honored even there, we may well feel some nostalgia for an epoch that effectively ended around 1930, when Edmund Wilson, the last and perhaps the greatest of that extinct race, the men of letters, was thirty-five years old and at the height of his powers.

Unlike most modern academic critics, Wilson was an excellent writer and had always at his command a strong, pure, unaffected English style. He was not, as a "creative" writer, in the first class, though he did not lack originality and talent. What he possessed abundantly were the qualities desirable in the best criticism. He was a marvelous reader with a contempt for translation few of us can afford; from early youth he had good Greek and Latin, he was perfectly at home in French, and in later life acquired a competence in Russian and a serviceable knowledge of Hebrew. All this makes him sound like a bookworm, but his interests were by no means merely literary; in his early years especially he was passionately interested in politics, and he was among the first lay critics to give intelligent consideration to the connections between psychoanalysis and literature.

He himself, it must be said, would not have regarded

these interests as separable from his literary activities. His first major critical work, *Axel's Castle* (1931) deals with the relations between the Symbolist aesthetic and the assumptions of such modern writers as Proust and Eliot— a topic that might be thought of as having little political resonance; yet *Axel's Castle* is impregnated by the political and moral views of Wilson at that time. *To the Finland Station* (1940) is a remarkably researched history of the origins and growth of Russian Communism; but the mind that examines the documents and controls the narration is always a literary mind. It is always, moreover, an American mind. Wilson came increasingly to see himself as representing a sort of patriotism that could not survive the mechanization and vulgarity of the modern world, though it had deep roots. Patrician, isolated, independent of opinion, this patriot was often at odds with authority, and in his last years felt somewhat lonely and alien in his own country; he turned back to the past, and having been in his time a great advocate of modernity in art, dwelt more and more on the classics, and wished that literature as well as life had ceased to progress about the time of the invention of the bicycle.

Because he turned away from the here and now, Wilson's influence and authority waned in his last years, and they have not yet recovered. It is as certain as anything can be that they will be restored, provided, of course, that we retain any taste for literary culture. Nobody who has even dabbled in Wilson's trade can fail to be astonished at the efficiency of his preparations, the prodigiousness of his reading in any subject that caught his imagination, from Marx to the Dead Sea Scrolls, and his skill in presenting, explaining, illuminating. Fullness and clarity were the hallmarks of his manner; and he was lucky to have started his work at a time when the United States had journals and publishers who valued such qualities and encouraged such a man to do as he wished.

Though he so often introduced and explained avant-garde writing, Wilson was not as a critic especially "advanced." He admired Sainte-Beuve and Saintsbury, critics more anathematized than read by many of his critical contemporaries. His essay, "The Historical Interpretation of Literature" in *The Triple Thinkers,* will suffice to show how little he would have cared for modern critical theory. He believed that good literature gave quality to life, and that it was therefore of importance in a world which by its economic arrangements imposed terrible privations on the poor and a false bourgeois consciousness on the rest. And he also considered, after the example of Freud, the strange means by which some human beings, though deeply wounded in their childhood, became the instruments of that grace which art can lend their partly ruined world.

Axel's Castle and *To the Finland Station,* usually thought to be his masterpieces, span the Thirties, the decade of the great Depression. The works collected and revised for *The Triple Thinkers* and *The Wound and the Bow* were also produced in that decade. They have the same qualities as the bigger books and reflect the same concerns. In *The Triple Thinkers* Wilson uses a great variety of reading, but is still thinking of himself as providing the kind of criticism the times require rather than simply following out his own interests, as he perhaps sometimes did in later years. It is a requirement calling for a high standard of performance and an individual talent no system of criticism could of itself supply. In "Marxism and Literature," for instance, he is quite clear that Marxist critics, though they might well have something useful to say, cannot dispense with a skill that has nothing to do with political philosophy, namely "literary competence." Literature is valuable not insofar as it complies with any set of beliefs but insofar as it has in it "the principle of life." The essay ends with an expression of a lingering Marxist utopianism, the hope that Communism might one day turn society itself into a work of art; but its deeper message is that the true critic is a disinterested detector of value, and must honor the individual creator.

When Wilson says of Flaubert that he abandoned the notion that there was "any non-bourgeois way out," he must, in a sense, have been thinking of himself; for he too transferred the guilt for the mess the world had got into from the Marxist class war to the human race as a whole. The essays on Paul Elmer More, John Jay Chapman, and "Mr Rolfe" remember an American past and hint at a future less hospitable to learning and dignity, when America, having lost the chance of building a communism acceptable to its great republican past, would choose instead not even a bourgeois culture but a populist substitute. Many future essays would echo this disillusion.

The other essays in *The Triple Thinkers* amply demonstrate the variety of Wilson's gifts. He was a good enough classic to be capable of writing well about A. E. Housman's genius as a classical scholar. The essay on Henry James founded a long tradition of critical inquiry into Jamesian "ambiguity" and particularly into the puzzles of *The Turn of the Screw*; the output of books and articles continues to this day, and all are descendants of Wilson's essay, however little he might have approved of them. The essay on Ben Jonson, boldly diagnosing the poet as anal-erotic, was an equally bold venture into an area jealously guarded by specialists; the test of its value, by the way, is not the correctness of the diagnosis but the use that diagnosis is put to as an instrument of literary criticism.

Finally, the essay "In Honor of Pushkin" is a model of its genre, the introductory essay. Wilson perfected this expository mode, which must both convey information and establish value. It sounds a great deal easier than it is; and of course it helped to be able to read Pushkin in Russian.

The Wound and the Bow, in which the essays are united by a single bonding agent—Wilson's interest in the psychological history of creative writers—is no less important as evidence of the spread of his interests and his energy in furthering them. The long Dickens essay was also a significant critical event, for it was written at a time when the academics showed very little interest in Dickens. They have certainly made up for their neglect by piling up books, but few of these have the vitality of their forerunner, and Wilson's piece is not superseded. Kipling also needed a fresh non-academic approach. George Orwell remarked that, in explaining Kipling's interest, Wilson had to make points that were "to us [the British] boringly obvious." But that is one of the things one may have to do in an introduction, which wasn't primarily meant for the British in any case, and which also makes critical comments—for instance on the stories "Mary Postgate" and "The Gardener"—that are very far from obvious.

"Uncomfortable Casanova" is an essay in which one may presume to see some autobiographical reference. In reading Wilson's accounts of his own childhood it is not difficult to see why he was interested in the connections between harsh childhood experience and adult talent. But here, in a more particular way, he seems to be thinking of the wild goings-on of the American Twenties, in which he played and also chronicled his part. It seemed important to distinguish between the sound and the bad kind of coarseness, to explain why Casanova may make us feel uncomfortable without forfeiting our respect. The *Memoirs* "required the courage of an individual point of view—and they required a capacity for feeling." And "how much of the world" he gets into his book!

There is surely a touch of Wilson in the portrait; not that his books could ever be called coarse. And although he traveled a lot and knew much of the world, the world he gets into his books is primarily the world of books. It is always exciting to watch him accept some great bookish challenge, as he does in his essay on *Finnegans Wake,* written very soon after the publication of that immense and baffling work, and, as so often, before the professors had turned their attention to it.

The final essay on Sophocles not only explains the title of *The Wound and the Bow* and provides the controlling psychological theme of the whole book, but once again demonstrates the ease and range of Wilson's powers of reading and exposition. He continued to practice the critical trade along with many others, and later achieved a new level of celebrity as the literary critic of the *New Yorker,* but it is fair to say that he was never to surpass the achievement of these two midlife collections.

                                        FRANK KERMODE

April 1984

PREFACE TO THE 1948 EDITION
OF THE TRIPLE THINKERS

THIS volume contains nine of the ten essays published under the same title in 1938, with three new ones: *Morose Ben Jonson,* '*Mr. Rolfe,*' and *The Historical Interpretation of Literature.* The old essays have been revised—in some cases, completely re-written. I have never changed seriously the substance of what I wrote in the first edition, but I have sometimes allowed myself references to books which had not then been published—as when I have given Joyce's *Work in Progress* its eventual title of *Finnegans Wake* or mentioned Auden's preface to the new edition of Henry James's *The American Scene.* When I have wanted to note a new event or to add a new idea, I have put it in a post-script or a footnote.

I may take this occasion to comment on certain criticisms that have been made of these essays and of those in *The Wound and the Bow.* It has sometimes been complained in connection with my studies of Dickens and Housman that, because I have had little to say about the humor of the former or the poetry of the latter, I must entirely have failed to appreciate the genius of my subjects. Now, my purpose has always been to try to contribute something new: I have aimed either to present some writer who was not well enough known or, in the case of a familiar writer, to call attention to some neglected aspect of his work or his career. I did not feel that there was anything fresh to say about either the humor of *Pickwick* or the pathos of the *Shropshire Lad.* I thought that I could assume that they were already well known to anyone with enough interest in literature to read a volume of literary criticism. But the classical scholarship of Housman in its bearing on his poetry and his personality and the social and moral criticism embodied in Dickens' later novels have not had justice done them. On the other hand, in the case of a writer like Pushkin or John Jay Chapman, I had to introduce him to a public who knew almost nothing about him, so I have started from the beginning and described his most obvious qualities.

Another objection is perhaps more valid. I have occasionally been accused of conveying a too favorable impression of certain rather imperfect works—notably, Dickens' later novels and Flaubert's *L'Education sentimentale*—by retelling them in such a way as to conjure out of sight their demerits. Well, it is true that it is pleasantly possible to go through a book that one has read before, skimming over the boring parts or disregarding some fundamental weakness, and that one can sometimes in this way arrive at the book that the author *intended* to write but did not quite fill in or rise to, and enjoy it as one could not do otherwise. When I reread *Our Mutual Friend*, for example, probably the weakest of Dickens' social novels, it is true that I leapt over the love scenes and the less successful grotesques, and got for the first time a good view of the general structure of the novel and the purport of its complicated parable, in such a way as is not always easy with even the best of Dickens, who so energetically plays on our interest with first one, then another, of his entertaining groups that we may miss the plan and the point. And so with *L'Education sentimentale*, if one can manage to displace one's attention from the hero, Frédéric Moreau, so that one is no longer bothered by his two-dimensional flatness and his lack of human development, one can survey for the first time the big canvas which Flaubert has animated, but to the historical and esthetic values of which—it is a real and grave fault—Frédéric tends to act as a nonconductor.

When I was writing about James, however, I did not review in this selective way the three long later novels that I had read first twenty years before; and it may be that, if I had done so, I should have given a somewhat different account. In looking into them again just now, I seemed sometimes to catch sight of qualities which I had not appreciated in my college days—at an age when James's lack of real 'love interest' is likely to prejudice one against him—and to which I feared I might not have done justice.

But there is really no way of considering a book independently of one's special sensations in reading it on a particular occasion. In this as in everything else one must allow for a certain relativity. In a sense, one can never read the book that the author originally wrote, and one can never read the same book twice.

1948

THE TRIPLE THINKERS
Twelve Essays on Literary Subjects

What is the artist if he is not a triple thinker?
FLAUBERT TO LOUISE COLET

MR. MORE AND THE MITHRAIC BULL *

I MET Mr. Paul Elmer More several times, but had an extended conversation with him only once. I wrote down a record of it at the time and give it here, as I wrote it then, embedded in a Princeton weekend.

I was taken to Mr. More's house by Dean Gauss, who was one of his closest friends at Princeton. Dean Gauss, on this Saturday afternoon, had a special reason for wanting to consult him.

At that time—this visit took place in the December of 1929—compulsory chapel had been partially abolished at Princeton, but it had been found desirable to make the students attend half the chapel services on Sundays in order to keep them in town over the weekends. Those students who professed unorthodox views—and who were often, as it turned out, the same ones that wanted to spend Saturday nights in Philadelphia or New York—were obliged to attend non-sectarian religious discussions which took place on Sunday evenings and were conducted by members of the faculty in rotation.

That month it had been Dean Gauss's turn, and he had begun on his first evening by attempting to find out how much the students knew about or were interested in religion. It had turned out that, though several boys believed in Heaven, nobody believed in the Devil; and when he had chalked up a list of theological words beginning with *infralapsarian* and *supralapsarian* and ending with *theism* and *deism*, it had been obvious that nobody knew anything about any of them. In dismissing the class,

* Written on the occasion of Paul Elmer More's death, March 9, 1937.

[3]

he had invited them to hand in questions which might stimulate discussion; and the sole response to this had been a letter written in Latin by a freshman and expressing a desire to learn something about Mithraism. Dean Gauss had decided to brush up on the subject by calling on Mr. More, who had the history of religions at his fingertips.

Mr. More had at that time just built himself a new house in the new residential section of Princeton near the Graduate School, and we approached it along a rainy new-laid pavement. The sitting room, where we waited a few moments, was comfortable but rather somber. With its walls densely lined with books, it was pre-eminently the room of a scholar—though there were a few carefully chosen articles of ornament: two small panes of Dutch stained glass, for example, which Mr. More had brought back from Europe and had had inlaid in the glass of a large window at the further end of the room.

But Mr. More did not make us wait long: he appeared almost at once, brisk enough, and greeted us with an alertness and an evident pleasure at having people come to see him, very attractive in a man of sixty-five. He was short and had picked up some of the plumpness that goes with a sedentary occupation. He had a Roman nose, a pale gray eye and an iron lock of hair on his forehead—in general, a peculiar iron-gray aspect. There was in his face much strength and some nobility, but a curious absence of color.

Affably he attended to the tea and began talking about T. S. Eliot, whom he had suggested inviting to Princeton to lecture. I was surprised to see how much he admired Eliot. He told us, in reply to our questions, that Eliot was 'tall and thin, quite strikingly good-looking,' and that he, More, had gone to Eliot's house in London and had met people there. He explained to us that Eliot's grandfather had been chancellor of Washington University in St. Louis at the time when he, More, had been a student there, so that he had already known the poet's family. And as he went on, I came to realize that it was for him a matter of deep gratification to have made the acquaintance of another writer of high intellectual distinction who had come like More himself out of that old Middle-Western world, who had the freedom of that

[4]

literary life of Europe from which More's provincialism had largely shut him out, and who had been kind enough to bring More into contact with it—a man who, with all his brilliant reputation, his position as a god of the young, was yet a scholar and a serious critic, preoccupied with problems of morality, and striving, although by a different route, just as More himself was, to find his way back to the Christian religion.

We talked about Eliot's influence among the students, and More demurred over Eliot's poetry. I asked him whether he didn't admire *The Waste Land*. 'Well, one can see,' he conceded, 'that it's written by a man of parts.' But it seemed to be *The Hippopotamus* which presented the most serious difficulties. 'I must say that it reads aloud very well,' he confessed; but he couldn't understand what Eliot meant by it. I suggested that it was a satire on the Church. 'But,' Mr. More protested, 'I can't understand how Eliot reconciles that with his present position.' I reminded him that Eliot had written the poem a good many years before; but Mr. More only shook his head and repeated that he could not reconcile those two things. Nor could he follow Eliot's enthusiasm for Baudelaire: 'It seems to me that he finds in Baudelaire . . . things that aren't there.' I admitted that there might be something in that, but asked him why he could not admire Baudelaire. 'Why,' he replied—he had an abrupt hesitation, as over the difficulty of dealing urbanely with a subject about which he felt so strongly, with an author of whom he so greatly disapproved, and upon whom, if he had been writing an essay, he would certainly have visited his stinging indignation —'I'm old-fashioned about Baudelaire. I recognize his power— and his significance in his time—but as a guide to life—!' He stopped, and neither Gauss nor I tried to debate the matter further.

It was the moment of the great controversy over Humanism, and we tried to draw him out on this subject. I had been hearing from a friend at Harvard of the belief of the fanatical Babbitt that his doctrine was gradually but surely taking possession of all the ablest minds of the time, and of the legend, circulated among his students, that the old man had a great map in his study and stuck a thumb-tack into it at every point where a Humanist center was supposed to have sprung up. But Mr. More was much more sensible and less pretentious. When Gauss asked him whether he felt it was true that a great tide of Humanism was rising: 'Well,' he replied, 'I'd rather say that it was having a great splurge just now, but it's partly based on misunderstanding.' Yet he spoke with evident satisfaction of an article on Stuart P. Sherman which Seward Collins had recently published in the *Bookman*. Sherman had been the favorite disciple who had turned renegade to the Humanist band—the split had come when Sherman praised Whitman—and Seward Collins had now repudiated Sherman. 'It seems,' remarked Mr. More, 'as if something like a conversion had taken place there.'

Gauss and More discussed their first acquaintance. The Dean in those now remote days had been an eager young journalist and poet, just back from the Paris of the nineties, with long yellow hair and a flowing Latin Quarter tie, and he had written a furious letter of protest to More over a review of some French life of Sainte-Beuve which the latter had published in the *Nation*. 'It wasn't a slating, was it?' said More, almost chuckling at the memory of past ferocity. 'It was just a bit—contemptuous.' He had answered Gauss's letter and received a second letter equally violent. Then he had invited Gauss to lunch and had found him, he said, quite amiable and mild. One of the great sources of More's strength, I realized, lay in the fact that he always knew precisely what he thought and was always ready to face anybody down, uncompromisingly and promptly. I looked at Gauss: his golden locks were gone and had left a prodigiously high domed bald forehead. With his fine profile of a blond South German Dante, in his Princetonian soft shirt and tweed golf suit, he sat today, lying back in his chair, the great expounder of French romanticism, hobnobbing with the great anti-romantic. So much subtler a mind than More, with so much wider a range of imaginative sympathy, and correspondingly so much less fixed in his opinions, he looked out coolly through his eyeglasses without rims on those prejudices and principles of More's which years ago had aroused his indignation. The amenities and responsibilities of Princeton had dimmed the flamboyance of his romanticism. But

Paul Elmer More, still just as positive, still nearly as narrow as then, sat attentively forward in his chair, still ready to face anybody down.

Dean Gauss now remembered Mithra and asked for light from Mr. More on the subject. Mr. More, who had the pride of learning, replied with immediate gusto: 'Why, I don't suppose I know any more about Mithraism than you do, Christian!'—At this moment there came into the room a sister of Mr. More's, who lived with him. She was a pleasant old lady, with none of her brother's asperity—dressed in black and very deaf. She had just been going through her bureau-drawers, she said—'And it's so hard to know what to throw away! It's really not worth the trouble trying to sort things!' Mr. More admitted rather perfunctorily and speaking loudly in order to make her hear, that this did constitute a perplexing problem, and quickly brought the conversation back to Mithra.

'Well,' he demanded in a brisk businesslike manner, pouring his sister a cup of tea, 'what d'ye want to know about Mithraism, Christian?' His voice, nasal, clear and Middle-Western, had a suggestion, not unattractive, of the homely plain-spoken manner of the old successful American merchant or banker. 'The Mithraic bee,' began Gauss, 'was a symbol of immortality—' 'I've never heard of that,' Mr. More caught him up. 'Where'd you find that?' 'I can't remember where,' replied Gauss. 'That's what I wanted to ask you. I read it years ago in some book and I can't remember now what it was. I thought you might know.' But Mr. More did not know: he mentioned all the books he had read that dealt with Mithraism and said that there was nothing in any of them about it. What he knew, it was plain, he knew: he needed to consult no index. 'I suppose,' Dean Gauss pursued, 'that the bee came to stand for immortality through the belief that bees were bred spontaneously in the carcasses of dead animals. It was really the carrion-fly. Virgil talks about it in the *Georgics*.' 'The "out of the strong came forth sweetness" of the Bible,' put in Mr. More. 'Yes,' said Gauss. 'Clovis was a Mithraist—' 'That I didn't know,' said Mr. More. 'Yes, Clovis was a Mithraist,' the Dean pursued, 'and his emblem before his conversion was the bee.' 'Is that a guess?'

[7]

demanded Mr. More. 'No,' said the Dean. 'I read it all some-where, but I can't remember where.' Clovis's bee, which Mr. More had never heard of and as to which, failing definite author-ity, he was not prepared to indulge in speculation, seemed to have made him a shade impatient. He delivered, however, a short lecture on what he did know about Mithraic myths; and it was amazing how much he knew and how accurately he was able to retail it. He traced Mithra, the God of Light, from the Vedic hymns into Persian mythology, and from the Orient into Greece, indicating his various transformations with confidence, lucidity and logic, but with a curious effect of his having retained them as ideas without their passing through the picture-making imagina-tion. And yet the Mithra he described was alive, devoid of mys-tery, form or color though he was. It reminded me of a book called *Error's Chains*, which I had used to look at in my grand-father's library and which had had many illustrations of the heathen gods, old line drawings done from paintings and statues. —Miss More was sitting beside me on the couch and could not hear the general conversation, so we talked separately from time to time while the discussion of Mithraism proceeded. 'You might just as well take it all out and burn it up!' she declared, still thinking of her bureau-drawers. 'When it's been accumulating as long as that, it's not worth the trouble to go through it and pick things out to save!'

At this point Mr. Frank Jewett Mather arrived. He was a cheer-ful little man in a checked vest and spats, with the cocky pointed mustache of an old beau and the rosiness of a child. And he turned out to know a lot about Mithraism. He told us that it had had a great success with the Roman soldiers because it had promised them a sure immortality, and that it had developed in the third century into a serious competitor to Christianity.—Mr. More's sis-ter suddenly got up: 'I'm going to burn up all that old stuff!' she announced, with the air of one who has finally arrived at a thor-oughly satisfactory resolution—and she said good-by and went upstairs.—Mr. Mather explained in detail the symbolism of Mithraic art. There was a Mithraic bull in the Museum, he said, which he had bought and brought back from Europe and which was one of the best things the Museum had. 'I didn't know that,' said Gauss with interest. 'I must go over and see it.' 'It's the best Mithraic bull on this side,' said Mather. 'The only really first-rate one.' It was a marble relief of the Sun-God holding a bull by the horns; there was a dog which was leaping at the throat of the bull and a snake which was attacking his testicles; the snake and the dog were Evil and Darkness. 'Let's go over and see it!' the Dean proposed to me.

Mr. More now reverted to the days of the *Nation*. He told us that Oswald Garrison Villard had sometimes disapproved of what he wrote but had always had somebody else speak to him about it. Mr. More seemed frankly delighted at this evidence that Villard had found him formidable. 'Afraid the "inner check" wouldn't work!' Frank Mather impishly put in. But Mr. More possessed no technique to deal with people who made jokes about Humanism and did not deign to reply to this. 'Who originated the term "inner check"? Was it you or Babbitt?' asked Mather. 'I was the first to use it,' said More. 'In the *Shelburne Essays*. But Babbitt has made much more of it than I have.' And he added, after a moment's pause: 'I think the phrase occurs once in Emerson.'

In the course of the conversation that followed, Mr. Mather ventured to remark that he didn't see how Humanism was going to get us very far by going back to the Council of Chalcedon. Mr. More was then nearing the completion of his series of volumes on Greek philosophy and Christianity. A man of true spiritual vocation, unable to remain a simple rationalist but prevented by a Protestant education and an obstinate hardheaded common sense from finding a basis in the mysticism of Rome, he had devoted long and diligent years to establishing an historical tradition which would justify his peculiar point of view. At that time he had just published the volume which brought the line of development to its climax with the promulgation at Chalcedon in the fifth century of the dogma of the Incarnation—a doctrine which, in laying down the dual nature of Christ, in representing him as both human and divine, had seemed to Mr. More to make it possible for him to preserve the philosophy of Plato, so attractive to his intellectual and esthetic side, and at the same time not to cut himself loose from the supernatural authority of religion. So he made no reply to this gibe—but presently, with a

[9]

touch of severity, accused Mather of being 'a half-way Platonist like Santayana.' He seemed to me that day very clear-cut against the background of the college community. He was himself not really typical of the American academic world: he was an independent scholar, who had denounced in the most vigorous language the lack of sincerity and the incompetence of the colleges. He stood out, not merely through his distinction of learning, his Greek and Sanskrit and Hebrew and Persian and the rest, but by reason of his unremitting seriousness, his stubborn insistence on the importance of maintaining in one's relation to literature a position which should be realistic in the sense that it would never lose contact with moral problems as he himself understood them, his refusal to allow himself to be seduced by purely esthetic or intellectual satisfactions. Gauss told him about a student at one of the Sunday-night meetings who had put himself down as a 'synthetic hedonist'; More smiled, but said, 'I wonder what he meant.'

We discussed an exhibition of modern art then on view in New York. Gauss thought Seurat essentially classical, but Mather insisted that he was decadent: Seurat's figures, he said, seemed to be perfectly realized, but actually they were hanging in the air, like the characters of Proust or Henry James, with no real connection with anything. And this led us to contemporary writing. Mr. More, who in a recent essay had allowed his intolerance of his contemporaries to go to lengths of positive ill temper in characterizing as 'an explosion in a cesspool' Dos Passos's *Manhattan Transfer*, conceded now, with an evident desire to be fair, that he 'recognized the element of protest in Dos Passos and Joyce.' I said that, though there was protest in Dos Passos, I did not believe there was any in Joyce, and thus unfortunately deprived Mr. More of his only excuse for being polite about *Ulysses*. He was afterwards to give more serious consideration to such writers as Joyce and Proust. His last volume of *Shelburne Essays* contained papers on these two novelists, which, uncongenial to More though the subjects were, show more grasp of what is really at issue in their books than most of the stuff which has been written to exalt them. The moralist in Paul Elmer More, who had always been at war with the poet and who had scored over him so crushing a victory, could usually be counted upon to formulate clearly—though of course a clear formulation may misrepresent a poet—the case of any writer, however abhorrent, who had a serious moral basis, even though the provincial prig who inseparably accompanied the moralist might prevent him from appreciating the artist's achievement. But at that time I do not think he had read *Ulysses*; and I myself was a little touchy on the subject, as my attention had just been called by Gauss to an editorial in *The New York Times* that morning in which one of their anonymous writers had ridiculed an article of mine on Joyce. Now I was further dismayed, as it seemed to me that these three men, in their fields of literature and art certainly among the ablest in the country, were themselves disposed to outlaw from literature the greatest literary artist then alive. The same confounded old academic inertia! I thought; the same old proprietary interest in the classics, which made them unwilling to believe that anything new could have great value! I remembered how thirteen years before it had been the same thing about Bernard Shaw, then already practically a classic. Dean Gauss had read *Ulysses*, but had not liked it much; and, though it turned out that Mather, the old rascal, had investigated Mrs. Bloom's soliloquy, he would not commit himself on the subject. Paul Elmer More, who, as I say, had evidently not yet read Joyce, began by trying to handle the matter without heat, but when I talked about the Homeric parallel—at the suggestion of such a fellow as Joyce's having the effrontery to associate himself with one of the major Greek classics—his arrogance suddenly started up from behind his deliberate urbanity, and he sharply cut down on the discussion—(it had also been a question of whether the characters in *Ulysses* were 'purposive' or mere passive recorders of impressions): 'But Homer's Ulysses knew what he wanted. He didn't need special explanations!' It seemed to me that there were so many misconceptions lodged behind this remark of Mr. More's that I had difficulty in knowing how to deal with it. The conversation became rather confused and took on a slightly acrimonious accent. Somebody changed the subject, and Mr. More proposed showing us his new house.

[11]

We went upstairs. On one side of the hallway which led to Mr. More's study was a bookcase entirely filled with detective stories, which I was told he systematically graded with A's, B's, C's and D's. On the shelves of his study were Plato and Plotinus and the Fathers of the Church. Frank Mather mischievously inquired where the Acts of the Council of Chalcedon were kept, and More as usual made no reply. The study was a small unpretentious room at the very top of the house: it had one large Morris chair and a table and a desk. On the walls hung two framed photographs, yellowish-brownish: one of Perugino's *Crucifixion* and the other of two battered Greek torsos, with both arms and legs broken off, awkwardly reclining together. They faced one another across the room, the Christian world and the Greek, and seemed to neutralize one another.

Then we descended and took our leave. Still chafing at More's attitude toward Joyce, I asked him, just as we were going out the door, whether he had ever read Eliot on *Ulysses*. He replied that he had not, and I told him that Eliot considered *Ulysses* a work of the highest importance. His whole attitude toward Eliot, so friendly before seemed, as if by reflex action, to stiffen. 'I don't see,' he retorted, 'what *Ulysses* has to do with Royalism, Anglo-Catholicism and Classicism!'—and added, 'That young man has a screw loose somewhere!' 'Would you agree with Huneker,' said Mather, 'that it's impossible for the same person really to like both Raphael and Goya?' 'I don't think,' Mr. More replied, 'that that pair is particularly well chosen; but I should say that a capacity for enjoying certain authors made it impossible to enjoy Dante or Shakespeare or Milton—or rather, I should say that, if a man liked certain things and claimed to enjoy Shakespeare and Dante, it would be impossible that he should really appreciate them!'

On this implacable dictum we went.

The next day I took a walk on the campus. It was dreary, misty and damp. I remembered the Mithraic bull and decided to look it up in the Museum. There it was, sure enough, right opposite the front door as I went in, shining in the dim afternoon: the white marble relief of Mithra, a naked youth in a peaked Phrygian cap, clasping the sacred bull, which had the dog and the snake that were Darkness and Evil threatening its throat and its balls. But the Sun-God was to kill the bull, and thereby to conquer the darkness and to make himself the creator of life, all the multiform life of the earth, which was to spring from the bull's ebbing blood. There they hung—once the light of those pagan caves to which the soldiers from their doomed legions had crept, once the Apollonian rivals of the Crucified—there they hung in the Princeton Museum on a Sunday afternoon! I went on to the glass-cases inside, but—Roman busts, Egyptian gods, Greek marbles—almost everything was a reproduction and gave me the impression of being denatured and canned. The afternoon light was gray, the rooms were becoming chill. I turned back and stood before the Mithra, which—round and complete and glowing—seemed the only thing alive in the Museum. I remembered with what amazement, a wonder that became exaltation, I had come upon the Apollo Belvedere when I had first visited Rome as a child—how I had turned back to stare at its beauty.

I went over to the University Library and sat down and wrote the *Times* a caustic letter about their sneering editorial on Joyce.

Then I went to see if Gauss were free. He had been busy all the afternoon and had evidently had a great many people: Sunday visitors, college officials, protesting parents of students whom he had disciplined. He always gave his closest attention to anything that was submitted for his decision and dealt with it according to his most scrupulous judgment; and I thought his mind was tired. And now he had to prepare his talk for the evening religious meeting. But he revived when I told him that I had been to see the bull and was all for going to the Museum at once. He got his hat and coat and stick, and we set out.

'It's curious,' he mused on the way, 'how closely it paralleled Christianity. They had a sacrifice, a communion and an atonement. The bull was killed in a cave, and that symbolized the resurrection.'—He spoke of his affection for More and told me a curious story. When More had come back recently from Italy, he had announced with gratification and assurance that he had discovered the finest picture in Florence. Gauss had said to him: 'I'll bet I can guess what it is! Don't tell me—I'll bet I can guess what you think is the finest picture in Florence!'—and he guessed Perugino's *Crucifixion*. He was right; More had been quite taken aback. 'But how did you know?' I asked. 'Why should he have liked that picture particularly?' 'Why, you see Christ way up there —so far above the world.'

But when we got to the Museum, it was dark, and we found that the front door had been locked. We squinted at the marble through the glass, but it was scarcely visible now: we could make out only a whitish blur at the bottom of the cavernous entrance hall. We walked around the building and found a side-door unlocked and went in. Obstinately, we climbed stairs, explored galleries, invaded classrooms and studios for classes, with their chalky plaster casts of famous statues; but all the doors into the Museum proper turned out to be locked tight for the night. A late student in one of the classrooms suggested that we might try to find the curator; but the curator was not in his office, and all the other offices were dark.

We walked back across the campus and parted. The Dean had to go to the library to look up some more about Mithra, and I remained in his office to type out my letter on Joyce.

The visit long haunted my memory, and now the news of Mr. More's death has brought it back into my mind: the empty academic week end, the new suburban house, the meetings for the discussion of religion designed to bring the students back to town, the Acts of the Council of Chalcedon, the nice old lady with her firm resolution to burn all that old stuff up, the argument over Joyce, More himself with his lifelong consecration to that great world of culture and thought which he had succeeded in making real to others but which he could never quite rejoin himself, and Gauss and I peering at Mithra through the glass.

IS VERSE A DYING TECHNIQUE?

THE MORE one reads the current criticism of poetry by poets and their reviewers, the more one becomes convinced that the discussion is proceeding on false assumptions. The writers may belong to different schools, but they all seem to share a basic confusion.

This confusion is the result of a failure to think clearly about what is meant by the words 'prose,' 'verse,' and 'poetry'—a question which is sometimes debated but which never gets straightened out. Yet are not the obvious facts as follows?

What we mean by the words 'prose' and 'verse' are simply two different techniques of literary expression. Verse is written in lines with a certain number of metrical feet each; prose is written in paragraphs and has what we call rhythm. But what is 'poetry,' then? What I want to suggest is that 'poetry' formerly meant one kind of thing but that it now means something different, and that one ought not to generalize about 'poetry' by taking all the writers of verse, ancient, medieval and modern, away from their various periods and throwing them together in one's mind, but to consider both verse and prose in relation to their functions at different times.

The important thing to recognize, it seems to me, is that the literary technique of verse was once made to serve many purposes for which we now, as a rule, use prose. Solon, the Athenian statesman, expounded his political ideas in verse; the *Works and Days* of Hesiod are a shepherd's calendar in verse; his *Theogony* is versified mythology; and almost everything that in contempo-

[15]

rary writing would be put into prose plays and novels was versified by the Greeks in epics or plays.

It is true that Aristotle tried to discriminate. 'We have no common name,' he wrote, 'for a mime of Sophron or Xenarchus and
a Socratic conversation; and we should still be without one even
if the imitation in the two instances were in trimeters or elegiacs
or some other kind of verse—though it is the way with people
to tack on "poet" to the name of a meter, and talk of elegiac-
poets and epic-poets, thinking that they call them poets not by
reason of the imitative nature of their work, but indiscriminately
by reason of the meter they write in. Even if a theory of medicine
or physical philosophy be put forth in a metrical form, it is usual
to describe the writer in this way; Homer and Empedocles, however, have really nothing in common apart from their meter; so
that, if the one is to be called a poet, the other should be termed
a physicist rather than a poet.'

But he admitted that there was no accepted name for the
creative—what he calls the 'imitative'—art which had for its me-
diums both prose and verse; and his posterity followed the custom of which he had pointed out the impropriety by calling anything in meter a 'poem.' The Romans wrote treatises in verse on
philosophy and astronomy and farming. The 'poetic' of Horace's
Ars Poetica applies to the whole range of ancient verse—though
Horace did think it just as well to mingle the 'agreeable' with the
'useful'—and this essay in literary criticism is itself written in
meter. 'Poetry' remained identified with verse; and since for centuries both dramas and narratives continued largely to be written
in verse, the term of which Aristotle had noticed the need—a term
for imaginative literature itself, irrespective of literary techniques
—never came into common use.

But when we arrive at the nineteenth century, a new conception of 'poetry' appears. The change is seen very clearly in the
doubts which began to be felt as to whether Pope were really a
poet. Now, it is true that a critic like Johnson would hardly have
assigned to Pope the position of pre-eminence he does at any
other period than Johnson's own; but it is *not* true that only a
critic of the latter part of the eighteenth century, a critic of an
'age of prose,' would have considered Pope a poet. Would not

Pope have been considered a poet in any age before the age of Coleridge?

But the romantics were to redefine 'poetry.' Coleridge, in the *Biographia Literaria*, denies that any excellent work in meter may be properly called a 'poem.' 'The final definition . . .' he says, 'may be thus worded. A poem is that species of composition which is opposed to works of science by proposing for its *immediate* object pleasure, not truth; and from all other species—(having *this* object in common with it)—it is discriminated by proposing to itself such delight from the *whole* as is compatible with a distinct gratification from each component part.' This would evidently exclude the *Ars Poetica* and the *De Rerum Natura*, whose immediate objects are as much truth as pleasure. What is really happening here is that for Coleridge the function of 'poetry' is becoming more specialized. Why? Coleridge answers this question in formulating an objection which may be brought against the first part of his definition: 'But the communication of pleasure may be the immediate object of a work not metrically composed; and that object may have been in a high degree attained, as in novels and romances.' Precisely; and the novels and romances were formerly written in verse, whereas they are now usually written in prose. In Coleridge's time, tales in verse were more and more giving place to prose novels. Before long, novels in verse such as *Aurora Leigh* and *The Ring and the Book* were to seem more or less literary oddities. 'Poetry,' then, for Coleridge, has become something which, unless he amends his definition, may equally well be written in prose: Isaiah and Plato and Jeremy Taylor will, as he admits, be describable as 'poetry.' Thereafter, he seems to become somewhat muddled; but he finally arrives at the conclusion that the 'peculiar property of poetry' is 'the property of exciting a more continuous and equal attention than the language of prose aims at, whether colloquial or written.'

The truth is that Coleridge is having difficulties in attempting to derive his new conception of poetry from the literature of the past, which has been based on the old conception. Poe, writing thirty years later, was able to get a good deal further. Coleridge had said—and it seems to have been really what he was principally trying to say—that 'a poem of any length neither can be,

[17]

nor ought to be, all poetry.' (Yet are not the *Divine Comedy* and Shakespeare's tragedies 'all poetry'? Or rather, in the case of these masterpieces, is not the work as a whole really a 'poem,' maintained, as it is, at a consistently high level of intensity and style and with the effects of the different parts dependent on one another?) Poe predicted that 'no very long poem would ever be popular again,' and made 'poetry' mean something even more special by insisting that it should approach the indefiniteness of music. The reason why no very long poem was ever to be popular again was simply that verse as a technique was then passing out of fashion in every department of literature except those of lyric poetry and the short idyl. The long poems of the past—Shakespeare's plays, the *Divine Comedy*, the Greek dramatists and Homer—were going to continue to be popular; but writers of that caliber in the immediate future were not going to write in verse.

Matthew Arnold was to keep on in Coleridge's direction, though by a route somewhat different from Poe's. He said, as we have heard so repeatedly, that poetry was at bottom a criticism of life; but, though one of the characteristics which true poetry might possess was 'moral profundity,' another was 'natural magic,' and 'eminent manifestations of this magical power of poetry' were 'very rare and very precious.' 'Poetry' is thus, it will be seen, steadily becoming rarer. Arnold loved quoting passages of natural magic and he suggested that the lover of literature should carry around in his mind as touchstones a handful of such topnotch passages to test any new verse he encountered. His method of presenting the poets makes poetry seem fleeting and quintessential. Arnold was not happy till he had edited Byron and Wordsworth in such a way as to make it appear that their 'poetry' was a kind of elixir which had to be distilled from the mass of their work—rather difficult in Byron's case: a production like *Don Juan* does not really give up its essence in the sequences excerpted by Arnold.

There was, to be sure, some point in what Arnold was trying to do for these writers: Wordsworth and Byron both often wrote badly and flatly. But they would not have lent themselves at all to this high-handed kind of anthologizing if it had not been that, by this time, it had finally become almost impossible to handle large subjects successfully in verse. Matthew Arnold could have done nothing for Dante by reducing him to a little book of extracts—nor, with all Shakespeare's carelessness, for Shakespeare. The new specialized idea of poetry appears very plainly and oddly when Arnold writes about Homer: the *Iliad* and the *Odyssey*, which had been for the Greeks fiction and scripture, have come to appear to this critic long stretches of ancient legend from which we may pick out little crystals of moral profundity and natural magic.

And in the meantime the ideas of Poe, developed by the Symbolists in France, had given rise to the *Art poétique* of Verlaine, so different from that of Horace: 'Music first of all . . . no Color, only the *nuance*! . . . Shun Point, the murderer, cruel Wit and Laughter the impure. . . Take eloquence and wring its neck! . . . Let your verse be the luck of adventure flung to the crisp morning wind that brings us a fragrance of thyme and mint—and all the rest is literature.'

Eliot and Valéry followed. Paul Valéry, still in the tradition of Poe, regarded a poem as a specialized machine for producing a certain kind of 'state.' Eliot called poetry a 'superior amusement,' and he anthologized, in both his poems and his essays, even more fastidiously than Arnold. He, too, has his favorite collection of magical and quintessential passages; and he possesses an uncanny gift for transmitting to them a personal accent and imbuing them with a personal significance. And as even those passages of Eliot's poems which have not been imitated or quoted often seemed to have been pieced together out of separate lines and fragments, so his imitators came to work in broken mosaics and 'pinches of glory'—to use E. M. Forster's phrase about Eliot— rather than with conventional stanzas.

The result has been an optical illusion. The critic, when he read the classic, epic, eclogue, tale or play, may have grasped it and enjoyed it as a whole; yet when the reader reads the comment of the critic, he gets the impression, looking back on the poem, that the *Divine Comedy*, say, so extraordinarily sustained and so beautifully integrated, is remarkable mainly for Eliot-like fragments. Once we know Matthew Arnold's essay, we find that the ἀνήριθμον γέλασμα of Aeschylus and the 'daffodils that come before the swallow dares' of Shakespeare tend to stick out from their contexts in a way that they hardly deserve to. Matthew Arnold, unintentionally and unconsciously, has had the effect of making the poet's 'poetry' seem to be concentrated in the phrase or the line.

Finally, Mr. A. E. Housman, in his lecture on *The Name and Nature of Poetry*, has declared that he cannot define poetry. He can only become aware of its presence by the symptoms he finds it producing: 'Experience has taught me, when I am shaving of a morning, to keep watch over my thought, because if a line of poetry strays into my memory, my skin bristles so that the razor ceases to act. This particular symptom is accompanied by a shiver down the spine; there is another which consists in a constriction of the throat and a precipitation of water to the eyes; and there is a third which I can only describe by borrowing a phrase from one of Keats's last letters, where he says, speaking of Fanny Brawne, "everything that reminds me of her goes through me like a spear." The seat of this sensation is the pit of the stomach.'

One recognizes these symptoms; but there are other things, too, which produce these peculiar sensations: scenes from prose plays, for example (the final curtain of *The Playboy of the Western World* could make one's hair stand on end when it was first done by the Abbey Theater), passages from prose novels (Stephen Daedalus' broodings over his mother's death in the opening episode of *Ulysses* and the end of Mrs. Bloom's soliloquy), even scenes from certain historians, such as Mirabeau's arrival in Aix at the end of Michelet's *Louis XVI*, even passages in a philosophical dialogue: the conclusion of Plato's *Symposium*. Though Housman does praise a few long English poems, he has the effect, like these other critics, of creating the impression that 'poetry' means primarily lyric verse, and this only at its most poignant or most musical moments.

Now all that has been said here is, of course, not intended to belittle the value of what such people as Coleridge and Poe, Arnold and Eliot have written on the subject of poetry. These men are all themselves first-class poets; and their criticism is very important because it constitutes an attempt to explain what they have aimed at in their own verse, of what they have conceived, in their age, to be possible or impossible for their medium.

Yet one feels that in the minds of all of them a certain confusion persists between the new idea of poetry and the old—between Coleridge's conception, on the one hand, and Horace's, on the other; that the technique of prose is inevitably tending more and more to take over the material which had formerly provided the subjects for compositions in verse, and that, as the two techniques of writing are beginning to appear, side by side or combined, in a single work, it is becoming more and more impossible to conduct any comparative discussion of literature on a basis of this misleading division of it into the departments of 'poetry' and of 'prose.'

One result of discussion on this basis, especially if carried on by verse-writers, is the creation of an illusion that contemporary 'poets' of relatively small stature (though of however authentic gifts) are the true inheritors of the genius and carriers-on of the tradition of Aeschylus, Sophocles and Virgil, Dante, Shakespeare and Milton. Is it not time to discard the word 'poetry' or to define it in such a way as to take account of the fact that the most intense, the most profound, the most beautifully composed and the most comprehensive of the great works of literary art (which for these reasons are also the most thrilling and give us most prickly sensations while shaving) have been written sometimes in verse technique, sometimes in prose technique, depending partly on the taste of the author, partly on the mere current fashion. It is only when we argue these matters that we become involved in absurdities. When we are reading, we appraise correctly. Matthew Arnold cites examples of that 'natural magic' which he regards as one of the properties of 'poetry' from Chateaubriand and Maurice de Guérin, who did not write verse but prose, as well as from Shakespeare and Keats; and he rashly includes Molière among the 'larger and more splendid luminaries in the poetical heaven,' though Molière was scarcely more 'poetic' in any sense except perhaps that of 'moral profundity' when he wrote verse than when he wrote prose and would certainly not have versified at all if the conventions of his time had not demanded it. One who has first come to Flaubert at a sensitive age when he is also

[21]

reading Dante may have the experience of finding that the paragraphs of the former remain in his mind and continue to sing just as the lines of the latter do. He has got the prose by heart unconsciously just as he has done with favorite passages of verse; he repeats them, admiring the form, studying the choice of words, seeing more and more significance in them. He realizes that, though Dante may be greater than Flaubert, Flaubert belongs in Dante's class. It is simply that by Flaubert's time the Dantes present their visions in terms of prose drama or fiction rather than of epics in verse. At any other period, certainly, *La Tentation de Saint Antoine* would have been written in verse instead of prose.

And if one happens to read Virgil's *Georgics* not long after having read Flaubert, the shift from verse to prose technique gets the plainest demonstration possible. If you think of Virgil with Tennyson, you have the illusion that the Virgilian poets are shrinking; but if you think of Virgil with Flaubert, you can see how a great modern prose-writer has grown out of the great classical poets. Flaubert somewhere—I think, in the Goncourt journal—expresses his admiration for Virgil; and, in method as well as in mood, the two writers are often akin. Flaubert is no less accomplished in his use of words and rhythms than Virgil; and the poet is as successful as the novelist in conveying emotion through objective statement. The *Georgics* were seven years in the writing, as *Madame Bovary* was six. And the fact that—in *Madame Bovary* especially—Flaubert's elegiac feeling as well as his rural settings run so close to the characteristic vein of Virgil makes the comparison particularly interesting. Put the bees of the *Georgics*, for example, whose swarming Virgil thus describes:

> *aethere in alto*
> *Fit sonitus, magnum mixtae glomerantur in orbem*
> *Praecipitesque cadunt*

beside the bees seen and heard by Emma Bovary on an April afternoon: 'quelquefois les abeilles, tournoyant dans la lumière, frappaient contre les carreaux comme des balles d'or rebondissantes.' Put

> *Et iam summa procul villarum culmina fumant,*
> *Maioresque cadunt altis de montibus umbrae*

[22]

beside: 'La tendresse des anciens jours leur revenait au cœur, abondante et silencieuse comme la rivière qui coulait, avec autant de mollesse qu'en apportait le parfum des seringas, et projetait dans leurs souvenirs des ombres plus démesurées et plus mélancoliques que celles des saules immobiles qui s'allongeaient sur l'herbe.' And compare Virgil's sadness and wistfulness with the sadness and nostalgia of Flaubert: the melancholy of the mountainous pastures laid waste by the cattle plague:

desertaque regna
Pastorum, et longe saltus lateque vacantes

with the modern desolations of Paris in L'*Education sentimentale*: 'Les rues étaient désertes. Quelquefois une charrette lourde passait, en ébranlant les pavés,' etc.; or Palinurus, fallen into the sea, swimming with effort to the coast of Italy, but only to be murdered and left there 'naked on the unknown sand,' while his soul, since his corpse lies unburied, must forever be excluded from Hades, or Orpheus still calling Eurydice when his head has been torn from his body, till his tongue has grown cold and the echo of his love has been lost among the river banks—compare these with Charles Bovary, a schoolboy, looking out on fine summer evenings at the sordid streets of Rouen and sniffing for the good country odors 'qui ne venaient pas jusqu'à lui'—('tendebantque manus ripae ulterioris amore')—or with the scene in which Emma Bovary receives her father's letter and remembers the summers of her girlhood, with the galloping colts and the bumping bees, and knows that she has spent all her illusions in maidenhood, in marriage, in adultery, as a traveler leaves something of his money at each of the inns of the road.

We find, in this connection, in Flaubert's letters the most explicit statements. 'To desire to give verse-rhythm to prose, yet to leave it prose and very much prose,' he wrote to Louise Colet (March 27, 1853), 'and to write about ordinary life as histories and epics are written, yet without falsifying the subject, is perhaps an absurd idea. Sometimes I almost think it is. But it may also be a great experiment and very original.' The truth is that Flaubert is a crucial figure. He is the first great writer in prose deliberately to try to take over for the treatment of ambitious subjects the delicacy, the precision and the intensity that have hitherto been identified with verse. Henrik Ibsen, for the poetic drama, played a role hardly less important. Ibsen began as a writer of verse and composed many short and non-dramatic poems as well as *Peer Gynt* and *Brand* and his other plays in verse, but eventually changed over to prose for the concentrated Sophoclean tragedies that affected the whole dramatic tradition. Thereafter the dramatic 'poets'—the Chekhovs, the Synges and the Shaws (Hauptmann had occasional relapses)—wrote almost invariably in prose. It was by such that the soul of the time was given its dramatic expression: there was nothing left for Rostand's alexandrines but fireworks and declamation.

In the later generation, James Joyce, who had studied Flaubert and Ibsen as well as the great classical verse-masters, set out to merge the two techniques. Dickens and Herman Melville had occasionally resorted to blank verse for passages which they meant to be elevated, but these flights had not matched their context, and the effect had not been happy. Joyce, however, now, in *Ulysses*, has worked out a new medium of his own which enables him to exploit verse metrics in a texture which is basically prose; and he has created in *Finnegans Wake* a work of which we cannot say whether it ought, in the old-fashioned phraseology, to be described as prose or verse. A good deal of *Finnegans Wake* is written in regular meter and might perfectly well be printed as verse, but, except for the interpolated songs, the whole thing is printed as prose. As one reads it, one wonders, in any case, how anything could be demanded of 'poetry' by Coleridge with his 'sense of novelty and freshness with old and familiar objects,' by Poe with his indefiniteness of music, by Arnold with his natural magic, by Verlaine with his nuance, by Eliot with his unearthliness, or by Housman with his bristling of the beard, which the *Anna Livia Plurabelle* chapter (or canto) does not fully supply.

If, then, we take literature as a whole for our field, we put an end to many futile controversies—the controversies, for example, as to whether or not Pope is a poet, as to whether or not Whitman is a poet. If you are prepared to admit that Pope is one of the great English writers, it is less interesting to compare him with

Shakespeare—which will tell you something about the development of English verse but not bring out Pope's peculiar excellence —than to compare him with Thackeray, say, with whom he has his principal theme—the vanity of the world—in common and who throws into relief the more passionate pulse and the solider art of Pope. And so the effort to apply to Whitman the ordinary standards of verse has hindered the appreciation of his careful and exquisite art.

If, in writing about 'poetry,' one limits oneself to 'poets' who compose in verse, one excludes too much of modern literature, and with it too much of life. The best modern work in verse has been mostly in the shorter forms, and it may be that our lyric poets are comparable to any who have ever lived, but we have had no imaginations of the stature of Shakespeare or Dante who have done their major work in verse. The horizon and even the ambition of the contemporary writer of verse has narrowed with the specialization of the function of verse itself. (Though the novelists Proust and Joyce are both masters of what used to be called 'numbers,' the verses of the first are negligible and those of the second minor.)

Would not D. H. Lawrence, for example, if he had lived a century earlier, probably have told his tales, as Byron and Crabbe did: in verse? Is it not just as correct to consider him the last of the great English romantic poets as one of the most original of modern English novelists? Must we not, to appreciate Virginia Woolf, be aware that she is trying to do the kind of thing that the writers of verse have done even more than she is trying to do what Jane Austen or George Eliot were doing?

Recently the techniques of prose and verse have been getting mixed up at a bewildering rate—with the prose technique steadily gaining. You have had the verse technique of Ezra Pound gradually changing into prose technique. You have had William Faulkner, who began by writing verse, doing his major work in prose fiction without ever quite mastering prose, so that he may at any moment upset us by interpolating a patch of verse. You have had Robinson Jeffers, in narrative "poems" which are as much novels as some of Lawrence's, reeling out yards of what are really prose dithyrambs with a loose hexametric base; and you have

[25]

had Carl Sandburg, of *The People, Yes,* producing a queer kind of literature which oscillates between something like verse and something like the paragraphs of a newspaper 'column.'

Sandburg and Pound have, of course, come out of the old *vers libre,* which, though prose-like, was either epigrammatic or had the rhythms of the Whitmanesque chant. But since the Sandburg-Pound generation, a new development in verse has taken place. The sharpness and the energy disappear; the beat gives way to a demoralized weariness. Here the 'sprung-rhythm' of Gerard Manley Hopkins has sometimes set the example. But the difference is that Hopkins' rhythms convey agitation and tension, whereas the rhythms of MacNeice and Auden let down the taut traditions of lyric verse with an effect that is often comic and probably intended to be so—these poets are not far at moments from the humorous rhymed prose of Ogden Nash. And finally—what is very strange to see—Miss Edna St. Vincent Millay in *Conversation at Midnight,* slackening her old urgent pace, dimming the ring of her numbers, has given us a curious example of metrics in full dissolution, with the stress almost entirely neglected, the lines running on for paragraphs and even the rhymes sometimes fading out. In some specimens of this recent work, the beat of verse has been so slurred and muted that it might almost as well have been abandoned. We have at last lived to see the day when the ballads of Gilbert and Hood, written without meter for comic effect in long lines that look and sound like paragraphs, have actually become the type of a certain amount of serious poetry.

You have also the paradox of Eliot attempting to revive the verse-drama with rhythms which, adapting themselves to the rhythms of colloquial speech, run sometimes closer to prose. And you have Mr. Maxwell Anderson trying to renovate the modern theater by bringing back blank verse again—with the result that, once a writer of prose dialogue distinguished by some color and wit, he has become, as a dramatic poet, banal and insipid beyond belief. The trouble is that no verse technique is more obsolete today than blank verse. The old iambic pentameters have no longer any relation whatever to the tempo and language of our lives. Yeats was the last who could write them, and he only because he inhabited, in Ireland and in imagination, a grandiose anachronistic world. You cannot deal with contemporary events in an idiom which was already growing trite in Tennyson's and Arnold's day; and if you try to combine the rhythm of blank verse with the idiom of ordinary talk, you get something—as in Anderson's *Winterset*—which lacks the merits of either. Nor can you try to exploit the worked-out rhythm without also finding yourself let in for the antiquated point of view. The comments on the action in *Winterset* are never the expression of sentiments which we ourselves could conceivably feel in connection with the events depicted: they are the echoes of Greek choruses and Elizabethan soliloquies reflecting upon happenings of a different kind.

Thus if the poets of the Auden-MacNeice school find verse turning to prose in their hands, like the neck of the flamingo in Lewis Carroll with which Alice tried to play croquet, Mr. Anderson, returning to blank verse, finds himself in the more awkward predicament of the girl in the fairy tale who could never open her mouth without having a toad jump out.

But what has happened? What, then, is the cause of this disuse into which verse technique has been falling for at least the last two hundred years? And what are we to expect in the future? Is verse to be limited now to increasingly specialized functions and finally to go out altogether? Or will it recover the domains it has lost?

To find out, if it is possible to do so, we should be forced to approach this change from the anthropological and sociological points of view. Is verse a more primitive technique than prose? Are its fixed rules like the syntax of languages, which are found to have been stiffer and more complicated the further back one goes? Aside from the question of the requirements of taste and the self-imposed difficulties of form which have always, in any period, been involved in the production of great works of art, does the easy flexibility, say, of modern English prose bear to the versification of Horace the same relation that English syntax bears to Horace's syntax, or that Horace's bears to that of the Eskimos?

It seems obvious that one of the important factors in the history of the development of verse must have been its relations with music. Greek verse grew up in fusion with music: verse and music were learned together. It was not till after Alexander the Great that prosody was detached from harmony. The Greek name for 'prose' was 'bare words'—that is, words divorced from music. But what the Romans took over and developed was a prosody that was purely literary. This, I believe, accounts for the fact that we seem to find in Greek poetry, if we compare it with Latin poetry, so little exact visual observation. Greek poetry is mainly for the ear. Compare a landscape in one of the choruses of Sophocles or Aristophanes with a landscape of Virgil or Horace: the Greeks are *singing* about the landscape, the Romans are fixing it for the eye of the mind; and it is Virgil and Horace who lead the way to all the later picture poetry down to our own Imagists. Again, in the Elizabethan age, the English were extremely musical: the lyrics of Campion could hardly have been composed apart from their musical settings; and Shakespeare is permeated with music. When Shakespeare wants to make us see something, he is always compelling and brilliant; but the effect has been liquefied by music so that it sometimes gives a little the impression of objects seen under water. The main stream of English poetry continues to keep fairly close to music through Milton, the musician's son, and even through the less organ-voiced Dryden. What has really happened with Pope is that the musical background is no longer there and that the ocular sense has grown sharp again. After this, the real music of verse is largely confined to lyrics—songs—and it becomes more and more of a trick to write them so that they seem authentic—that is, so that they sound like something sung. It was the aim of the late-nineteenth-century Symbolists, who derived their theory from Poe, to bring verse closer to music again, in opposition to the school of the Parnassians, who cultivated an opaque objectivity. And the excellence of Miss Millay's lyrics is obviously connected with her musical training, as the metrical parts of Joyce—such as the Sirens episode in *Ulysses*, which attempts to render music, the response to a song of its hearer—are obviously associated with his vocal gifts. (There is of course a kind of poetry which produces plastic effects not merely by picture-making through explicit descriptions or images, but by giving the language itself—as Allen Tate is able to do—a plastic quality rather than a musical one.)

We might perhaps see a revival of verse in a period and in a society in which music played a leading role. It has long played a great role in <u>Russia;</u> and in the Soviet Union at the present time you find people declaiming poetry at drinking parties or while traveling on boats and trains almost as readily as they burst into song to the accordion or the balalaika, and flocking to poetry-readings just as they do to concerts. It is possible that the Russians at the present time show more of an appetite for 'poetry,' if not always for the best grade of literature, than any of the Western peoples. <u>Their language, half-chanted and strongly stressed,</u> in many ways extremely primitive, provides by itself, as Italian does, a constant stimulus to the writing of verse.

Here in the United States, we have produced some of our truest poetry in the folk-songs that are inseparable from their tunes. One is surprised, in going through the collections of American popular songs (of Abbé Niles and W. C. Handy, of Carl Sandburg, of the various students trained by Professor Kittredge), which have appeared during the last ten or fifteen years, to discover that the peopling of the continent has had as a by-product a body of folk-verse not unworthy of comparison with the similar material that went to make Percy's *Reliques*. The air of the popular song will no doubt be carrying the words that go with it into the 'poetry' anthologies of the future when many of the set-pieces of 'poetry,' which strain to catch a music gone with Shakespeare, will have come to seem words on the page, incapable of reverberation or of flight from between the covers.

Another pressure that has helped to discourage verse has undoubtedly been the increased demand for reading matter which has been stimulated by the invention of the printing press and which, <u>because ordinary prose is easier to write than verse,</u> has been largely supplied by prose. Modern journalism has brought forth new art-forms; and you have had not only the masterpieces of fiction of such novelists as <u>Flaubert and Joyce,</u> who are also consummate artists in the sense that the great classical poets were, but also the work of men like <u>Balzac and Dickens</u> which lacks the tight organization and the careful attention to detail of the classical epic or drama, and which has to be read rapidly in bulk. The novels of such writers are the epics of societies: they have neither the concision of the folk-song nor the elegance of the forms of the court; they sprawl and swarm over enormous areas like the city populations they deal with. Their authors, no longer schooled in the literary tradition of the Renaissance, speak the practical everyday language of the dominant middle class, which has destroyed the Renaissance world. Even a writer like Dostoevsky rises out of this weltering literature. You cannot say that his insight is less deep, that his vision is less noble or narrower, or that his mastery of his art is less complete than that of the great poets of the past. You can say only that what he achieves he achieves by somewhat different methods.

The technique of prose today seems thus to be absorbing the technique of verse; but it is showing itself quite equal to that work of the imagination which caused men to call Homer 'divine': that re-creation, in the harmony and logic of words, of the cruel confusion of life. Not, of course, that we shall have Dante and Shakespeare redone in some prose form any more than we shall have Homer in prose. In art, the same things are not done again or not done again except as copies. The point is that literary techniques are tools, which the masters of the craft have to alter in adapting them to fresh uses. To be too much attached to the traditional tools may be sometimes to ignore the new masters.

1948. The recent work of W. H. Auden has not shown a running-to-seed of the tendencies mentioned above, but has on the contrary taken the direction of returning to the older tradition of serviceable and vigorous English verse. His *New Year Letter* must be the best specimen of purely didactic verse since the end of the eighteenth century, and the alliterative Anglo-Saxon meter exploited in *The Age of Anxiety* has nothing in common with prose. It may, however, be pointed out, for the sake of my argument above, that in the speech of the girl over the sleeping boy in the fifth section of the latter poem, the poet has found it easy to slip into the rhythms and accents of Mrs. Earwicker's half-prose soliloquy at the end of *Finnegans Wake*.

IN HONOR OF PUSHKIN

I. Evgeni Onegin *

ANYONE who has read criticism by foreigners, even well-informed criticism, of the literature of his own country knows what a large part of it is likely to be made up of either banalities or errors. In the case of a novice at Russian like the writer, this danger is particularly great; and I shall probably be guilty of many sins in the eyes of Russian readers who should happen to see this essay. But Pushkin, the hundredth anniversary of whose death is being celebrated this year by the Soviets, has in general been so little appreciated in the English-speaking countries that I may, perhaps, be pardoned for however imperfect an attempt to bring his importance home to English-speaking readers. And Evgeni Onegin, who has played such a role for the Russian imagination, really belongs among those figures of fiction who have a meaning beyond their natìonal frontiers for a whole age of Western society. The English Hamlet was as real, and as Russian, to the Russians of the generations that preceded the Revolution as any character in Russian literature. Let us receive Evgeni Onegin as a creation equally real for us.

It has always been difficult for Westerners—except perhaps for the Germans, who seem to have translated him more successfully than anyone else—to believe in the greatness of Pushkin. We have always left him out of account. George Borrow, who visited Russia in the course of his work for the Bible Society, published some translations of Pushkin in 1835; but the conven-

* Written for the centenary of Pushkin's death, January 29, 1937.

tional world of literature knew little or nothing about him. Three years after Pushkin's death (and when Lermontov's career was nearly over), Carlyle, in *Heroes and Hero Worship*, described Russia as a 'great dumb monster,' not yet matured to the point where it finds utterance through the 'voice of genius.' Turgenev struggled vainly with Flaubert to make him recognize Pushkin's excellence; and even Renan was so ignorant of Russian literature that it was possible for him to declare on Turgenev's death that Russia had at last found her voice. Matthew Arnold, in writing about Tolstoy, remarked complacently that 'the crown of literature is poetry' and that the Russians had not yet had a great poet; and T. S. Eliot, not long ago, in a discussion of the importance of Greek and Latin, was insisting on the inferior educational value of what he regarded as a merely modern literature like Russian, because 'half a dozen great novelists'—I quote from memory—'do not make a culture.' Even today we tend to say to ourselves, 'If Pushkin is really as good as the Russians think he is, why has he never taken his place in world literature as Dante and Goethe have, and as Tolstoy and Dostoevsky have?'

The truth is that Pushkin *has* come through into world literature—he has come through by way of the Russian novel. Unlike most of the poets of his period, he had the real dramatic imagination, and his influence permeates Russian fiction—and theater and opera as well. Reading Pushkin for the first time, for a foreigner who has already read later Russian writers, is like coming for the first time to Voltaire after an acquaintance with later French literature: he feels that he is tasting the pure essence of something which he has found before only in combination with other elements. It is a spirit whose presence he has felt and with whom in a sense he is already familiar, but whom he now first confronts in person.

For the rest, it is true that the poetry of Pushkin is particularly difficult to translate. It is difficult for the same reason that Dante is difficult: because it says so much in so few words, so clearly and yet so concisely, and the words themselves and their place in the line have become so much more important than in the case of more facile or rhetorical writers. It would require a translator himself a poet of the first order to reproduce Pushkin's peculiar combination of intensity, compression and perfect ease. A writer like Pushkin may easily sound 'flat,' as he did to Flaubert in French, just as Cary's translation of Dante sounds flat. Furthermore, the Russian language, which is highly inflected and able to dispense with pronouns and prepositions in many cases where we have to use them and which does without the article altogether, makes it possible for Pushkin to pack his lines (separating modifiers from substantives, if need be) in a way which renders the problem of translating him closer to that of translating a tightly articulated Latin poet like Horace than any modern poet that we know. Such a poet in translation may sound trivial just as many of the translations of Horace sound trivial— because the weight of the words and the force of their relation have been lost with the inflections and the syntax.

So that, failing any adequate translation, we have tended, if we have thought about Pushkin at all, to associate him vaguely with Byronism: we have heard that *Evgeni Onegin* is an imitation of *Don Juan*. But this comparison is very misleading. Pushkin was a great artist: he derived as much from André Chénier as from Byron. *Don Juan* is diffuse and incoherent, sometimes brilliant, sometimes silly; it has its unique excellence, but it is the excellence of an improvisation. Byron said of some of the cantos that he wrote them on gin, and essentially it is a drunken monologue by a desperately restless, uncomfortable man, who does not know what is the matter with him or what he ought to do with himself, who wants to tell stories about other things or to talk about himself in such a way as to be able to laugh and curse and grieve without looking into anything too closely. Byron's achievement, certainly quite remarkable, is to have raised the drunken monologue to the dignity of a literary form. But the achievement of Pushkin is quite different. He had, to be sure, learned certain things from Byron—for example, the tone of easy negligence with which *Evgeni Onegin* begins and the habit of personal digression; but both of these devices in Pushkin are made to contribute to a general design. *Evgeni Onegin* is the opposite of *Don Juan* in being a work of unwavering concentration. Pushkin's 'novel in verse' came out of Pushkin's deepest self-knowledge and was given form by a long and exacting discipline. The poet had adopted a compact speech and a complicated stanza-form as different as possible from Byron's doggerel; and he worked over the three hundred and eighty-nine stanzas which fill about two hundred pages through a period of eight years (1823-31) and was still, with every successive edition, revising them and cutting them down up to the time of his death.

One can convey a much more accurate impression of what Pushkin's actual writing is like by comparing him to Keats than to Byron. There are passages in *Evgeni Onegin*, such as those that introduce the seasons, which have a felicity and a fullness of detail not unlike Keats's *Ode to Autumn*—or, better perhaps, the opening of *The Eve of St. Agnes*, which resembles them more closely in form:

> St. Agnes' Eve—Ah, bitter chill it was!
> The owl, for all his feathers, was a-cold;
> The hare limp'd trembling through the frozen grass,
> And silent was the flock in woolly fold:
> Numb were the Beadsman's fingers while he told
> His rosary, and while his frosted breath,
> Like pious incense from a censer old,
> Seem'd taking flight for heaven without a death,
> Past the sweet Virgin's picture, while his prayer he saith.

Here is Pushkin's description of the coming of winter:

'Already now the sky was breathing autumn, already the dear sun more seldom gleamed, shorter grew the day, the forest's secret shadow was stripped away with sighing sound, mist lay upon the fields, the caravan of loud-tongued geese stretched toward the south: drew near the duller season; November stood already at the door.

'Rises the dawn in cold murk; in the fields the sound of work is still; the wolf with his hungry mate comes out upon the road; sniffing, the road-horse snorts—and the traveler who is wise makes full speed up the hill; the herdsman now at last by morning light no longer drives his cattle from the byre; at mid-day to their huddle his horn no longer calls them; inside her hut, the farm girl, singing, spins, while—friend of winter nights—her little flare of kindling snaps beside her.

'And now the heavy frosts are snapping and spread their silver through the fields . . . smoother than a smart parquet glistens the ice-bound stream. The merry mob of little boys with skates cut ringingly the ice; on small red feet the lumbering goose, hoping to float on the water's breast, steps carefully but slips and topples; gaily the first snow flashes and whirls about, falling in stars on the bank.'

If you can imagine this sort of thing, which I have translated more or less literally, done in something like Keats's marrowy line, you will get some idea of what Pushkin is like. He can make us see and hear things as Keats can, but his range is very much greater: he can give us the effect in a few lines of anything from the opening of a bottle of champagne or the loading and cocking of pistols for a duel to the spinning and skipping of a ballet girl— who 'flies like fluff from Aeolus' breath'—or the falling of the first flakes of snow. And as soon as we put *The Eve of St. Agnes* (published in 1820) beside *Evgeni Onegin*, it seems to us that Keats is weakened by an element of the conventionally romantic, of the mere storybook picturesque. But Pushkin can dispense with all that: here everything is sharp and real. No detail of country life is too homely, no phase of city life too worldly, for him to master it by the beauty of his verse. Artistically, he has outstripped his time; and neither Tennyson in *In Memoriam* nor Baudelaire in *Les Fleurs du Mal* was ever to surpass Pushkin in making poetry of classical precision and firmness out of a world realistically observed.

I should note also—what I have never seen mentioned—that the passages of social description often sound a good deal more like Praed than like Byron. It is not likely that Pushkin was influenced by Praed, since Praed's poems began to appear in *Knight's Quarterly* only in 1823, the year that *Onegin* was begun, and his characteristic vein of *vers de société* seems to date only from 1826, in which year Pushkin completed his sixth chapter. But the stanza in Chapter Two, with its epitaph, on the death of Tatyana's father might have been imitated from Praed's poem *The Vicar*, and if you can imagine Praed's talent raised to a higher power and telling a long story in his characteristically terse and witty stanzas (Pushkin's measure is shorter than Byron's, a rapid tetrameter like Praed's), you will be closer to Pushkin than *Don Juan* will take you:

> Good night to the Season!—the dances,
>   The fillings of hot little rooms,
> The glancings of rapturous glances,
>   The fancyings of fancy costumes;
> The pleasures which Fashion makes duties,
>   The praisings of fiddles and flutes,
> The luxury of looking at Beauties,
>   The tedium of talking to Mutes;
> The female diplomatists, planners
>   Of matches for Laura and Jane;
> The ice of her Ladyship's manners,
>   The ice of his Lordship's champagne.

To have written a novel in verse, and a novel of contemporary manners, which was also a great poem was Pushkin's unprecedented feat—a feat which, though anticipated on a smaller scale by the tales in verse of Crabbe and several times later attempted by nineteenth-century poets, was never to be repeated. And when we think of *Evgeni Onegin* in connection with *Don Juan* or *The Ring and the Book* or *Aurora Leigh* or *Evangeline*, we find that it refuses to be classed with them. Pushkin's genius, as Maurice Baring has said, has more in common with the genius of Jane Austen than with the general tradition of the nineteenth-century novel. It is classical in its even tone of comedy which is at the same time so much more serious than the tragedies of Byron ever are, in its polishing of the clear and rounded lens which focuses the complex of human relations.

But Pushkin is much more vigorous than Jane Austen: the compression and rigor of the verse cause the characters to seem to start out of the stanzas. And he deals with more violent emotions. *Evgeni Onegin* is occupied with Byronism in a different way than that of deriving from Byron: it is among other things an objective study of Byronism. Both in the poem itself and in a letter that Pushkin wrote while he was working on it, he makes significant criticisms of Byron. 'What a man this Shakespeare is!' he exclaims. 'I can't get over it. How small the tragic Byron seems beside him!—that Byron who has been able to imagine but a single character: his own. . . Byron simply allots to each of his characters some characteristic of his own: his pride to one, his hatred to another, his melancholy to a third, etc., and thus out of a character which is in itself rich, somber and energetic, he makes several insignificant characters; but that is not tragedy.' And in *Evgeni Onegin*, he speaks of Byron's 'hopeless egoism.' Pushkin has been working away from his early romantic lyricism toward a Shakespearean dramatization of life, and now he is to embody in objective creations, to show involved in a balanced conflict, the currents of the age which have passed through him. Evgeni Onegin is presented quite differently from any of the romantic heroes of Byron or Chateaubriand or Musset: when Byron dropped the attitudes of Childe Harold, the best he could do with Don Juan was to give him the innocence of Candide. Evgeni differs even from his immediate successor and kinsman, Lermontov's Hero of Our Time—because Lermontov, though he tells his story with the distinctive Russian realism absent in the other romantic writers, is really involved to a considerable degree with the attitudes of his hero; whereas Pushkin, in showing us Evgeni, neither exalts him in the perverse romantic way nor yet, in exposing his weakness, hands him over to conventional morality. There is, I think, but one creation of the early nineteenth century who is comparable to Evgeni Onegin: Stendhal's Julien Sorel; and the poem is less akin to anything produced by the romantic poets than it is to *Le Rouge et le Noir* and *Madame Bovary*.

Our first glimpse of Pushkin's hero is not an ingratiating one: he has just been summoned to the bedside of a dying uncle, whose estate he is going to inherit, and he is cursing at the tiresome prospect of sitting around till the old man dies. But the scene is shifted at once to his previous life in St. Petersburg. He has been a young man about town, who has had everything society can give him. We see him at the restaurant, the opera, the ball; in one masterly passage we are shown him falling asleep after a round of the pleasures of the capital while the Petersburg of

[37]

the merchants and cabmen and peddlers is just waking up for the day. But Evgeni is intelligent: he gets tired of his friends, tired of his love affairs. He is infected with the 'English spleen' and grows languid and morose like Childe Harold. He shuts himself up to write, but he finds it terribly hard and gives it up. Then his uncle dies, and he inherits the estate and goes to live in the country.

The country bores him, too. Being a man of liberal ideas, he tries to lighten the lot of his serfs, and the neighbors decide he is a dangerous fellow. Then there appears in the neighborhood a young man named Lensky with whom Evgeni finds he has something in common. Lensky has just come back from Göttingen and is saturated with German idealism; and he is a poet in the German-romantic vein. Evgeni thinks him callow and naïve, but tries not to throw cold water on his illusions. He likes Lensky, and they go riding and have long arguments together.

Lensky is in love in the most idealistic fashion with a girl whom he has known since childhood and to whom he has always been faithful. She is pretty but entirely uninteresting: Pushkin tells us that she is just like the heroines of all the popular love stories of the day. Lensky goes to see her every evening—she lives with her sister and her widowed mother on a nearby estate—and one day takes Evgeni with him. Evgeni has sarcastically told Lensky in advance what the refreshments and the conversation will be like—the Larins will be just a 'simple Russian family'; and on the drive back home he remarks that the face of Lensky's worshiped sweetheart is lifeless, red, and round 'like this silly moon over this silly horizon,' and remarks that if *he* were a poet like Lensky, he would have preferred the older sister, who had sat sadly by the window and said nothing.

This older sister, Tatyana, is 'wild, melancholy, silent, and shy' and not so pretty as Olga. As a child, she hadn't liked games and hadn't been fond of dolls; she had thought it was funny to mimic her mother by lecturing her doll on how young ladies ought to comport themselves. Now her head is full of Richardson and Rousseau, and she likes to get up before dawn and watch the stars fade and the distance grow bright and feel the morning wind. And now, from the first moment she sees him, she falls furiously in love with Evgeni. She waits for a time in silence; then, as Evgeni does not come to call again, she sits down and writes him a letter, in which, painfully, uncontrollably, innocently, she confesses to him her love. This chapter, which deals with Tatyana's letter, is one of the great descriptions of first love in literature. Pushkin renews for us as we read all the poignancy and violence of those moments when for the first time the emotional forces of youth are released by another human being and try to find their realization through him. All the banal and deluded things that young people say and feel—that Evgeni is the one man in the world for her, the man for whom she has been waiting all her life, that he has been appointed by God to be her protector, that she is all alone and that no one understands her—poor Tatyana believes them all and puts them all into her letter; and Pushkin has succeeded in giving them to us in all their banality and deludedness, with no romantic sentimentalization, and yet making them move us profoundly. We enter into the emotions of Tatyana as we do into those of Juliet, yet at the same time Pushkin has set the whole picture in a perspective of pathetic irony which is not in that early play of Shakespeare's: there is nothing to indicate that Shakespeare's lovers might not have been ideally happy if it had not been for the family feud; but, in the case of Tatyana, we know from the first moment that her love is hopelessly misplaced in Evgeni. And the whole thing is set off and rooted in life by a series of marvelous touches—Tatyana's conversation with the nurse, the song she hears the serf-girls singing—and saturated with the atmosphere of the country estate where Tatyana has spent her whole life and where—so amazing is Pushkin's skill at evoking a complete picture through suggestion, needing only a few hundred lines where a novelist would take as many pages—we feel by the time she leaves it that we have lived as long as she.

Evgeni does not answer the letter, but two days afterwards he comes to see her. The role of the seducer is *passé*: it went out with periwigs and red heels; and for Evgeni the time for great passions is past: it is too much trouble to do anything about Tatyana. He conducts himself honorably, he talks to her kindly. He tells her that, if he had any desire for family life, she would certainly be the woman he would choose for a wife. But he was not created for happiness, such satisfactions are foreign to his soul. As a husband, he would be gloomy and disagreeable, and he would eventually cease to love her. He makes quite a long speech about it. And he tells her that she ought to learn to control herself: another man might not understand as he does. Tatyana listens silently, in tears. He gives her his arm and leads her back to the house.

But now Evgeni takes an unexpected turn. The Larins give a big evening party to celebrate Tatyana's Saint's Day. Evgeni goes and sits opposite Tatyana and realizes that she is still in love with him and frightened to death in his presence. He thinks that he is angry with Lensky because the party has turned out a bore and Lensky has brought him there on false pretenses. He has for months been watching Lensky moon over Olga with his eternal romantic devotion which treats the beloved object with a reverence almost religious and never makes any practical advances; and he sets out now to annoy the young poet by getting Olga away from him for the evening. Evgeni makes Olga dance with him repeatedly, pays her animated attentions—to which, as she is incapable of saying no, she almost automatically responds. Lensky is deeply hurt and furious; he leaves the party and goes straight home and writes Evgeni a note calling him out.

Evgeni's first impulse, when he receives the challenge, is to set things right with Lensky, not to let the young man make a fool of himself. But then he is moved, as he tells himself, by the fear of public opinion: the second by whom Lensky has sent the challenge, though a thoroughly disreputable individual, is an old-fashioned fancier and promoter of duels. The night before they are to meet, Lensky sits up till morning writing poetry. Evgeni sleeps sound and late; he arrives on the field with his French valet, whom he insolently presents as his second. The adversaries are stationed by their seconds and take their paces toward one another. Evgeni, as he is still approaching, quietly raises his pistol, and he shoots while Lensky is aiming. Lensky falls: in a remarkable simile, characteristically realistic and exact, Pushkin tells us how the young man's heart, in which a moment before all the human passions were dwelling, becomes suddenly like an abandoned house blinded and dark and silent, with the windows covered with chalk and the owner gone away. Evgeni has killed in the most cynical fashion a man whose friend he had believed himself to be and whom he had thought he did not want to kill. Now at last we are sure of what Pushkin, who has always given us Evgeni's version of his own motives, has only so far in various ways suggested: that, for all Lensky's obtuseness and immaturity, Evgeni has been jealous of him, because Lensky has been able to feel for Olga an all-absorbing emotion whereas Evgeni, loved so passionately by Tatyana, has been unable to feel anything at all. Lensky, the author now tells us, might or might not have become a good poet; but the point is, as he lets us know without telling us, that it is the poet in Lensky whom Evgeni has hated. Evgeni had wanted to write; but when he had sat down with the paper before him, he had found it was too much trouble.

After the duel, Evgeni leaves the countryside. Lensky is soon forgotten by Olga. She says yes to an uhlan, who takes her off when he goes to join his regiment. Tatyana is left alone. She walks over to Evgeni's house and gets the caretaker to let her in; and there she returns day after day and reads the books—so much more up to date than Richardson and Rousseau—which she has found in Evgeni's library. There are a picture of Byron on the wall and a little iron statue of Napoleon; and, for the first time, Tatyana reads Byron, as well as several fashionable novels which reflect the fashionable attitudes of the day. Evgeni has marked them and made notes in the margin: and now his lecture to her after her letter begins to have the sound of an echo of all the things he has read.

But Tatyana continues to languish, doesn't get married. Her mother decides to take her to Moscow. There follows a wonderful description of the Larin family traveling to Moscow. Pushkin, with his infinite sympathy and his equally universal detachment, puts on record characteristics and customs of the Russians which are still striking to a foreigner today. The Larins set several dates to get off, but they never get off on those dates. Then at last they do get off and get there. Now the leafy and mazy and timeless estate is far behind Tatyana, and she sees the gold crosses of the churches and then the people and shops and palaces of

Moscow. The shift from country to town is beautifully handled by Pushkin; and there is nothing in fiction more remarkable in its way than the account of Tatyana's first days in Moscow. It is the forerunner of the social scenes in *War and Peace,* and Natasha Rostova and her family seem related to Tatyana and hers, just as Tolstoy's Moscow originals must have been to Pushkin's. The Moscow cousin, to whose house Tatyana and her mother first go and where an old Kalmuck in a ragged caftan and spectacles lets them in, had been in love before she was married with a dandy whom she had thought another Sir Charles Grandison; and now the first thing she says to Tatyana's mother, in whom she had used to confide, is, 'Cousin, do you remember Grandison?' 'What Grandison? Oh, Grandison!—of course, I remember: where is he?' 'He's living in Moscow now; he came to see me at Christmas; he married off his son not long ago.'—But the fashion of the younger generation—we are not told whether or not Tatyana makes this reflection—is for Byron instead of Grandison.

Tatyana cannot at first take her place in this world. Her cousins, though urban, are nice; they look her over and decide she is nice. They confide in her, but she cannot return their confidences: she moves among them detached, distracted. She goes to dinner to be shown to her grandparents: ' "How Tanya has grown!" they say. "Wasn't it just the other day I christened you? and I used to carry you in my arms! And I boxed your ears! And I used to feed you gingerbread!" And the old ladies in chorus would keep repeating: "How our years fly by!"—But they—in them she could see no change; it was all on the same old pattern: her aunt, the Princess Helena, still had the same tulle bonnet, Lukerya Lvovna still powdered herself just as much, Lyubov Petrovna still told the same lies, Ivan Petrovich was still just as silly, Semen Petrovich was still just as stingy, Pelagya Nikolavna still had the same friend, M. Finemouche, and the same Pomeranian and the same husband; and her husband was just as punctual at his club and just as meek and just as deaf as ever, and still ate and drank enough for two.' One night at a ball, her solicitous aunt whispers to her to look to the left. An important-looking general is staring at her. 'Who?' she asks. 'That fat general?'

When Evgeni returns from his travels and goes into society again, he sees at a ball an extraordinarily smart lady who combines perfect naturalness with great dignity, whom everybody wants to speak to and to whom everybody defers; and he gasps at her resemblance to Tatyana. He inquires who she is of a man he knows. 'My wife,' the friend replies. It is Tatyana, now a princess; the man is the pompous general. Tatyana meets Evgeni without batting an eyelash: she asks him whether he has been long in St. Petersburg and whether he doesn't come from her part of the world.

Evgeni pays her court, follows her everywhere; but she refuses to recognize him. He writes her a letter, which is the counterpart of hers: now the roles are reversed—it is he who is putting himself at her mercy. She doesn't answer: he writes again and again. Then he shuts himself up in his house, cuts himself off from society and gives himself up to serious reading: history and moral philosophy. But Lensky gets between him and the page, and he hears a voice that says, 'What, killed?' and he sees all the malicious gossips and the mean cowards and the young jilts and bitches whom he has known in Petersburg society and whom he has wanted to get away from and forget, and he sees Tatyana in the country house, sitting silent beside the window, as on the day when he first called.

Suddenly, one day when the winter snow is melting, he gets into his sleigh and drives off to her house. There is no one in the hall: he walks in. He finds her reading his letters. He throws himself at her feet. She looks at him without anger or surprise; she sees how sick and pitiful he is; the girl who loved him so in the country wakens again in her heart; she does not take her hand from his lips. Then, after a moment, she makes him get up. 'I must be frank with you,' she tells him. 'Do you remember in the orchard how submissively I listened to your rebuke? Now it's my turn. I was younger then, and better. I loved you, and you were severe with me. The love of a humble country girl was not exciting for you. Good heavens! my blood still chills when I remember the cold look and the sermon you gave me. You didn't like me then in the country, and why do you run after me now? Because I'm rich and well known? because my husband has been wounded on the battlefield? because we're in favor at court? Isn't it because my shame would now be known to everybody, and would give you a reputation as a rake? Don't you think I would a thousand times rather be back with the orchard and my books and the places where I first saw you and the graveyard with my nurse's grave, than play this role in this noisy masquerade? But it's too late to do anything now. From the moment when you wouldn't have me, what did it matter to me what became of me? And now you're a man of honor; and although I love you still— why should I pretend?—I've given myself to another and I shall always be faithful to him.'

She goes; and Evgeni stands thunderstruck, and then he hears the clank of the general's spurs. And there Pushkin leaves him.

The truth about Evgeni's fatal weakness has for the first time been fully driven home in Tatyana's speech: he has never been able to judge for himself of the intrinsic value of anything; all his values are social values; he has had enough independence, he has been enough superior to his associates, to be dissatisfied with the life of society, but, even in his disaffection, he has only been able to react into the disaffected attitude that is fashionable; his misanthropy itself has been developed in terms of what people will think of him, and, even trying to escape to the country, he has brought with him the standards of society. He had had enough sense of real values to know that there was something in Tatyana, something noble about her passion for him, to recognize in his heart that it was she who was the true unquiet brooding spirit, the true rebel against the conventions, where his quarrel with the world had been half a pose; but he had not had quite enough to love her just as she was: he had only been able to shoot Lensky.

Pushkin has put into the relations between his three central characters a number of implications. In one sense, they may be said to represent three intellectual currents of the time: Evgeni is Byronism turning worldly and dry; Lensky, with his Schiller and Kant, German romantic idealism; Tatyana, that Rousseauist Nature which was making itself heard in romantic poetry, speaking a new language and asserting a new kind of rights. And from another point of view they represent different tendencies in Russia itself: both Evgeni and Lensky are half foreigners, they think in terms of the cultures of the West, whereas Tatyana, who has spent her whole life on the wild old feudal estate, is for Pushkin the real Russia. Tatyana, like Pushkin, who said he owed so much to the stories of his Russian nurse, has always loved old wives' tales and is full of country superstitions. Before the fatal Saint's-Day party and after her conversation with Onegin, she has an ominous dream, which is recounted at length. Tatyana's subconscious insight, going to the bottom of the situation and clothing it with the imagery of folk-tales, reveals to her a number of things which the others do not yet know about themselves: that there is something bad about Evgeni and that there is an antagonism between him and Lensky; in her dream, she sees Onegin stab Lensky. It is the sensitive though naïve Russian spirit, always aware of the hidden realities, with which Tolstoy and Dostoevsky were later on still attempting to make contact in their reaction against Western civilization. Yet with Pushkin, as Gide says of Dostoevsky, the symbols are perfectly embodied in the characters; they never deform the human being or convert him into an uninteresting abstraction. *Evgeni Onegin* has been popular because it has for generations been read by young Russians as a story— a story in which the eternal reasoning male is brought up against the eternal instinctive woman—like Elizabeth Bennet and Mr. Darcy; and in which the modest heroine—who, besides, is Cinderella and will end up expensively dressed and with the highest social position—gets morally all the best of it.

But there is still another aspect which the characters in *Evgeni Onegin* present. Pushkin speaks, at the end, of the years which have elapsed since he first saw Evgeni dimly, before the 'free novel' which was to shape itself could be discerned 'through the magic crystal.' This magic crystal was Pushkin's own mind, which figures in the poem in a peculiar way. The poet, when he talks about himself, is not willful and egoistic like Byron; his digressions, unlike Byron's or Sterne's, always contribute to the story: they will begin by sounding like asides, in which the author is merely growing garrulous on the subject of some personal experience, but they will eventually turn out to merge into the experience of one of his characters, which he has been filling-in in this indirect way. Yet the crystal sphere is always there: it is inside it that we see the drama. Pushkin, throughout this period, had been tending to get away from his early subjective lyricism and to produce a more objective kind of art. After *Evgeni Onegin*, he was to write principally stories in prose. And in *Evgeni Onegin* it is almost as if we had watched the process—as we can see in the life-cell the nucleus splitting up into its separate nuclei and each concentrating its filaments and particles about it—by which the several elements of his character, the several strands of his experience, have taken symmetry about the foci of distinct characters. Pushkin had finally transfused himself into a dramatic work of art as none other of his romantic generation had done—for his serenity, his perfect balance of tenderness for human beings with unrelenting respect for reality, show a rarer quality of mind than Stendhal's.

Yet *Evgeni Onegin*, for all its lucidity, all its objectification, has behind it a conflict no less desperate than those which the other romantics were presenting so much more hysterically. Though Pushkin had triumphed as an artist as Byron was never able to do, he is otherwise a figure more tragic than the man who died at Missolonghi. For, after all, the chief disaster of *Evgeni Onegin* is not Evgeni's chagrin or Lensky's death: it is that Tatyana should have been caught up irrevocably by that empty and tyrannical social world from which Evgeni had tried to escape and which she had felt and still feels so alien. Pushkin married, the same year that *Onegin* was finished, a young and pleasure-loving wife who submerged him in the expenses of social life; and before he was out of his thirties, he got himself killed in a duel by a man whom he suspected of paying her attentions. It was as if in those generations where Byron, Shelley, Keats, Leopardi and Poe were dead in their twenties or thirties or barely reached forty, where Coleridge and Wordsworth and Beddoes and Musset burned out while still alive, where Lermontov, like Pushkin, was killed in a duel, before he was twenty-seven—it was as if in that great age of the bourgeois ascendancy—and even in still feudal Russia—it were impossible for a poet to survive. There was for the man of imagination and moral passion a basic maladjustment to society in which only the student of society—the social philoso-

pher, the historian, the novelist—could find himself and learn to
function. And to deal with the affairs of society, he had to learn
to speak its language: that is, giving up the old noble language,
he had—as Goethe and Hugo did, and as Pushkin did just before
he died—to train himself to write in prose.

Yet Pushkin, who had done for the Russian language what
Dante had done for Italian and who had laid the foundations of
Russian fiction, had, in opposing the natural humanity of Tatyana
to the social values of Evgeni, set a theme which was to be developed through the whole of Russian art and thought, and to
give it its peculiar power. Lenin, like Tolstoy, could only have
been possible in a world where this contrast was acutely felt.
Tatyana, left by Pushkin with the last word, was actually to
remain triumphant.

II. THE BRONZE HORSEMAN

In attempting a new translation of A. S. Pushkin's great poem,
The Bronze Horseman, it may be useful to make a few explanations.

The poem deals with the tragic contradiction between the right
to peace and happiness of the ordinary man and the right to
constructive domination of the state. (The Bronze Horseman,
which symbolizes the latter, is Falconet's well-known statue of
Peter the Great, which has figured in several Soviet films.) What
is present to the minds of Russian readers but what may not be
equally familiar to foreign ones is the background of the history
of St. Petersburg. This new capital was built by Peter the Great—
the 'He' of the first part of the poem—at the beginning of the
eighteenth century, on the swampy shores and islands of the
Neva. The difficulties involved in the feat were prodigious, and
neither then nor with a view to the future did Peter stint himself
in the expenditure of human life. Of the artisans whom he compelled to come north to lay the foundations of the city, thousands
died of hardship and disease; and the city, in its unnatural location, was at the mercy of terrible floods caused by the breaking-up
of the ice of Lake Ladoga just east of it or—as on the occasion
described in the poem—by the west wind blowing back the Neva.

There had been one such flood in 1777, there was another in 1824, and they continued after Pushkin's time.

Pushkin contributed anonymously to the victims of 1824, and it is with this disaster that *The Bronze Horseman* deals. But the poem was not written until 1833. The poet, who had spent seven of the best years of his youth in exile and under surveillance as a result of his revolutionary verses and who, finally allowed to return to St. Petersburg, was still obliged to submit all his writings and movements to the obstructive control of the Tsar, knew well what it was to have one's life in the hands of a ruthless authority. And he had recently married a young wife who was bringing him into the circle of the Court, where the obligations imposed by the Tsar were weighing on him more heavily than ever and where, it has been supposed, the attentions of the Tsar to his wife were one of the factors in the sequence of events which drove Pushkin, hardly more than three years later, to issue the challenge to his fatal duel.

In *The Bronze Horseman*, as in *Evgeni Onegin*, we can see very clearly the process by which the creations which Pushkin in the beginning has identified more or less with himself become detached from the author, turn into sharply outlined characters and dramatize the impulse which engendered them in a purely objective way. The original intention of Pushkin had been to continue *Evgeni Onegin*. In this sequel Evgeni was to have played some role in connection with the Decembrist revolt of 1825, in consequence of which so many of Pushkin's friends had been executed or sent to Siberia. He wrote this tenth canto in cipher and then, still fearing that it might get him into trouble, burned most of the manuscript. Then he embarked on an entirely new poem in the same stanza-form as *Evgeni Onegin* and with a hero whose first name was still Evgeni, but whose family name was different and who was in fact a quite different person. The new Evgeni is the descendant of an illustrious old boyar family—Pushkin begins with a long genealogy—whose possessions and credit have terribly dwindled. Evgeni himself is a clerk; and Pushkin in his original draft conducted a long argument with imaginary opponents over his right to choose so humble a personage, in defiance of the romantic fashion, as the hero of a

narrative poem. The situation of the new Evgeni was a caricature of Pushkin's own. He himself was the descendant of boyars—
the early Pushkins had been among the electors of the first
Romanov—and now he found himself a socially insignificant person in a *haut monde* where neither his ancient blood nor his
genius as a poet was much respected. He had been put under a
terrible strain since his marriage to keep up his establishment from
his literary earnings.

And, as Pushkin begins to develop his real theme, the new
Evgeni evolves entirely out of the *Evgeni Onegin* frame. Pushkin drops the genealogy, the *vers de société* stanza-form, the amusing man-of-the-world digressions. He drops the imaginary argument, of which he has apparently gotten the better. The former
family glories of the hero, which we are told he spends no time
regretting, are alluded to in half a dozen lines; and the poet in
two words says curtly that Evgeni avoids the nobility. The life
of upper-class St. Petersburg figures only in an introduction, in
which Pushkin describes its attractions in his own conventional
character; and his deeper feelings have obviously been canalized
in the character of the unfortunate desk-worker who hopes to
own two chairs and a table. Indeed, Pushkin has used already
in regard to himself, in one of the rejected parts of *Evgeni Onegin*,
exactly the same phrases about wanting only to be master in his
own house with a pot of cabbage soup, which he now assigns to
the second Evgeni. At the beginning of *Evgeni Onegin*, we see
Evgeni, the Petersburg dandy, returning home after a night of gaiety
just as the common people of the capital are getting up and going
about their tasks. The new Evgeni is now one of these common
people: Pushkin has dropped even the literary avocations which
he gave him in his original version. And he has made out of
Evgeni's collision with the power and pride of St. Petersburg a
poem which has been put by Russian critics beside the longer
masterpiece that preceded it—which has indeed been described
by D. S. Mirsky as probably the greatest Russian poem ever
written.

It would be impossible to reproduce in English the peculiar
poetic merits of *The Bronze Horseman*. The terseness and com-

pactness of Pushkin's style, which constitute one of the chief difficulties of translating him, reach a point in this poem where, as Mirsky says, 'the words and their combinations' are 'charged to breaking-point with all the weight of meaning they can bear.' The two terrific themes of violence: the oppressive power of the city, made solid in stone and metal, the liquid force and fury of the flood, are embodied in language of a density and energy which are hardly to be found in English outside the first books of *Paradise Lost:*

> *He scarce had finisht, when such murmur fill'd*
> *Th' assembly, as when hollow rocks retain*
> *The sound of blust'ring winds, which all night long*
> *Had rous'd the sea, now with hoarse cadence lull*
> *Sea-faring men o'er watcht. . .*

Or,

> *Rocks, caves, lakes, fens, bogs, dens, and shades of death. . .*

Yet I believe it is worth while to make an attempt to present *The Bronze Horseman* in English. There has, so far as I know, been only one English translation—that of Professor Oliver Elton, included by Mr. Avrahm Yarmolinsky in his *Poems, Prose and Plays of Pushkin*. This translation is a very respectable performance: it has certain merits which mine cannot pretend to. Professor Elton, following Pushkin's rhymed verse, has been able to succeed far better than I in catching the tumult and movement of the poem, and he has occasionally struck off a fine Pushkinian line; but he has blurred the effect of the whole by diluting it with a kind of stock romantic verbiage.

I have tried the experiment of translating the poem into prose with an iambic base. This at least makes it possible to avoid the woolliness which is the bane of translations of Pushkin—who is the least woolly of poets—since one is not obliged to pad out the spare and rapid phrases of the original with half-a-dozen words or more for every two of the text and with adjectives and images which are not Pushkin's. (I have used a different text from Professor Elton's: that of P. E. Shchegolev.)

But the main point is that this tale in verse is certainly one of the most enlightening things ever written about Russia by a Russian. It is not only in the portrayal of chaos, the resounding accents of power, that Pushkin is comparable to Milton. Pushkin's poor clerk Evgeni, too, is defying Eternal Order. But his defiance no longer appears under the aspect of a theological struggle; it is the great theme of the nineteenth century: the struggle of the individual with society—the theme of which, in terms of the bourgeois world, the great artistic presentation is in Ibsen. But Pushkin had dramatized it in terms of a society partly modernized and yet basically and belatedly feudal. Evgeni has lost his position as a gentleman through the incompetence of his father as a landlord (this appears from the genealogical fragment which Pushkin broke off and published separately), but he has not become a middle-class man. He is the pettiest of *petits bourgeois*; with his two chairs and his pot of cabbage soup, he has been reduced practically to a working-class level. The distance between him and the Statue, and what the Statue represents, is immense. He will be crushed, and his protest will never be heard—or rather, it would never have been heard if it had not been transmitted by Pushkin, whose poet's vocation it was to hear and to give a voice to the voiceless.

The Tsar was to do his best to prevent it from being heard: *The Bronze Horseman* was suppressed by the censorship and not published till after Pushkin's death. And one wonders, in reading it today, what repercussions it may have in Soviet Russia. After all, the construction of the White Sea canal has been accomplished by forced labor not much different from the forced labor with which Peter the Great built St. Petersburg; and, after all, Peter the Great is the figure to whom the laureates of Stalin most willingly compare him and to whom he is said to be most willing to be compared. The dissident and the irreverent, like Evgeni, hear behind them a horseman, not of bronze but of steel, and no matter where they go, they cannot escape him; he drives them into the prisons of the GPU just as surely as he drove Evgeni into the Gulf of Finland; and just as Evgeni took off his hat and slunk aside where he had formerly hissed a threat, so the guilt of simple opposition puts them ultimately at the mercy of the

'Idol' and compels them to confess to crimes which they have un questionably never committed. Between the power that builds the State and the Idol that represents it, on the one hand, and the ordinary man, on the other, the distance is still very great.

Not of course that Soviet Russia is not an advance beyond Tsarist Russia. The gains of the Revolution and the potentialities of its program should be no more destructible by the policies of however narrow and harsh an administration than the gains of the American Revolution and the potentialities of our republic were destroyed by Harding and Hoover. And not, on the other hand, that government of any sort, whether tsarist or capitalist or socialist, may not give rise to the same kind of conflict between the individual and the corporate interest which Pushkin presents in this poem. But it is well to remember nowadays that the attempt to establish socialism in Russia has had to be carried out in a society conditioned by despotism.

It is also well to remember that Pushkin makes Evgeni's defiance take place in Senate Square, the scene of the Decembrist revolt, which occurred the year after the flood; and that, however discouraged the poet may have been by the suppression of the revolt and by his own eclipse, that defiance was ultimately made good—in November, 1917.

THE BRONZE HORSEMAN

A Petersburg Tale

The incident described in this tale is based on fact. The details are taken from contemporary magazines. The curious may verify them from the material compiled by V. I. Berkh.—Foreword by Pushkin.

Beside the desolate waves stood *He*, and, thronged with mighty thoughts, stared out. Before him, broad, the river rushed along; a poor skiff plied upon it, solitary. Along the mossy marshy bank, the cabins, here and there, showed black: roofs for the wretched Finn; and forests, never brightened by the mist-enshrouded sun, were roaring all around.

Thought *He*: 'We shall from hence strike terror to the Swede. Here shall a town be reared to that arrogant neighbor's woe. Here, for our greatness, Nature has ordained that we shall break a window through to Europe; shall stand with foot set firm beside the sea. Hither, by waters they have never known, all flags shall come to be our guests, and we shall glory in our scope.'

A hundred years went by, and that young city, of northern lands the beauty and the marvel, from dark of forests, damp of bogs, rose up in all its grandeur and its pride; where once the Finnish fisher, Nature's sullen stepchild, had all alone beside low-lying shores let down his ragged nets, today by bustling docks, crowd, strong and shapely, bulks of tower and palace; ships swarm from all earth's ends to that rich port; Neva has clothed herself in stone; bridges have spanned her waters; her isles with groves dark-green are covered over; and now before the younger capital, old Moscow dims—as, before the new Tsarina, the widow of the purple.

I love thee, masterpiece of Peter—I love thine aspect, graceful and severe, Neva's mighty stream, her granite banks, stiff lace of iron fences, the limpid dusk and moonless radiance of nights so full of thought, when lampless in my room I write and read, and sleeping masses of deserted streets show clear, and the Admiralty's needle gleams, and, never suffering the shade of night to dim the golden sky, one glow makes haste to take the other's place, leaves night but half an hour. I love thy cruel winters, the frost and moveless air, the racing of the sleighs beside broad Neva, the girls with faces brighter bit than roses, the balls with all their glitter, stir and chatter, and bachelor feasts, with fizz of foaming goblets and azure flame of punch. I love the warlike liveliness of playing-fields of Mars, monotonous beauty of the Horse and Foot in ranks that sway in rhythm, streaming triumphant banners, the glinting of their bronze war-riddled helmets. I love, O martial capital, thy fort's loud smoke and thunder, when the Empress of the North gives the Imperial house a son, or Russia greets, exulting, her foeman's fresh defeat, or Neva, breaking through the dark blue ice, forth sweeps it to the sea and, smelling spring days, rejoices.

Be splendid, Peter's City, and stand, like Russia, strong—for lo,

the very conquered element has made her peace with thee at last;
their ancient hate and bondage may the Finnish waves forget, nor
vex with impotent anger Peter's eternal sleep!

A dreadful time there *was*—of that I tell. And may my story,
friends, be but, for you, a grisly fireside tale, no legend of bad
omen. . .

I

On Petrograd, all clouded over, November breathed the autumn
cold. Splashing with loud waves against her handsome banks,
Neva threshed about, a sick man on his restless bed. The hour
was late and dark; angry, the rain against the window beat, the
dolorous wind drove howling. That evening from the house of
friends returned the young Evgeni. We shall call our hero so:
the name rings nicely; my pen is friendly to it from of old. No
need to give his surname—though in former times it may have
shone, and sounded from the pen of Karamzin among our country's annals; today the world of gossip has forgot it. Our hero
lodges in a little room. He works somewhere or other, shuns the
gentry, pines after neither his departed relatives nor old days
now forgotten.

And so, come home, he shook his overcoat, undressed and went
to bed, but long he could not sleep, disturbed by divers thoughts.
What thoughts? That he was poor; that he had to work for decent
independence; that God might make him cleverer and richer; that
there were certain lucky idle fellows, who loafed and took no
thought and found life light enough!; that he must wait two
years perhaps to get promotion; that the river was all bloated, that
the weather got no better; that the bridges might perhaps be
taken up, and that in that case his Parasha would surely miss
him. . . Here he was filled with ardent tenderness, his fancy,
like a poet's, soared away.

Get married? Well, why not? Why not, indeed? 'I shall make
myself a modest little corner and there I shall give Parasha peace.
A bed, two chairs, a pot of cabbage soup, and I the master of the
house. . . What more should I want? We shall coddle no
caprices; I shall take Parasha out for country walks on summer
Sundays; humble I'll be and sly: they'll give me a snug berth;

Parasha will keep house, bring up the children. . . And so we'll live and so go down to death, still hand in hand, and be buried by our grandsons. . ."

So he mused. And yet that night he was melancholy, and he wished that the wind would not sound so dreary, that the rain would not sound so angry, as it beat against the pane.

Sleepy, he closed his eyes at last. And lo! the dark of that foul night is thinning, and pale day is at hand. . . Ah, dreadful day!

All night had Neva plunged against the storm to reach the sea, but, worsted by that fury, she now could fight no more. . . At morning to her shores the people flocked in crowds, in wonder at the spray, the mountainous swell, the foam of raging waters. But Neva, by the Gulf winds' driving taxed now beyond her force, fell back in rage and tumult; flooded the islands; fiercer and fiercer grew; reared up and roared; like a caldron, boiled, breathed steam; and, frenzied, fell at last upon the town. All fled before her—all was left abandoned—and now the waves were breaking through the streets, and now invading basements; Neva's canals were all one sea with her, and like a Triton, Petropol emerged, waist-deep in water.

A siege! A storming! Waves, like savage beasts, climb to the windows. Boats, pell-mell borne along, strike the glass with their sterns. Bridges swept loose by the deluge, fragments of cabins, timbers, roofs, the thrifty merchant's wares, the wretched chattels of the poor, the wheels of city droshkies, the coffins from the graveyard, washed afloat—all these drift through the town!

The people see the wrath of God and wait their execution. Alas! all ruined: roof and food! Where will it end?

The late Tsar in that terrible year still gloriously ruled Russia. Distressed and baffled now, he sought the balcony and spoke: 'To tsars it is not given to curb the elements, for they belong to God.' With mournful brooding eyes, he watched the dreadful work. The public squares were lakes, and into them the streets were pouring rivers. The palace seemed a dismal isle. The Tsar's command went forth: his generals, far and wide, through stormy waters on a perilous course, plunged through the streets and sought to save the people, gone mad with panic, drowning in their houses.

[55]

Now at this time in Peter's Square, where a new corner-house had risen, where on the perron high, lifelike with lifted paw, two ornamental lions stand—astride one marble beast, hatless, with arms tight folded, rigid and deathly pale, Evgeni perched. Not for himself, poor fellow, did he fear. He did not notice how the greedy billows rose till they lapped his soles nor how his face was dashed with rain nor how the wildly howling wind had suddenly snatched his hat. His eyes were fixed far out in one strained desperate stare. *There* reared and raged the waves, like mountains, from the outraged deep; *there* raved the storm, *there* broken things were tossed. . . And *there*—God! God!—alas! within the billows' reach, by the Gulf's very brink—the paintless fence, the willow, the little flimsy house—and they, the widow and her daughter, *there*—his dear Parasha, all his hope. . . Or is it all a dream that he beholds? Or is our life, then, nothingness—as empty as a dream, Fate's mockery of man? As if bewitched, fast rooted to the marble, he can't dismount! About him stretches water—water now and nothing else. And, back turned toward him, steady on its height above defiant Neva, rears on its steed of bronze, with outstretched arm, the idol.

II

But now, with ruin sated, with insolent uproar spent, Neva crept back, well pleased to have wreaked her fury and heedlessly abandoning her booty. So, with his villainous band invading town, the ruffian breaks in, wrecks, ransacks, cuts throats: cries, grindings, violence, oaths, alarms and howls! . . . And, burdened with their plunder, fearing pursuit and tired, the robbers hurry home and drop their loot along the road.

The water sank, the pavements cleared again, and my Evgeni hastes with fainting spirit, hoping, fearing, yearning, to the river scarce grown tame. But, still exulting fiercely in the fullness of their triumph, still wickedly the waters boil; still does the foam o'erspread them, and like a warhorse running from a battle, heavily Neva breathes. Evgeni looks: he sees a boat, a godsend; he runs, calls out to the boatman—and this man, with no heed to danger, is ready enough to take him across the terrible waters for ten kopecks.

And long the practiced oarsman contends with the tossing waves, and momently the skiff with its rash sailors seems like to plumb the abyss between their ranks—and now at last it makes the land.

The poor wretch runs along the familiar street to find the familiar place. He looks—oh, dreadful sight!—he knows it not. All lies a heap before him; part tumbled down, part swept away; some of the little houses knocked awry, some quite destroyed, some shifted by the waves—and all about, as on a field of battle, bodies are strewn. Evgeni rushes headlong—uncomprehending, faint with horror—where Fate awaits him with the unseen tidings as if with a sealed letter. And now he is in that last outlying suburb, and here's the Gulf, and here's the house hard by it. . . What's this? . . . He stops—goes back, returns. He stares . . . advances . . . stares again. Here is the place their house stood; here is the willow. Here were the gates—so they've been carried off. But where's the house? And, full of black foreboding, he prowls and prowls about, talks loudly to himself—then suddenly, striking his brow, he bursts out laughing.

Night's darkness fell upon the frightened town; and long the people did not sleep, but talked of the day just past.

The morning's ray, from pale and haggard clouds, shone on a quiet capital and found no trace of yesterday's disaster; with royal purple now the hurt was overspread. And all took up the old routine. Already through the streets, now clear again, with cold indifference flowed the crowd. The clerks, quitting their lodgings, went to their desks. Hardy trade, not downed, explored his cellars, plundered by the river, preparing to revenge his heavy losses out of his neighbor's pocket. And people took the boats out of the courtyards.

And Khostov, poet, favorite of the heavens, already sang in verses never to die the griefs of Neva's shores.

But ah, my poor Evgeni . . . alas! his baffled wits gave way before these blows. The mutinous roar of Neva and the winds were now resounding in his ears. Possessed by dreadful thoughts he could not utter, he strayed from place to place. Some dream was preying on him. A week, and then a month had passed—he never from that day went home. His empty lodging, when the lease expired, the landlord rented out to a poor poet. Evgeni never came to claim his things. The world forgot him soon. All day he tramped, at night slept on the docks; his food was morsels handed out from windows. His shabby clothes were torn and wearing out. The cruel children stoned him as he passed. Often he felt the coachmen's whips, for all was thoroughfare to him alike—courtyard or street, he never paid attention, always submerged in some strange inner terror. And so he dragged his miserable life, not beast nor man, not this nor that, no dweller on the earth nor yet departed spirit. . .

One night he slept on a landing of the Neva. The summer days inclined toward fall. A foul wind blew. The dark surf dashed on the wharf, muttering grief and beating the smooth steps, like a suppliant at the door of a deaf court. The poor wretch fell asleep. The dark had come; the rain was dripping down; the wind was dreary; from far away the sentry through the thickness of the night returned its cry. . . Evgeni leapt from sleep; his horror had come on him; quickly he rose and started on his wandering. Then suddenly he stopped and, standing very still, his face aghast with terror, began to gaze about. The great house with its columns rose before him. And on the perron high, lifelike with lifted paw, the ornamental lions stood; and right before him, from its fenced-in rock, with outstretched arm, uprearing in the darkness, the idol sat its copper steed.

A shudder shook Evgeni. His thoughts grew terribly clear. He knew this place where the flood had had its sport, where the waves had flocked like beasts of prey about him, ruthless, in full rebellion—and he knew these lions and this square, and him he knew who, fixed and still forever, held high in the murk of night his copper head—himself whose fateful will had based the city on the sea. . . How dreadful now in all-enveloping mist! What power of thought upon his brow! What force within! And in that steed what fire! Where dost thou gallop, haughty steed? And where wilt thou plant thy hoof? O thou who, in thy might, didst master Destiny! Didst not just so, aloft, above the very precipice, with iron curb make Russia rear?

The poor crazed fellow prowled about the pedestal, cast wild looks on the image of the lord of half the world. His chest grew tight. He pressed his brow against the cold grate; his eyes blurred with mist; a flame flashed through his heart; his blood boiled up. Somber he stood before the arrogant statue, and, clinching teeth and fists, possessed by some black force: 'Good! wonderworking builder!' with quivering hate, he hissed. 'You'll reckon with me yet!'—And headlong took to flight. The terrible Tsar, on the instant hot with wrath, had seemed all soundlessly to turn his head.

And through the empty square he plunges wildly, and hears behind—like rattling thunder.clap—against the pounded pave a heavy-ringing gallop. And, dark in the pale moon, one arm flung up, the Copper Horseman comes behind, his charger's gallop ringing brass; and all night long, turn where Evgeni will, the Copper Horseman's clattering hoofbeats hammer—pursuing, still impend.

Thereafter, if he chanced upon the Square, his face, dismayed, would darken. Quick he would press his hand against his heart as if to calm its fluttering, remove his shabby cap, cast down his gaze and slink away.

A little isle there is that lies offshore. Sometimes the fisher moors there with his net, belated at the haul, and cooks his humble supper, or some dreaming Sunday boatman puts in at the desert place. No blade of grass has ever sprouted there. But there the sportive flood had brought a flimsy cottage. Like a blackened bush it showed above the water. Last spring they took it up aboard a barque. It was empty, all a wreck; but on its threshold they dragged up my madman, and there for Charity's sake they buried his cold corpse.

A. E. HOUSMAN

The Voice, Sent Forth, Can Never Be Recalled

WHEN A. E. Housman's *Introductory Lecture* delivered in 1892 'Before the Faculties of Arts and Laws and of Science in University College, London' was reprinted in 1933, Housman characteristically wrote of it as follows: 'The Council of University College, not I, had the lecture printed.' He described it as 'rhetorical and not wholly sincere' and put upon the title page, *Nescit vox missa reverti.*

The little essay is curious in largely evading the questions it raises and taking the direction of a piece of special pleading for the author's own pursuits. Both the sciences and the arts, says Housman, are ordinarily defended by arguments which make their interests appear mutually antagonistic. But the arguments on both sides are mistaken. Science is said to be useful; but what is the use, for example, of a great deal of astronomical research? And the businessmen who make practical use of the results of scientific study are usually not scientists at all. (They do make use of them, nevertheless; and the results of the most gratuitous researches are always likely to turn out to be useful.) The Humanities, on the other hand, are supposed to 'transform and beautify our inner nature by culture.' Yet the proportion of the human race capable of being benefited by classical studies is certainly very small, and these 'can attain the desired end without that minute and accurate study of the classical tongues which affords Latin professors their only excuse for existing.' Not even the great critics of the classics are genuine classical scholars: 'When it comes to literary criticism, heap up in one scale all the literary criticism that the whole nation of professed scholars ever wrote, and drop into the other the thin green volume of Matthew Arnold's *Lectures on Translating Homer,* which has long been out of print because the British public does not care to read it, and the first scale, as Milton says, will straight fly up and kick the beam.' (We shall look into the assumptions here in a moment.)

The arts and the sciences alike are only to be defended, says Housman, on the ground that the desire for knowledge is one of the normal human appetites, and that men suffer if they do not have it gratified. And 'once we have recognized that knowledge in itself is good for man, we shall need to invent no pretexts for studying this subject or that; we shall import no extraneous considerations of use or ornament to justify us in learning one thing rather than another. If a certain department of knowledge specially attracts a man, let him study that, and study it because it attracts him; and let him not fabricate excuses for that which requires no excuse, but rest assured that the reason why it most attracts him is that it is best for him.'

This is certainly true in so far as it means that we should follow the direction of our aptitudes; but it seems to imply that there is no difference in value between one department of learning and another or between the different points of view from which the various kinds of research can be conducted. There is no conception in Housman's mind, as there would have been in Whitehead's, for example, of relating the part to the whole, understanding the organism through the cell. Knowledge seems to be regarded by Housman as a superior sort of pastime—'good for man' because it gives him pleasure and at most because 'it must in the long run be better for a man to see things as they are than to be ignorant of them; just as there is less fear of stumbling or of striking against corners in the daylight than in the dark.' (*The thoughts of others Were light and fleeting, Of lovers' meeting Or luck or fame; Mine were of trouble And mine were steady, So I was ready When Trouble came.*') The disillusionment of western man in regard to his place in the universe, finding 'that he has been deceived alike as to his origin and his expectations, that he neither springs of the high lineage he fancied, nor will inherit the vast estate he looked for,' is described in an eloquent passage; and the activities of the 'Arts and Laws and Science' are finally char-

acterized as 'the rivalry of fellow soldiers in striving which can
most victoriously achieve the common end of all, to set back the
frontier of darkness.'

In other words, there is no role for creation in Housman's
scheme of things. Indeed, if one had read only his poetry, one
might be surprised to find that he even believed that it was possible or of any importance to set back the frontier of darkness. In
this poetry, we find only the realization of man's smallness on his
turning globe among the other revolving planets and of his
own basic wrongness to himself, his own inescapable anguish. No
one, it seems, can do anything about this universe which 'ails
from its prime foundation': we can only, like Mithridates, render
ourselves immune to its poisons by compelling ourselves to ab-
sorb them in small quantities in order that we may not succumb
to the larger doses reserved for us by our fellows, or face the
world with the hard mask of stoicism, 'manful like the man of
stone.' For the rest, 'let us endure an hour and see injustice done.'
And now we learn that for Housman knowledge itself meant at
most the discovery of things that were already there—of those
sharp corners which it was just as well not to bump into, of facts
that were as invariable and as inert as the astronomical phenomena which are always turning up in his poems and which form
the subject of the poem of Manilius to which he devoted so much
of his life. He does not look to the sciences and arts for the births
of new worlds of thought, of new possibilities for men themselves.
It is characteristic of him that he should speak, in this essay, of
Milton as a greater artist than Shakespeare, of Shakespeare, in
fact, as not 'a great artist'—as if the completeness and richness of
Shakespeare's dramatic imagination, a kind of genius which Milton, by comparison, seems hardly to possess at all, were not important enough to be taken into account in estimating his greatness as an artist—as if those stretches of *Paradise Lost* where everything is dead but the language were not the result of artistic deficiency. Again, the creation of life has no place in the universe
of Housman.

Housman's practice in his own field of scholarship is an astonishing proof of this. The modern English classical scholar of the

type of A. W. Verrall or Gilbert Murray is a critic not merely of texts but of the classics in their quality as literature and of literature in its bearing on history. This school on one of its sides sometimes merges with the anthropology of J. G. Frazer; and it deals with ancient Greece and Rome in relation to the life of its own time, restates them in terms of its own time. The danger, of course, with a Verrall or a Murray is that, with something of the poet's imagination himself, he may give way, in the case of Greek drama, for example, to inventing new plays of his own and trying to foist them on Euripides or Aeschylus. With Housman we do not run this danger. Housman is the opposite kind of scholar; he is preoccupied with the emendation of texts. He could never have been guilty of the extravagances of a Gilbert Murray or a Verrall, but he was not capable of their kind of illumination. Note his assumption, in the passage quoted above, that 'the minute and accurate study of the classical tongues,' with which he himself is exclusively preoccupied, 'affords Latin professors their only excuse for existing.' Have those classical scholars who write history, who write criticism, who make translations— Gibbon and Renan and Verrall and Murray and Jowett and Mackail (to take in the whole field of the classics)—no excuse for existing, then? Is it so certain that, if their literary criticism were put into the scales with Matthew Arnold on Homer, the scholars would kick the beam? Or are such persons not scholars at all? In either case, it is plain that, for Housman, their activities lie outside the periphery of the sphere which he has chosen for himself.

Not, however, that Housman in this limited sphere has left the poet of *The Shropshire Lad* behind him. On the contrary, the peculiar genius which won him a place beside Porson and Bentley, which established him in his own time as almost supreme, with, apparently, only Wilamowitz as a rival, was derived from his ability to combine with the most 'minute and accurate' mastery of language a first-hand knowledge of how poets express themselves. 'The task of editing the classics,' he wrote in his preface to Juvenal, 'is continually attempted by scholars who have neither enough intellect nor enough literature. Unless a false reading chances to be unmetrical or ungrammatical they have no means of knowing that it is false.' And he himself seemed able with a miraculous sureness to give the authors back their lines as they had written them. So, for example, despite a unanimity of manuscripts which read 'Omnis ab hac cura mens relavata mea est,' Housman restored to Ovid from an inscription one of the latter's characteristic turns of style: 'Omnis ab hac cura cura levata mea est.' ('And set you at your threshold down, Townsman of a stiller town'; 'Runners whom renown outran And the name died before the man'; 'By Sestos tower, in Hero's town, On Hero's heart Leander lies.') So, slightly emending the text, he turned a meaningless accepted reading of Juvenal, 'Perditus ac vilis sacci mercator olentis,' into a characteristically vivid satiric stroke: 'Perditus ac similis sacci mercator olentis'—the money-chasing merchant, on a stormy voyage, turns as yellow as his bag of saffron. ('They shook, they stared as white's their shirt: Them it was their poison hurt.') So, without even an emendation and simply by indicating a new relation between three words of Virgil's, he was able to save Virgil's style in a phrase—fallax herba veneni—which had always up to then been read as if it had been written with neither style nor grammar: substituting for 'the deceitful plant of poison,' 'the plant that dissembles its venom.' ('And bear from hill and valley The daffodil away That dies on Easter day'; 'Lie long, high snowdrifts in the hedge That will not shower on me'; 'Snap not from the bitter yew His leaves that live November through.') Several of his readings, I understand, have been confirmed by the subsequent discovery of manuscripts which Housman had never seen.

To this rescue of the Greek and Roman poets from the negligence of the Middle Ages, from the incompetence and insensitivity of the scholars, A. E. Housman brought an unremitting zeal which may almost be described as a passion. It has been said of the theorems of Newton that they cause the pulse to beat faster as one follows them. But the excitement and satisfaction afforded by the classical commentary of Housman must be unique in the history of scholarship. Even the scraping of the rust from an old coin is too tame an image to convey the experience of pursuing one of his arguments to its climax. It is as if, from the ancient author, so long dumb with his language itself, his very identity blurred or obliterated, the modern classicist were striking a new spark of life—as if the poet could only find his tongue at the touch across Time of the poet. So far is Housman the scholar a giver of life—yet it is only as re-creator. He is only, after all, again, discovering things that were already there. His findings do not imply a new vision.

It was a queer destiny, and one that cramped him—if one should not say rather that he had cramped himself. (Not to dispute, however, with Housman, who thought that human beings were all but helpless, the problem of natural fate and free will.)
The great work of A. E. Housman's life in the field of classical scholarship was his edition of the five books of Manilius, the publication of which alone extended from 1903 to 1930. We are told in a memoir of Housman by his colleague, Professor A. S. F. Gow of Cambridge, that Housman regarded Manilius as 'a facile and frivolous poet, the brightest facet of whose genius was an eminent aptitude for doing sums in verse.' And the layman may be disposed to assume that by Housman's time the principal Latin poets had already been covered so completely that there was nobody left except third-rate ones like Manilius. But it turns out from Professor Gow that Housman's real favorite was Propertius, and that he had done a great deal of valuable work on him and had at one time contemplated a complete edition. Professor Gow says that presumably Housman saw in Manilius and Lucan (Lucan he seems also to have despised) 'more opportunity than in Propertius of displaying his special gifts, and more hope of approaching finality in the solution of the problems presented,' but adds that he 'cannot help regretting that he [Housman] abandoned a great and congenial poet on whom so much time had already been lavished.'
The elegist of *The Shropshire Lad*, then, deliberately and grimly chose Manilius when his real interest was in Propertius. There is an element of perversity, of self-mortification, in Housman's career all along. (Gow tells how up to the time of his death 'he would be found reading every word of books whose insignificance must have been apparent in ten pages, and making remorseless catalogues of their shortcomings.') And his scholarship, great as it is in its way, is poisoned in revenge by the instincts which

[65]

it seems to be attempting to destroy, so that it radiates more hatred for his opponents than love for the great literature of antiquity. Housman's papers on classical subjects, which shocked the sense of decorum of his colleagues, are painful to the admirers of his poetry. The bitterness here *is* indecent as in his poetry it never is. In a prose, old-fashioned and elaborate, which somewhat resembles Pope's, he will attack the German professors who have committed the unpardonable sin of editing the Latin authors inadequately with sentences that coil and strike like rattlesnakes, or that wrap themselves around their victims and squeeze them to death like boa constrictors. When English fails, he takes to scurrilous Latin. And the whole thing is likely at any moment to give way to some morose observation on the plight of the human race: 'To believe that wherever a best *ms* gives possible readings it gives true readings, and that only when it gives impossible readings does it give false readings, is to believe that an incompetent editor is the darling of Providence, which has given its angels charge over him lest at any time his sloth and folly should produce their natural results and incur their appropriate penalty. . . How the world is managed, and why it was created, I cannot tell; but it is no feather-bed for the repose of sluggards.' And not only, he continues, has the notion been imposed that 'inert adhesion to one authority is methodical criticism,' but 'rational criticism has been branded with a term of formal reprobation.' 'But still there is a hitch. Competent editors exist; and side by side with those who have embraced "the principles of criticism," there are those who follow the practice of critics: who possess intellects, and employ them on their work. Consequently their work is better done, and the contrast is mortifying. This is not as it should be. As the wise man dieth, so dieth the fool: why then should we allow them to edit the classics differently? If nature, with flagitious partiality, has given judgment and industry to some men and left other men without them, it is our evident duty to amend her blind caprice; and those who are able and willing to think must be deprived of their unfair advantage by stringent prohibitions. In Association football you must not use your hands, and similarly in textual criticism you must not use your brains. Since we cannot make fools behave like wise men, we will insist that wise men should behave like fools: by these means only can we redress the injustice of nature and anticipate the equality of the grave.'

And here is the somber and threatening, the almost Isaian, utterance to which he is moved by the failure of one of the compilers of a German-Latin dictionary to include in the article on *aelurus,* the Latinized Greek word for *cat,* any mention of an instance of its occurrence arrived at by an emendation in Juvenal and believed by Housman to be the first extant: 'Everyone can figure to himself the mild inward glow of pleasure and pride which the author of this unlucky article felt while he was writing it and the peace of mind with which he said to himself, when he went to bed that night, "Well done, thou good and faithful servant." This is the felicity of the house of bondage, and of the soul which is so fast in prison that it cannot go forth; which commands no outlook on the past or the future, but believes that the fashion of the present, unlike all fashions heretofore, will endure perpetually and that its own flimsy tabernacle of second-hand opinions is a habitation for everlasting.'

Even when Housman is saying something positive the emotion is out of proportion to its object: he speaks feverishly, seems unnaturally exalted. Here is a passage on Bentley from the preface to the first volume of his Manilius: '*Lucida tela diei:* these are the words that come into one's mind when one has halted at some stubborn perplexity of reading or interpretation, has witnessed Scaliger and Gronovius and Huetius fumble at it one after another, and then turns to Bentley and sees Bentley strike his finger on the place and say *thou ailest here, and here. . .* The firm strength and piercing edge and arrowy swiftness of his intellect, his matchless facility and adroitness and resource, were never so triumphant as where defeat seemed sure; and yet it is other virtues that one most admires and welcomes as one turns from the smoky fire of Scaliger's genius to the sky and air of Bentley's: his lucidity, his sanity, his great and simple and straightforward fashion of thought.' Transferring Arnold's words for Goethe to Bentley is not perhaps comparing great things with small, but in the substitution for the 'physician of the Iron Age' of the physician of mangled texts, there is a narrowing of scope almost comic. The preface to the first book of Manilius, from which the above passage has been quoted, magnificent as it is in its way, has also something monstrous about it.

Yet some acquaintance with the classical work of Housman greatly increases one's estimate of his stature. One encounters an intellectual pride almost Dantesque or Swiftian. 'You would be welcome to praise me,' he writes, 'if you did not praise one another'; and 'the reader whose good opinion I desire and have done my utmost to secure is the next Bentley or Scaliger who may chance to occupy himself with Manilius.' His arrogance is perhaps never more ferocious than when he is judging himself severely: when a friend who had ventured to suggest the publication of a paper on Swinburne which Housman had read before a college literary society had been told by Housman that he was leaving directions to have it destroyed after his death and had retorted that if the writer really thought it so bad, he would already himself have destroyed it, Housman replied: 'I do not think it bad: I think it not good enough for me.' And he put on the title page of his edition of Juvenal, *editorum in usum edidit*, to indicate that this feat of erudition—according to his own announcement, unprecedented—was merely intended as a hint to future scholars who might tackle the subject as to how they might accomplish their task in a thoroughgoing fashion.

Is this the spectacle of a great mind crippled? Certainly it is the spectacle of a mind of remarkable penetration and vigor, of uncommon sensibility and intensity, condemning itself to duties which prevent it from rising to its full height. Perhaps it is the case of a man of genius who has never been allowed to come to growth. Housman's anger is tragic like Swift's. He is perhaps more pitiable than Swift, because he has been compelled to suppress himself more completely. Even when Swift had been exiled to Ireland, he was able to take out his fury in crusading against the English. But A. E. Housman, giving up Greek in order to specialize in Latin because he 'could not attain to excellence in both,' giving up Propertius, who wrote about love, for Manilius, who did not even deal with human beings, turning away from the lives of the Romans to rivet his attention to the difficulties of their texts, can only flatten out small German professors with weapons which would have found fit employment in the hands of a great reformer or a great satirist. He is the hero of *The Grammarian's Funeral*—the man of learning who makes himself impressive through the magnitude, not the importance, of his achievement. After all, there was no need for another Bentley.

It is only in the Latin verses—said to have been called by Murray the best since the ancient world—which Housman prefixed to his Manilius, in his few translations from Latin and Greek, and in his occasional literary essays, that the voice of the Shropshire Lad comes through—that voice which, once sped on its way, so quickly pierced to the hearts and the minds of the whole English-speaking world and which went on vibrating for decades, disburdening hearts with its music that made loss and death and disgrace seem so beautiful, while poor Housman, burdened sorely forever, sat grinding and snarling at his texts. Would he have called back that voice if he could, as he recalled, or tried to recall, so much else? There are moments when his ill humor and his pedantry, his humility which is a perverse kind of pride, almost make us think that he would.

At this point Professor Gow is able to throw some further light on his friend. It seems that Housman had marked the following passage from Colonel Lawrence's *Seven Pillars of Wisdom*, which he had come across in a review:

'There was my craving to be liked—so strong and nervous that never could I open myself friendly to another. The terror of failure in an effort so important made me shrink from trying; besides, there was the standard; for intimacy seemed shameful unless the other could make the perfect reply, in the same language, after the same method, for the same reasons.

'There was a craving to be famous; and a horror of being known to like being known. Contempt for my passion for distinction made me refuse every offered honor. I cherished my independence almost as did a Beduin, but my impotence of vision showed me my shape best in painted pictures, and the oblique overheard remarks of others best taught me my created impression. The eagerness to overhear and oversee myself was my assault upon my own inviolate citadel.'

Housman had written in the margin, 'This is me.' Both had

been compelled by their extreme sensibility to assume in the presence of their fellows eccentric or repellent masks. Both had been led by extreme ambition to perform exploits which did not do them justice, exploits which their hearts were but half in: Professor Gow says that Housman's prime motive in undertaking his edition of Manilius was the ambition to 'build' himself 'a monument.' And just as Lawrence was always losing the manuscripts of his books, limiting their circulation, making the pretense of suppressing them altogether, so Housman kept his poems out of anthologies, made the gestures of a negative attitude in regard to the reprinting of his other writings, and left instructions that his classical papers, of which Gow says there are something like a hundred, should never be collected in a volume (instructions which it is to be hoped will be disobeyed).

Both were products of the English universities; and it would take an Englishman properly to account for them. But their almost insane attempts to conceal their blazing lights under bushels are recognizable as exaggerations of the Englishman's code of understatement in connection with his achievements and conquests. And both obviously belong to the monastic order of English university ascetics. The company to which Housman refers himself is that of Walter Pater, Lewis Carroll, Edward Fitzgerald and Gerard Manley Hopkins—and, earlier, Thomas Gray. Hopkins, converted at Oxford, entered the Jesuit order; Pater and Dodgson stayed on there as dons; Fitzgerald and Gray, when they had finished at Cambridge, continued to haunt the place: they remained men of the monastery all their lives. Are their humility, which seems imposed by moral principles, their shyness in relation to the extra-collegiate world, derived from the ages when learning was the possession of pious brotherhoods and shut away between the walls of foundations?

Certainly their failure to develop emotionally is due to that semi-monastic training. All seem checked at some early stage of growth, beyond which the sensibility and the intellect—even, in Lawrence's case, the ability to manage men—may crystallize in marvelous forms, but after which there is no natural progress in the experience of human relationships. Their works are among the jewels of English literature rather than among its great springs of life; and Alice and the Shropshire Lad and Marius the Epicurean are all the beings of a looking-glass world, either sexless or with an unreal sex which turns only toward itself in the mirror of art. Isn't the state of mind indicated by Lawrence in the first of the paragraphs quoted above essentially an adolescent one? We are told, in a recent memoir, that Housman used to rail against marriage and child-bearing. 'My father and my mother,' he makes one of his hanged heroes say, 'They had a likely son, And I have none.'

It would not be true to say of Housman, as it would be of Fitzgerald or Gray, that his achievement has been merely to state memorably certain melancholy commonplaces of human existence without any real presentation of that existence as we live it through. There *is* immediate emotional experience in Housman of the same kind that there is in Heine, whom he imitated and to whom he has been compared. But Heine, for all his misfortunes, moves at ease in a larger world. There is in his work an exhilaration of adventure—in travel, in love, in philosophy, in literature, in politics. Doleful though his accents may sometimes be, he always lets in air and light to the mind. But Housman is closed from the beginning. His world has no opening horizons; it is a prison that one can only endure. One can only come the same painful cropper over and over again and draw from it the same bitter moral.

And Housman has managed to grow old without in a sense ever knowing maturity. He has somehow never arrived at the age when the young man decides at last to summon all his resources and try to make something out of this world he has never made.

THE POLITICS OF FLAUBERT

GUSTAVE FLAUBERT has figured for decades as the great glorifier and practitioner of literary art at the expense of human affairs both public and personal. We have heard about his asceticism, his nihilism, his consecration to the search for *le mot juste*. His admirers have tended to praise him on the same assumption on which his critics have found him empty and sterile: the assumption that he had no moral or social interests. At most, *Madame Bovary* has been taken as a parable of the romantic temperament.

Really Flaubert owed his superiority to those of his contemporaries—Gautier, for example, who professed the same literary creed—to the seriousness of his concern with the large questions of human destiny. It was a period when the interest in history was intense; and Flaubert, in his intellectual tastes as well as in his personal relations, was almost as close to the historians Michelet, Renan and Taine, and to the biographical critic Sainte-Beuve, as to Gautier and Baudelaire. In the case of Taine and Sainte-Beuve, he came to deplore their preoccupation in their criticism with the social aspects of literature at the expense of all its other values; but he himself seems always to see humanity in social terms and historical perspective. His point of view may be gauged pretty accurately from his comments in one of his letters on Taine's *History of English Literature*: 'There is something else in art beside the milieu in which it is practiced and the physiological antecedents of the worker. On this system you can explain the series, the group, but never the individuality, the special fact which makes him this person and not another. This method results inevitably in leaving *talent* out of consideration. The masterpiece has no longer any significance except as an historical document. It is the old critical method of La Harpe exactly turned around. People used to believe that literature was an altogether personal thing and that books fell out of the sky like meteors. Today they deny that the will and the absolute have any reality at all. The truth, I believe, lies between the two extremes.'

But it was also a period in France—Flaubert's lifetime, 1820-81—of alternating republics and monarchies, of bogus emperors and defeated revolutions, when political ideas were in much confusion. The French historians of the Enlightenment tradition, which was the tradition of the Revolution, were steadily becoming less hopeful; and a considerable group of the novelists and poets held political and social issues in contempt and staked their careers on art as an end in itself: their conception of their relation to society was expressed in their damnation of the bourgeois, who gave his tone to all the world, and their art was a defiance of him. The Goncourts in their journal have put the attitude on record: 'Lying phrases, resounding words, hot air—that's just about all we get from the political men of our time. Revolutions are a simple *déménagement* followed by the moving-back of the same ambitions, corruptions and villainies into the apartment which they have just been moved out of—and all involving great breakage and expense. No political morals whatever. When I look about me for a disinterested opinion, I can't find a single one. People take risks and compromise themselves on the chance of getting future jobs. . . You are reduced, in the long run, to disillusion, to a disgust with all beliefs, a tolerance of any power at all, an indifference to political passion, which I find in all my literary friends, and in Flaubert as in myself. You come to see that you must not die for any cause, that you must live with any government that exists, no matter how antipathetic it may be to you—you must believe in nothing but art and profess only literature. All the rest is a lie and a booby-trap.' In the field of art, at least, it was possible, by heroic effort, to prevent the depreciation of values.

This attitude, as the Goncourts say, Flaubert fully shared. 'Today,' he wrote Louise Colet in 1853, 'I even believe that a thinker (and what is an artist if he is not a triple thinker?) should have neither religion nor fatherland nor even any social conviction. It seems to me that absolute doubt is now indicated so unmistakably that it would almost amount to an absurdity to take the trouble to formulate it.' And: 'The citizens who work themselves up for or against the Empire or the Republic,' he wrote George Sand in 1869, 'seem to be just about as useful as the ones who used to argue about efficacious grace and efficient grace.' Nothing exasperated him more—and we may sympathize with him today—than the idea that the soul is to be saved by the profession of correct political opinions.

Yet Flaubert is an idealist on a grandiose scale. 'The idea' which turns up in his letters of the fifties—'genius like a powerful horse drags humanity at her tail along the roads of the idea,' in spite of all that human stupidity can do to rein her in—is evidently, under its guise of art, none other than that Hegelian 'Idea' which served Marx and so many others under a variety of different guises. There are great forces in humanity, Flaubert feels, which the present is somehow suppressing but which may some day be gloriously set free. 'The soul is asleep today, drunk with the words she has listened to, but she will experience a wild awakening, in which she will give herself up to the ecstasies of liberation, for there will be nothing more to constrain her, neither government nor religion, not a formula; the republicans of all shades of opinion seem to me the most ferocious pedagogues, with their dreams of organizations, of legislations, of a society constructed like a convent.'

When he reasons about society—which he never does except in his letters—his conceptions seem incoherent. But Flaubert, who believed that the artist should be triply ('to the n*th* degree') a thinker and who had certainly one of the great minds of his time, was the kind of imaginative writer who works directly in concrete images and does not deal at all in ideas. His informal expressions of his general opinions are as unsystematized and impromptu as his books are well-built and precise. But it is worth while to quote a few from his letters, because, though he never came anywhere near to expounding a social philosophy—when George Sand accused him of not having one, he admitted it—they do indicate the instincts and emotions which are the prime movers in the world of his art.

Flaubert is opposed to the socialists because he regards them as materialistic and because he dislikes their authoritarianism, which he says derives straight from the tradition of the Church. Yet they have 'denied *pain*, have blasphemed three-quarters of modern poetry, the blood of Christ, which quickens in us.' And: 'O socialists, there is your ulcer: the ideal is lacking to you; and that very matter which you pursue slips through your fingers like a wave; the adoration of humanity for itself and by itself (which brings us to the doctrine of the useful in Art, to the theories of public safety and reason of state, to all the injustices and all the intolerances, to the immolation of the right, to the leveling of the Beautiful), that cult of the belly, I say, breeds wind.' One thing he makes clear by reiteration through the various periods of his life: his disapproval of the ideal of equality. What is wanted, he keeps insisting, is 'justice'; and behind this demand for justice is evidently Flaubert's resentment, arising from his own experience, against the false reputations, the undeserved rewards and the stupid repressions of the Second Empire. And he was skeptical of popular education and opposed to universal suffrage.

Yet among the men of his time whom Flaubert admired most were democrats, humanitarians and reformers. 'You are certainly the French author,' he wrote Michelet, 'whom I have read and reread most'; and he said of Victor Hugo that Hugo was the living man 'in whose skin' he would be happiest to be. George Sand was one of his closest friends: *Un Cœur simple* was written for her—apparently in answer to her admonition that art was 'not merely criticism and satire' and to show her that he, too, had a heart.

When we come to Flaubert's books themselves, we find a much plainer picture of things.

It is not true, as is sometimes supposed, that he disclaimed any moral intention. He deliberately refrained in his novels from commenting on the action in his own character: 'the artist ought not to appear in his work any more than God in nature.' But, like

[75]

God, he rules his universe through law; and the reader, from what he hears and sees, must infer the moral system.

What *are* we supposed to infer from Flaubert's work? His general historical point of view is, I believe, pretty well known. He held that 'the three great evolutions of humanity' had been 'paganisme, christianisme, muflisme [muckerism],' and that Europe was in the third of these phases. Paganism he depicted in *Salammbô* and in the short story *Hérodias*. The Carthaginians of *Salammbô* had been savage and benighted barbarians: they had worshiped serpents, crucified lions, sacrificed their children to Moloch, and trampled armies to death with herds of elephants; but they had slaughtered, lusted and agonized superbly. Christianity is represented by the two legends of saints, *La Tentation de Saint Antoine* and *La Légende de Saint Julien l'Hospitalier*. The Christian combats his lusts, he expiates human cruelty; but this attitude, too, is heroic: Saint Anthony, who inhabits the desert, Saint Julien, who lies down with the leper, have pushed to their furthest limits the virtues of abnegation and humility. But when we come to the *muflisme* of the nineteenth century—in *Madame Bovary* and *L'Education sentimentale*—all is meanness, mediocrity and timidity.

The villain here is, of course, the bourgeois; and it is true that these two novels of Flaubert ridicule and damn the contemporary world, taking down its pretentions by comparing it with Carthage and the Thebaid. But in these pictures of modern life there is a complexity of human values and an analysis of social processes which does not appear in the books that deal with older civilizations; and this social analysis of Flaubert's has, it seems to me, been too much disregarded—with the result that *L'Education sentimentale*, one of his most remarkable books, has been rather underestimated.

In *Madame Bovary*, Flaubert is engaged in criticizing that very longing for the exotic and the faraway which played such a large part in his own life and which led him to write *Salammbô* and *Saint Antoine*. What cuts Flaubert off from the other romantics and makes him primarily a social critic is his grim realization of the futility of dreaming about the splendors of the Orient and the brave old days of the past as an antidote to bourgeois society. Emma Bovary, the wife of a small country doctor, is always seeing herself in some other setting, imagining herself someone else. She will not face her situation as it is, and the result is that she is eventually undone by the realities she has been trying to ignore. The upshot of all Emma's yearnings for a larger and more glamorous life is that her poor little daughter, left an orphan by Emma's suicide and the death of her father, is sent to work in a cotton mill.

The socialist of Flaubert's time might perfectly have approved of this: while the romantic individualist deludes himself with unrealizable fantasies, in the attempt to evade bourgeois society, and only succeeds in destroying himself, he lets humanity fall a victim to the industrial-commercial processes, which, unimpeded by his dreaming, go on with their deadly work.

Flaubert had more in common with, and had perhaps been influenced more by, the socialist thought of his time than he would ever have allowed himself to confess. In his novels, it is never the nobility—indistinguishable for mediocrity from the bourgeoisie —but the peasants and working people whom he habitually uses as touchstones to show up the pretensions of the bourgeois. One of the most memorable scenes in *Madame Bovary* is the agricultural exhibition at which the pompous local dignitaries award a medal to an old farm servant for forty-five years of service on the same farm. Flaubert has told us about the bourgeois at length, made us listen to a long speech by a town councilor on the flourishing state of France; and now he describes the peasant—scared by the flags and drums and by the gentlemen in black coats, and not understanding what is wanted of her. Her long and bony hands, with which she has worked all her life in stable dust, lye and greasy wool, still seem dirty, although she has just washed them, and they hang at her sides half open, as if to present a testimony of toil. There is no tenderness or sadness in her face: it has a rigidity almost monastic. And her long association with animals has given her something of their placidity and dumbness. 'So she stood up before those florid bourgeois, that half-century of servitude.' And the heroine of *Un Cœur simple*, a servant who devotes her whole life to the service of a provincial family and gets not one ray of love in return, has the same sort of dignity and pathos.

It is, however, in *L'Education sentimentale* that Flaubert's account of society comes closest to socialist theory. Indeed, his presentation here of the Revolution of 1848 parallels in so striking a manner Marx's analysis of the same events in *The Eighteenth Brumaire of Louis Napoleon* that it is worth while to focus together the diverse figures of Flaubert and Marx in order to recognize how two of the most searching minds of the century, pursuing courses so apparently divergent, arrived at almost identical interpretations of the happenings of their own time.

When we do this, we become aware that Marx and Flaubert started from very similar assumptions and that they were actuated by moral aims almost equally uncompromising. Both implacably hated the bourgeois, and both were resolved at any cost of worldly success to keep outside the bourgeois system. And Karl Marx, like Flaubert, shared to some degree the romantic bias in favor of the past. The author of *Das Kapital* can hardly, of course, be said to have had a very high opinion of any period of human history; but in comparison with the capitalist nineteenth century, he did betray a certain tenderness for Greece and Rome and the Middle Ages. He pointed out that the slavery of the ancient world had at least purchased the 'full development' of the masters, and that a certain Antipater of Thessalonica had joyfully acclaimed the invention of the water wheel for grinding corn because it would set free the female slaves who had formerly had to do this work, whereas the bourgeois economists had seen in machinery only a means for making the workers work faster and longer in order 'to transform a few vulgar and half-educated upstarts into "eminent cotton spinners," "extensive sausage makers" and "influential blacking dealers." ' And he had also a soft spot for the feudal system before the nobility had revolted against the Crown and while the rights of all classes, high and low, were still guaranteed by the king. Furthermore, the feudal lords, he insisted, had spent their money lavishly when they had it, whereas it was of the essence of capitalism that the capitalist saved his money and invested it, only to save and reinvest the profits.

[78]

Karl Marx's judgment on his age was the *Communist Manifesto*. Let us examine the implications of Flaubert's political novel. The hero of *L'Education sentimentale*, Frédéric Moreau, is a sensitive and intelligent young man equipped with a moderate income; but he has no stability of purpose and is capable of no emotional integrity. He becomes aimlessly, will-lessly, involved in love affairs with different types of women and he is unable to make anything out of any of them: they simply get in each other's way till in the end he is left with nothing. Frédéric is most in love from the very beginning of the story with the virtuous oval-faced wife of a sort of glorified drummer, who is engaged in more or less shady business enterprises; but, what with his timidity and her virtue, he never gets anywhere with her—even though she loves him in return—and leaves her in the hands of the drummer. Flaubert makes it plain to us, however, that Frédéric and the vulgar husband at bottom represent the same thing: Frédéric is only the more refined as well as the more incompetent side of the middle-class mediocrity of which the dubious promoter represents the more flashy and active aspect. And so in the case of the other characters, the journalists and the artists, the members of the various political factions, the remnants of the old nobility, Frédéric finds the same shoddiness and lack of principle which are gradually revealed in himself—the same qualities which render so odious to him the banker M. Dambreuse, the type of the rich and powerful class. M. Dambreuse is always ready to trim his sails to any political party, monarchist or republican, which seems to have a chance of success. 'Most of the men who were there,' Flaubert writes of the guests at the Dambreuse house, 'had served at least four governments; and they would have sold France or the human race in order to guarantee their fortune, to spare themselves an anxiety or a difficulty, or even from simple baseness, instinctive adoration of force.' 'Je me moque des affaires!' cries Frédéric when the guests at M. Dambreuse's are complaining that criticism of the government hurts business; but he cannot give up going to the house, because he always hopes to profit by Dambreuse's investments and influence.

The only really sympathetic characters in *L'Education senti-*

[79]

mentale are, again, the representatives of the people. Rosanette, Frédéric's mistress, is the daughter of poor workers in the silk mills, who sold her at fifteen as mistress to an old bourgeois. Her liaison with Frédéric is a symbol of the disastrously unenduring union between the proletariat and the bourgeoisie, of which Karl Marx had written in *The Eighteenth Brumaire*. After the suppression of the workers' insurrection during the June days of '48, Rosanette gives birth to a weakly child, which dies at the same time that Frédéric is already arranging a love affair with the dull wife of the banker. Frédéric believes that Mme Dambreuse will be able to advance his interests. And bourgeois socialism gets a very Marxist treatment—save in one respect, which we shall note in a moment—in the character of Sénécal, who is eternally making himself unpleasant about communism and the welfare of the masses, for which he is ready to fight to the last barricade. When, later, Sénécal gets a job as foreman in a pottery factory, he at once becomes a harsh little tyrant; and as soon as it begins to appear, after the putting-down of the June riots, that the reaction is sure to triumph, he decides, like certain radicals turned fascists, that the strong centralization of the government is already a kind of communism and that authority is in itself a great thing.

You have, on the other hand, the clerk Dussardier, a strapping and obtuse fellow, who is one of the few honest characters in the book. When we first see him, he has just knocked down a policeman in a political brawl on the street. Later, when the National Guard, of which Dussardier is a member, turns against the proletariat in the interests of law and order, Dussardier fells one of the insurgents from the top of a barricade and gets at the same time a bullet in the leg, thereby becoming a great hero of the bourgeois. But the poor fellow himself is unhappy. The boy that he had knocked down had wrapped the tricolor around him and shouted to the National Guard: 'Are you going to fire on your brothers?' Dussardier is not at all sure that he ought not to have been on the other side. His last appearance is at the climax of the story, constitutes, indeed, the climax: he turns up in a proletarian street riot, which the cavalry and the police are putting down. Dussardier refuses to move, crying 'Vive la République!'; and Frédéric comes along just in time to see one of the policemen kill him. Then he recognizes this policeman: it is the socialist, Sénécal.

L'Education sentimentale, unpopular when it first appeared, is likely, if we read it in youth, to prove baffling and even repellent. The title may have given the impression that we are going to get a love story, but the love affairs turn out invariably to be tepid or incomplete, and one finds oneself depressed or annoyed. Is it a satire? The characters are too close to life, and a little too well rounded, for satire. Yet they are not quite vitalized enough, not quite responsive enough, to seem the people of a straight novel. But we find that it sticks in our crop. If it is true, as Bernard Shaw has said, that *Das Kapital* makes us see the nineteenth century 'as if it were a cloud passing down the wind, changing its shape and fading as it goes,' so that we are afterwards never able to forget that 'capitalism, with its wage slavery, is only a passing phase of social development, following primitive communism, chattel slavery and feudal serfdom into the past'—so Flaubert's novel plants deep in our mind an idea which we never quite get rid of: the suspicion that our middle-class society of manufacturers, businessmen and bankers, of people who live on or deal in investments, so far from being redeemed by its culture, has ended by cheapening and invalidating all the departments of culture, political, scientific, artistic and religious, as well as corrupting and weakening the ordinary human relations: love, friendship and loyalty to cause—till the whole civilization seems to dwindle.

But fully to appreciate the book, one must have had time to see something of life and to have acquired a certain interest in social and political dramas as distinct from personal ones. If one rereads it in middle age, one finds that the author's tone no longer seems quite so acrid, that one is listening to a muted symphony of which the varied instrumentation and the pattern, the marked rhythms and the melancholy sonorities, had been hardly perceptible before. There are no hero, no villain, to arouse us, no clowns to entertain us, no scenes to wring our hearts. Yet the effect is deeply moving. It is the tragedy of nobody in particular, but of the poor human race itself reduced to such ineptitude, such cowardice, such commonness, such weak irresolution—arriving, with so many fine notions in its head, so many noble words on its lips, at a failure which is all the more miserable because those who have failed in their roles have even forgotten what roles they were cast for. We come to understand the statement of Mr. Ford Madox Ford that he has found it is not too much to read the book fourteen times. Though *L'Education sentimentale* is less attractive on the surface and less exciting as a story than *Madame Bovary*, it is certainly the book of Flaubert's which is most ambitiously planned and into which he has tried to put most. And once we have got the clue to the immense and complex drama which unrolls itself behind the half-screen of the detached and monotonous style, we find it as absorbing and satisfying as a great play or a great piece of music.

The one conspicuous respect in which Flaubert's point of view on the events of 1848 *diverges* from that of Marx has been thrown into special relief by the events of our own time. For Marx, the evolution of the socialist into a proletarian-persecuting policeman would have been blamed on the bourgeois in Sénécal; for Flaubert, it is a development of socialism implicit in socialist beginnings. He distrusted, as I have shown above, the authoritarian aims of the socialists. It is Flaubert's conception that Sénécal, given his bourgeois hypocrisy, is still carrying out a socialist principle—or rather, that his behavior as a policeman and his yearnings toward socialist control are both derived from his impulse toward despotism.

We may not be prepared to conclude that the evolution of Sénécal represents the whole destiny of socialism, but we must recognize that Flaubert had here brought to attention a danger of which Marx was not aware. We have had the opportunity to see how even a socialism which has come to power as the result of a proletarian revolution can breed a political police of almost unprecedented ruthlessness—how the example of Marx himself, with his emphasis on dictatorial control rather than on democratic processes, has contributed to produce this disaster. Flaubert, who believed that the artist should rid himself of social convictions, has gauged the tendencies of a political doctrine as the greatest of doctrinaires could not; and here the attitude he proposed has been justified.

The war of 1870 was a terrible shock to Flaubert: the nervous disorders of his later years have been attributed to it. He had the Prussians in his house at Croisset and had to bury his manuscripts. When he made a trip to Paris after the Commune, he came back to the country deeply shaken. 'This would never have happened,' he said when he saw the wreck of the Tuileries, 'if they had only understood *L'Education sentimentale*.' What Flaubert meant, no doubt, was that if the French had seen the falsity of their politics, they would never have fought about them so fiercely. 'Oh, how tired I am,' he writes George Sand, 'of the ignoble worker, the inept bourgeois, the stupid peasant and the odious ecclesiastic.'

But in his letters of this period, which are more violent than ever, we see him taking a new direction. The effect of the Commune on Flaubert, as on so many of the other French intellectuals, was to bring out in him the class-conscious bourgeois. Basically bourgeois his life had always been, with his mother and his little income. He had, like Frédéric Moreau himself, been 'cowardly in his youth,' he wrote George Sand. 'I was *afraid* of life.' And, even moving amongst what he regarded as the grandeurs of the ancient world, he remains a moderate Frenchman of the middle nineteenth century, who seems to cultivate excess, systematically and with a certain self-consciousness, in the hope of horrifying other Frenchmen. Marcel Proust has pointed out that Flaubert's imagery, even in books which do not deal with the bourgeois, tends to be rather banal. It was the enduring tradition of French classicism which had saved him from the prevailing shoddiness: by discipline and objectivity, by heroic application to the mastery of form, he had kept the enemy at a distance. But now when a working-class government had held Paris for two months and a half and had wrecked monuments and shot bourgeois hostages, Flaubert found himself as fierce against the Communards as any respectable 'grocer.' 'My opinion is,' he wrote George Sand, 'that the whole Commune ought to have been sent to the galleys, that

[83]

those sanguinary idiots ought to have been made to clean up the ruins of Paris, with chains around their necks like convicts. That would have wounded *humanity*, though. They treat the mad dogs with tenderness, but not the people whom they have bitten.' He raises his old cry for 'justice.' Universal suffrage, that 'disgrace to the human spirit,' must first of all be done away with; but among the elements of civilization which must be given their due importance he now includes 'race and even money' along with 'intelligence' and 'education.'

For the rest, certain political ideas emerge—though, as usual, in a state of confusion. 'The mass, the majority, are always idiotic. I haven't got many convictions, but that one I hold very strongly. Yet the mass must be respected, no matter how inept it is, because it contains the germs of an incalculable fecundity. Give it liberty, but not power. I don't believe in class distinctions any more than you do. The castes belong to the domain of archeology. But I do believe that the poor hate the rich and that the rich are afraid of the poor. That will go on forever. It is quite useless to preach the gospel of love to either. The most urgent need is to educate the rich, who are, after all, the strongest.' 'The only reasonable thing to do—I always come back to that—is a government of mandarins, provided that the mandarins know something and even that they know a great deal. The people is an eternal minor, and it will always (in the hierarchy of social elements) occupy the bottom place, because it is unlimited number, mass. It gets us nowhere to have large numbers of peasants learn to read and no longer listen to their priest; but it is infinitely important that there should be a great many men like Renan and Littré who can live and be listened to. Our salvation now is in a *legitimate aristocracy*, by which I mean a majority which will be made up of something other than numerals.' Renan himself and Taine were having recourse to similar ideas of the salvation of society through an 'élite.' In Flaubert's case, it never seems to have occurred to him that his hierarchy of mandarins and his project for educating the rich were identical with the notions of Saint-Simon, which he had rejected with scorn years before on the ground that they were too authoritarian. The Commune has stimulated in Flaubert a demand for his own kind of despotism.

He had already written in 1869: 'It's no longer a question of imagining the best form of government possible, because they are all alike, but of making sure that science prevails. That is the most urgent problem. Everything else will inevitably follow. The purely intellectual type of man has done more for the human race than all the Saint Vincent de Pauls in the world! And politics will remain idiotic forever so long as it does not derive from science. The government of a country ought to be a department of the Institute, and the least important of all.' 'Politics,' he reiterated in 1871, 'must become a positive science, as war has already become'; and, 'The French Revolution must cease to be a dogma and become part of the domain of science, like all the rest of human affairs.' Marx and Engels were not reasoning otherwise; but they believed, as Flaubert could not do, in a coming-of-age of the proletariat which would make possible the application of social science. To Flaubert the proletariat made a certain pathetic appeal, but it seemed to him much too stupid to act effectively in its own behalf; the Commune threw him into such a panic that he reviled the Communards as criminals and brutes. At one moment he writes to George Sand: 'The International may end by winning out, but not in the way that it hopes, not in the way that people are afraid of'; and then, two days later, 'the International will collapse, because it is on the wrong path. No ideas, nothing but envy!'

Finally, he wrote her in 1875: 'The words "religion" or "Catholicism," on the one hand, "progress," "fraternity," "democracy," on the other, no longer answer the spiritual needs of the day. The dogma of equality—a new thing—which the radicals have been crying up, has been proved false by the experiments of physiology and by history. I do not at the present time see any way of setting up a new principle, any more than of still respecting the old ones. So I search unsuccessfully for the central idea from which all the rest ought to depend.'

In the meantime, his work becomes more misanthropic. 'Never, my dear old chap,' he had written Ernest Feydeau, 'have I felt so colossal a disgust for mankind. I'd like to drown the human race under my vomit.' His political comedy, *Le Candidat*, produced in 1874, is the only one of his works which does not include a single character for whom one can feel any sympathy. The rich parvenu who is running for deputy not only degrades himself by every form of truckling and trimming in order to win the election, but sacrifices his daughter's happiness and allows himself to be cuckolded by his wife. The audiences would not have it; the actor who played the candidate came off the stage in tears. And, reading the play today, one cannot but agree with the public. It has some amusing and mordant passages, but one's gorge rises against it.

Flaubert then embarked on *Bouvard et Pécuchet*, which occupied him—with only one period of relief, when he indulged his suppressed kindliness and idealism in the relatively human *Trois Contes*—for most of the rest of his life. Here two copyists retire from their profession and set out to cultivate the arts and sciences. They make a mess of them all. The book contains an even more withering version of the events of 1848, in which the actors and their political attitudes are reduced to the scale of performing fleas. (There is one bitter scene, however, which has a terrible human force: that in which, the revolution having failed and the reaction having entrusted to the clergy the supervision of public education, the village priest visits the village schoolmaster, a freethinker who has been on the revolutionary side, and compels him, by threatening to dismiss him from the job which he needs to support his children, to consent to betray his principles by teaching catechism and sacred history.) When Bouvard and Pécuchet find at last that everything has 'cracked in their hands,' they go back to copying again. Flaubert did not live to finish the book; but he had already compiled some of the materials which he had intended to use in the second part: a collection of ridiculous statements and idiotic sentiments that Bouvard and Pécuchet were to find in the works they should copy.

This last uncompleted novel has somewhat mystified those critics who have taken it for an attack on the bourgeois like *L'Education sentimentale*—though there would not have been much point in Flaubert's simply doing the same thing again in a smaller and drier way. But M. René Dumesnil, one of the principal authorities on Flaubert, believes that *Bouvard et Pécuchet* was to have had a larger application. The anthology of 'idées reçus' was to have been not merely a credo of the bourgeois: it was to have included, also, many lapses by distinguished men of the past as well as the present, of writers, in certain cases, whom Flaubert immensely admired, and some passages, even, from Flaubert himself (in the first part of the book, it is obvious that the author is caricaturing his own ideas along with those of everybody else). Bouvard and Pécuchet, having realized the stupidity of their neighbors and discovered their own limitations, were to be left with a profound impression of the general imbecility and ignorance. They were themselves to assemble this monument to the inanity of the human mind.

If this be true—and the papers left by Flaubert seem to make his intention clear—he had lifted the blame from a social class and for the first time written a work of the type of _Gulliver's Travels_: a satire on the human race. The bourgeois has ceased to preach to the bourgeois: as the first big cracks begin to show in the structure of the nineteenth century, he shifts his complaint to the incompetence of humanity, for he is unable to believe in, or even to conceive, any non-bourgeois way out.

THE AMBIGUITY OF HENRY JAMES

A DISCUSSION of Henry James's ambiguity may appropriately begin with *The Turn of the Screw*. This story, which seems to have proved more fascinating to the general reading public than anything else of James's except *Daisy Miller*, perhaps conceals another horror behind the ostensible one. I do not know who first suggested this idea; but I believe that Miss Edna Kenton, whose insight into James is profound, was the first to write about it,* and the water-colorist Charles Demuth did a set of illustrations for the tale that were evidently based on this interpretation.

The theory is, then, that the governess who is made to tell the story is a neurotic case of sex repression, and that the ghosts are not real ghosts but hallucinations of the governess.

Let us see how the narrative runs. This narrative is supposed to have been written by the governess herself, but it begins with an introduction in which we are told something about her by a man whose sister's governess she had been after the time of the story. The youngest daughter of a poor country parson, she struck him, he explains, as 'awfully clever and nice . . . the most agreeable woman I've ever known in her position' and 'worthy of any whatever.' (Now, it is a not infrequent trick of James's to introduce sinister characters with descriptions that at first sound flattering, so this need not throw us off.) Needing work, she had come up to London to answer an advertisement and had found someone who wanted a governess for an orphaned nephew and niece. 'This

* In *The Arts*, November, 1924. This issue contains also photographs of the Demuth illustrations.

prospective patron proved a gentleman, a bachelor in the prime of life, such a figure as had never risen, save in a dream or an old novel, before a fluttered, anxious girl out of a Hampshire vicarage.' It is made clear that the young woman has become thoroughly infatuated with her employer. He is charming to her and lets her have the job on condition that she will take all the responsibility and never bother him about the children; and she goes down to the house in the country where they have been left with a housekeeper and some other servants.

The boy, she finds, has been sent home from school for reasons into which she does not inquire but which she colors, on no evidence at all, with a significance somehow ominous. She learns that her predecessor left, and that the woman has since died, under circumstances which are not explained but which are made in the same way to seem queer. The new governess finds herself alone with the good but illiterate housekeeper and the children, who seem innocent and charming. As she wanders about the estate, she thinks often how delightful it would be if one should come suddenly round the corner and see the master just arrived from London: there he would stand, handsome, smiling, approving.

She is never to meet her employer again, but what she does meet are the apparitions. One day when his face has been vividly in her mind, she comes out in sight of the house and, looking up, sees the figure of a man on a tower, a figure which is not the master's. Not long afterwards, the figure appears again, toward the end of a rainy Sunday. She sees him at closer range and more clearly: he is wearing smart clothes but is obviously not a gentleman. The housekeeper, meeting the governess immediately afterwards, behaves as if the governess herself were a ghost: 'I wondered why she should be scared.' The governess tells her about the apparition and learns that it answers the description of one of the master's valets, who had stayed down there and who had sometimes stolen his clothes. The valet had been a bad character, had used 'to play with the boy . . . to spoil him'; he had finally been found dead, having apparently slipped on the ice coming out of a public house—though one couldn't say he hadn't been murdered. The governess cannot help believing that he has come back to haunt the children.

Not long afterwards, she and the little girl are out on the shore of a lake, the child playing, the governess sewing. The latter becomes aware of a third person on the opposite side of the lake. But she looks first at little Flora, who is turning her back in that direction and who, she notes, has 'picked up a small flat piece of wood, which happened to have in it a little hole that had evidently suggested to her the idea of sticking in another fragment that might figure as a mast and make the thing a boat. This second morsel, as I watched her, she was very markedly and intently attempting to tighten in its place.' This somehow 'sustains' the governess so that she is able to raise her eyes: she sees a woman 'in black, pale and dreadful.' She concludes that it is the former governess. The housekeeper, questioned, tells her that this woman, although a lady, had had an affair with the valet. The boy had used to go off with the valet and then lie about it afterwards. The governess concludes that the boy must have known about the valet and the woman—the boy and girl have been corrupted by them.

Observe that there is never any reason for supposing that anybody but the governess sees the ghosts. She believes that the children see them, but there is never any proof that they do. The housekeeper insists that she does not see them; it is apparently the governess who frightens her. The children, too, become hysterical; but this is evidently the governess' doing. Observe, also, from the Freudian point of view, the significance of the governess' interest in the little girl's pieces of wood and of the fact that the male apparition first takes shape on a tower and the female apparition on a lake. There seems here to be only a single circumstance which does not fit into the hypothesis that the ghosts are mere fancies of the governess: the fact that her description of the masculine ghost at a time when she knows nothing of the valet should be identifiable as the valet by the housekeeper. And when we look back, we see that even this has perhaps been left open to a double interpretation. The governess has never heard of the valet, but it has been suggested to her in a conversation with the housekeeper that there has been some other male about who 'liked everyone young and pretty,' and the idea of this other person has been ambiguously confused with the master and with the master's possible interest in her, the present governess. And may she not, in her subconscious imagination, taking her cue from this, have associated herself with her predecessor and conjured up an image who wears the master's clothes but who (the Freudian 'censor' intervening) looks debased, 'like an actor,' she says (would he not have to stoop to love her)? The apparition had 'straight, good features' and his appearance is described in detail. When we look back, we find that the master's appearance has never been described at all: we have merely been told that he was 'handsome,' and it comes out in the talk with the housekeeper that the valet was 'remarkably handsome.' It is impossible for us to know how much the phantom resembles the master—the governess, certainly, would never tell.

The new apparitions now begin to be seen at night, and the governess becomes convinced that the children get up to meet them, though they are able to give plausible explanations of the behavior that has seemed suspicious. The housekeeper now says to the governess that, if she is seriously worried about all this, she ought to report it to the master. The governess, who has promised not to bother him, is afraid he would think her insane; and she imagines 'his derision, his amusement, his contempt for the breakdown of my resignation at being left alone and for the fine machinery I had set in motion to attract his attention to my slighted charms.' The housekeeper, hearing this, threatens to send for the master herself; the governess threatens to leave if she does. After this, for a considerable period, the visions no longer appear.

But the children become uneasy: they wonder when their uncle is coming, and they try to communicate with him—but the governess suppresses their letters. The boy finally asks her frankly when she is going to send him to school, intimates that if he had not been so fond of her, he would have complained to his uncle long ago, declares that he will do so at once.

This upsets her: she thinks for a moment of leaving, but decides that this would be deserting them. She is now, it seems, in love with the boy. Entering the schoolroom, after her conversation with him, she finds the ghost of the other governess sitting with her head in her hands, looking 'dishonored and tragic,' full of 'unutterable woe.' At this point the new governess feels— the morbid half of her split personality is now getting the upper hand of the other—that it is she who is intruding upon the ghost: 'You terrible miserable woman!' she cries. The apparition disappears. She tells the housekeeper, who looks at her oddly, that the soul of the woman is damned and wants the little girl to share her damnation. She finally agrees to write to the master, but no sooner has she sat down to the paper than she gets up and goes to the boy's bedroom, where she finds him lying awake. When he demands to go back to school, she embraces him and begs him to tell her why he was sent away; appealing to him with what seems to her desperate tenderness but in a way that disquiets the child, she insists that all she wants is to save him. There is a sudden gust of wind—it is a stormy night outside—the casement rattles, the boy shrieks. She has been kneeling beside the bed: when she gets up, she finds the candle extinguished. 'It was I who blew it, dear!' says the boy. For her, it is the evil spirit disputing her domination. She cannot imagine that the boy may really have blown out the candle in order not to have to tell her with the light on about his disgrace at school. (Here, however, occurs a detail which is less easily susceptible of double explanation: the governess has *felt* a 'gust of frozen air' and yet sees that the window is 'tight.' Are we to suppose she merely fancied that she felt it?)

The next day, the little girl disappears. They find her beside the lake. The young woman for the first time now speaks openly to one of the children about the ghosts. 'Where, my pet, is Miss Jessel?' she demands—and immediately answers herself: 'She's there, she's there!' she cries, pointing across the lake. The housekeeper looks with a 'dazed blink' and asks where she sees anything; the little girl turns upon the governess 'an expression of hard, still gravity, an expression absolutely new and unprecedented and that appeared to read and accuse and judge me.' The governess feels her 'situation horribly crumble' now. The little girl breaks down, becomes feverish, begs to be taken away from the governess; the housekeeper sides with the child and hints that the governess had better go. But the young woman forces her, instead, to take the little girl away; and she tries to make it impossible, before their departure, for the children to see one another.

She is now left alone with the boy. A strange and dreadful scene ensues. 'We continued silent while the maid was with us—as silent, it whimsically occurred to me, as some young couple who, on their wedding-journey, at the inn, feel shy in the presence of the waiter.' When the maid has gone, and she presses him to tell her the reason for his expulsion from school, the boy seems suddenly afraid of her. He finally confesses that he 'said things'— to 'a few,' to 'those he liked.' It all sounds sufficiently harmless: there comes to her out of her 'very pity the appalling alarm of his being perhaps innocent. It was for the instant confounding and bottomless, for if he *were* innocent, what then on earth was I?' The valet appears at the window—it is 'the white face of damnation.' (But is it really the spirits who are damned or the governess who is slipping to damnation herself?) She is aware that the boy does not see it. 'No more, no more, no more!' she shrieks to the apparition. 'Is she *here?*' demands the boy in panic. (He has, in spite of the governess' efforts, succeeded in seeing his sister and has heard from her of the incident at the lake.) No, she says, it is not the woman: 'But it's at the window— straight before us. It's *there!*' . . . 'It's *he?*' then. Whom does he mean by 'he'? ' "Peter Quint—you devil!" His face gave again, round the room, its convulsed supplication. "Where?" ' 'What does he matter now, my own?' she cries. 'What will he *ever* matter? I have you, but he has lost you forever!' Then she shows him that the figure has vanished: 'There, *there!*' she says, pointing toward the window. He looks and gives a cry; she feels that he is dead in her arms. From the governess' point of view, the final disappearance of the spirit has proved too terrible a shock for the child and 'his little heart, dispossessed, has stopped'; but if we study the dialogue from the other point of view, we see that he must have taken her 'There, *there!*' as an answer to his own 'Where?' Instead of persuading him that there is nothing to be frightened of, she has, on the contrary, finally convinced him either that he has actually seen or that he is just about to see

[93]

some horror. He gives 'the cry of a creature hurled over an abyss.' She has literally frightened him to death.

When one has once got hold of the clue to this meaning of *The Turn of the Screw*, one wonders how one could ever have missed it. There is a very good reason, however, in the fact that nowhere does James unequivocally give the thing away: almost everything from beginning to end can be read equally in either of two senses. In the preface to the collected edition, however, as Miss Kenton has pointed out, James does seem to want to give a hint. He asserts that *The Turn of the Screw* is 'a fairy-tale pure and simple'—but adds that the apparitions are of the order of those involved in witchcraft cases rather than of those in cases of psychic research. And he goes on to tell of his reply to one of his readers who objected that he had not characterized the governess sufficiently. At this criticism, he says, 'One's artistic, one's ironic heart shook for the instant almost to breaking'; and he answered: 'It was *"déjà trés-joli"* . . . please believe, the general proposition of our young woman's keeping crystalline her record of so many intense anomalies and obscurities—*by which I don't of course mean her explanation of them, a different matter. . .* She has "authority," which is a good deal to have given her. . .' The italics above are mine: these words seem impossible to explain except on the hypothesis of hallucination (though this is hardly consistent with the intention of writing 'a fairy-tale pure and simple'). And note too, that in the collected edition James has not included *The Turn of the Screw* in the volume with his other ghost stories but with stories of another kind: between *The Aspern Papers* and *The Liar*—the first a study of a curiosity which becomes a mania and menace (to which we shall revert in a moment), the second a study of a pathological liar, whose wife protects his lies against the world, acting with very much the same sort of 'authority' as the governess in *The Turn of the Screw*.

When we look back in the light of these hints, we are inclined to conclude from analogy that the story is primarily intended as a characterization of the governess: her somber and guilty visions and the way she behaves about them seem to present, from the moment we examine them from the obverse side of her narrative, an accurate and distressing picture of the poor country parson's daughter, with her English middle-class class-consciousness, her inability to admit to herself her natural sexual impulses and the relentless English 'authority' which enables her to put over on inferiors even purposes which are totally deluded and not at all in the other people's best interests. Remember, also, in this connection, the peculiar psychology of governesses, who, by reason of their isolated position between the family and the servants, are likely to become ingrown and morbid. One has heard of actual cases of women who have frightened a household by opening doors or smashing mirrors and who have succeeded in torturing parents by mythical stories of kidnappers. The traditional 'poltergeist' who breaks crockery and upsets furniture has been for centuries a recurring phenomenon. First a figure of demonology, he later became an object of psychic research, and is now a recognized neurotic type.

Once we arrive at this conception of *The Turn of the Screw*, we can see in it a new significance in its relation to Henry James's other work. We find now that it is a variation on one of his familiar themes: the thwarted Anglo-Saxon spinster; and we remember unmistakable cases of women in James's fiction who deceive themselves and others about the origins of their aims and emotions. One of the most obvious examples is that remarkable and too little read novel, *The Bostonians*. The subject of *The Bostonians* is the struggle for the daughter of a poor evangelist between a young man from the South who wants to marry her and a well-to-do Boston lady with a Lesbian interest in her. The strong-minded and strong-willed spinster is herself apparently quite in the dark as to the real character of her feeling for the girl: she is convinced that her desire to dominate her, to have her always living with her, to teach her to make speeches on women's rights and to prevent the young Southerner from marrying her, is a disinterested ardor for the Feminist cause. But the reader is not left in doubt; and Olive Chancellor is shown us in a setting of other self-deluded New England idealists.

There is a theme of very much the same kind in the short story called *The Marriages*, which amused R. L. Stevenson so hugely. But here the treatment is frankly comic. A young and rather stupid girl, described as of the unmarriageable type, but much attached to her widower father and obsessed by the memory of her mother, undertakes to set up an obstacle to her father's proposed second marriage. Her project, which she carries out, is to go to his fiancée and tell this lady that her father is an impossible character who had made her late mother miserable. She thus breaks up the projected match; and when her brother calls her a raving maniac, she is not in the least disquieted in her conviction that, by frustrating her father, she has proved faithful in her duty to her mother.

James's world is full of these women. They are not always emotionally perverted. Sometimes they are apathetic—like the charming Francie Dosson of *The Reverberator*, who, though men are always falling in love with her, seems not really ever to have grasped what courtship and marriage mean and is apparently quite content to go on all the rest of her life eating *marrons glacés* with her family in a suite in a Paris hotel. Or they are longing, these women, for affection but too inhibited or passive to obtain it for themselves, like the pathetic Milly Theale of *The Wings of the Dove*, who wastes away in Venice and whose doctor recommends a lover.

II

James's men are not precisely neurotic; but they are the masculine counterparts of his women. They have a way of missing out on emotional experience, either through timidity or prudence or through heroic renunciation.

The extreme and fantastic example is the hero of *The Beast in the Jungle*, who is finally crushed by the realization that his fate is to be the man in the whole world to whom nothing at all is to happen. Some of these characters are presented ironically: Mr. Acton of *The Europeans*, so smug and secure in his clean-swept house, deciding not to marry the baroness who has proved such an upsetting element in his little New England community, is an amusing and accurate portrait of a certain kind of careful Bostonian. Others are made sympathetic, such as the starved Lambert Strether of *The Ambassadors*, who comes to Paris too late in life.

Sometimes, however, the effect is ambiguous. Though the element of irony in Henry James is often underestimated by his readers, there are stories which leave us in doubt as to whether or not the author could foresee how his heroes would strike the reader. Is the fishy Bernard Longueville, for example, of the early novel called *Confidence* really intended for a sensitive and interesting young man or is he a prig in the manner of Jane Austen? This is not due to a beginner's uncertainty, for some of James's later heroes make us uneasy in a similar way. The very late short story *Flickerbridge,* in which a young American painter decides not to marry a young newspaper woman (the men are always deciding *not* to marry the women in Henry James) because he fears that she will spoil by publicizing it a delightful old English house, the property of a cousin of hers, which she herself has not yet seen but at which he has enjoyed visiting—this story is even harder to swallow, since it is all too evident here that the author approves of his hero.

But what are we to think of *The Sacred Fount?* This short novel, surely James's most curious production, inspired when it first appeared a parody by Owen Seaman which had a certain historical significance because the book seemed to mark the point at which James, for the general public, had definitely become unassimilable, and therefore absurd or annoying. *The Sacred Fount* was written not long after *The Turn of the Screw* and is a sort of companionpiece to it. Here we have the same setting of an English country house, the same passages of a strange and sad beauty, the same furtive subversive happenings in an atmosphere of clarity and brightness, the same dubious central figure, the same almost inscrutable ambiguity. As in the case of *The Turn of the Screw,* the fundamental question presents itself and never seems to get properly answered: What is the reader to think of the protagonist? —who is here a man instead of a woman.

It would be tedious to analyze *The Sacred Fount* as I have done *The Turn of the Screw*—and it would prove, I think, somewhat more difficult. The book is not merely mystifying but maddening. Yet I believe that if one got to the bottom of it, a good deal of light would be thrown on the author. Rebecca West, in her little book on James, has given a burlesque account of this novel as the story of how 'a week-end visitor spends more intellectual force than Kant can have used on *The Critique of Pure Reason* in an unsuccessful attempt to discover whether there exists between certain of his fellow-guests a relationship not more interesting among these vacuous people than it is among sparrows.' This visitor, who himself tells the story, observes that, among the other guests, a man and a woman he knows, both of them middle-aged, appear to have taken a new lease on life, whereas a younger man and woman appear to have been depleted. He evolves a theory about them: he imagines that the married couples have been forming new combinations and that the younger man and woman have been feeding the older pair from the sacred fount of their youth at the price of getting used up themselves.

This theory seems rather academic—and does James really mean us to accept it? Do not the narrator's imaginings serve to characterize the narrator just as the governess' ghosts serve to characterize the governess? As this detached and rather eerie individual proceeds to spy on and question his friends in order to find out whether the facts fit his hypothesis, we decide, as we do with *The Turn of the Screw*, that there are two separate stories to be kept distinct: a romance which the narrator is spinning and a reality which we are supposed to divine from what he tells us about what actually happens. We remember the narrator of *The Aspern Papers*, another prying and importunate fellow, who is finally foiled and put to rout by the old lady whose private papers he is trying by fraud to get hold of. In the case of *The Aspern Papers*, there is no uncertainty whatever as to what we are to think of the narrator: the author is quite clear that the papers were none of the journalist's business and that the rebuff he received served him right. Now, the amateur detective of *The Sacred Fount* is also foiled and rebuffed, and in very much the same manner, by one of his recalcitrant victims. 'My poor dear, you *are* crazy, and I bid you good-night!' she says to him at the end of the story. 'Such a last word,' the narrator remarks, 'the word that put me altogether nowhere—was too inacceptable not to prescribe afresh that prompt test of escape to other air for which I had earlier in the evening seen so much reason. I *should* certainly never again, on the spot, quite hang together, even though it wasn't really that I hadn't three times her method. What I too fatally lacked was her tone.' But *why* did he lack her tone?—*why* would he not hang together? What view are we supposed to take of the whole exploit of this singular being?

Mr. Wilson Follett, the only writer, so far as I know, who has given special attention to *The Sacred Fount*,* believes that the book is a parable—even a conscious parody—of James's own role as an artist. The narrator may or may not have been right as to the actual facts of the case. The point is that, in elaborating his theory, he has constructed a work of art, and that you cannot test the validity of works of art by checking them against actuality. The kind of reality that art achieves, made up of elements abstracted from experience and combined in a new way by the artist, would be destroyed by a collision with the actual, and the artist would find himself blocked.

Now it may very well be true that James has put himself into *The Sacred Fount*—that he has intended some sort of fable about the brooding imaginative mind and the material with which it works. But it seems to me that Mr. Follett's theory assumes on James's part a conception of artistic truth which would hardly be worthy of him. After all, the novelist must pretend to know what people are actually up to, however much he may rearrange actuality; and it is not clear in *The Sacred Fount* whether the narrator really knows what he is talking about. If the book is, then, merely a parody, what is the point of the parody? Why should James have represented the artist as defeated by the breaking-in of life?

The truth is, I believe, that Henry James was not clear about the book in his own mind. Already, with *The Turn of the Screw*, he has carried his ambiguous procedure to a point where we almost feel that the author does not want the reader to get through to the hidden meaning. See his curious replies in his letters to correspondents who write him about the story: when they chal-

* *Henry James's 'Portrait of Henry James'* in the *New York Times Book Review*, August 23, 1936. (Since my own essay was first written, Mr. Edward Sackville West, in the *New Statesman and Nation* of October 4, 1947, has taken issue with the views here expressed in the best defense of this book I have seen.)

lenge him with leading questions, he seems to give evasive answers, dismissing the tale as a mere 'pot-boiler,' a mere *jeu d'esprit*. There was no doubt in *The Bostonians*, for example, as to what view the reader was intended to take of such a character as Olive Chancellor: Olive, though tragic perhaps, is definitely unhealthy and horrid, and she is vanquished by Basil Ransom. But James does leave his readers uncomfortable as to what they are to think of the governess. And now, in *The Sacred Fount*, we do not know whether the week-end guest, though he was unquestionably obnoxious to the other guests, is intended to be taken as one of the élite, a fastidious, highly civilized sensibility, or merely as a little bit cracked and a bore. The man who tried to get the Aspern papers was a fanatic, a cad and a nuisance; but many of James's inquisitive observers who never take part in the action are presented as superior people, and Henry James had confessed to being an inquisitive observer himself. Ambiguity was certainly growing on him. It was eventually to pass all bounds in those scenes in his later novels (of which the talks in *The Turn of the Screw* between the housekeeper and the governess are only comparatively mild examples) in which he compels his characters to carry on long conversations with each of the interlocutors always mistaking the other's meaning and neither ever yielding to the impulse to say one of the obvious things that would clear the situation up.

What if the hidden theme of *The Sacred Fount* is simply sex again? What if the real sacred fount, from which the narrator's acquaintances have been drawing their new vitality, is love, sexual love, instead of youth? They have something which he has not had, know something which he does not know; and, lacking the clue of experience, he can only misunderstand them and elaborate pedantic hypotheses; while they, having the forces of life on their side, are in a position to frighten him away. This theory may be dubious, also; but there is certainly involved in *The Sacred Fount*, whether or not Henry James quite meant to put it there, the conception of a man shut out from love, condemned to peep at other people's activities and to speculate about them rather barrenly, who will be shocked and put to rout when he touches the live current of human relations.

Hitherto, as I have said, it has usually been plain what James wanted us to think of his characters; but now there appears in his work a relatively morbid element which is not always handled objectively and which seems to have invaded the storyteller himself. It is as if at this point he had taken to dramatizing the frustrations of his own life without quite being willing to confess it, without fully admitting it even to himself.

But before we go further with this line of inquiry, let us look at Henry James in another connection.

III

Who *are* these characters of James's about whom we come to be less certain as to precisely what we ought to think?

The type of Henry James's observers and sometimes of his heroes is the cultivated American bourgeois, like Henry James himself, who lives on an income derived from some form of business activity, usually left rather vague, but who has rarely played any part in the efforts which have created the business. These men turn their backs on the commercial world; they disdain its vulgarity and dullness, and they attempt to enrich their experience through the society and art of Europe. But they bring to these the bourgeois qualities of timidity, prudence, primness, the habits of mind of a puritan morality, which, even when they wish to be men of the world, make it too easy for them to be disconcerted. They wince alike at the brutalities of the aristocracy and at the coarseness of the working class; they shrink most of all from the 'commonness' of the less polished bourgeoisie, who, having acquired their incomes more recently, are not so far advanced in self-improvement. The women have the corresponding qualities: they are innocent, conventional and rather cold—sometimes they suffer from Freudian complexes or a kind of arrested development, sometimes they are neglected or cruelly cheated by the men to whom they have given their hearts. And even when James's central characters are English, they assimilate themselves to these types.

It is enlightening in this connection to compare James's point of view with Flaubert's. The hero of *L'Education sentimentale* is a perfect Henry James character: he is sensitive, cautious, afraid

[101]

of life; he lives on a little income and considers himself superior to the common run. But Flaubert's attitude toward Frédéric Moreau is devastatingly ironic. Frédéric has his aspects of pathos, his occasional flashes of spirit: but Flaubert is quite emphatic in his final judgment of Frédéric. He considers Frédéric a worm.

Now, James has his own kind of irony, but it is not Flaubert's kind. Frédéric Moreau, in a sense, is the hero of many of James's novels, and you can see how the American's relation to him usually differs from the Frenchman's if you compare certain kinds of scenes which tend to recur in Henry James with certain scenes in L'Education sentimentale of which they sometimes seem like an echo: those ominous situations in which we find the sensitive young man either immersed in some sort of gathering or otherwise meeting successively a number of supposed friends, more worldly and unscrupulous persons, who are obviously talking over his head, acting behind his back, without his being able, in his innocence, quite to make out what they are up to. You have this same situation, as I say, in James and in Flaubert; but the difference is that, whereas with James the young man is made wondering and wistful and is likely to turn out a pitiful victim, with Flaubert he is quietly and cruelly made to look like a fool and is as ready to double-cross these other people who seem to him so inferior to himself as they are to double-cross him.

In this contrast between Flaubert's treatment of Frédéric Moreau and James's treatment of, say, Hyacinth Robinson in The Princess Casamassima is to be found perhaps one of the reasons for James's resentment of Flaubert. James had known Flaubert, had read him when young, had obviously been impressed by his work; he had it in common with the older man that he wanted to give dignity and integrity to the novel of modern life by imposing on it rigorous esthetic form. Yet there is something about Flaubert that sticks in his crop, and he keeps up a sort of running quarrel with him, returning to the subject again and again in the course of his critical writing. But though it is plain that James cannot help admiring the author of Madame Bovary, he usually manages before he has done to give the impression of belittling him—and he is especially invidious on the subject of L'Education sentimentale. His great complaint is that Flaubert's characters are intrinsically so ignoble that they do not deserve to be treated at length or to have so much art expended on them and that there must have been something wrong with Flaubert for him ever to have supposed that they did. James does not seem to understand that Flaubert *intends* all his characters to be 'middling' and that the greatness of his work arises from the fact that it constitutes a criticism of something bigger than they are. James praises the portrait of Mme Arnoux: let us thank God, at least, he exclaims, that Flaubert was able here to command the good taste to deal delicately with a fine-grained woman! He does not seem to be aware that Mme Arnoux is treated as ironically as any of the other characters—that the virtuous bourgeois wife with her inhibitions and superstitions is pathetic only as a part of the failure of a civilization. Henry James mistakes Mme Arnoux for a refined American woman and he is worried because Frédéric isn't one of his own American heroes, quietly vibrating and scrupulously honorable. Yet it probably makes him uncomfortable to feel that Flaubert is flaying remorselessly the squeamish young man of this type; and it may be that Henry James's antagonism to Flaubert has something to do with the fact that the latter's all-permeating criticism of the pusillanimity of the bourgeois soul has touched Henry James himself. The protagonists of the later James are always regretting having lived too meagerly; and James distills from these non-participants all the sad self-effacing nobility, all the fine wan beauty, they are good for. Flaubert extracts something quite different from Frédéric Moreau—a kind of acrid insecticide: when Frédéric and his friend, both middle-aged by now, recall at the end of the book their first clumsy and frightened visit to a brothel as the best that life has had to offer them, it is a damnation of their whole society.

But there was another kind of modern society which Gustave Flaubert did not know and which Henry James did. Henry James was himself that new anomalous thing, an American. He had, to be sure, lived a good deal in Europe both in childhood and early manhood, and he had to a considerable extent become imbued with the European point of view—so that the monuments of antiquity and feudalism, the duchesses and princesses and princes who seem to carry on the feudal tradition, are still capable of having the effect for him of making modern life look undistinguished. But the past, in the case of James, does not completely dwarf the present, as the vigil of Flaubert's Saint Anthony and the impacts of his pagan armies diminish Frédéric Moreau. The American in Henry James asserts himself insistently against Europe. After all, Frédéric Moreau and the respectable Mme Arnoux are the best people of Albany and Boston!—but in America they are not characters in Flaubert. Their scruples and renunciations have a real moral value here—for Frédéric Moreau at home possesses a real integrity; and when these best people come over to Europe, they judge the whole thing in a quite new way. James speaks somewhere of his indignation at an Englishwoman's saying to him in England, in connection with something they were discussing: 'That is true of the aristocracy, but in one's own class it is quite different.' As an American and the grandson of a millionaire, it had never occurred to James that anyone could consider him a middle-class person. When Edith Wharton accused him in his later years of no longer appreciating Flaubert and demanded of him why Emma Bovary, the choice of whom as a heroine he had always deplored, was not just as good a subject for fiction as Tolstoy's Anna Karenina, he replied: 'Ah, but one paints the fierce passions of a luxurious aristocracy; the other deals with the petty miseries of a little bourgeoise in a provincial town!' But if Emma Bovary is small potatoes, what about Daisy Miller? Why, Daisy Miller is an American girl! Emma Bovary has her longings and her debts and her adulteries, but she is otherwise a conventional person, she remains in her place in the social scheme even when she dreams of rising out of it. So great is the prestige for her of the local nobility that when she goes to the château for the ball, the very sugar in the sugar bowl seems to her whiter and finer than the sugar she has at home; whereas a girl like Daisy Miller as well as one like Isabel Archer represents a human species that had been bred outside of Europe and that cannot be accommodated or judged inside the European frame. When this species comes back to Europe, it tends to disregard the social system. Europe is too much for Daisy Miller: she catches cold in the Coliseum, where according to European conventions she oughtn't to have been at that hour. But the great popularity of her story was certainly due to the fact that her creator had somehow conveyed the impression that her spirit went marching on.

There evidently went on in the mind of James a debate that was never settled between the European and the American points of view; and this conflict may have had something to do with his inability sometimes to be clear as to what he wants us to think of a certain sort of person. It is quite mistaken to talk as if James had uprooted himself from America in order to live in England. He had traveled so much from his earliest years that he had never had real roots anywhere. His father had himself been a wandering intellectual, who had oscillated back and forth between Europe and the United States; and even in America the Jameses were always oscillating between New York and Boston. They were not New Englanders even by ancestry, but New Yorkers of Irish and Scotch-Irish stock, and they had none of the tight New England local ties—they always came to Boston from a larger outside world and their point of view about it was objective and often rather ironical. To this critical attitude on Henry's part was probably partly due the failure of *The Bostonians*; and this failure seems to mark the moment of his abandonment of his original ambition of becoming the American Balzac, as it does that of his taking up his residence in England and turning, for the subjects of his fiction, from the Americans to the English. He had been staying for some time in London, and he found he liked living in London better than in New York or New England, better than in Paris or Rome. His parents in the States had just died, and his sister came over to join him.

IV

And this brings us to what seems to have been the principal crisis in Henry James's life and work. We know so little about his personal life from any other source than himself, and even in his memoirs and letters he tells us so little about his emotions, that it is impossible to give any account of it save as it reflects itself in his writings.

Up to the period of his playwriting, his fiction has been pretty plain sailing. He has aimed to be a social historian, and, in a limited field, he has succeeded. His three long novels of the later eighties—*The Bostonians, The Princess Casamassima* and *The Tragic Muse*—are, indeed, as social history, his most ambitious undertakings, and from the conventional point of view—that of the reporting of the surface of life—by far his most successful. The first hundred pages of *The Bostonians,* with the arrival of the young Southerner in Boston and his first contacts with the Boston reformers, is, in its way, one of the most masterly things that Henry James ever did. *The Princess Casamassima,* with its opening in the prison and its revolutionary exiles in London, deals with issues and social contrasts of a kind that James had never before attempted. The familiar criticism of Henry James—the criticism made by H. G. Wells: that he had no grasp of politics or economics—does not, in fact, hold true of these books. Here his people do have larger interests and functions aside from their personal relations: they have professions, missions, practical aims; and they also engage in more drastic action than in his novels of any other period. Basil Ransom pursues Verena Tarrant and rescues her from the terrible Olive Chancellor; Hyacinth Robinson pledges himself to carry out a political assassination, then commits suicide instead; Miriam Rooth makes her career as a great actress. One finds in all three of these novels a will to participate in life, to play a responsible role, quite different from the passive ones of the traveler who merely observes or the victim who merely suffers, that had seemed characteristic of James's fiction. Up to a point these books are brilliant.

But there is a point—usually about half way through—at which every one of these novels begins strangely to run into the sands; the excitement of the story lapses at the same time as the treatment becomes more abstract and the color fades from the picture. The ends are never up to the beginnings. This is most obvious—even startling—in *The Tragic Muse,* the first volume of which, as we read it, makes us think that it must be James's best novel, so solid and alive does it seem. Here are areas of experience and types of a kind that James has never before given us: a delicately comic portrait of a retired parliamentarian, which constitutes, by implication, a criticism of British Liberal politics; a really charged and convincing scene between a man and a woman (Nick Dormer and Julia Dallow) in place of the mild battledore-and-shuttlecock that we are accustomed to getting from James; and, in Miriam Rooth, the Muse, a character who comes nearer to carrying the author out of the bounds of puritan scruples and prim prejudices on to the larger and more dangerous stage of human creative effort than any other he has hitherto drawn. Here at last we are among complete people, who have the appetites and ambitions that we recognize—and in comparison, the characters of his earlier works only seem real in a certain convention. Then suddenly the story stops short: after the arrival of Miriam in London, *The Tragic Muse* is almost a blank. Of the two young men who have been preoccupied with Miriam, one renounces her because she will not leave the stage and the other doesn't, apparently, fall in love with her. Miriam herself, to be sure, makes a great success as an actress, but we are never taken into her life, we know nothing at first hand of her emotions. The only decisions that are looming are negative ones, and the author himself seems to lose interest.

These earlier chapters of *The Tragic Muse* are the high point of the first part of James's career, after which something snaps. He announces that he will write no more long novels, but only fiction of shorter length; and it may be that he has become aware of his failure in his longer novels to contrive the mounting-up to a climax of intensity and revelation which, in order to be effective, this kind of full-length fiction demands. At any rate, he applied himself to writing plays, and for five years he produced little else; but one wonders when one reads these plays—in the two volumes he called *Theatricals*—why James should have sacrificed not only his time but also all the strength of his genius for work that was worse than mediocre. He had had reason to complain at this period that he had difficulty in selling his fiction, and he confessed that his plays were written in the hope of a popular success, and that they were intended merely as entertainment and were not to be taken too seriously—seeking to excuse that which 'would otherwise be inexplicable' by invoking 'the uttermost regions of dramatic amiability, the bland air of the little domestic fairy-tale.' Yet the need for money and even for fame is surely an insufficient explanation for the phenomenon of a novelist of James's gifts almost entirely abandoning the art in which he has perfected himself to write plays that are admittedly trivial.

That there was something insufficient and unexplained about James's emotional life seems to appear unmistakably from his novels. I believe that it may be said that there have not been up to this point any consummated love affairs in his fiction—that is, none among the principal characters and while the action of the story is going on; and this deficiency must certainly have contributed to his increasing loss of hold on his readers. It is not merely that he gave in *The Bostonians* an unpleasant picture of Boston, and in *The Tragic Muse*, on the whole, a discouraging picture of the English; it is not merely that *The Princess Casamassima* treated a social-revolutionary subject from a point of view that was non-political and left neither side a moral advantage. It was not merely that he was thus at this period rather lost between America and England. It was also that you cannot enchant an audience with stories about men wooing women in which the parties either never get together or are never seen functioning as lovers. And you will particularly dampen your readers with a story—*The Tragic Muse*—which deals with two men and a girl but in which neither man ever gets her. There is, as I have said, in *The Tragic Muse*, one of his more convincing man-and-woman relationships. Julia Dallow is really female and she behaves like a woman with Nick Dormer; but here the woman's political ambitions get between Nick and her, so that this, too, never comes to anything: here the man, again, must renounce. (In Henry James's later novels, these healthily female women—Kate Croy and Charlotte Stant—are to take on a character frankly sinister.) Years later, Henry James explained in his preface to *The Tragic Muse* that the prudery, in the eighties, of the American magazines had made it impossible for Miriam Rooth to follow the natural course of becoming Nick Dormer's mistress; and certainly the skittishness of a public that was scandalized by *Jude the Obscure* is not to be underestimated. But, after all, Hardy did write about Jude, and Meredith about Lord Ormont and his Aminta, and let the public howl; and it might well have enhanced Henry James's reputation—to which he was by no means indifferent—if he had done the same thing himself. Problems of sexual passion in conflict with convention and law were beginning to be subjects of burning interest. But it is probable that James had by this time—not consciously, perhaps, but instinctively—come to recognize his unfittedness for dealing with them and was far too honest to fake.

One feels about the episode of his playwriting that it was an effort to put himself over, an effort to make himself felt, as he had never succeeded in doing. His brother William James wrote home in the summer of 1889, at the beginning of this playwriting period, that Henry, beneath the 'rich sea-weeds and rigid barnacles and things' of 'strange heavy alien manners and customs' with which he had covered himself like a 'marine crustacean,' remained the 'same dear old, good, innocent and at bottom very powerless-feeling Harry.' He had seriously injured his back in an accident in his boyhood, and it was necessary for him still, in his forties, to lie down for regular rests. And now it is as if he were trying to put this 'broken back,' as he once called it, into making an impression through the drama as he had never been able to put it into a passion. His heroine Miriam Rooth has just turned away from the Philistine English world which rejects her and taken into the theater the artist's will with which she is to conquer that world; and her creator is now to imitate her.

But his plays were either not produced or not well received. At the first night of *Guy Domville* (January 5, 1895), he ran foul of a gallery of hooligans, who booed and hissed him when he came before the curtain. Their displeasure had evidently been partly due to a feeling of having been let down by one of James's inevitable scenes of abdication of the lover's role: the hero, at the end of the play, had rejected a woman who adored him and an estate he had just inherited in order to enter the Church. These five years of unsuccessful playwriting had put Henry James under a strain, and this was the final blow. When he recovers from his disappointment, he is seen to have passed through a crisis.

Now he enters upon a new phase, of which the most obvious feature is a subsidence back into himself. And now sex *does* appear in his work—even becoming a kind of obsession—in a queer and left-handed way. We have *The Turn of the Screw* and *The Sacred Fount*; *What Maisie Knew* and *In the Cage*. There are plenty of love affairs now and plenty of irregular relationships, but there are always thick screens between them and us; illicit appetites, maleficent passions, now provide the chief interest, but they are invariably seen from a distance.

For the Jamesian central observer who has become a special feature of his fiction—the reflector by whose consciousness is registered all that we know of events—has undergone a diminution. This observer is less actively involved and is rarely a complete and a full-grown person: we have a small child who watches her elders, a female telegraph operator who watches the senders of telegrams and lives vicariously through them, a week-end guest who seems not to exist in any other capacity whatever except that of week-end guest and who lives vicariously through his fellow guests. The people who surround this observer tend to take on the diabolic values of the specters of *The Turn of the Screw*, and these diabolic values are almost invariably connected with sexual relations that are always concealed and at which we are compelled to guess. The innocent Nanda Brookenham of *The Awkward Age*, a work of the same period and group, is hemmed in by a whole host of goblins who beckon and hint and whisper and exhale a creepy atmosphere of scandal. It has for the time become difficult for James to sustain his old objectivity: he has relapsed into a dreamy interior world, where values are often uncertain and where it is not even possible any longer for him to judge his effect on his audience—on the audience which by this time has shrunk to a relatively small band of initiated readers. One is dismayed, in reading his comments on *The Awkward Age*, which he regarded as a technical triumph, to see that he was quite unaware of the inhuman aspect of the book which makes it a little repellent. The central figure of *The Sacred Fount* may perhaps have been presented ironically; but James evidently never suspected how the ordinary reader would feel about this disemboweled gibbering crew who hover around Nanda Brookenham with their shadowy sordid designs.

This phase of Henry James's development is also distinguished by a kind of expansion of the gas of the psychological atmosphere —an atmosphere which has now a special flavor. With *What Maisie Knew*, James's style, as Ford Madox Ford says, first becomes a little gamey. He gets rid of some of his old formality and softens his mechanical hardness; and, in spite of the element of abstraction which somewhat dilutes and dims his writing at all periods, his language becomes progressively poetic.

With all this, his experience of playwriting has affected his fiction in a way which does not always seem quite to the good. He had taken as models for his dramatic work the conventional 'well made' French plays of the kind that Bernard Shaw was ridiculing as 'clock-work mice'; and when he took to turning his plays into novels (*Covering End* and *The Outcry*), their frivolity and artificiality became even more apparent (it was only in *The Other House*, which he also made into a novel, that he had dared to be at all himself, and had produced a psychological thriller that had something in common with *The Turn of the Screw; Guy Domville*, too, was evidently more serious, but the text has never been published). Even after he had given up the theater, he went on casting his novels in dramatic form—with the result that *The Awkward Age*, his supreme effort in this direction, combines a lifeless trickery of logic with the equivocal subjectivity of a nightmare.

In this period also originates a tendency on James's part to exploit his sleight-of-hand technique for the purpose of diverting attention from the inadequacies of his imagination. This has imposed on some of James's critics and must of course have imposed on James himself. One can see from his comments at various periods how a method like that of Tolstoy became more and more distasteful to him. Tolstoy, he insisted, was all over the shop, never keeping to a single point of view but entering the minds of all his characters and failing to exercise sufficiently the principle of selection, and James was even reckless enough, in his preface to *The Tragic Muse*, to class *War and Peace* with *Les Trois Mousquetaires* and *The Newcomes*, as 'large loose baggy monsters, with . . . queer elements of the accidental and the arbitrary'—though the truth was, of course, that Tolstoy had spent six years on his novel, had reduced it by a third of its original length and made of every little scene a masterpiece of economy and relevance. He speaks in the same preface of the difficulty he has found himself in handling a complex subject—though it is only a problem here of going into the minds of two of the characters. The truth is, of course, that the question of whether or not the novelist enters into a variety of points of view has nothing necessarily to do with his technical mastery of his materials or even with his effect of concentration. Precisely one trouble with *The Tragic Muse* is that James does not get inside Miriam Rooth; and if he fails even to try to do so, it is because, in his experience of the world and his insight into human beings, he is inferior to a man like Tolstoy. So, in *The Wings of the Dove*, the 'messengering,' as the drama courses say, of Kate Croy's final scene with Merton Densher is probably due to James's increasing incapacity for dealing directly with scenes of emotion rather than to the motives he alleges. And so his recurring complaint that he is unable to do certain things because he can no longer find space within his prescribed limits has the look of another excuse. Henry James never seems aware of the amount of space he is wasting through the long abstract formulations that do duty for concrete details, the unnecessary circumlocutions and the gratuitous meaningless verbiage—the *as it were's* and *as we may say's* and all the rest—all the words with which he pads out his sentences and which themselves are probably symptomatic of a tendency to stave off his main problems, since they are a part of the swathing process with which he makes his embarrassing subjects always seem to present smooth contours.

V

But after this a new process sets in. In *The Ambassadors*, *The Wings of the Dove* and *The Golden Bowl*, the psychological atmosphere thickens and fills up the structure of the novel, so carefully designed and contrived, with the fumes of the Jamesian gas; and the characters, though apprehended as recognizable human entities, loom obscurely through a phantasmagoria of dreamlike similes and metaphors that seem sometimes, as Miss West has said, more vivid and solid than the settings.

But a positive element reappears. The novels of *The Awkward Age* period were written not merely from an international limbo between Europe and the United States but in the shadow of defeat and self-doubt. Yet in these queer and neurotic stories (some of them, of course—*The Turn of the Screw* and *What Maisie Knew*—among James's masterpieces) moral values begin to reassert themselves. These present themselves first in an infantile form, in Maisie Farrange and in Nanda Brookenham, whose innocence is a touchstone for the other characters. Then, in the longer novels that follow, embodied in figures of a more mature innocence, they come completely to dominate the field. These figures are <u>now always Americans</u>. We have returned to the pattern of his earlier work, in which the typical dramatic conflict took place between glamorous people who were worldly and likely to be wicked, and people of superior scruples who were more or less homely, and in which the glamorous characters usually represented Europe and the more honorable ones the United States. In those earlier novels of James, it had not been always—as in *The Portrait of a Lady*—the Americans who were left with the moral advantage; the Europeans—as in the story with that title—had been sometimes made the more sympathetic. But in these later ones it is always the Americans who command admiration and respect—where they are pitted against a fascinating Italian prince, a charming and appealing French lady, and a formidable group of rapacious English. Yes: there *was* a beauty and there was also a power in the goodness of these naïve but sensitive people—there *were* qualities which did not figure in Flaubert's or Thackeray's picture. This *was* something new in the world which did not fit into the formulas of Europe. What if poor Lambert Strether *had* missed in Woollett, Mass., many things he would have enjoyed in Paris: he had brought to Paris something it lacked. And the burden of James's biography of William Wetmore Story, which came out at the same time as these novels, the early years of the century—rather different from that of his study of Hawthorne, published in 1880—is that artists like Story who left Boston for Europe eventually found themselves in a void and might better have stayed at home.

And now Henry James revisits America, writes *The American Scene*, and, for the first time since the rejected *Bostonians*, lays the scene of a novel—*The Ivory Tower*, which he dropped and did not live to finish—entirely in the United States.

In another unfinished novel, the fantasia called *The Sense of the Past*, he makes a young contemporary American go back into eighteenth-century England. Here the Jamesian ambiguity serves an admirable artistic purpose. Is it the English of the past who are ghosts or the American himself who is only a dream?—will the moment come when *they* will vanish or will he himself cease to exist? And, as before, there is a question of James's own asking at the bottom of the ambiguity: Which is real—America or Europe?—a question which was apparently to be answered by the obstinate survival of the American in the teeth of the specters who would drag him back. (It is curious, by the way, to compare *The Sense of the Past* with Mark Twain's *Connecticut Yankee:* the two books have a good deal in common.)

Yes: in spite of the popular assumption, founded on his expatriation and on his finally becoming a British citizen, it is the ideals of the United States which triumph in James's work. His warmest tributes to American genius come out of these later years. Though he could not, in *Notes of a Son and Brother*, resist the impulse to remove references to Lincoln as 'old Abe' from William James's early letters of the wartime, this autobiographical revery contains pages on Lincoln's death of a touching appreciation and pride. 'It was vain to say,' he writes of Andrew Johnson, of whom he declares that the American people felt him unworthy to represent them, 'that we had deliberately invoked the "common" in authority and must drink the wine we had drawn. No countenance, no salience of aspect nor composed symbol, could superficially have referred itself less than Lincoln's mold-smashing mask to any mere matter-of-course type of propriety; but his admirable unrelated head had itself revealed a type—as if by the very fact that what made in it for roughness of kind looked out only less than what made in it for splendid final stamp; in other words for commanding Style.' And of the day when the news reached Boston: 'I was fairly to go in shame of its being my birthday. These would have been the hours of the streets if none others had been—when the huge general gasp filled them like a great earth-shudder and people's eyes met people's eyes without the vulgarity of speech. Even this was, all so strangely, part of the lift and the swell, as tragedy has but to be of a pure enough strain

[114]

and a high enough connection to sow with its dark hand the seed of greater life. The collective sense of what had occurred was of a sadness too noble not somehow to inspire, and it was truly in the air that, whatever we had as a nation produced or failed to produce, we could at least gather round this perfection of classic woe.' In *The American Scene*, he writes of Concord: 'We may smile a little as we "drag in" Weimar, but I confess myself, for my part, much more satisfied than not by our happy equivalent, "in American money," for Goethe and Schiller. The money is a potful in the second case as in the first, and if Goethe, in the one, represents the gold and Schiller the silver, I find (and quite putting aside any bimetallic prejudice) the same good relation in the other between Emerson and Thoreau. I open Emerson for the same benefit for which I open Goethe, the sense of moving in large intellectual space, and that of the gush, here and there, out of the rock, of the crystalline cupful, in wisdom and poetry, in *Wahrheit* and *Dichtung*; and whatever I open Thoreau for (I needn't take space here for the good reasons) I open him oftener than I open Schiller.' Edith Wharton says that he used to read Walt Whitman aloud 'in a mood of subdued ecstasy' and with tremendous effect on his hearers.

James's visit to the United States in 1904-05, after nearly a quarter of a century's absence, had been immensely exciting to him. He had plunged into his sensations with a gusto, explored everything accessible with a voracity and delivered himself of positive ideas (the presence and the opinions of William must partly have stimulated this, as a passage in Henry's note-books suggests) at a rate that seems almost to transform the personality of the modest recluse of Lamb House, with his addiction to the crepuscular and the dubious. One realizes now for the first time, as he was realizing for the first time himself, how little of America he had seen before. He had never been West or South. He had known only New York, Boston and Newport. But he now traveled all the way south to Florida and all the way west to California, apparently almost drunk with new discoveries and revelations. His account of his trip in *The American Scene*, published in 1907, has a magnificent solidity and brilliance quite different from the vagueness of impressionism which had been making the backgrounds of his novels a little unsatisfactory; and the criticism of the national life shows an incisiveness, a comprehensiveness, a sureness in knowing his way about, a grasp of political and economic factors, that one might not have expected of Henry James returning to Big Business America. It is probably true that James —as W. H. Auden has suggested—had never approached Europe with anything like the same boldness. In Italy, France, or England, he had been always a 'passionate pilgrim' looking for the picturesque. But with long residence abroad, as he tells us, the romance and the mystery had evaporated, and America, of which he had been hearing such sensational if sometimes dismaying news, had in its turn been coming to seem romantic. What is exhilarating and most surprising is the old-fashioned American patriotism which—whether he is admiring or indignant—throbs in every pulse of *The American Scene*. It would be difficult to understand why James should have been credited in the United States with being an immoderate Anglophile—even if the implications of *The Wings of the Dove* had been missed—after *The American Scene* had appeared, if one did not have to allow for the shallowness of professional criticism and the stupid indifference of the public that marked that whole period in the United States. The truth is that he returns to America with something like an overmastering homesickness that makes him desire to give it the benefit of every doubt, to hope for the best from what shocks or repels him. He is not at the mercy of his wincings from the elements that are alien and vulgar. The flooding-in of the new foreign population, though he has to make an effort to accept it, does not horrify him or provoke him to sneers, as it did that professional explorer but professional Anglo-Saxon, Kipling—after all, the James family themselves had not been long in the United States and were so nearly pure Irish that Henry speaks of their feeling a special interest in the only set of their relatives that represented the dominant English blood. He thinks it a pity that the immigrants should be standardized by barren New York, but he is gratified at the evidence that America has been able to give them better food and clothing. The popular consumption of candy, in contrast to the luxury and privilege that sweets have always been in Europe, seems to please him when he attends the

Yiddish theater. He is angry over the ravages of commercialism—the exploitation of real-estate values and the destruction of old buildings and landmarks that followed the Civil War—but he is optimistic enough to hope that the time is approaching when the national taste will have improved sufficiently to check this process. And in the meantime at Mount Vernon he feels awe at the memory of Washington, invokes in the Capitol the American eagle as a symbol of the republican idealism, and writes one of the most eloquent and most moving pages to be found in the whole range of his work in celebration of the Concord bridge and the shot heard round the world. It is as if, after the many books which James had written in countries not native to him, under the strain of maintaining an attitude that should be rigorously international, yet addressing himself to an audience that rarely understood what he was trying to do and in general paid little attention to him—it is as if, after a couple of decades of this, his emotions had suddenly been given scope, his genius for expression liberated, as if his insight had been confronted with a field on which it could play without diffidence; and he produced in *The American Scene*, one of the very best books about modern America.

The point is that James's career—given his early experience of Europe—had inevitably been affected by the shift in American ambitions which occurred after the Civil War. It has been shown by Mr. Van Wyck Brooks in his literary history of the United States how the post-Revolutionary American had been stimulated—much like the Russian of the first years of the Soviet regime—to lay the foundations for a new humanity, set free from the caste-barriers and the poverties of Europe, which should return to the mother-continent only to plunder her for elements of culture that might be made to serve the new aim; but how, with the growth of industry, the ascendancy of business ideals, the artists and the other intellectuals found it difficult to function at home and discouraged with the United States, more and more took refuge in Europe. James explains, in *The American Scene*, that the residence abroad of Americans like himself, of small incomes and non-acquisitive tastes, had by this time become merely a matter of having found oneself excreted by a society with whose standards of expenditure one was not in a position to keep up, at the same time that one could not help feeling humiliated at being thrust by it below the salt. But though his maturity belonged to this second phase, he had grown up during the first—the brothers of his grandmother James had fought in the Revolution and been friends of Lafayette and Washington, and his James grandfather had come to America from Ireland and made a fortune of three million dollars—and he had never lost the democratic idealism, the conviction of having scored a triumph and shown the old world a wonder, that were characteristic of it. This appears at the beginning of James's career in the name of 'the American,' Newman, and at the end in his magnificent phrase about <u>Lincoln's 'mold-smashing mask.'</u>

VI

But Henry James is a reporter, not a prophet. With less politics even than Flaubert, he can but chronicle the world as it passes, and in his picture the elements are mixed. In the Americans of Henry James's later novels (those written before his return)—the Milly Theales, the Lambert Strethers, the Maggie Ververs—he shows us all that was magnanimous, reviving and warm in the Americans at the beginning of the new century along with all that was frustrated, sterile, excessively refined, depressing—all that they had in common with the Frédéric Moreaus and with the daughters of poor English parsons. Here they are with their ideals and their blights: <u>Milly Theale</u>, for example, quite real at the core of her cloudy integument, probably the best portrait in fiction of a rich New Yorker of the period. It is the period of the hey-day of Sargent; but compare such figures of James's with the fashionable paintings of <u>Sargent,</u> truthful though these are in their way, and see with what profounder insight as well as with what <u>superior delicacy Henry James</u> has caught the monied distinction of the Americans of this race.

But between the first blooming and the second something tragic has happened to these characters. What has become of Christopher Newman? What has become of Isabel Archer? They are Lambert Strether and Milly Theale—the one worn out by Woollett, Mass., the other overburdened with money and dying for lack of love. Neither finds any fulfilment in Europe, neither ever gets his money's worth. Maggie Verver has her triumph in the end, but she, too, is much too rich for comfort. These people look wan and they are more at sea than the people of the earlier novels. They have been tumbled along or been ground in the sand by the surf of commercial success that has been running in the later part of the century, and in either case are very much the worse for it. It seems to me foolish to reproach Henry James for having neglected the industrial background. Like sex, we never get very close to it, but its effects are a part of his picture. James's tone is more often old-maidish than his sense of reality is feeble; and the changes in American life that have been going on during his absence are implied in these later books.

When he revisits the States at last, he is aroused to a new effort in fiction as well as to the reporting of *The American Scene*. The expatriate New Yorker of *The Jolly Corner* comes back to the old house on Fifth Avenue to confront the apparition of himself as he would have been if he had stayed and worked 'downtown.' 'Rigid and conscious, spectral yet human, a man of his own substance and stature waited there to measure himself with his power to dismay.' At first this *alter ego* covers its face with its hands; then it advances 'as for aggression, and he knew himself give ground. Then harder pressed still, sick with the force of his shock, and falling back as under the hot breath and the sensed passion of a life larger than his own, a rage of personality before which his own collapsed, he felt the whole vision turn to darkness and his very feet give way.' He faints.

Yet at contact with this new America which is extravagant at the same time as ugly, the old Balzac in James revives. I do not know why more has not been made in the recent discussion of James—especially by the critics of the Left, who are so certain that there is nothing in him—of the unfinished novel called *The Ivory Tower*. The work of James's all but final period has been 'poetic' rather than 'realistic'; but now he passes into a further phase in which the poetic treatment is applied to what is for James a new kind of realism. The fiction of his latest period is occupied in a special way with the forgotten, the poor and the old, even—what has been rare in James—with the uncouth, the grotesque. It is perhaps the reflection of his own old age, his own lack of worldly success, the strange creature that he himself has become. This new vein had already appeared in the long short story *The Papers*, with its fantastically amusing picture of the sordid lives of journalists in London; and he later wrote *Fordham Castle*, in which he said he had tried to do something for the parents of the Daisy Millers whose children had left them behind —a curious if not very successful glimpse of the America of Sinclair Lewis; and *The Bench of Desolation*, the last story but one that he published, surely one of the most beautifully written and wonderfully developed short pieces in the whole range of James's work: a sort of prose poem of loneliness and poverty among the nondescript small shopkeepers and retired governesses of an English seaside resort.

But in the meantime the revelation of Newport, as it presented itself in the nineteen hundreds—so different from the Newport which James had described years ago in *An International Episode* —stimulates him to something quite new: a kind of nightmare of the American *nouveaux riches*. Here his appetite for the varied forms of life, his old interest in social phenomena, seem brusquely to wake him up from revery. The appearances of things become vivid again. To our amazement, there starts into color and relief the America of the millionaires, at its crudest, corruptest and phoniest: the immense amorphous mansions, complicated by queer equipment which seems neither to have been purchased by personal choice nor humanized by personal use; the old men of the Rockefeller-Frick generation, landed, with no tastes and no interests, amidst a limitless magnificence which dwarfs them; the silly or clumsy young people of the second generation with their dubious relationships, their enormous and meaningless parties, their touching longings and resolute strivings for an elegance and cultivation which they have no one to guide them in acquiring. The specter of *The Jolly Corner* appeared to the expatriate American 'quite as one of those expanding fantastic images projected by the magic lantern of childhood'; and in somewhat the same way, for the reader of James, with the opening of *The Ivory Tower*, there emerges the picture of old Abner Gaw, a kind of monster from outside the known Jamesian world, sitting and rocking his

foot and looking out on the sparkling Atlantic while he waits for
his business partner to die. *The Ivory Tower,* in dealing with the
newest rich, is comic and even homely; but it is also, like all this
later work of Henry James, poetic in that highest sense that its
characters and scenes and images shine out with the incandescence which shows them as symbols of phases through which the
human soul has passed. The moral of the novel—which seems
quite plain from the scenario left by James—is also of particular
interest. The ivory tower itself, a fine piece of Chinese carving, is
to represent, for the young American who has just returned from
Europe and inherited his uncle's fortune, that independence of
spirit, that private cultivation of sensations and that leisure for
literary work, which the money is to make possible for him;
but it fatally contains, also, the letter in which Abner Gaw, out
of vindictiveness toward the partner who has double-crossed him,
has revealed all the swindles and perfidies by which the fortune
has been created. So that the cosmopolitan nephew (he has always
had a *little* money) is finally to be only too glad to give up the
independence with the fortune.

Henry James dropped *The Ivory Tower* when the war broke
out in 1914, because he felt it was too remote from the terrible
contemporary happenings. These events seem to have presented
themselves to James as simply a critical struggle between, on
the one hand, French and English civilization and, on the other,
German barbarity. He had believed in and had invoked rather
vaguely the possible salutary effect for the world of an influential
group of international élite made up of the kind of people with
whom he associated and whom he liked to depict in his novels; but
now he spoke of the past as 'the age of the mistake,' the period
when people had thought that the affairs of the world were sufficiently settled for such an élite to flourish. He was furiously nationalistic, or at least furiously pro-Ally. He railed against Wood-
row Wilson for his delay in declaring war, and he applied in 1915,
in a gesture of rejection and allegiance, to become a British subject.
'However British you may be, I am more British still!' he is said to
have exclaimed to Edmund Gosse, when the process had been
completed—something which, Gosse is supposed to have remarked,
'nobody wanted him to be.' He had hitherto refrained from this

step, feeling, as we gather from *The American Scene*, some pride and some advantage in his status as a citizen of the United States. But he had been thrown off his balance again, had been swung from his poise of detachment, always a delicate thing to maintain and requiring special conditions. It never occurred to James that he had been, in *The Ivory Tower*, much closer to contemporary realities than he was when he threw up his hat and enlisted in a holy war on Germany; that the partnership of Betterman and Gaw was not typical merely of the United States but had its European counterparts—any more than it was present to him now that the class antagonisms of *The Princess Casamassima*, his response to the depression of the eighties, must inevitably appear again and that the events he was witnessing in Europe were partly due to that social system whose corruption he had been consciously chronicling, and were expediting the final collapse which he had earlier half-predicted.

But as Hyacinth Robinson had died of the class struggle, so Henry James died of the war. He was cremated, and a funeral service was held—on March 3, 1916—at Chelsea Old Church in London; but his ashes, as he had directed, were brought to the United States and buried in the Cambridge cemetery beside his parents and sister and brother. One occasionally, however, finds references to him which assume that he was buried in England—just as one sometimes also finds references which assume that he was born in New England—so that even Henry James's death has been not without a suggestion of the equivocal.

The English had done him the honor, not long before he died, of awarding him the Order of Merit. But I do not think that anybody has yet done full justice to his genius as an international critic of manners, esthetic values and morals. The strength of that impartial intelligence of which his hesitating and teasing ambiguity sometimes represented a weakness had prompted him to find his bearings among social gravitational fields which must at the time have seemed almost as bewildering as the astronomical ones with which the physics of relativity were just beginning to deal. It had fortified him to meet and weather the indifference or ridicule of both the two English-speaking peoples to whom he had addressed himself and whose historian he had trained himself to be; and it had stimulated him, through more than half a hundred books, a long life of unwearying labor, to keep re-creating himself as an artist and even to break new ground at seventy.

For Henry James *is* a first-rank writer in spite of certain obvious deficiencies. His work is incomplete as his experience was; but it is in no respect second-rate, and he can be judged only in company with the greatest. I have been occupied here with the elements that travail or contend or glow beneath the surface of his even fiction, and my argument has not given me occasion to insist, as ought to be done in any 'literary' discussion of James, on his classical equanimity in dealing with diverse forces, on his combination, equally classical, of hard realism with formal harmony. These are qualities—I have tried to describe them in writing about Pushkin—which have always been rather rare in American and English literature and of which the fiction of James is one of the truest examples.

1948. I have left my description of *The Turn of the Screw* mainly as I originally wrote it. In going over it again, however, it has struck me that I forced a point in trying to explain away the passage in which the housekeeper identifies, from the governess' description, the male apparition with Peter Quint. The recent publication of Henry James's note-books seems, besides, to make it quite plain that James's conscious intention, in *The Turn of the Screw*, was to write a *bona fide* ghost story; and it also becomes clear that the theme of youth feeding age was to have been the real subject of *The Sacred Fount*. I should today restate my thesis as follows:

At the time that James wrote these stories, his faith in himself had been somewhat shaken. Though he had summoned the whole force of his will and brought his whole mind to bear on writing plays, he had not made connections with the theater. The disastrous opening night of *Guy Domville* had occurred on January 5, 1895. On the evening of January 10, we learn from an entry in the note-books, James had heard from Archbishop Benson the story that suggested *The Turn of the Screw*. On January 23, he writes:

'I take up my *own* old pen again—the pen of all my old unfor-
gettable efforts and sacred struggles. To myself—today—I need
say no more. Large and full and high the future still opens. It
is now indeed that I may do the work of my life. And I will. . .
I have only to face my problems.' *The Turn of the Screw* was begun in the fall of 1897 (*The Spoils of Poynton* and *What Maisie
Knew* had been written in between). Now, to fail as James had
just done is to be made to doubt one's grasp of reality; and the
doubts that some readers feel as to the soundness of the governess' story are, I believe, the reflection of James's doubts, com-
municated unconsciously by James himself (in sketching out his
stories in his note-books—as for *The Friends of the Friends*, described below—he sometimes shifts over without a break from a
first person which refers to himself to a first person which refers
to the imaginary teller). An earlier story, *The Path of Duty*, published in 1884, is perhaps the most obvious example of James's
interest in cases of self-deception and his trick of presenting
them from their own points of view; and it is given a special
relevance to the problem of *The Turn of the Screw* by the entry
about it in the note-books. This entry is simply a notation of a
curious piece of gossip which James had heard in London, with a
discussion of the various ways in which it could be treated in
fiction; but the story that James afterwards wrote depends for its
effectiveness on an element which James does not mention there.
The original anecdote is used, but it here gets another dimension
from the attitude of the woman who is supposed to be telling it.
This American lady in London is enamored of an attractive nobleman in line for a desirable baronetcy, with whom she is on fairly
close terms but who takes no serious interest in her. She therefore
intervenes in a mischievous way, under the pretense of keeping
him to the 'path of duty,' to prevent him from marrying the
woman he loves and induce him to marry one he doesn't—a situation in which everybody else is to be left as dissatisfied as she is.
She has never admitted to herself her real motives for what she
is doing, and they gradually dawn on the reader in the form of
intermittent suspicions like the suspicions that arise in one's mind
in reading *The Turn of the Screw*. But in the case of *The Path
of Duty*, we are quite clear as we finish the story, as to what

role the narrator has actually played. She has written her account, we realize, though ostensibly to satisfy a friend who has been asking her about the episode, really as a veiled confession; and then she has decided to withhold it, ostensibly to shield the main actors, but really to shield herself. Here James, having noted down an anecdote, as he was also to do for *The Turn of the Screw* and had already done with the notion that was to be used in *The Sacred Fount*, has produced a psychological study for which the anecdote is only a pretext. Another story, *The Friends of the Friends*, the idea for which James first noted in the December of 1895 and which he immediately afterwards wrote, also offers a clue to the process which I believe was at work in *The Turn of the Screw*. *The Friends of the Friends* is a ghost story, which involves, like *The Marriages* and *The Path of Duty*, a mischievous intervention prompted by interested motives on the part of a woman narrator; and the ghost is presumably a product of this narrator's neurotic jealousy. *Maud-Evelyn*, a story written later and first published in 1900, though the first suggestion of it seems also to occur in the note-books of 1895, presents a young man who from interested motives lends himself to the spiritualistic self-deceptions of parents who have lost their daughter. One is led to conclude that, in *The Turn of the Screw*, not merely is the governess self-deceived, but that James is self-deceived about her.

A curious feature of these note-books is the tone that Henry James takes in collecting his materials and outlining his plots. It is not, as with the notes of most writers, as if James were sitting in the workshop of his mind, alone and with no consciousness of an audience, but exactly as if he were addressing a letter to a friend who took a keen interest in his work but with whom he is not sufficiently intimate to discuss his personal affairs. He calls himself *mon bon* and *caro mio*—'Causons, causons, mon bon,' he will write—and speaks to himself with polite depreciation—referring to 'the narrator of the tale, as I may in courtesy call it.' But, though he talks to himself a good deal—and sometimes very excitedly and touchingly—about his relation to his work, his 'muse,' he never notes down personal emotions in relation to anything else as possible subjects for fiction. One comes to the conclusion that Henry James, in a special and unusual way, was what is nowadays called an 'extrovert'—that is, he did not brood on himself and analyze his own reactions, as Stendhal, for example, did, but always dramatized his experience immediately in terms of imaginary people. One gets the impression here that James was not introspective. Nor are his characters really so. They register, as James himself registered, a certain order of perceptions and sensations; but they justify to some degree the objection of critics like Wells that his psychology is superficial—though it would be more correct to put it that, while his insight is not necessarily superficial, his 'psychologizing' tends to be so. What we are told is going on in the characters' heads is a sensitive reaction to surfaces which itself seems to take place on the surface. We do not often see them grappling with their problems in terms of concrete ambitions or of intimate relationships. What we see when we are supposed to look into their minds is something as much arranged by James to conceal, to mislead and to create suspense as the actual events presented. These people, so far as the 'psychologizing' goes, are not intimate even with themselves. They talk to themselves about what they are doing and what is happening to them even a good deal less frankly than James talks to himself about them, and that is already with the perfect discretion of an after-dinner conversation between two gentlemanly diners-out. As Henry James gets further away—beginning with *What Maisie Knew*—from the realism of his earlier phases, his work—as Stephen Spender has said in connection with *The Golden Bowl*—becomes all a sort of ruminative poem, which gives us not really a direct account of the internal workings of his characters, but rather James's reflective feelings, the flow of images set off in his mind, as he peeps not impolitely inside them. Not, however, that his sense of life—of personal developments and impacts—is not often profound and sure. The point is merely that it is not always so, and that the floor of the layer of consciousness that we are usually allowed to explore sometimes rings rather hollow. Where motivations are rarely revealed, we cannot always tell how much the author knows; and it is on this account that arguments occur —and not only in the case of *The Turn of the Screw* but also in that of *The Golden Bowl*—as to what is supposed to be happening in a given situation or as to what kind of personalities the characters are supposed to be. Carefully though, from one point of view, the point of view of technical machinery, Henry James always planned his novels, he seems sometimes to falter and grope in dealing with their human problems. The habits he imposed on himself in his attempt to write workable plays was unfortunate in this connection. The unperformed comedies that he published in the two volumes of *Theatricals*, which are almost the only things he wrote that can really be called bad, show a truly appalling self-discipline in sterile and stale devices and artificial motivations. In the stage world of Henry James, young men are always prepared to marry, regardless of personal taste or even of close acquaintance, from an interest in a property or an inheritance, or because they have been told that they have compromised girls or simply because women have proposed to them; and an element of this false psychology was afterwards carried by James through the whole of his later fiction along with his stage technique. It is true that in this later fiction there is a good deal of illicit passion, as had not been the case in his plays; but his adulteries seem sometimes as arbitrary as the ridiculous engagements of *Theatricals*. They are not always really explained, we cannot always be sure they are really there, that the people have been to bed together. But, on the other hand, we sometimes feel the presence, lurking like 'the beast in the jungle,' of other emotional factors with which the author himself does not always appear to have reckoned.

I once gave *The Turn of the Screw* to the Austrian novelist Franz Höllering to see what impression he would get of it. It did not occur to him that it was not a real ghost story, but he said to me, after he had read it: 'The man who wrote that was a *Kinderschänder*'; and I remembered that in all James's work of this period—which extends from *The Other House* through *The Sacred Fount*—the favorite theme is the violation of innocence, with the victim in every case (though you have in *The Turn of the Screw* a boy as well as a girl) a young or a little girl. In *The Other House* a child is murdered; in *What Maisie Knew* and *The Awkward Age*, a child and a young virgin are played upon by forces of corruption which, though they do not destroy the girls' innocence, somewhat harm them or dislocate their emotions by

[127]

creating abnormal relationships; in *The Turn of the Screw*, whichever way you take it, the little girl is either hurt or corrupted. (The candid and loyal young heroines of *The Spoils of Poynton* and *In the Cage*, though they can hardly be said to be violated, are both, in their respective ways, represented as shut out from something.) This, of course, in a sense, is an old theme for James: *Washington Square* and *The Portrait of a Lady* were studies in innocence betrayed. But there is something rather peculiar, during this relatively neurotic phase, in his interest in and handling of this subject. The real effectiveness of all these stories derives, not from the conventional pathos of a victim with whom we sympathize but from the excitement of the violation; and if we look back to Henry James's first novel, *Watch and Ward*, serialized when he was twenty-eight, we find a very queer little tale about a young man of twenty-six who becomes the guardian of a girl of ten and gradually falls in love with her but is for a long time debarred from marrying her, when she comes of age to marry, by a complication of scruples and misunderstandings. The relationship clearly connects itself with the relationship, in *The Awkward Age*, between Nanda and Mr. Langdon, in which, also, the attitude of the pseudo-father is given a flavor of unavowed sex. We are not in a position to explain, on any basis of early experience, this preoccupation of James with immature girls who are objects of desire or defilement; but it seems clear what symbolic role they played from time to time in his work. He seems early to have 'polarized' with his brother William in an opposition of feminine and masculine. This appears in a significant anecdote which he tells in his autobiography about William's having left him once to go to play, as he said, with 'boys that curse and swear'; and in his description of his feeling from the first that William was "occupying a place in the world to which I couldn't at all aspire—to any approach to which in truth I seem to myself ever conscious of having signally forfeited a title'; and one finds it in their correspondence and in everything one has heard of their relations. There was always in Henry James an innocent little girl whom he cherished and loved and protected and yet whom he later tried to violate, whom he even tried to kill. He must have felt particularly helpless, particularly unsuited for the battle with the world, particularly exposed to rude insult, after the failure of his dramatic career, when he retreated into his celibate solitude. The maiden innocent of his early novels comes to life again; but he now does not merely pity her, he does not merely adore her: in his impotence, his impatience with himself, he would like to destroy or rape her. The real dramatic and esthetic values of the stories that he writes at this period are involved with an equivocal blending of this impulse and an instinct of self-pity. (The conception of *innocence excluded* is a reaction to the same situation: Fleda Vetch, in *The Spoils of Poynton*, misses marrying the man she loves and misses inheriting the spoils, which in any case go up in flames; the girl in the telegraph office finds that it is not she who is 'in the cage' but the dashing young captain whose amours she has fascinatedly watched from afar—just as James must have had to decide that the worldly success he had tried for was, after all, not worth having. So the innocents in certain of the other stories, too, are left with a moral advantage.) This is not in the least, on the critic's part, to pretend to reduce the dignity of these stories by reading into them the embarrassments of the author. They do contain, I believe, a certain subjective element which hardly appears to the same degree elsewhere in James's mature work; but he has expressed what he had to express—disappointments and dissatisfactions that were poignantly and not ignobly felt—with dramatic intensity and poetic color. These are fairy-stories, but fairy-stories that trouble, that get a clear and luminous music out of chords very queerly combined. They are unique in literature, and their admirable style and form are not quite like anything else even in the work of James. In *The Wings of the Dove*, of course, which follows *The Awkward Age*, he is still occupied with violated innocence, but now his world is firm again on its base, and we are back on the international stage of *The Portrait of a Lady*. Milly Theale, though languishing and fatally ill, is a real and full-grown woman dealing with a practical conspiracy, not a tender little girl or *jeune fille* jeopardized by an ambiguous dream.*

* The immaturity of the heroines in James serves sometimes to provide one of his many pretexts for making it impossible for the heroes to marry

It is of course no longer true, as is implied in the above essay, that the stature and merits of James are not fully appreciated in the English-speaking world. Since the centenary of James's birth in 1943, he has been celebrated, interpreted, reprinted, on a scale which, I believe, is unprecedented for a classical American writer. There have contributed to this frantic enthusiasm perhaps a few rather doubtful elements. A novelist whose typical hero invariably decides not to act, who remains merely an intelligent onlooker, appeals for obvious reasons to a period when many intellectuals, formerly romantic egoists or partisans of the political Left, have been resigning themselves to the role of observer or of passive participant in activities which cannot command their whole allegiance. The stock of Henry James has gone up in the same market as that of Kafka, and the recent apotheosis of him has sometimes been conducted as uncritically as the prayers and contemplations of the Kafka cult. At the same time, in a quite different way, he has profited from—or, at any rate, been publicized by—the national propaganda movement which has been advertising Amer-

them. The whole question of the motif of impotence in James has been discussed very suggestively and interestingly—though on the basis of an incomplete acquaintance with Henry James's work—in a paper called *The Ghost of Henry James: A Study in Thematic Apperception* by Dr. Saul Rosenzweig (*Character and Personality*, December 1943). Dr. Rosenzweig suggests that the accident in which Henry James sprained his back at eighteen—'a horrid even if an obscure hurt,' as James himself calls it—and from which he suffered, sometimes acutely, all the rest of his life, may have been partly neurotic not only in its results but even in its origin—since it offers a strangely close parallel with the accident in which the elder Henry James had lost his leg—also in extinguishing a fire—at the age of thirteen. The son's accident had occurred, as he tells us himself, at the beginning of the Civil War and put it out of the question for him to answer Lincoln's first call for volunteers. Dr. Rosenzweig has brought to light a very early story of James, the first he ever published: *The Story of a Year*, which appeared in the *Atlantic Monthly* in March 1865. Here you have a young man of the North who, just before going off to the war, becomes engaged to a girl but makes her promise that, if he should die, she will forget him and marry someone else. She dreams, when he has gone, that she is walking in a wood with a man who calls her wife and that they find a dead man covered with wounds. They lift the corpse up to bury it, and it opens its eyes and says 'Amen'; they stamp down the dirt of the grave. The lover is actually wounded, lingers for some time between life and death, and then dies, leaving the fiancée to marry another man. Another factor in the story is the young man's mother, who comes between him and the girl, being unwilling to have him marry her and ican civilization under stimulus of our needs in the war and our emergence into the international world. The assumption seems to be that Henry James is our counterpart to Yeats, Proust and Joyce, and he has been tacitly assigned to high place in the official American Dream along with 'Mr. Jefferson,' the *Gettysburg Address*, Paul Bunyan, the Covered Wagon, and Mom's Huckleberry Pie. He will doubtless be translated for the Japanese, who were fascinated before the war by the refinements of Paul Valéry and Proust.*

Yet we do well to be proud of him, and there are very good reasons for young people to read him straight through, as—incredible though it would have sounded at the time he was still alive— they seem more and more to be doing. Henry James stands out today as unique among our fiction writers of the nineteenth century in having devoted wholeheartedly to literature the full span of a long life and brought to it first-rate abilities. Beside James's half century of achievement, with its energy, continuity and va-

---

trying to prevent her seeing him after he has been brought home wounded— Henry James, it seems, was his mother's favorite child. Dr. Rosenzweig might also have cited another early short story, *An Extraordinary Case* (1868), in which another returned soldier, suffering from an unspecified ailment, loses his girl to another man and dies.

One can agree with Dr. Rosenzweig that a castration theme appears here— one recognizes it as the same that figures through the whole of James's work; but that work does not bear out the contention put forward by Dr. Rosenzweig that James was to suffer all his life from unallayed feelings of guilt for not having taken part in the war. The only real pieces of evidence that Dr. Rosenzweig is able to produce are the short story, *Owen Wingrave*, which deals with the deliberate pacifism of a young man from a military family and leaves the moral advantage all with the pacifist, who dies in the cause of peace; and Henry James's excitement at the beginning of World War I and his memories at this time of the Civil War. He must certainly be right, however, in assuming that well before the age when *The Story of a Year* was written, a state of mind in which 'aggression and sexuality were repressed' had been 'established as a *modus vivendi*.' One of James's most curious symbols for his chronic inhibition occurs in a very early story called first *Théolinde*, then *Rose-Agathe*, in which a man falls in love with a dummy in a Parisian hairdresser's window and finally buys her and takes her home to live with. The wax dummy is cut off at the waist.

* Since writing this, I have found in a book catalogue—along with a Japanese translation of *Ulysses*—a volume of James's short stories translated into Japanese (1924), and a Japanese book about James (1934).

riety, the production of Hawthorne looks furtive and meager and the work of Poe's brief years fragmentary. Alone among our novelists of the past, Henry James managed to master his art and to practice it on an impressive scale, to stand up to popular pressures so as not to break down or peter out, and to build up what the French call an *œuvre*.

1959. Since writing the above, I have become convinced that James knew exactly what he was doing and that he intended the governess to be suffering from delusions. The story, in the New York Edition, is placed, as I have mentioned above, not among the ghost stories but between *The Aspern Papers* and *The Liar*. My description above of *The Liar*, which I had not reread in years, really misses the point of the title, which, as has been noted by Mr. Marius Bewley, is that the liar is not the harmless romancer who is adored and protected by his wife, but the painter who is telling the story. This narrator has been in love with the wife and is still unable to forgive her for having married someone else, so, in painting a portrait of the husband, he falsifies the latter's personality by representing him as more false than he is. The parallel with the governess is thus complete. In both cases, the mind of the narrator is warped, and the story he tells untrue. The narrator of *The Aspern Papers*, in a somewhat similar way, is presenting his impudent activities in quite a different light from that in which they appear to his victims. As for the explanation of the governess' describing correctly the person of Peter Quint, it is so clear that—though slily contrived—one wonders how one could ever have missed it; yet it had never, so far as I know, been brought out before the publication, in *American Literature* of May, 1957, of a paper by John Silver called 'A Note on the Freudian Reading of *The Turn of the Screw*.' The governess, Mr. Silver suggests, had learned about Quint's appearance from the people in the village with whom we know she had talked and who had presumably also told her of the manner of Quint's death.

JOHN JAY CHAPMAN

The Mute and the Open Strings

Mr. M. A. DeWolfe Howe has done an excellent job with the letters and papers of the late John Jay Chapman.* Mr. Howe enjoyed the advantages of having known Chapman personally and of already being thoroughly at home in the latter's period and circle.

One's only complaint about Mr. Howe's book is that there is not anywhere near enough of it. I understand that he was induced by his publishers to cut down his original manuscript; and this seems to me to have been a mistake. Anybody interested in Chapman at all would be able to read a book twice as long as the present one. My own impression from what is here published is that John Jay Chapman was probably the best letter-writer that we have ever had in this country. And it seems to me a pity that Mr. Howe did not include the whole text of the autobiographical document which Chapman prepared not long before his death, instead of only selections from it. My hope and belief is, in fact, that the future will be sufficiently interested in Chapman to print and read his letters as eagerly as has been done with Horace Walpole's—as well as to go back to his published works as we have done to those of Thoreau.

Yet at the present time hardly one reader in a million has heard of even the name of John Jay Chapman. His later books have had no circulation, and most of his earlier ones are out of print. How, then, is it possible to attach so much importance to a writer who has been persistently ignored by the historians of American literature and who has been read by almost nobody,

* *John Jay Chapman and His Letters.*

even during these last twenty years when so much rummaging has been going on in the attic of our literary history? How has it been possible thus for a writer who was at one time a conspicuous figure and who is still valued so highly by a few readers, to become completely invisible to the general reading public even while he was still living and writing?

This essay will attempt to answer that question, on which Mr. Howe's biography has thrown a great deal of light.

I

Perhaps our most vivid impression as we read about Chapman in this book—especially through the first half of his life—is that we have encountered a personality who does not belong in his time and place and who by contrast makes us aware of the commonness, the provinciality and the timidity of most of his contemporaries. 'Yes,' we say to ourselves in our amazement, 'people ought to be more like this!'

When John Jay Chapman was twenty-five and studying law at Harvard—it was the winter of 1886-7—he made the acquaintance of the half-Italian niece of the Brimmer family of Boston: 'a swarthy, fiery large-eyed girl, who looked like the younger Sibyl of Michael Angelo' and 'had the man-minded seriousness of women in classic myths, the regular brow, heavy dark hair, free gait of the temperament that lives in heroic thought and finds the world full of chimeras, of religious mysteries, sacrifice, purgation' —such a woman as had hardly existed outside 'the imagination of Aeschylus and the poets.'

'I had never abandoned my reading of Dante'—it would be a pity not to give it in his own words—'and it somehow came about that I read Dante with Minna. There was a large airy room at the top of the old Athenaeum Library in Boston whose windows looked out on the churchyard. It was a bare and quiet place: no one ever came there. And during the winter we read Dante there together, and in the course of this she told me of her early life in Milan. There were five children, three of them boys, and there were tempestuous quarrels between the parents. I saw that it was from her mother that she had inherited her leonine temperament.

The mother had been a fury. I could see this, though she did not say it. . . The Dante readings moved gradually like a cloud between me and the law, between me and the rest of life. It was done with few words. I had come to see that she was in love with someone. It never occurred to me that she might be in love with me. An onlooker might have said, "You loved her for the tragedies of her childhood and she loved you that you did pity them."

'The case was simple, but the tension was blind and terrible. I was completely unaware that I was in love.'

But he did come to be aware that something was making her unhappy, and he decided that 'an acquaintance of hers, a friend in whom she had little interest,' had been trifling with her affections. One evening at 'the most innocent kind of party that you can imagine at a country house,' he suddenly, without conscious premeditation, invited the man outside and beat him.

'The next thing I remember is returning late at night to my room. At that time I was rooming alone in a desolate side-street in Cambridge. It was a small, dark, horrid little room. I sat down. There was a hard-coal fire burning brightly. I took off my coat and waistcoat, wrapped a pair of suspenders tightly on my left forearm above the wrist, plunged the left hand deep in the blaze and held it down with my right hand for some minutes. When I took it out, the charred knuckles and finger bones were exposed. I said to myself, "This will never do." I took an old coat, wrapped it about my left hand and arm, slipped my right arm into an overcoat, held the coat about me and started for Boston in the horsecars. On arriving at the Massachusetts General Hospital I showed the trouble to a surgeon, was put under ether, and the next morning waked up without the hand and very calm in my spirits. Within a few days I was visited by the great alienist, Dr. Reginald Heber Fitz, an extremely agreeable man. He asked me among other things whether I was insane. I said, "That is for you to find out." He reported me as sane. I took no interest in the scandal which my two atrocious acts must have occasioned.'

He knew now that he was in love with Minna and that it was he whom Minna loved. 'Do you know, Minna,' he wrote her, before they were married, in the summer of the same year, 'the one time in my life during which I lived was that twenty days of

pain. I read *Henry Esmond*, Dickens' *Christmas Stories*, one
morning—I never shall forget them—*Mr. Barnes of New York*.
Every word of it is glowing with life and love. There was fire in
everything I touched—the fire of the activity of that part of me
which was meant to be used, which got suppressed all my life till
it broke. The depth of the intentions and remote unkempt wells
of life and feeling. Browning I used to read anywhere. . . Somehow I have known the meaning of things, if not for long, and all
the while I thought I need rest, I need sleep. You see life is an
experiment. I had not the least idea but what [if] I met you all
this would run the other way and the pain turn into pleasure. I
thought I had opened life forever—what matter if the entrance
was through pain.'

And later, three years after they were married, he wrote her
in an extraordinary love letter on one of his business trips to the
West: 'It was not a waste desert in Colorado. It is not a waste
time, for you are here and many lives packed into one life, and
the green shoot out of the heart of the plant, springing up blos-
soms in the night, and many old things have put on immortality
and lost things have come back knocking within, from before the
time I was conceived in the womb, there were you, also. And what
shall we say of the pain! it was false—and the rending, it was
unnecessary. It was the breaking down of the dams that ought not
to have been put up—but being up it was the sweeping away of
them that the waters might flow together.'

They lived in New York, where he had been born. Chapman
practiced and hated law. He was, on the other hand, passionately
interested in politics. He had been a member of the City Reform
Club, founded by Theodore Roosevelt and others, almost from
its beginning in 1882; and later became president of the Good
Government Club, which had grown out of the City Reform
Club. The Good Government Club had been founded by another Harvard man, Edmond Kelly, for the purpose of fighting
Tammany Hall. When Kelly found out that it was impossible
to recruit the working-class to his movement, he gave it up and
became a socialist. But Chapman and another Harvard man assumed the leadership of the Good Government movement, and

from 1895 through 1900 he had an odd and very interesting career as a non-socialist political radical.

In the election of 1895, the 'Goo-Goo's,' unable to agree with
the Republicans on a common ticket against Tammany, ran a
campaign of their own and were defeated; and in all this John
Jay Chapman played a spirited and provocative part. He made
speeches from the cart-tail in the streets and created a great impression by getting down and manhandling hecklers who were trying to break him up—he was a man of formidable build—then going back and finishing his speech and afterwards buying his opponents drinks; and he was able, also, to upset the routine of
such accepted professional reformers as Joseph Choate and God-
kin of the *Post*. His announced policy at political dinners was
'to say nothing that he would not regret'; and he is reported to
have been the only person who ever caused the venerable and
cultivated Choate to lose his urbanity in public—by pointing out
to him that the anti-Tammany organization to which Mr. Choate
belonged had been guilty of a deal with the enemy. John Jay
Chapman did not understand politics even as the political reformers did. He combined the extreme exhilaration of hope with the
utmost contempt of compromise. He had at this period what the
poet Yeats calls 'the purity of a natural force,' and he disturbed
and frightened people.

But he was presently to collide with another personality, with
whom he had supposed himself to be traveling, but of whom he
turned out to be crossing the path. In the autumn of 1898, John
Jay Chapman was one of the leaders of a group of political Independents who wanted to nominate Theodore Roosevelt for the
governorship of New York. Chapman had an interview with
Roosevelt: the latter accepted the nomination and continued to
affirm his willingness to be run by the Independents even after
the Republican Party had offered to nominate him, too. But, in
the meantime, the Independents had drawn up a whole Independent ticket; and the Republican boss, Tom Platt, told Roosevelt
that if he wanted the Republicans to run him, he would have to
throw over the Independents—which Roosevelt immediately did.
Chapman had been so unwary as to fail to extract a written promise from Roosevelt, because he had supposed a gentleman's word

was enough. He had happened to start down to Oyster Bay to call on his supposed candidate just before the news of the defection broke in New York; and when he got there, he found there was no train back, so that he had to spend the evening with Roosevelt. It seems to have been a harrowing occasion, 'for I was not going home leaving any mist or misunderstandings in the air as to how the Good Government Club group viewed the situation. But I went further. I unloaded the philosophy of agitation upon Roosevelt and pictured him as the broken-backed half-good man, the successor of the doughface and Northern man with Southern principles of Civil War times, the trimmer who wouldn't break with his party and so, morally speaking, it ended by breaking him.'

Chapman knew very well what Roosevelt had promised him; and the incident gave him seriously to think. He observed that Roosevelt presently persuaded himself that he had never understood the original proposal; and that he thereafter became very vociferous over the damage done progressive movements by fanatics on their 'lunatic fringe.' Chapman had been publishing since March 1897 a review called the *Political Nursery* (originally, simply the *Nursery*), and he now used it to attack Roosevelt's subsequent activities and those of the reformist mayor, Seth Low, formerly a candidate of the Independents. It was the McKinley-Roosevelt era of American imperialist expansion, and Chapman fought the policy of the United States in Cuba and in the Philippines, as well as denounced the British in South Africa.

This review, which he carried on through January 1901, is one of the best written things of the kind which has ever been published anywhere. Chapman wrote most of it himself, and he dealt with philosophical and literary, as well as with political, subjects. Here he began the characteristic practice which William James described when he wrote of him: 'He just looks at things and tells the truth about them—a strange thing even to *try* to do, and he doesn't always succeed.' But he did succeed pretty often, and he is at his best during this early period. As I have not the files of the *Political Nursery* by me, I shall quote some portraits and comments from the letters of his later as well as of his earlier years.

Of James Russell Lowell, he wrote in 1896:

'I don't dislike the man. I think him a fine man, a little dandi-fied and genteel perhaps, but still a good story character. His poetry is nothing but a fine talent, a fine ear, a fine facility—too much morality and an incredible deftness at imitating everybody from Milton down. I cannot read his poems with any comfort—but his early essays I still think the best things he ever did, witty, snappy, "smart" to a degree, and quite natural—they are the only things he ever did that were quite natural. In later life he got all barnacled with quotations and leisure. He pulls out pocket-books and gold snuff boxes and carbuncled cigarette-cases, and emerald eye-glasses, and curls and pomatums himself and looks in pocket looking glasses, and smoothes his Vandyke beard and is a literary fop—f-o-p, fop. Too much culture—overnourished as Waddy Longfellow says—too many truffled essays and champagne odes and lobster sonnets, too much Spanish olives, potted prov-erbs—a gouty old cuss in his later essays. But in '54-'65 he wrote rapidly and most clearly. Belles Lettres is the devil after all. It spoils a man. His prefaces—sometimes very nice, in spirit—but his later prefaces are so expressive— O my! so expressive of hems and haws and creased literary trousers. I feel like running him in the belly and singing out Hulloo! old cockolorum.'

Of President Eliot of Harvard (1898):

'Read the essays of (Pres.) Eliot. There's no offense in them. Two by six. Everything in Massachusetts is deal boards. You can put every man in a box—Smug, Smug. He has a good word for poetry too. It's the Dodgedom of Culture. My God, how I hate it. He's the very highest type of a most limited and inspiring pork-chopism. My God, he is hopeful—calls his book *American Contributions to Civilization*—thinks we don't understand small parks and drainage—but will learn and are doing nicely. Has a chapter on "the pleasures of life." It's all one size. Every word in this work is the same size. The Puritans—the war—the prob-lems of labor and capital—education—all excite the same emotion—i.e. that of a woodchuck eating a carrot.'

Of Eliot and J. Pierpont Morgan (1907):

'Pierpont Morgan is the actual apex as well as the type, of the commercial perversions of the era. The political corruption, etc., the power behind all. . . Now then, at the dedication of the New Medical School, Eliot goes about in a cab with Pierpont, hangs laurel wreaths on his nose, and gives him his papal kiss. Now what I want to know is this—what has Eliot got to say to the young man entering business or politics who is about to be corrupted by Morgan and his class? How eloquently can Eliot present the case for honesty? Can he say anything that will reverberate through the chambers of that young man's brain more loudly than that kiss?

'If Eliot is a great man, I want a small man.'

Of Roosevelt and Wilson (1930):

'I have just read in type-writing a book about Roosevelt—which ought to be called the Night Side of T. R.; for it is wholly malignant—and to that extent ineffective. But it's true. He was very nearly mad at times—and broke down his mind by his egotism and mendacity. I had a quarrel with him—political, and personal, and deadly. He was a great genius for handling a situation, and with men, in such a way as to get credit—but he was a damned scoundrel. His genius was to flash a light, put someone down a well, raise a howl to heaven about honesty, and move on to the next thing. Such a genius for publicity as never was—and our people being boy-minded and extremely stupid found him lovely. His feebleness of intellect appears in his writings—which are dull and bombastic—and I doubt whether he will go down as a great man. He's more like a figure out of Dumas. Wilson, a character more odious still, will go down to history as the father of the League of Nations. Drat him! His writings also are dull and he also had the power of hypnotizing men. They idolized him—even those who didn't like him—obeyed—worshiped.

'Apropos—aren't great men apt to be horrid?'

In 1898, he published a volume of literary papers called *Emerson and Other Essays*. In this collection and in the *Political Nursery*, he wrote a commentary on authors then popular—Stevenson, Kipling, Browning, etc.—of which in our day the acumen seems startling. I cannot remember any other American critic of that period—except, in his more specialized field and his more circumlocutionary way, Henry James—who had anything like the same sureness of judgment, the same freedom from current prejudices and sentimentalities. Chapman was then, as, it seems to me, he was to remain, much our best writer on literature of his generation—who made the Babbitts and the Mores and the Brownells, for all the more formidable rigor of their systems and the bulkier mass of their work, look like colonial schoolmasters.

It is worth while to rescue a passage from one of his more ephemeral papers—an article on Kipling in the *Political Nursery* of April 1899—for its statement of his organic ideal for literature:

'Permanent interest cannot attach to anything which does not consist, from rind to seeds, of instructive truth. A thing must be interesting from every point of view, as history, as poetry, as philosophy; good for a sick man, just the thing for Sunday morning. It must be true if read backwards, true literally and true as a parable, true in fragments and true as a whole. It must be valuable as a campaign document, and it must make you laugh or cry at any time, day or night. Lasting literature has got to be so very good as to fulfill all these conditions. Kipling's work does not do so since the time he began making money out of it.'

But the long study of Emerson had a special importance. It was something other than a mere essay on Emerson. It was rather an extension of Emerson, a re-creation of Emerson for a new generation, for it was really an expression—the first full expression—of Chapman's own point of view. And what Chapman got out of Emerson was something entirely different from the gentle and eupeptic personality—though that was a part of the real Emerson, too —of Van Wyck Brooks's recent portrayals. What Chapman got out of Emerson was a sort of beneficent Nietzscheanism, as electrical as Nietzsche's but less rhetorical. It had seemed to him at college, Chapman wrote, 'as if Emerson were a younger brother of Shakespeare. . . I was intoxicated with Emerson. He let loose something within me which made me in my own eyes as good as anyone else.' It was Emerson who had first made it possible for him to say to himself: 'After all, it is just as well that there should be *one* person like *me* in the world.' John Jay Chapman was thus a continuator of the individualist tradition of Emerson, which is also the tradition of Thoreau. (Chapman speaks of Thoreau less often, though it seems to me that he is in some ways even more closely akin to him.) He had carried this tradition to New York—for, in spite of the influence on his thought of Cambridge and Concord and Boston, he was distinctly to remain a New Yorker; and in his hands it was to undergo here an interesting variation.

'As I look back over my past,' he writes, 'the figure of Emerson looms up in my mind as the first modern man, and the city of Boston as the first living civilization which I knew. New York is not a civilization; it is a railway station.' Yet the New Yorker, though beside the New Englanders, with their Concord flavor and color, he may seem a little abstract and steely (as Henry James does, also, beside Hawthorne), is the man of a larger world. He was to bring against Emerson a new criticism. 'Our people are as thin-skinned as babies,' he wrote in one of his lectures, 'and the Massachusetts crowd has never been criticized.' No one had ventured to stand up to Emerson on the issue of the sexual emotions since Walt Whitman had walked with him on Boston Common and, after listening to all his remonstrances against the *Children of Adam* section of *Leaves of Grass*, had replied that he couldn't answer Emerson's arguments, but that he felt sure of being right just the same. 'If an inhabitant of another planet,' wrote Chapman, 'should visit the earth, he would receive, on the whole, a truer notion of human life by attending an Italian opera than he would by reading Emerson's volumes. He would learn from the Italian opera that there were two sexes; and this, after all, is probably the fact with which the education of such a stranger ought to begin. In a review of Emerson's personal character and opinions, we are thus led to see that his philosophy, which finds no room for the emotions, is a faithful exponent of his own and of the New England temperament, which distrusts and dreads the emotions. Regarded as a sole guide to life for a young person of strong conscience and undeveloped affections, his works might conceivably be even harmful because of their unexampled power of purely intellectual stimulation.

And he was to take the Thoreauvian intransigence into society instead of into solitude. John Jay Chapman's attitude toward politics is to develop with a curious logic, which is set forth in two other remarkable books: *Causes and Consequences* (1898) and *Practical Agitation* (1900). *Causes and Consequences* is one of the most powerful tracts ever written on the debasement of our politics and government by unscrupulous business interests. It begins with a pungent fable about the gradual but complete domination of a small American town by a railroad which passes through it. This, says Chapman, when he has told his story, is the whole history of America since the Civil War. And he shows the results of this process in the general cultural life with a force which was not later surpassed by Mencken or Van Wyck Brooks:

'We have seen that the retailer in the small town could not afford to think clearly upon the political situation. But this was a mere instance, a sample of his mental attitude. He dare not face any question. He must shuffle, qualify and defer. Here at last we have the great characteristic which covers our continent like a climate—intellectual dishonesty. This state of mind does not merely prevent a man having positive opinions. The American is incapable of taking a real interest in anything. The lack of passion in the American—noticeable in his books and in himself—comes from the same habitual mental distraction; for passion is concentration. Hence also the flippancy, superficiality and easy humor for which we are noted. Nothing except the dollar is believed to be worthy the attention of a serious man. People are even ashamed of their tastes. Until recently, we thought it effeminate for a man to play on the piano. When a man takes a living interest in anything, we call him a "crank." There is an element of self-sacrifice in any honest intellectual work which we detect at once and score with contumely.

'It was not solely commercial interest that made the biographers of Lincoln so thrifty to extend and veneer their book. It was that they themselves did not, could not, take an interest in the truth about him. The second-rate quality of all our letters and verse is due to the same cause. The intellectual integrity is undermined. The literary man is concerned for what "will go," like the reformer who is half politician. The attention of everyone in the United States is on someone else's opinion, not on truth.'

What is one to do in such a world? The diagnosis of *Causes and Consequences* is followed by a program of action in *Practical*

Agitation; but Chapman's practical agitation is of a special and unexpected kind. As a result of his experience as a reformer, he has ceased to believe in the possibility of organized political reform under the American conditions of the time. One of the most amusing and searching passages of *Practical Agitation* describes the rapid absorption and the complete neutralization of a reform movement by the forces it has set out to correct. The commercial solidarity of society has rendered such crusading futile.

Once arrived at such a recognition, one might expect a man like Chapman to turn socialist; but his position on socialism is stated as follows:

'The function of Socialism is clear. It is a religious reaction going on in an age which thinks in terms of money. We are very nearly at the end of it, because we are very nearly at the end of the age. Some people believe they hate the wealth of the millionaire. They denounce corporations and trusts, as if these things hurt them. They strike at the symbol. What they really hate is the irresponsible rapacity which these things typify, and which nothing but moral forces will correct. In so far as people seek the cure in property-laws they are victims of the plague. The cure will come entirely from the other side; for as soon as the millionaires begin to exert and enjoy the enormous power for good which they possess, everybody will be glad they have the money.'

He does not, therefore, believe much in economics:

'The economic laws are valuable and suggestive, but they are founded on the belief that a man will pursue his own business interests exclusively. This is never entirely true even in trade, and the doctrines of the economists become more and more misleading when applied to fields of life where the money motive becomes incidental. The law of supply and demand does not govern the production of sonnets.'

But, 'when you see cruelty going on before you, you are put to the alternative of interposing to stop it, or of losing your sensibility.'

What then? Here is where Emerson comes in. 'If a soul,' he wrote, 'be taken and crushed by democracy till it utter a cry, that cry will be Emerson.' And: 'The thing seems to me about this,' he wrote in a letter of this time, after finishing an essay on the *Social Results of Commercialism*—'Emerson made coherent. It's all Emerson. I should have had neither the ideas reduced so clearly nor the public to understand them if it hadn't been for Emerson. I can't imagine what I should have been if it hadn't been for Emerson.' For he is thrown back on the individual conscience. Here is the situation with which the citizen finds himself confronted:

'Remember . . . that there is no such thing as abstract truth. You must talk facts, you must name names, you must impute motives. You must say what is in your mind. It is the only means you have of cutting yourself free from the body of this death. Innuendo will not do. Nobody minds innuendo. We live and breathe nothing else. If you are not strong enough to face the issue in private life, do not dream that you can do anything for public affairs. This, of course, means fight, not tomorrow, but now. It is only in the course of conflict that anyone can come to understand the system, the habit of thought, the mental condition, out of which all our evils arise. The first difficulty is to see the evils clearly; and when we do see them it is like fighting an atmosphere to contend against them. They are so universal and omnipresent that you have no terms to name them by. You must burn a disinfectant.'

And one can take only individual action:

'You yourself cannot turn Niagara; but there is not a town in America where one single man cannot make his force felt against the whole torrent. He takes a stand on a practical matter. He takes action against some abuse. What does this accomplish? Everything. How many people are there in your town? Well, every one of them gets a thrill that strikes deeper than any sermon he ever heard. He may howl, but he hears. The grocer's boy, for the first time in his life, believes that the whole outfit of morality has any place in the practical world.'

There can have been few codes of morality ever formulated so individualistic as John Jay Chapman's:

'If you want a compass at any moment in the midst of some

difficult situation, you have only to say to yourself, "Life is larger than this little imbroglio. I shall follow my instinct." As you say this, your compass swings true. You may be surprised to find what course it points to. But what it tells you to do will be practical agitation.'

This code, with high courage and immense energy, he attempted to put into practice. These were intent and tumultuous years, during which he was shaken by many emotions. At the beginning of 1897, after the birth of their second son, his wife suddenly and unexpectedly died while he was reading to her aloud as she lay in bed. The next year he married his friend, Elizabeth Chanler. Through all this he had been speaking, writing, organizing, getting out his paper, practicing law and leading an active social life—while the immovable magnitude of the forces against him was gradually but inexorably becoming clear to him. 'My own family and connections,' he wrote, 'being a lot of well-meaning bourgeois, are horrified at me. But I enjoy it.' Yet, 'Politics takes physique,' he wrote at another time, 'and being odious takes physique. I feel like Atlas, lifting the entire universe. I hate this community and despise 'em—and fighting, fighting, fighting, fighting an atmospheric pressure gets tiresome.' When his friends expressed apprehension: 'As for insanity,' he replied, 'why, I was once examined for insanity by the two most distinguished physicians in Boston [at the time when he had burned off his hand]. It has no terrors. I talked to them like Plato.'

In the summer of 1900, he went out to attend a convention in Indianapolis which nominated 'Gold Democrat' candidates to run against both McKinley and Bryan; and he worked hard to organize a 'National Party,' the candidates proposed for which refused to run. That winter, after an attack of grippe, at the time when his wife was expecting a baby, he suddenly broke down in the midst of a speech in a small town in Pennsylvania. 'Too much will and self-will,' he wrote his mother.

He retreated to a darkened room. For a year he did not leave his bed, and when he was finally able to get up, remained for two or three years longer under the delusion that he was unable to walk without crutches. Turned in on his own blackness, the

sight of a beautiful sunset or the interior of an Italian church,
which he had been induced to come out to see, would excite him
to the point of collapse.

II

The second half of John Jay Chapman's life is quite distinct
from the first. In the August of 1903, one of his sons by his first
wife Minna was drowned in an Austrian river; and the shock seems
to have brought him to himself. He went back to the United
States without his crutches.

He recovered, and thereafter for thirty years led the life of a
well-to-do country squire at Barrytown on the Hudson. His second wife's family, the Chanlers, were among the most adventurous
and gifted of that special race, the Hudson River gentry; and John
Jay Chapman took his place in their world. Chapman's father
had been president of the New York Stock Exchange, but had
lost heavily in the panic of the seventies, so that John Jay had
had partly to put himself through college by tutoring, and he
seems to have had a certain amount of difficulty in supporting
his family on his earnings from the law. In his youth he had had
a variety of social experience which verged at moments on the
picaresque. In the course of a trip to Europe after his graduation
from Harvard, he had gone to visit an aunt who had married the
German minister to Russia and had attended a ball at the Winter
Palace, where he saw through the eyes of Tolstoy the Grand
Dukes and 'the gorgeous ministers holding glittering staves' and
the 'consoling duplicities' of the diplomats, and rescued a pair
of toboggans which seemed about to become untied on a chute
by throwing himself between them and holding them together
while he was dragged on his belly to the bottom; and not long
afterwards, when he had returned to America, he went to Canada
and hired himself out as a farm-hand: he 'did chores, digged
holes for posts, picked cherries on a ladder' till his 'head swam'
and 'the landscape reeled,' but was so bad at it that one farmer
refused to pay him, and he finally came back to his family in
such a condition of raggedness and shagginess that they were unable to recognize him; his whole exploit had netted him a dollar.

On the eve of his second marriage, he had been troubled by

apprehensions at the prospect of being well-to-do. 'The first thing you know we'll be drowned in possessions,' he wrote at that time to Miss Chanler, 'and then by thinking of our horses' health. It is not so easy to keep the keen vision which an empty stomach lends, if you have footmen. I fear a footman. I tremble before a man with hot water. . . Let's keep the New Testament open before us. The losing of wrath is to be feared. . . If I become classed with men at ease about money, the Lord protect me. It is a steel corselet against the heart of mankind and the knowledge of life.' And there are indications in his later letters that he continued to shrink from allowing himself to be 'classed with men at ease about money.' 'I take rides on the busses—for 4d.,' he wrote a friend from London. 'You can go at the rate of 10 m. per hour for half an hour. These things recall London—and student days. The cheap things give one most pleasure—when one is old and rich like me.' And: 'The food of the rich is disgusting to me . . . messes. Last night I had to go to Childs and eat cornbeef hash and poached eggs, which pulled me round.'

Yet he is haunted by ideas of his affinities with royalty and aristocracy. 'I never saw children like them,' he wrote of his sons by his first wife. 'They are King's children in disguise, and I am a stepfather to them.' And, during a visit to an Italian noble, 'I am having some gold fringe put on my pants and I have assumed the title of Monsignore. It is amazing how easily gentility sits on me. I believe some people are just naturally swells—you know what I mean—and fit well in palaces and eat good food naturally and without effort. I remember the first royal palace I saw—seemed to me—gave me a feeling—just like the old homestead. I often think that Grandma Jones used to say, 'the Chapmans were once Kings.' Dear old Grandpa, with his old cotton socks, wouldn't he be proud if he could see me he-hawing and chaw-chawing with Roman princes!' His plays are full of princes and counts and kings. He had himself something of a kingly presence, especially adorned with the magnificent beard with which he had emerged from his illness. And it is impossible to escape the impression that the comfort and security of his later years did to some degree dull his responses and cut him off from the active world. He succumbed to the Hudson Valley in becoming one of its principal ornaments—to Dutchess County, with its cupolaed castles on their towering dark-wooded hills, which do their best to give work or give alms to the humble feudal villages on the riverbank, to the thunderstorms that seem to crack the firmament and the heavy and slumbrous summers, to the tradition of public responsibility which Hamilton Fish shares with Franklin D. Roosevelt, to the culture which, where it occurs, is likely to range so much more widely and to seem to have so much more authenticity than that of most wealthy communities in America, and to the naturalness and amiability which merge quietly and not unpleasantly with smugness—and all, as it were, walled-in from the rest of the United States and alone with the noble river.

The young John Jay Chapman had plunged into the thick of the conflicts of his time. *Emerson* and *Causes and Consequences* had been talked about and read, had had their influence. In both his political and his literary writing, he had dealt with matters of current interest. But now, in his second period, he seems to have withdrawn from contemporary life, and tends to confine himself to history and the classics. He seems almost to be talking to himself, he seems hardly to expect or hope for an audience; and so people cease to listen to him. The second half of Chapman's career must inevitably be surprising and depressing, though not entirely disappointing, to one who has been stirred by the first. Though he had been able to throw away his crutches, he was to remain, in a deeper sense, a crippled man all the rest of his life. Yet the alternative to survival on these terms would, one supposes, have been madness or death; and it is the proof of the authenticity of his genius that, throughout this long period when he is turned toward the past, when, as a rule, he emerges into the present to raise only trivial or unreal issues, he keeps his power not merely to charm but also sometimes to stimulate.

The Americans who graduated from college in the eighties had to contend with a world that broke most of them. One can see the situation very clearly if one compares the men of the eighties even with those of the seventies. In the seventies, the universities were still turning out admirable professional men, who had had the old classical education, a culture much wider

[149]

than their profession and the tradition of political idealism and public conscience which had presided at the founding of the Republic. The world which they had found when they got out had not yet become different enough from the world for which their education had fitted them so that they were not able, on the terms of that old education, to make for themselves positions of dignity in it. But by the later years of the eighties, the industrial and commercial development which followed the Civil War had reached a point where the old education was no longer an equipment for life. It had, in fact, become a troublesome handicap. The best of the men who had taken it seriously were launched on careers of tragic misunderstanding. They could no longer play the role in the professions of a trained and public-spirited caste: the new society did not recognize them. The rate of failure and insanity and suicide in some of the college 'classes' of the eighties shows an appalling demoralization.

Some set themselves to learn the new methods and choked their scruples and did their best to cash in; but John Jay Chapman— who had John Jay among his ancestors—was too honest, too fastidious, too proud, and too violently impulsive, for this. Others compromised shrewdly, like Roosevelt; but the merest suggestion of compromise seems at that period to have driven Chapman into a frenzy. Almost all were compelled to accept in some way the values of the world of business; but how little this was possible for Chapman is indicated in one of his late letters when he insists that, let people say what they please, business can never be a profession. (I have heard a college man of as late as the nineties, who had spent fifty years with an importing firm, tell of his feelings of humiliation when he first started in to work there at a time when the business men, on their side, were supposed to have no use for college graduates. By the second decade of our century, probably the majority of college students had no higher object, on graduating, than to qualify for selling bonds or to slip behind some desk in a family concern and present a well-brushed appearance; and the movement for business courses in the colleges and the talk of the university as a 'big business' were already well under way.)

Given the fineness of Chapman's equipment, the overpowering

nature of his emotions and the relentless clarity of his insight—
and given the inescapable conviction of his superiority which
made him, for all the ardor of his patriotism, talk about 'a soul
crushed by democracy'—there was nothing for him to do but
break. And the permanent psychological damage which he had
inflicted upon himself by beating his head against the gilt of the
Gilded Age was as much one of the scars of the heroism of his
passionate and expiatory nature as the hand he had burnt off in
his youth.

Let us see how he occupies himself. He begins by writing little
plays for children—then, later, tries longer plays. *The Treason and
Death of Benedict Arnold* (1910) is perhaps the best of these and
has a certain personal interest—with its Coriolanian picture of a
man of touchy pride and strong self-will driving through a perverse
course of action, which will bring him, among his enemies, honor
but no comfort and which will separate him forever from the
cause for which he has fought:

> *They must pet me then,*
> *To show that loyal treason reaps reward.*
> *'Twas policy, not liking for my face,*
> *That made King George so sweet.*
> *What in this world of savage Englishmen,*
> *Strange monsters that they are, have you and I*
> *Found of a country? Friends, good hearts and true;*
> *But alien as the mountains of the moon,*
> *More unrelated than the Polander,*
> *Are Englishmen to us. They are a race,*
> *A selfish, brawling family of hounds,*
> *Holding a secret contract on each fang,*
> *'For us,' 'for us,' 'for us.' They'll fawn about;*
> *But when the prey's divided;—Keep away!*
> *I have some beef about me and bear up*
> *Against an insolence as basely set*
> *As mine own infamy; yet I have been*
> *Edged to the outer cliff. I have been weak,*
> *And played too much the lackey. What am I*
> *In this waste, empty, cruel, land of England,*

Save an old castaway,—a buccaneer,—
The hull of derelict Ambition,—
Without a mast or spar, the rudder gone,
A danger to mankind!

But, on the whole, as his biographer says, Chapman is unable to transmit to his characters his own power of self-dramatization. He shrank from and had little comprehension of the new dramatic forms of Ibsen and Shaw, as he shrank from the world they reflected. The companion of Shakespeare and Aeschylus, he followed their methods as a matter of course, with results which are not hopelessly academic only because he could not help getting some reality into everything that he wrote. His plays were mostly in verse; and his verse—he also made some translations from the Greeks and published a certain amount of miscellaneous poetry—is usually only effective when it approximates to the qualities of his prose. There are a few exceptions to this, such as his fine translations from Dante; but the poet that there undoubtedly was in Chapman—perhaps some Puritan heritage had its blighting effect here—found expression chiefly in preaching. As a moralist, John Jay Chapman is a highly successful artist; and it is mainly as a moralist now that he will continue to hold our attention.

With his illness, there emerges a new point of view—really a sort of rarefication of his earlier one. It was before the days of psychoanalysis, and he had been helped through his breakdown by 'faith healers.' In a peculiar and personal way, he now becomes religious. 'There was never anyone with less practical notions, or less under the belief that he was religious in his aims, than I,' he wrote to a friend in 1922 of his early political experience. 'I wanted to attack practical evils—find out about them anyway, affront and examine them, understand them—and I set out by experiment and analysis to deal with them as a workaday problem. And gradually under inspection and ratiocination they turned into spiritual things—mystical elements, and went back into the envelope of religious truth. Nothing else but religious truth was involved. It happened to me apropos of reform movements, to the next man in medicine, to the next in hygiene, in education, in literary work—(look at Winston Churchill). Surely all of us were toys in a shop, and were being turned by the same dynamo— we all approach more nearly all the time to a common frame of mind and temperament—a common sense of helplessness—we who were going to be so powerful and triumphant.' He had announced his new attitude in 1913 at the end of his book on William Lloyd Garrison: 'At first,' he says, 'we desire to help vigorously, and we do all in our power to assist mankind. As time goes on, we perceive more and more clearly that the advancement of the world does not depend upon us, but that we, rather, are bound up in it, and can command no foothold of our own. At last we see that our very ambitions, desires and hopes in the matter are a part of the Supernal Machinery moving through all things, and that our souls can be satisfied and our power exerted only in so far as we are taken up into that original motion, and merged in that primal power. Our minds thus dissolve under the grinding analysis of life, and leave behind nothing except God. Towards him we stand and look: and we, who started out with so many gifts for men, have nothing left in our satchel for mankind except a blessing.'

To one who, like the present writer, is fundamentally unsympathetic with all modern manifestations of religion, the books of John Jay Chapman on this subject—*Notes on Religion* (1922) and *Letters and Religion* (1924)—seem genuine and impressive in a way that most other such recent writings do not. There have been lately in fashion among literary people two main ways of being religious: one historical, philosophical and ritualistic—the convert turns to the Catholic Church; the other through a substitute pseudo-religion, like that proposed by H. G. Wells. But in the flashes of revelation that were intermittently noted by Chapman, we seem to touch a live spiritual experience as we do not often do with these writers. It is, of course, intensely Protestant: it is Emersonianism again. We are not to look for direction to any established church; each is to trust his own instinct and to interpret the Scriptures for himself:

'Christianity accomplishes itself; and this not through a grand, frontal attack on humanity, but rather through the story and sayings of Christ which dart through the earth, pierce men's ears and heal them, run like elixirs through the languages and habits of men. They are couriers, arrows that live in the ether and need no inns or baiting-places between their flights. The sayings have inexhaustible meanings, and many depths of meaning which the comfortable people of the world cannot hope to fathom—meanings that lie in ambush in the texts, and enter men's hearts in the wake of grief. A man must have been disgraced and in jail to know many of them.' Yet the instincts of individuals are to unite in communion the whole of mankind. With the capacity for deep humility and the sympathy with American life which saved his sense of superiority from snobbery, he was able to interest himself in philanthropies and popular churches:

'I believe that if we could see the invisible church as it actually exists in the interlacing of all men in God and with each other through the force that makes them live, the alarm of those who are fostering religion for fear it will die out would appear ridiculous. Even the half-charlatan, half-illiterate American religious cults deserve our interest and respect.'

'The new American mysticism, for all its eccentricities, dropped an anchor for a generation that had been living in continuous flotation; and being at anchor, the waves of life began to play against the souls of that generation, and beat them into faith. The breakdown of the older ecclesiastical authorities proved a blessing. All the barriers, the interpretations, the shopworn catechisms, the churchy miasmas of many centuries, had been blown away, and the bare text of the New Testament began to convert a new generation and to bring them rest. The new faith was purest in the most humble, as has been the case with all Christian revivals.'

The later Chapman is a lesser Tolstoy, fighting out on his estate on the Hudson the same kind of long war with his conscience which Tolstoy fought at Yasnaya Polyana. And we feel about him somewhat as the contemporaries of Tolstoy seem to have felt about him: that, whatever his inconsistencies and his crusadings for mistaken causes, his spirit and example were a force of incalculable value.

'Truly,' he wrote in one of his letters, 'it is the decay in the American brain that is the real danger, and in my narrow philoso-

phy I see the only cure in self-expression, passion, feeling—
spiritual reality of some sort. We're about dead spiritually—that's
my illusion.' William James, the one of Chapman's contemporaries who probably appreciated him most, called him 'a profound
moralist.' 'I have a notion,' he once wrote James, 'that I could tell
you what is the matter with pragmatism—if you would only stand
still. A thing is not truth till it is so strongly believed in that the
believer is convinced that its existence does not depend upon
him. This cuts off the pragmatist from knowing what truth is.'
And: 'It is utter nonsense,' he wrote another correspondent, 'this
great passion and little passion—this upper clef and lower clef.
All life is nothing but passion. From the great passion of love
to the regard for a passing stranger is all one diapason, and is
the same chord. The whole of it vibrates no matter where you
touch it—tho' in different degrees.' His ideal of practical agitation
has in his later phase subsided to this: 'I am saying things which
will some day be thought of, rather than trying to get the attention of anyone.' 'It is an accident when I *do* right, but I *am* right,'
he once declared.

This rightness was due to some influence which took possession
of him and was stronger than he. We may be puzzled at first by
the language in which he writes to Minna Timmins, his future
wife, after the experience of burning off his hand: 'I do think
there was something Promethean in it, in the capacity to yield.'
What fire had Chapman snatched from Heaven? And is it Promethean to yield? He means that a divine revelation had caused
him to mutilate himself—the revelation of his love for Minna,
which was unable to break through into his consciousness and
to assert its authority over him save by compelling him to recognize, and hence to punish himself for, his mistake. And he wrote
later on to Miss Chanler: 'I . . . have broken and battered down
the doors of silence once and forever years ago, and go about the
world escaped from that prison, I thank the powers of life.' Yet he
must break out of prison again and again; and his language is always that of giving himself up to something that invades him from
outside: 'I'll tell you my philosophy—that there's only one real joy
in life . . . —the joy of casting at the world the stone of an unknown world.' His first love, his first wife and her children, with

their fierce natures and their sudden or violent deaths, is itself like a power that seizes upon him, a current for which he acts as conductor and which will leave him partially shattered. And when it is not love, he calls it God.

Besides these religious *pensées*, Chapman publishes during this period several volumes of essays, literary, historical and social, and some memoirs of New York and Boston. He perfects himself now as a writer: in these books, the 'style all splinters,' of which William James wrote at the time of *Practical Agitation*, is hammered out into an instrument of perfect felicity, economy, limpidity, precision and point. Some of his most beautiful prose is in his very latest writings. And he can still take our breath away by laying hold of the root of some subject, by thrusting through, with a brusque direct gesture, all the familiar conventions and pretensions with which it has been enclosed.

In his relation to the literary classics, he was that almost unprecedented phenomenon, a highly intelligent and well-educated American who paid almost no attention to European criticism and scholarship. Well as he knew Europe, he was never afflicted with the nostalgia for it which seized so many of the cultivated Americans of his time. In his opinions on European culture, he was as naturally and uncompromisingly American as Walt Whitman or Mark Twain. The accepted apparatus of learning he either quarreled with or disregarded—characterizing, for example, the taking-over of Greek literature by the mandarins of the English universities as an incident in the expansion of the British Empire.

To Chapman, the great writers of the past were neither a pantheon nor a vested interest. He approached them openmindedly and boldly, very much as he did living persons who he thought might entertain or instruct him. Not that he judged them by contemporary standards; but he would go straight to them across the ages in the role of an independent traveler, who was willing to pay his toll to the people that kept the roads but wished to linger with them as little as possible. He sometimes committed blunders: he got the relationships mixed up in the *Antigone*, and he never grasped the simple enough principles which govern, in the *Divine Comedy*, the assignment of the souls to the different worlds—complaining that Dante's arrangements involved a good deal of injustice. 'You know,' he says in a letter, 'I've never known the literature of the subjects I wrote on. I never knew the Emerson literature—except Emerson himself.' But Chapman has at least always got there and had a good look at the man; and he can always tell you about him something that you have not heard before. To me, Chapman's flashlighting and spotlighting in his studies of the Greeks, Dante, Shakespeare and Goethe (this last left unpublished at his death and unfortunately not yet published) are among the few real recent contributions to the knowledge of these familiar subjects. He cannot help bumping into aspects which, though they bulk very large in these authors, have so often been ignored or evaded that many people have never noticed they were there. He saw the basic barbarity of Greek tragedy, which he denounced Gilbert Murray for sentimentalizing; he saw the importance of the pederasty of Plato: Diotima, he writes, is 'an odious creature, being a man in disguise'; he saw, through all the Dante commentaries, how impossible it is to interpret Dante in terms of medieval theology.

Here are passages from some of the latest of these essays, which show the freshness of Chapman's mind in his sixties:

'Plato soothes and rests. He takes the mind off its troubles and supplies it with imaginative solutions for problems which do not press. To read him is a solace and to write commentaries on him is an entrancing and enduring preoccupation. He is the patron saint of those who sit in armchairs and speculate. His wealth of information, myth and anecdote, the amenity and fluidity of his procedure, endear him to all book-lovers. He is enshrined in a civilization which will interest the world as long as intelligent men shall be born into it. Even the limitations and defects of the Athenians are stimulating. "Athens," we say, and surrender ourselves to romance. We sleep while awake; and if you point out that Plato deceives us by intellectual legerdemain which cheats the mind, nay, if you should prove it, this will make you no friends; for, as Mr. Barnum discovered to his profit many centuries later, the public likes to be fooled. A vision of truth which does not call upon us to get out of our armchair—why, this is the desideratum of mankind.'

[157]

'Dante's frailty is the source of his power. Had he been truly a medieval theologian, or philosopher, or moralist, or historian, he would today be as dead as the rest of them. . . [His philosophy] is full of whimsies and cobwebs, private significances and key-words; and there is no philosophic instrument of thought which he does not distort as he touches it—even as all poets do, and must do.' 'The conceptions of Greek mythology spring out of a Supermind which harmonizes the fantasies of childhood with the thought of mature age. They are embedded in the ganglia of the brain as music is: no explanation touches them. They defy analysis, and Dante himself fails to interpret them: his metaphysics will not stick to them.' 'To raise the question whether Dante was technically or virtually a heretic . . . is to miss the human and important point of the whole question. Dante's attitude toward the Empire and the Papacy was that of a super-autocrat who is above both of them, and holds a commission from on high to regulate the affairs of each.' 'The truth is that one must gather Dante's meanings, as one gathers the meanings of other men, by putting two and two together, not by drawing pictures of his Supposed Universe, and then hanging his phrases on them as on a Christmas Tree.' 'He had invented the *terza rima*, a form in which a continuous lyric can float and be indefinitely sustained upon the narrative below it.'

What a pity, one is moved to exclaim, that John Jay Chapman remained a dilettante! Yet 'dilettante' is not the proper word for one who worked at his writing so diligently and so seriously. And his literary essays, after all, are only a part of his general commentary, which possesses a sort of center of its own, independent of the various subjects treated.

Aside from this purely literary activity, he carried on a certain amount of agitation, sporadically and in behalf of a strange diversity of causes. His rejection of economics, his failure, when he had recognized political corruption as a mere by-product of the industrial-commercial system, to study the mechanics and the history of that system, had left him without bearings in the political world.

First of all, he went back to the Civil War—he was very proud of one of his grandmothers, who had been a prominent Abolitionist—and in his book on William Lloyd Garrison fought the battle of slavery all over again with a spirit that would have been employed more usefully in fighting the battle of labor. It was the period of the rise of Bill Haywood's Wobblies, of the growth of Eugene Debs's Socialist Party, of Lincoln Steffens' muck-raking movement.

On August 13, 1911, a Negro who had shot and killed a special officer of the Worth Brothers Steel Company in Coatesville, Pennsylvania, was burned alive by a mob under circumstances of special horror. Chapman, who was full of the Civil War, brooded upon this incident till he 'felt as if the whole country would be different if any one man did something in penance, and so I went to Coatesville and declared my intention of holding a prayer meeting to the various business men I could buttonhole.' He had difficulty in getting a hall, but finally, four days after the anniversary of the lynching, succeeded in finding a place to speak. The address he delivered was strange and moving. He said that, when he had read in the papers how 'hundreds of well-dressed American citizens' had stood by and watched the torture of the Negro, he had seemed to see into 'the unconscious soul' of America. And what he had seen there was death—'the paralysis of the nerves about the heart in a people habitually and unconsciously given over to selfish aims.' They had 'stood like blighted things, like ghosts about Acheron, waiting for someone or something to determine their destiny for them.' It was the old wickedness, not yet purged, of the slave trade, and all America was to blame for it. They could but open their hearts to God and pray that new life might flow into them.—The only persons who attended the meeting were an educated Negro woman from Boston and a stool pigeon sent by the police.

The World War, when it first broke out, aroused him to a new burst of agitation. He was in Europe in August 1914, and went immediately to Balfour, Haldane and Sir Edward Grey, and told them that it was of vital importance, in order to elicit the sympathy of the world, that the Allies should declare their aims to be non-aggressive and announce their intention, in the event of their victory, of calling a world disarmament congress; and he seems to have been deceived by the intelligence and kindness with which these statesmen heard him out. Later, he went to Wilson and urged him to elicit such a declaration. He also published a book, *Deutschland über Alles* (1914), in which he pointed out the propaganda methods by which the Germans had been worked up to the war, and advised the United States to stay out. 'If America should enter the war, the world would lose the benevolence and commonsense which we now possess, and which is a strong factor in the whole situation. You and I would, in that case, become partisans, cruel, excited and bent on immediate results.'

In the meantime, however, his son Victor, one of his children by his first wife, had, against his father's wishes, enlisted in the Foreign Legion and had later become one of the most daring pilots of the Lafayette Escadrille. He was killed—the first American aviator to die—on June 23, 1916; and his father now fell a victim to that war psychology which he had foreseen and dreaded for the country. Chapman was even betrayed temporarily into applauding his old enemy Roosevelt, whose pro-Ally bellowings and pawings of the ground were certainly no more to be taken seriously than the other Rooseveltian impostures which Chapman had so relentlessly exposed. Later, in 1920, when Siegfried Sassoon came to New York, and read his poems and made an anti-war speech at the Cosmopolitan Club, the former opponent of wartime fanaticism—who, no doubt, felt it a duty to speak for his dead son—got up and aroused consternation and hisses by denouncing what he characterized as a philosophy of fear and self-pity. The next day he tried to call on Sassoon and finally wrote him a letter: 'Sorry to miss you this morning. It was a suffering occasion last night. I think I suffered as much as you did. If you will do it, why, you must.' Had he remembered his early gospel of the value of the individual gesture and reflected that the young Sassoon had, after all, only been doing what he himself had done when, for example, at that political dinner in 1895, he had spoken out in a way that had made old Mr. Choate turn pale?

The most wrongheaded of all his crusades, but the one to which he devoted most energy, was his attack on the Roman Catholic Church. He had received no doubt a terrifying impression of the bad influence of the Catholics in Boston; but he exaggerated its importance in the United States as a whole, and he

had become, by 1925, so almost monomaniacally obsessed by it
that it was thought best for him to go abroad to distract his mind
from the subject and avoid another breakdown.* At one period he
was inclined to believe—in spite of the admiration for Jewish culture which had caused him once to call himself a 'Hebraist'—
that the Jews, also, were coming to be a sinister influence, and
he even contributed a sonnet, anti-Catholic and anti-Semitic,
to the organ of the Ku Klux Klan. ('The Jews,' he had written in 1897, 'have in my experience more faith than the Chris-
tians. They have clever heads, better hearts, and more belief
in the power of good every way. They gave to the world all
the religion it has got and are themselves the most religious
people in it. I work with them day and night and most of the
time is spent in prying up some Christian to do a half day's work.')

For two years he and Mrs. Chapman conducted a club-room
for young people in the Hell's Kitchen section of New York.
On one occasion, two boys whom he had had to put out, came
back and blew kerosene in his beard and tried to set it afire. When
they had failed, he handed them a handkerchief and told them to
wipe themselves off.

Besides all this, he was continually agitating against the influence of big business at Harvard and harrying with scolding letters
the Head Master of St. Paul's School, as well as old friends in
positions of prominence of whose activities he disapproved. One
of his correspondents, Mr. T. B. Wells, the editor of *Harper's
Magazine*, was finally goaded to ask what Chapman himself had
accomplished any more than 'a lot of other brilliant fellows who
did not make full use of their talents' to give him the right to
call everyone else to account over the way they handled their jobs.
And it is true that one feels a touch of envy in his tone toward
men like Shaw and Wells, even toward William James, whom
he undoubtedly liked and admired—who were doing a kind of
work that one would think he might have applauded. There is
even an occasional accent of the ignorant and cutting Boston
snootiness that he had disliked and ridiculed. As one goes through

* Since this was written, the Catholic Church has become in the United
States a formidable pressure group, exercising the retrograde and repressive
force that Chapman at that time ascribed to it.

his later letters—as in reading his work of this period—one is made more and more uncomfortable by the feeling that one has been shut up in a chamber from which the air is being gradually withdrawn—shut in with a chafing spirit who, baffled of finding an outlet, is sometimes furious and sometimes faint. Then suddenly one recoils and stands outside the cell: one sees how Chapman's outlook has narrowed. One remembers all the things that have happened in the world of which there is almost no mention in these letters—almost the whole significant life of the time; and one realizes that Chapman's interests have come to be almost entirely confined to the horizons of his old Harvard circle. It is all Harvard College and St. Paul's School, Porcellian Club and Tavern Club. He writes to Dr. Drury of St. Paul's and E. S. Martin of *Life* as if they were among the great molders of thought of their age. We have the suspicion that even William James, as distinct from Wells and Shaw, is only admitted to the sphere of Chapman's interest because he, too, belongs to Harvard. It is the lost traveler's dream under the hill—the old conception of the caste of trained 'college men' who were to preside over the arts and professions. It is the same point of view—we had not recognized it at first—that seemed so fatuous, that became so unconsciously comic, in Owen Wister's memoirs of Roosevelt. Mr. Wister, whose claim to celebrity consists in his having written novels, is wonderful when, after telling of his acquaintance with various personages of Philadelphia and Harvard of whom we have never heard, he says that, 'Huysmans (if I recall the right name) had recently published a novel, in which were described the rites of the Black Mass'—and he is even more wonderful when, after a life 'chiefly passed,' as he says, 'among the Alexander Cassatts, the George Baers and the Weir Mitchells' of Philadelphia, he goes West and discovers Coxey's army and the stoppage of trains due to the Pullman strike, and is obliged to spend two dreadful nights sleeping on the floor of a boat from San Pedro. But this failure of response to contemporary events, either artistic or economic is, in Chapman's case, simply depressing. Owen Wister thinks them still important, Olympians who dominate the world —Roosevelt and Henry Adams and Henry Cabot Lodge and the rest. John Jay Chapman has no illusions about them, but he has to go on nagging at them and abusing them. He does not seem to realize that they have all been either absorbed or left behind by a new world never contemplated by old Harvard. He himself—for all the piercing intuitions which still at moments strike through age and class—has been left behind by that world.

He believed in these later days that the society of the period after the war was on the eve of a great religious reawakening:

'Who shall say that this present era, when all the idols are broken, all the great traditions dead, and the fine arts have become mere wandering lights, while the mind of man seems to have passed into a tunnel of transition—who shall say that these apparent extinguishments and this twilight are not necessary? Our present incredulity as to all the explanations of life is very favorable to a direct vision of life itself. The floods have carried away our mills, and a thunderstorm has destroyed the wiring of our houses; but the powers of gravity and electricity are not abolished for a moment. The contrivances on which we had set so much store served but to obscure the phenomena. Like Job in the wreck of his homestead, we have been humbled. The war humbled that spirit which had ruled the nineteenth century. In scale the drama differed from the Book of Job, but in plot it was similar.

'In the meantime, though the arts have lost their message, religion stalks in upon us. The auld wives' tales about prayer and healing, which during many centuries had been regarded as ecstatic parables, are now taken literally: we live in them. This tunnel into which the age is running is one of the clairvoyant periods of history in which men are seen as trees walking. The actual world does not disappear, nor is it relegated to a life to come, or disparaged, or condemned as evil. It remains perfectly real, and yet visibly penetrated by the rays of an inner universe which are at play everywhere.'

One used to see him, during those years, in New York, in company a figure of a distinction almost exotic for the United States, with his fine manners, his sensitive intelligence, his clothes with their attractive suggestion of the elegance of another era, his almost Jove-like beard and brow, his deep and genial laugh; or for a moment under a quite different aspect, when one had hap-

[163]

pened to meet him in the street: walking alone, head drooping and brooding, with his muffler around his neck, in his face dreadful darkness and sadness and fear, as if he were staring into some lidless abyss.

He died, after an operation, on November 4, 1933. He had loved music, and when he was a student at Harvard had had what he described as 'an obsession, a sort of self-willed mania for learning to play the violin, for which I had no talent.' He had worked at it two years, but his fellow students had discouraged him by throwing coal scuttles at his door and hanging alarm-clocks outside his windows. After his father's financial failure, he wrote home, 'I shall sell the violin: it's no halfway business.' But at the time he was recovering from his breakdown, he had taken up the study of harmony and tried to compose a little. Now two days before his death, writes Mrs. Chapman, he kept murmuring, 'A soldier lay dying, a soldier lay dying.' 'I bent over him to catch the words, and he repeated the first four lines of "A soldier of the Legion lay dying in Algiers," adding, "*But there is lack of nothing here*," in a voice of deep feeling.' But later, when semi-conscious, he began saying, 'plucking at my fingers, "I want to take it away, I want to take it away!" "What?" I asked. "The pillow?" "No," he said. "The mute, the mute. I want to play on the open strings." '

BERNARD SHAW AT EIGHTY

Time has shifted our point of view on Bernard Shaw, yet he is still worth our contemplation. Let us cast a look back over his career.

George Bernard Shaw was born in Dublin, July 26, 1856, the son of shabby-genteel parents who had connections with the Irish nobility. The elder Shaw became an alcoholic, and the boy had to go to work as a clerk at the age of fifteen. Mrs. Shaw finally left her husband and went to London, where she made a living by teaching music. Her son came to live with her when he was twenty and wrote novels which he was unable to sell and picked up through journalism such money as he could. He remained with his mother till he was forty-two.

In the fall of 1882 he happened to attend a lecture on land nationalization delivered by Henry George in London. The result was a revelation: It flashed on me,' he writes, 'that "the conflict between religion and science" . . . the overthrow of the Bible, the higher education of women, Mill on Liberty and all the rest of the storm that raged around Darwin, Tyndall, Huxley, Spencer and the rest, on which I had brought myself up intellectually, was a mere middle-class business. . . The importance of the economic basis dawned on me.' He read George's *Progress and Poverty*—then someone told him to read *Das Kapital*. 'Karl Marx,' he once said, 'made a man of me.'

The result of the depression of the eighties was a revival of socialist agitation. Bernard Shaw became a socialist and spoke in halls, on street corners, in Hyde Park. The 'insurrectionism' of the period reached a climax in the 'Bloody Sunday' of November

1887, when the socialists, at the head of a working-class demonstration, invaded Trafalgar Square and were routed by the police. After this, business revived and took up the slack of unemployment, and the agitation quieted down.

In the meantime, Shaw had attached himself to the socialist statistician, Sidney Webb, and with others they had founded the Fabian Society, which had 'agreed to give up the delightful ease of revolutionary heroics and take to the hard work of practical reform on ordinary parliamentary lines.' Webb was a civil servant with a post in the colonial office and later a member of the London County Council; Shaw became a vestryman, then a borough councilor. The Fabians continued to treat Marx with respect, but the polite and reasonable criticism to which they subjected him was designed to discredit some of his main assumptions. Marx had asserted that the value of commodities was derived from the labor which had gone to produce them; and the Fabians, by elaborating a counter-theory that made value depend on demand, shifted the emphasis from the working class to the 'consumer.' They also repudiated the class war, showed that it would never occur. Socialist nationalization was to be accomplished by a corps of experts who should 'permeate' government and business, quietly invading Whitehall and setting up state departments which, unassisted by the action of the masses, should put socialist ideas into effect. Shaw boasted that the Fabians had made socialism respectable.

This variation of Marxism in England was natural to the place and time. A period of prosperity during the seventies had deflated the Chartist agitation (I am indebted to Mr. Mark Starr for a Marxist analysis of Fabian Marxism); and it was not until the eighties, when British commercial domination was being challenged by the United States and Germany, that the dangers of the capitalist system began to become generally plain. But now attention was principally directed toward the evils of competition. The development of large-scale industry was eliminating competition and making municipal ownership seem desirable, not only to the lower layers of the middle class, but even to private enterprise itself, which benefited from good housing and cheap tram-lines. The professional middle class were in a position to see the value of nationalization, and the working class had not yet discovered that for them there was not very much difference between being exploited by a private employer and being exploited by a government that was controlled by the propertied classes. The Fabians looked no further than their reforms.

In Bernard Shaw's case, this compromise Marxism played in with the elements of his character and influenced its subsequent development. Coming to London, as he has recently told us, with a conviction of his own superiority and a snobbish family tradition, but with no money and no social experience, Shaw was himself one of the dispossessed, and the socialist criticism of the class system based on property strongly recommended itself to him. Yet at the same time that in all good faith he was working to destroy that system, there is apparent in his career a tendency in the inverse direction to this. At the same time that he was spurred by a moral need to work for a future society consistent with his sense of justice, he was spurred, also, by a social need to vindicate his rightful position in the society in which he lived. He has told us that his father's bad habits had caused his family to be dropped socially in Dublin and that when he first came to London he was so shy that he would not accept dinner invitations and would 'sometimes walk up and down the Embankment for twenty minutes or more before venturing to knock at the door' of a house to which he had been asked. He goes on to say, 'The house and its artistic atmosphere were most congenial to me; and I liked all the Lawsons; but I had not mastered the art of society at that time and could not bear making an inartistic exhibition of myself; so I soon ceased to plague them.' There has always been thus in Shaw a certain amount of social snobbery mixed up with his intellectual snobbery.

The confusion produced in his thought by these two conflicting tendencies is curiously illustrated in a passage from his autobiographical preface to the collected edition of his works: 'Finding one's place may be made very puzzling,' he writes, 'by the fact that there is no place in ordinary society for extraordinary individuals. For the worldly wiseman, with common ambitions, the matter is simple enough: money, title, precedence, a seat in parliament, a portfolio in the cabinet, will mean success both to him and to his circle. But what about people like St. Francis and St. Clare? Of what use to them are the means to live the life of the country house and the West End mansion? They have literally no business in them, and must necessarily cut an unhappy and ridiculous figure there. They have to make a society of Franciscans and Poor Clares for themselves before they can work or live socially. It is true that those who are called saints are not saintly all the time and in everything. In eating and drinking, lodging and sleeping, chatting and playing: in short, in everything but working out their destiny as saints, what is good enough for a plowman is good enough for a poet, a philosopher, a saint or a higher mathematician. But Hodge's work is not good enough for Newton, nor Falstaff's conversation holy enough for Shelley. Christ adapted himself so amicably to the fashionable life of his time in his leisure that he was reproached for being a gluttonous man and a winebibber, and for frequenting frivolous and worthless sets. But he did not work where he feasted, nor flatter the Pharisees, nor ask the Romans to buy him with a sinecure. He knew when he was being entertained, well treated, lionized: not an unpleasant adventure for once in a way; and he did not quarrel with the people who were so nice to him. Besides, to sample society is part of a prophet's business: he must sample the governing class above all, because his inborn knowledge of human nature will not explain the anomalies produced in it by Capitalism and Sacerdotalism. But he can never feel at home in it.'

But which is true: that the St. Francis or the St. Clare can't 'live socially' till they have 'made a society of Franciscans and Poor Clares' or that 'in eating and drinking, lodging and sleeping, chatting and playing,' 'what is good enough for a plowman is good enough for a saint'? And as for Shaw's description of Christ, it evokes an incongruous picture: what one sees is the preacher of the Sermon on the Mount very much pleased with himself on the beach at the Riviera or playing Santa Claus at Lady Astor's Christmas party.

And other influences, from his early education, came to deflect the straight line of his socialism.

The escapades of the romantic hero, from Childe Harold through Don César de Bazan, with his 'Tant pis! C'est moi!,' to

Siegfried, had been a protest against the meanness and dullness of the commercial bourgeois world; but this revolt was itself merely a further phase of the tradition of individual assertion which, deriving from the Protestant conscience, had produced the anarchic individualism of the competitive commercial system. The romantic, like the old-fashioned capitalist, proclaimed the power of the personal will in defiance of society and God.

William Archer tells us that the first time he ever saw Shaw, the latter was sitting in the British Museum studying alternately the French translation of *Das Kapital* and the score of *Tristan und Isolde*. When Shaw first came before the public, he fell instinctively into dramatizing himself as a semi-romantic character—and this in spite of the fact that he was managing to figure at the same time as the arch-enemy and blasphemer of romanticism. The impulse to satirize romanticism implies, as in the case of Flaubert, a strong predisposition toward it; and the exploded romantic, Captain Brassbound, is offset by the Devil's Disciple. It is true that Shaw's conscious intention was to ridicule and shame his audience out of exclusive preoccupation with the emotions of their personal lives—especially, with romantic love—and to interest them in the problems of society. Here is the fine and well-known passage from *Man and Superman,* in which he defends what he calls the 'artist-philosophers' against the 'mere artists': 'This is the true joy in life, the being used for a purpose recognized by yourself as a mighty one; the being thoroughly worn out before you are thrown on the scrap heap; the being a force of Nature instead of a feverish selfish little clod of ailments and grievances complaining that the world will not devote itself to making you happy.' Yet is this not, too, a kind of romanticism—romanticism *par excellence?* The ego has now, to be sure, identified itself with a force of Nature, but this simply makes the ego seem godlike. There is nothing to guarantee that it will respect either the feelings or the interests of others. The ideal artist-philosopher of Bernard Shaw has always a strong social conscience, and his heroes are likely to be philosopher-statesmen or social prophets or saviors of society; but there is nothing to guarantee that they shall be, in the socialist sense, genuine popular leaders, deriving their power from, as well as guiding, the dispossessed: they may be simply

despot-heroes—as Shaw's *Julius Caesar* actually is—acting in the
right of their own superiority and giving people what they know
to be good for them.

And finally, of course, Bernard Shaw was not only a political
prophet struggling for socialist ideas, but an artist trying to realize
himself through art. There was a poet in Shaw, still partly suppressed, or at any rate terribly overtaxed, by the round of political
meetings, the functions of vestryman and borough councilor, and
the years of theatergoing and weekly article-writing about the
theater, which he had come to judge almost exclusively in terms
of the sort of thing that he wanted to do himself. His own
plays he had been writing in note-books while traveling on the
tops of buses between one engagement and another. Now in
1898, when he was forty-two, he had what seems to have been
a general collapse as the result of a bad fall and a serious injury
to his foot. When he recovered, he married an Irish lady, well-
to-do but belonging like Shaw to the general 'advanced' movement, who gave him for apparently the first time in his life a
comfortable place to live and took the most excellent care of
him. Thereafter, he was able to give up the journalism on which
he had depended for a living and to devote all his best energies
to his plays. He remained a public man, but he spoke no more
at dockers' strikes.

By 1905 he was writing *Major Barbara*, in which the type of
Christian sainthood, an aristocratic Salvation Army worker, is
confronted with a self-made munitions manufacturer, the type
of successful capitalism; and ending the play with an alliance
between them. In his preface, he made out a ringing case for the
man who recognizes poverty as the worst of all the evils and
consequently the worst of all the sins, and who saves himself
from it at any cost. *Major Barbara* contains one of the best expo-
sitions of the capitalist point of view ever written. Bernard Shaw,
like his hero, Andrew Undershaft, had come by that time to
know what it was to make one's way in capitalist society and to
occupy a position of power. He had himself become the type of
the critic, who, by scolding the bourgeoisie, makes good with it
and becomes one of its idols. He was gradually, for all the scandal
of his début, turning into a dependable member of the British

[170]

propertied classes; and he was to end as an esteemed public figure in a country where an aristocratic governing class was still able to contribute to public life a certain distinction and glamor.

II

The real Shaw has thus never been the single-minded crusader that people at one time used to think him. Except for a limited period during the eighties and early nineties—when he wrote his only straight socialist plays, *Widowers' Houses* and *Mrs. Warren's Profession*—he has never really been a practicing socialist. And I am inclined to believe that the future will exactly reverse the opinion which his contemporaries have usually had of him. It used always to be said of Shaw that he was primarily not an artist, but a promulgator of certain ideas. The truth is, I think, that he is a considerable artist, but that his ideas—that is, his social philosophy proper—have always been confused and uncertain. As he has grown older and as the world has been shaken out of the pattern to which he had adapted his attitudes, the inadequacy of those attitudes has been exposed.

One is struck, as one goes through the volumes of the collected edition of Shaw, which includes a good deal of his journalism, by the fact that, though his writing on musical and theatrical and literary subjects remains remarkably fresh, the pieces on public affairs and on social questions in general prove very much less satisfactory than one had remembered their seeming when they first came out. There are passages of admirable exposition and passages of wonderful eloquence—some of which, such as the peroration to *The Intelligent Woman's Guide to Socialism and Capitalism*, will probably always stand among the classics of socialist literature. But the political writing of Shaw does not drive you into taking up a position as the greatest socialist writing does: indeed, before he has finished—and he is likely to go on talking too long—he has often seemed to compromise the points which you had imagined he was trying to make, and has produced, with much earnestness and emphasis, an impression rather blurred by rhetoric. Both his intelligence and his sense of justice have prevented him from assailing the capitalist system with such intolerant resentment and unscrupulous methods as Voltaire trained on the Church. With Voltaire, it *is* the crusader that counts; with Shaw, it is the dramatic poet.

The volume which covers the wartime exposes Bernard Shaw's contradictions in a particularly striking manner. Though he was perfectly familiar with the Marxist theory of capitalist expansion and aggression, and had expounded it on many occasions, he had always been liable to fits of admiration for the exploits of the British Empire. Irishman though he was, he had never been an Irish patriot; and, critical though he was of the English, he had in *John Bull's Other Island*—which was written for but declined by the Abbey Theater—backed them against the Irish on account of what he regarded as their superior enterprise and practicality. And though he denounced the Denshawai massacre in Egypt, he supported the British against the Boers at the time of the South African war, because the Boers represented for him a backward civilization and the British a progressive one. When the civilizing forces of the various nations had finally collided in 1914, it was Lenin, the revolutionary exile, not Shaw, the successful British citizen, who wrote *Imperialism: The Last Stage of Capitalism*.

What Bernard Shaw did write was *Common Sense About the War*, which, although it raised a terrible outcry in the fall of 1914 on the part of certain elements of the British public who thought that Shaw ought to be put in the Tower, seems today rather a double-facing document. Shaw, to be sure, makes a certain amount of effort still to keep before the minds of his readers the socialist interpretation of the War. 'Will you,' he writes, 'now at last believe, O stupid British, German and French patriots, what the Socialists have been telling you for so many years: that your Union Jacks and tricolors and Imperial Eagles ("where the carcase is, there will the eagles be gathered") are only toys to keep you amused, and that there are only two real flags in the world henceforth: the red flag of Democratic Socialism and the black flag of Capitalism, the flag of God and the flag of Mammon? What earthly or heavenly good is done when Tom Fool shoots Hans Narr? The plain fact is that if we leave our capital to be dealt with according to the selfishness of the private man he will send it where wages are low and workers enslaved and docile:

that is, as many thousand miles as possible from the Trade Unions and Trade Union rates and parliamentary Labour parties of civilization; and Germany, at his sordid behest, will plunge the world into war for the sake of disgracing herself with a few rubber plantations, poetically described by her orators and journalists as "a place in the sun." When you do what the Socialists tell you by keeping your capital jealously under national control and reserving your shrapnel for the wasters who not only shirk their share of the industrial service of their country, but intend that their children and children's children shall be idle wasters like themselves, you will find that not a farthing of our capital will go abroad as long as there is a British slum to be cleared and rebuilt or a hungry, ragged and ignorant British child to be fed, clothed and educated.'

This sounds spirited enough by itself, yet the burden of *Common Sense About the War* is that the war must be supported and vigorously prosecuted. Shaw afterwards visited and wrote about the front at the invitation of Sir Douglas Haig and even did some work for the propaganda department of the government. In his discussion of compulsory military service in *Common Sense About the War*, he defends his position as follows: 'In my own case, the question of conscientious objection did not arise: I was past military age. I did not counsel others to object, and should not have objected myself if I had been liable to serve: for intensely as I loathed the war, and free as I was from any illusion as to its character, and from the patriotic urge (patriotism in my native country taking the form of an implacable hostility to England), I knew that when war is once let loose, and it becomes a question of kill or be killed, there is no stopping to argue about it: one must just stand by one's neighbors and take a hand with the rest. If England had adopted me, as some of my critics alleged in their attempts to convict me of gross ingratitude, I could have pleaded that she must take the consequences without claiming any return; but as I had practically adopted England by thrusting myself and my opinions on her in the face of every possible rebuff, it was for me to take the consequences, which certainly included an obligation to help my reluctant ward in her extremity as far as my means allowed.'

Frank Harris, in his book about Shaw, reproached him for supporting the war; and Shaw retorted in a postscript that Harris 'could not stop to ask himself the first question . . . of the intellectually honest judicious critic, "What else could I have done had it been my own case?"' Yet surely there were other courses open to a man of Shaw's opinions. He could have expressed his disapproval and shut up, as John Morley and others did. But it is impossible for Shaw to shut up, and he went on talking incessantly through the whole four years of slaughter. Much of what he had to say was intelligent, and it required some courage to say it. Compared with most of the British writers, he seemed at the time to an American remarkably cool and sagacious. The atmosphere was feverish with panic and stupefying with the fumes of propaganda, and Shaw did do something to clear the air for a discussion of the origin and aims of the war. But when we reread what he wrote today, he looks a little foolish. The old socialist has gone down into the mêlée and sacrificed something of his moral dignity: we hear him remonstrating, scolding, exhorting, making fun of the politicians and at the same time lending a hand to the government, pleading for the conscientious objectors and at the same time 'joy-riding at the front'—and doing everything with equal cocksureness.

Before the Peace Conference, he had great hopes of Wilson. Before the Washington Disarmament Conference, he was cynical. Later, he spoke a kind word for the League of Nations. And in the meantime the Russian Revolution had set him off on a different tack. He would alternately lecture Lenin and Trotsky on the futility of what they were trying to do and applaud them for succeeding in doing it: he was alternately a middle-class socialist using Fabianism against the Marxists and a Marxist using Lenin and Trotsky against the British governing class. (It is interesting to note that Lenin characterized him as 'a good man fallen among Fabians,' and that Trotsky, of whom Shaw wrote enthusiastically as 'the Prince of Pamphleteers,' expressed the wish, apropos of his own exclusion from England, that 'the Fabian fluid that ran in [Bernard Shaw's] veins' might have 'been strengthened by even so much as five per cent of the blood of Jonathan Swift.' It is amusing to see Trotsky's indignation in his *Where Is*

Britain Going? over Shaw's cavalier suggestion that Marx had been superseded by H. G. Wells's *Outline of History*: Trotsky had gone to the trouble of procuring and looking into Wells.)

In his political utterances since the war, it is hardly too much to say that Bernard Shaw has behaved like a jackass. In the autumn of 1927, he was staying in Italy on the Lago Maggiore and throwing bouquets at Mussolini. It was his old admiration for the romantic hero, his old idealization—which was as likely to be set off by an imperialist as a Marxist theme—of the practical Caesarean statesman who makes people stand around. Mussolini had, according to Shaw, 'achieved a dictatorship in a great modern state without a single advantage, social, official or academic, to assist him, after marching to Rome with a force of Black Shirts which a single disciplined regiment backed by a competent government could have routed at any moment. . . After the war the government of Italy' had been 'so feeble that silly Syndicalists were seizing factories, and fanatical devotees of that curious attempt at a new Catholic church called the Third International were preaching a *coup d'état* and a Crusade in all directions, and imagining that this sort of thing was Socialism and Communism. Mussolini, without any of Napoleon's prestige, has done for Italy what Napoleon did for France, except that for the Duc d'Enghien you must read Matteotti.' When Gaetano Salvemini reminded Shaw that, so far from being 'without a single advantage,' Mussolini had had behind him 'the money of the banks, the big industrialists and the landowners,' and that his Black Shirts had been 'equipped with rifles, bombs, machine-guns, and motor-lorries by the military authorities, and assured of impunity by the police and the magistracy, while their adversaries were disarmed and severely punished if they attempted resistance,' Shaw's rebuttal was almost unbelievable: Why, he demanded, had Mussolini been able to command the support of the army officers and capitalists 'instead of Signors Salvemini, Giolitti, Turati, Matteotti and their friends, in spite of the fact that he was farther to the Left in his political opinions than any of them? The answer, as it seems to me, is that he combined with extreme opinions the knowledge that the first duty of any Government, no matter what its opinions are, is to carry on, and make its citizens carry on, liberty or no liberty, de-

mocracy or no democracy, socialism or no socialism, capitalism
or no capitalism. Until Salvemini and his friends convince Italy
that they understand this necessity as well as Mussolini does they
will never shake his hold on the situation. To rail at him as Shelley
railed at Castlereagh and Eldon, Marx at Napoleon III and Thiers,
Kautsky at Lenin, is to play the amusing but inglorious part of
Thersites.' Now a dramatist in his capacity of dramatist may make
out a very interesting case for a Castlereagh or a Napoleon III;
but why should Shaw in his capacity as a political writer take the
part of such politicians against their philosophical opponents?
He is himself of the company of Shelley and Marx—the company
of the poets and prophets; and railing at the Castlereaghs and
Napoleons—of which Shaw himself has done plenty on occasion
—is by no means the least valuable of their functions. The analogy between these other cases and Kautsky complaining of Lenin
is certainly a silly and dishonest one.

That spring he had finished a long treatise—*The Intelligent
Woman's Guide*—in which he had made a more comprehensive
effort than he had ever done in his socialist days in the eighties
to analyze capitalist society and to argue the case for socialism.
Perhaps the book should have been written in the eighties. Ramsay Macdonald and Sidney Webb had come to power with the
Labour Government in 1924, and Macdonald had not yet definitely sold out; and the whole story is repeated in general in the
familiar Fabian terms—to which Shaw, without Fabian sanction,
had added equality of income as a prime item of his socialist program. Through many pages of swift exposition, perhaps Shaw's
most precise and limpid writing, which, together with the magnificent close, give the book an enduring value, he makes his way
to conclusions that perplex us in proportion as the reasoning becomes more fine-spun and that do not seem finally to land us in
any very realistic relation to the England of after the war. 'A series
of properly prepared nationalizations may not only be understood
and voted for by people who would be quite shocked if they
were called Socialists, but would fit in perfectly with the habits of
the masses who take their bread as it comes and never think about
anything of a public nature.' And in the meantime the road to
socialism remains for a good part of the way—through 'national-

izations, expropriative taxation and all the constructive political machinery'—identical with the road to state capitalism. So that Lenin, says Shaw, had been quite in the wrong when he had denounced the methods of the Fabians as state capitalism.

But Lenin had been aware of the psychological pitfalls in the approach of the Fabians toward socialism—pitfalls which no amount of lucid explanation was able to get them over and which Shaw continued to stumble into himself. From the moment that you propose to benefit people from the point of view of imposing upon them what is best for them rather than of showing them the way to what they ought to have and awaiting the moment when they will know that they must have it, what is to prevent your slipping—the post-Lenin period in Russia has proved it as much as the Ramsay Macdonald Labour Government—into imposing upon the people something which will benefit you yourself?

I shall not here pursue the story of the subsequent career of the Fabians, as I want to show further on how it was reflected in Bernard Shaw's later plays. But I will note here that in 1931 he visited Soviet Russia in company with the Tory Lady Astor and with the liberal Marquess of Lothian, had an audience with Stalin, at which, as he said, they treated Stalin like 'a friendly emperor,' and, on his return, began loudly endorsing Russia and especially scolding the United States for not following the Soviet example. Later, in his *Preface on Bosses* in his volume of plays of 1936, he was back praising Mussolini again and even throwing a few kind words to Hitler, whom he described as 'not a stupid German' (did Bernard Shaw prefer a crazy Austrian?) and whose persecution of the Jews he characterized considerately as 'a craze, a complex, a bee in his bonnet, a hole in his armor, a hitch in his statesmanship, one of those lesions which sometimes prove fatal.' Of the systematic persecution by the Nazis of Communists, Socialists and Pacifists, of everybody—including critics and artists—who belonged to Bernard Shaw's own camp, he had nothing whatever to say save to mention it and minimize it in passing as 'plundering raids and *coups d'état* against inconvenient Liberals or Marxists.' At the time of the Ethiopian War, he came out strongly for Mussolini on the same grounds on which he had formerly defended the behavior of the British in South Africa, and insisted that the League of Nations, on behalf of which in 1928 he had written a Fabian pamphlet, should never have tried to interfere.

Thus in this period of disastrous dictatorships, when it was very important for a socialist to keep clear in the eyes of the public the difference between the backing and aims of Lenin and the backing and aims of Mussolini, Bernard Shaw has done a good deal to confuse them and, parliamentary socialist though he claims to be, to exalt the ideal of the dictator. When the socialist dictatorship of Lenin gave way to the despotism of Stalin, Shaw did not seem to know the difference, but applauded the suppression of the old Leninists, on the ground that most professional revolutionists ought to be shot the morning after the revolution, and, on the principle that the socially harmful had to be got out of the way, gave his blessing to the Russian concentration camps, with their millions of political prisoners.

All this he has handled, of course, with his marvelous cleverness and style. Analyzing everybody perpetually, he is a great master of the smoke-screen against criticism. It is done partly by sheer personal hypnotism and Irish gift of gab. Before you arrive at any book of Bernard Shaw's—from *What I Really Wrote About the War* to his correspondence with Ellen Terry—you have almost invariably been told what to think of it in a preface by which Shaw has protected himself against your possible perception of his weakness. If you submit to his spell, you will allow him to manipulate the lights in such a way that, by the time the curtain goes up, you find Shaw looking noble in the center of the stage with everything else left in semi-obscurity, and yourself with your discriminatory powers in a temporary state of suspension, under the illusion that you must either accept or reject him. (Of late the exhibitionistic vanity which seemed dashing in his early days when he was assailing the philistines with such spirit has come to be tiresome and even repellent—as, for example, when his comment on the death of one of his distinguished contemporaries takes the form of the irrelevant reflection, 'I'll be dead very soon myself!')

But there has been also an odd kind of trickery involved in the whole of Bernard Shaw's career. It depends on a technique which he has mastered of functioning on three distinct planes and of shifting from one to another. His air of certainty, his moralist's tone, his well-drilled sentences, his regular emphasis, all go to create an impression of straightforwardness. But actually the mind of Shaw is always fluctuating between various emotions which give rise to various points of view.

The mechanics seem to be somewhat as follows: At the bottom of Shaw is a commonsense sphere of practical considerations; above this is a plane of socialism, of the anticipated reorganization of society in the interest of ideal values; and above this, a poet-philosopher's ether from which he commands a longer view of life *sub specie aeternitatis* and where the poet allows himself many doubts which neither the socialist nor the bourgeois citizen can admit. Shaw has never really taken up his residence for any great length of time on any one of these three planes of thinking. The socialist, for example, denounces war; but when England actually goes to war, the respectable householder backs her. The moralist denounces marriage; but the conventional married man always advises young people to get married. The socialist takes sword in hand to battle for a sounder society based on a redistribution of income; and the long-view philosopher-poet comes to sap the socialist's faith with misgivings as to the capacity for intellect and virtue of the material of common humanity as contrasted with philosopher-poets. The poet gets a good way above the earth in the ecstasy of imaginative vision; but the socialist reminds him that it is the duty of art to teach a useful social lesson, and the householder damps the fires of both by admonishing them that the young people in the audience oughtn't to be told anything that will get them into trouble. The result is that reading Shaw is like looking through a pair of field glasses of which the focus is always equally sharp and clear but the range may be changed without warning.

So adroit are Shaw's transitions that we are usually unaware of what has happened; and when we have come to be conscious of them, we wonder how much Shaw is aware. It is curious to go back over his work and see him juggling with his various impersonations: the socialist, the fascist, the saint, the shrewd businessman, the world genius, the human being, the clever journalist who knows how to be politic, the popular speaker who knows how to be tactful. It is quite as if they were the characters in a comedy, each of whom he can pick up where he has dropped him and have him go on with his part.

III

But comedies are best presented in the theater; and in the theater Shaw's conflicts of impulse, his intellectual flexibility and his genius for legerdemain—all the qualities that have had the effect of weakening his work as a publicist—have contributed to his success as an artist.

One of the prime errors of recent radical criticism has been the assumption that great novels and plays must necessarily be written by people who have everything clear in their minds. People who have everything clear in their minds, who are not capable of identifying themselves imaginatively with, who do not actually embody in themselves, contrary emotions and points of view, do not write novels or plays at all—do not, at any rate, write good ones. And—given genius—the more violent the contraries, the greater the works of art.

Let us consider Shaw as an artist.

Bernard Shaw's great role in the theater has been to exploit the full possibilities of a type of English comedy which had first been given its characteristic form during the seventies of the nineteenth century in the comedies of W. S. Gilbert. The comedy of the Restoration, which had culminated in Congreve, had been the product of an aristocratic society, which depended for its ironic effects on the contrast between artificial social conventions and natural animal instincts, between fine manners and fine intelligence, on the one hand, and the crudest carnal appetites, on the other. The comedy of the nineteenth century—setting aside Oscar Wilde—depended on the contrast between the respectable conventions of a pious middle-class society and the mean practical realities behind them, between the pretension to high moral principles and the cold complacency which underlay it. As with the dramatists of the Restoration, it was always the pursuit of pleasure that emerged from behind the formalities, so,

in the comedies of Gilbert which preceded his Savoy operas and
of which the most famous and successful was *Engaged* (1877), it
is always the greed for money that extrudes from behind the screen
of noble words and discreet behavior. 'Dear papa,' says the
Victorian young lady in one of the scenes of *Engaged*, when she
has just heard of the failure of a bank in which the fortune of
her fiancé was invested, 'I am very sorry to disappoint you,
but unless your tom-tit is very much mistaken, the Indestructible
was registered under the Joint Stock Companies Act of '62 and
in that case the stockholders are jointly and severally liable to
the whole extent of their available capital. Poor little Minnie
don't pretend to have a business head; but she is not quite such
a little donkey as that, dear papa!' The characters of Gilbert's
comedies, who talk the language of Victorian fiction, are never
for a moment betrayed by emotion into allowing themselves to be
diverted from the main chance; and the young men are perfectly ready, not from appetite but from sheer indifference, to
make equally passionate professions to any number of young ladies at the same time. It is not far from the Symperson family
and Cheviot Hill of *Engaged* to Shaw's *The Philanderer* and
Widowers' Houses.

But neither Gilbert nor Dickens nor Samuel Butler—those two
other great satirists of the money-minded English, to whom,
also, Shaw is indebted—could teach him to analyze society in
terms of economic motivation or to understand and criticize the
profit system. This he learned to do from Karl Marx, whose work
during his English residence, the period when *Das Kapital* was
written, was itself of course a product of and an ironical protest
against English nineteenth-century civilization. Bernard Shaw
thus brought something quite new into English imaginative literature. His study of economics had served him, as he said, for his
plays as the study of anatomy had served Michael Angelo. And
with economic insight and training he joined literary qualities of
a kind that had never yet appeared in combination with them—
qualities, in fact, that, since the century before, had been absent from English literature entirely.

The Irish of Bernard Shaw's period enjoyed, in the field of literature, certain special advantages over the English, due to the fact

[181]

that, since Irish society was still mainly in the pre-industrial stage, they were closer to eighteenth-century standards. If we compare Shaw, Yeats and Joyce to, say, Galsworthy, Wells and Bennett, we are struck at once by the extent to which these latter writers have suffered from their submergence in the commercial world. In their worst phases of sentimentality and philistinism, there is almost nothing to choose between them and the frankly trashy popular novelist; whereas the Irish have preserved for English literature classical qualities of hardness and elegance.

Bernard Shaw has had the further advantage of a musical education. 'Do not suppose for a moment,' he writes, 'that I learnt my art from English men of letters. True, they showed me how to handle English words; but if I had known no more than that, my works would never have crossed the Channel. My masters were the masters of a universal language; they were, to go from summit to summit, Bach, Handel, Haydn, Mozart, Beethoven and Wagner. . . For their sakes, Germany stands consecrated as the Holy Land of the capitalistic age.' Einstein has said that Shaw's plays remind him of Mozart's music: every word has its place in the development. And if we allow for some nineteenth-century prolixity, we can see in Shaw's dramatic work a logic and grace, a formal precision, like that of the eighteenth-century composers.

Take *The Apple Cart*, for example. The fact that Shaw is here working exclusively with economic and political materials has caused its art to be insufficiently appreciated. If it had been a sentimental comedy by Molnar, the critics would have applauded its deftness; yet Shaw is a finer artist than any of the Molnars or Schnitzlers. The first act of *The Apple Cart* is an exercise in the scoring for small orchestra at which Shaw is particularly skillful. After what he has himself called the overture before the curtain of the conversation between the two secretaries, in which the music of King Magnus is foreshadowed, the urbane and intelligent King and the 'bull-roarer Boanerges' play a duet against one another. Then the King plays a single instrument against the whole nine of the cabinet. The themes emerge: the King's disinterestedness and the labor government's sordid self-interest. The development is lively: the music is tossed from one instrument to another, with, to use the old cliché, a combination of inevitable-ness and surprise. Finally, the King's theme gets a full and splendid statement in the long speech in which he declares his principles: 'I stand for the great abstractions: for conscience and virtue; for the eternal against the expedient; for the evolutionary appetite against the day's gluttony,' etc. This silver voice of the King lifts the movement to a poignant climax; and now a dramatic reversal carries the climax further and rounds out and balances the harmony. Unexpectedly, one of the brasses of the ministry takes up the theme of the King and repeats it more passionately and loudly: 'Just so! . . . Listen to me, sir,' bursts out the Powermistress, 'and judge whether I have not reason to feel everything you have just said to the very marrow of my bones. Here am I, the Powermistress Royal. I have to organize and administer all the motor power in the country for the good of the country. I have to harness the winds and the tides, the oils and the coal seams.' And she launches into an extraordinary tirade in which the idea of political disinterestedness is taken out of the realm of elegant abstraction in which it has hitherto remained with the King and reiterated in terms of engineering: 'every little sewing machine in the Hebrides, every dentist's drill in Shetland, every carpet sweeper in Margate,' etc. This ends on crashing chords, but immediately the music of the cabinet snarlingly reasserts itself. The act ends on the light note of the secretaries.

This music is a music of ideas—or rather, perhaps, it is a music of moralities. Bernard Shaw is a writer of the same kind as Plato. There are not many such writers in literature—the *Drames philosophiques* of Renan would supply another example—and they are likely to puzzle the critics. Shaw, like Plato, repudiates as a dangerous form of drunkenness the indulgence in literature for its own sake; but, like Plato, he then proceeds, not simply to expound a useful morality, but himself to indulge in an art in which moralities are used as the motifs. It is partly on this account, certainly, that Bernard Shaw has been underrated as an artist. Whether people admire or dislike him, whether they find his plays didactically boring or morally stimulating, they fail to take account of the fact that it is the enchantment of a highly accomplished art which has brought them to and kept them in the playhouse. It is an art that has even had the power to preserve such pieces as *Getting Married*, of which the 1908 heresies already seemed out of date twenty or thirty years later but of which the symphonic development still remains brilliant and fresh. So far from being relentlessly didactic, Shaw's mind has reflected in all its complexity the intellectual life of his time; and his great achievement is to have reflected it with remarkable fidelity. He has *not* imposed a cogent system, but he has worked out a vivid picture. It is, to be sure, not a passive picture, like that of Santayana or Proust: it is a picture in which action plays a prominent part. But it does not play a consistent part: the dynamic principle in Shaw is made to animate a variety of forces.

Let us see what these forces are and to what purpose they interact.

IV

What are the real themes of Bernard Shaw's plays?

He has not been a socialist dramatist in the sense that, say, Upton Sinclair has been a socialist novelist. His economics have served him, it is true, as anatomy served Michael Angelo; but to say that is to give as little idea of what kind of characters he creates and what his plays are about as it would of the figures of the sculptor to say that they were produced by an artist who understood the skeleton and the muscles. It is quite wrong to assume, as has sometimes been done, that the possession of the social-economic intelligence must imply that the writer who has it writes tracts for social reform.

Shaw is himself partly responsible for this assumption. In his early days, when he *was* a social reformer, he wrote books about Wagner and Ibsen which introduced them to the English-speaking public as primarily social reformers, too. There is of course a social revolutionist, a man of 1848, in Wagner, and a critic of bourgeois institutions in Ibsen. But Bernard Shaw, in his brilliant little books, by emphasizing these aspects of their work at the expense of everything else, seriously misrepresents them. He appreciates Siegfried and Brunhilde in their heroic and rebellious phases; but Wagner's tragedies of love he pooh-poohs; and it is sometimes just when Ibsen is at his strongest—as in *Brand* or *Rosmersholm*—that Bernard Shaw is least satisfactory on him, be-

cause the tragic spirit of Ibsen does not fit into Shaw's precon-
ception. In Ibsen's case, Shaw is particularly misleading, because
Ibsen disclaimed again and again any social-reforming intentions.
His great theme, characteristic though it is of nineteenth-century
society, is not a doctrine of social salvation: it is the conflict between one's duty to society as a unit in the social organism and
the individual's duty to himself. Ibsen treats this theme over and
over but in a number of different ways, sometimes emphasizing
the validity of social claims as opposed to the will of the individual (*Little Eyolf*), sometimes showing them as unjustified and oppressive (*Ghosts*); sometimes showing the individual undone by
self-indulgence or perverse self-assertion (*Peer Gynt* and *Brand*),
sometimes showing him as noble and sympathetic (the hero and
heroine of *Rosmersholm*); sometimes dramatizing the two poles
of conduct in the career of a single individual, like Dr. Stockman
in *An Enemy of the People*, who begins by trying to save society
but who later, when society turns against him, is driven back into
an individualistic vindication of the social conscience itself with
the realization that 'the strongest man is he who stands most
alone.' But the conflict is always serious; and it usually ends in
disaster. Rarely—*A Doll's House* is the principal example—does it
result in a liberation. Ibsen is hardly ever a social philosopher: he
goes no further than the conflict itself.

Now is there any such basic theme in Bernard Shaw? Has he
been creating a false impression not only about Ibsen but also
about himself? Certainly the prefaces he prefixes to his plays do
not really explain them any more than *The Quintessence of
Ibsenism* really explains Ibsen.

The principal pattern which recurs in Bernard Shaw—aside from
the duel between male and female, which seems to me of much
less importance—is the polar opposition between the type of the
saint and the type of the successful practical man. This conflict,
when it is present in his other writing, has a blurring, a demoralizing effect, as in the passage on Saint Francis *et al.* which I
quoted at the beginning of this essay; but it is the principle of life
of his plays. We find it in its clearest presentation in the opposition between Father Keegan and Tom Broadbent in *John Bull's
Other Island* and between Major Barbara and Undershaft—where

the moral scales are pretty evenly weighted and where the actual predominance of the practical man, far from carrying ominous implications, produces a certain effect of reassurance: this was apparently the period—when Bernard Shaw had outgrown his early battles and struggles and before the war had come to disturb him—of his most comfortable and self-confident exercise of powers which had fully matured. But these opposites have also a tendency to dissociate themselves from one another and to feature themselves sometimes, not correlatively, but alternatively in successive plays. In *The Devil's Disciple* and *The Shewing-up of Blanco Posnet*, the heroes are dashing fellows who have melodramatic flashes of saintliness; their opponents are made comic or base. *Caesar and Cleopatra* is a play that glorifies the practical man; *Androcles and the Lion* is a play that glorifies the saint. So is *Saint Joan*, with the difference that here the worldly antagonists of the saint are presented as intelligent and effective.

Certainly it is this theme of the saint and the world which has inspired those scenes of Shaw's plays which are most moving and most real on the stage—which are able to shock us for the moment, as even the 'Life Force' passages hardly do, out of the amiable and objective attention which has been induced by the bright play of the intelligence. It is the moment when Major Barbara, brought at last to the realization of the power of the capitalist's money and of her own weakness when she hasn't it to back her, is left alone on the stage with the unregenerate bums whose souls she has been trying to save; the moment when Androcles is sent into the arena with the lion; the moment in the emptied courtroom when Joan has been taken out to be burned and the Bishop and the Earl of Warwick are trying each to pin the responsibility on the other. It is the scene in *Heartbreak House* between Captain Shotover and Hector, when they give voice to their common antagonism toward the forces that seem to have them at their mercy: 'We must win powers of life and death over them. . . There is enmity between our seed and their seed. They know it and act on it, strangling our souls. They believe in themselves. When we believe in ourselves, we shall kill them. . . We kill the better half of ourselves every day to propitiate them.' It is the scene in *Back to Methuselah* when the Elderly Gentleman declares to the Oracle: 'They have gone back to lie about your answer [the political delegation with whom he has come]. I cannot go with them. I cannot live among people to whom nothing is real!'—and when she shows him her face and strikes him dead.

But now let us note—for the light they throw on Bernard Shaw in his various phases—the upshots of these several situations. In *Major Barbara*, the Christian saint, the man of learning, and the industrial superman form an alliance from which much is to be hoped. In *Androcles and the Lion*, written in 1913, in Shaw's amusing but least earnest middle period, just before the war, Androcles and the lion form an alliance, too, of which something is also to be hoped, but go out arm in arm after a harlequinade on the level of a Christmas pantomime. In *Heartbreak House*, which was begun in 1913 and not finished till 1916, the declaration of war by the unworldlings takes place in the midst of confusion and does not lead to any action on their part.

In *Back to Methuselah*, of the postwar period, the Elderly Gentleman is blasted by the Oracle in a strange scene the implications of which we must stop to examine a moment. The fate of the Elderly Gentleman is evidently intended by Shaw to have some sort of application to himself: though a member of a backward community in which people have not yet achieved the Methuselah-span of life, he differs from his fellows at least in this: that he finds he cannot bear any longer to live among people to whom nothing is real. So the Oracle shrivels him up with her glance.

But what is this supposed to mean? What *is* this higher wisdom which the Elderly Gentleman cannot contemplate and live? So far as the reader is concerned, the revelation of the Oracle is a blank. The old system of Bernard Shaw, which was plausible enough to pass before the war, has just taken a terrible blow, and its grotesque and gruesome efforts to pull itself together and function give the effect of an umbrella, wrecked in a storm, which, when the owner tries to open it up, shows several long ribs of steel sticking out. The Life Force of the man and woman in *Man and Superman* no longer leads either to human procreation or to social-revolutionary activity. The Life Force has been finally detached from socialism altogether. In the *Intelligent Woman's Guide*, Shaw will reject the Marxist dialectic as a false religion of social salvation; but the Life Force is also a religious idea, which we have always supposed in the past to be directed toward social betterment, and now, in *Back to Methuselah*, we find that it has misfired with socialism. Socialism has come and gone; the planet has been laid waste by wars; the ordinary people have all perished, and there is nobody left on earth but a race of selected supermen. And now the race of superior human beings, which was invoked in *Man and Superman* as the prime indispensable condition for any kind of progress whatever but which was regarded by Shaw at that time as producible through eugenic breeding, has taken here a most unearthly turn. It has always been through the superman idea that Shaw has found it possible to escape from the implications of his socialism; and he now no longer even imagines that the superior being can be created by human idealism through human science. The superior beings of *Back to Methuselah* are people who live forever; but they have achieved this superiority through an unconscious act of the will. When they have achieved it, what the Life Force turns out to have had in store for them is the mastery of abstruse branches of knowledge and the extra-uterine development of embryos. Beyond this, there is still to be attained the liberation of the spirit from the flesh, existence as a 'whirlpool in pure force.' 'And for what may be beyond, the eyesight of Lilith is too short. It is enough that there is a beyond.'

Humanity, in *Back to Methuselah*, has dropped out for the moment altogether. The long-livers of the period of progress contemporary with the Elderly Gentleman are not the more 'complete' human beings, with lives richer and better rounded, which Marx and Engels and Lenin imagined for the 'classless society': they are Shavian super-prigs who say the cutting and dampening things which the people have always said in Shaw's plays but who have been abstracted here from the well-observed social setting in which Shaw has always hitherto presented them. And the beings of the later epoch are young people playing in an Arcadia and ancients immersed in cogitations, alike—both cogitations and Arcadia—of the bleakest and most desolating description. There is in *Back to Methuselah* nothing burning or touching, and there is nothing genuinely thrilling except the cry of the Elderly Gentleman; and that, for all the pretense of revelation, is answered by a simple extinction.

In the *Tragedy of an Elderly Gentleman*, the Elderly Gentleman is frightened, but his tragedy is not a real tragedy. *Saint Joan* (1924) is an even more frightened play, and, softened though it is by the historical perspective into which Shaw manages to throw it through his epilogue, it was the first genuine tragedy that Shaw had written. The horror of *Back to Methuselah* is a lunar horror; the horror of *Saint Joan* is human. The saint is suppressed by the practical man; and even when she comes back to earth, though all those who exploited or destroyed her are now obliged to acknowledge her holiness, none wants her to remain among them: each would do the same thing again. Only the soldier who had handed her the cross at the stake is willing to accept her now, but he is only a poor helpless clown condemned to the dungeon of the flesh.

V

Back to Methuselah is a flight into the future; *Saint Joan* is a flight into the past. But with *Heartbreak House* Bernard Shaw had already begun a series of plays in which he was to deal with the postwar world and his own relation to it in terms of contemporary England—a section of his work which, it seems to me, has had too little appreciation or comprehension.

Heartbreak House has the same sort of setting and more or less the same form as such Shavian conversations as *Getting Married* and *Misalliance*; but it is really something new for Shaw. There is no diagram of social relations, no tying-up of threads at the end. *Heartbreak House*, Shaw says in his preface, is 'cultured leisured Europe before the War'; but the play, he told Archibald Henderson, 'began with an atmosphere and does not contain a word that was foreseen before it was written,' and it is the only one of his plays which he has persistently refused to explain. 'How should I know?' he replied, when he was asked by his actors what it meant. 'I am only the author.' Heartbreak House, built like a ship, with its old drunken and half-crazy master, the retired adventurer

Captain Shotover, is cultured and leisured England; but the characters are no longer pinned down and examined as social specimens: in an atmosphere heavily charged, through a progression of contacts and collisions, they give out thunder and lightning like storm-clouds. Brooding frustrations and disillusions, childlike hurts and furious resentments, which have dropped the old Shavian masks, rush suddenly into an utterance which for the moment has burst out of the old rationalistic wit. For once, where Bernard Shaw has so often reduced historical myths to the sharp focus of contemporary satire, he now raises contemporary figures to the heroic proportions of myth.—An air-raid brings down the final curtain: Heartbreak House has at last been split wide. The capitalist Mangan gets killed, and there is a suggestion that they may all be the better for it.

But in 1924 the Labour Party came to power, with Ramsay Macdonald as Prime Minister. Macdonald had been a member of the Executive Committee of the Fabian Society, and he brought with him two other Fabians, Sidney Webb and Sydney Olivier, who took the portfolios of Minister of Labour and Secretary of State for India. When Macdonald was re-elected in 1929, he was accompanied by no less than twenty Fabians, of whom eight were cabinet members. The Fabians had now achieved the aim which was to have been the condition for the success of their ideas: they had 'interpenetrated' the government. But in the meantime the competition of the British Empire with the German had culminated in a four years' war; and in England of after the war, with the top manhood of her society slaughtered and the lower classes laid off from their wartime jobs, and with English commercial domination further damaged by the United States, the influence of the Fabians could do little to bridge over the abyss which had been blasted between the extremes of the British class society. The best measures of the Labour Government were able to accomplish no more than just to keep the unemployed alive; and when the capitalists began to feel the pinch, they openly took over control. Ramsay Macdonald, in 1931, became Prime Minister in a Nationalist government and cleared his socialists out of office.

At the moment of the second accession of the Labour Party to power, Shaw had written *The Apple Cart*, in which Macdonald is caricatured as Proteus, the Prime Minister of a labor government. This government is represented as really controlled by Breakages, Limited, a great monopoly which opposes industrial progress for the reason that it has an interest in perpetuating the inferior and less durable machinery that requires more frequent repairs. But one finds in *The Apple Cart* no comment on the Fabianism, which, after all, has been partly responsible for Proteus: the blame is laid at the door, not of that socialism by interpenetration which has ended by itself being interpenetrated, but of something which Shaw calls 'democracy'; and what is opposed to the corrupt socialism of Proteus is not socialism of a more thoroughgoing kind, but the super-constitutional-monarch, King Magnus. Again, Shaw has given the slip to his problems through recourse to the cult of the superior person.

Yet in 1931, after the final collapse of the Labour Government, Bernard Shaw visited Russia and, by applauding the Soviet system, incurred unpopularity in England for the first time since the war. In the same year, he wrote *Too True to Be Good*, a curious 'political extravaganza,' in which he turns back upon and criticizes his own career. Here the theme of the bourgeois radical of the eighties, disillusioned with himself under stress of the disasters of the twentieth century, is treated in the same vein, with the same kind of idealist poetry, now grown frankly elegiac and despairing, which Shaw had opened in *Heartbreak House* and which had made the real beauty of *The Apple Cart*.

A rich young English girl of the upper middle class is languishing with an imaginary illness in a gloomy Victorian chamber, fussed over by a Victorian mother. Into this sickroom erupt two rebels: a young preacher and a former chambermaid, who is an illegitimate child of the aristocracy. The chambermaid has been masquerading as the heiress's trained nurse, and she and the preacher have a plot to steal the heiress's pearl necklace. The girl comes to from her megrims and puts up an unexpected struggle. The preacher becomes interested in his victim and says that he has always wondered why she does not steal the necklace herself. Why doesn't she take it and go and do what she pleases, instead of staying home with her mother, moping and fancying

[191]

herself sick? Why doesn't she let him and his accomplice sell the necklace for her, taking 25 per cent of the price apiece and giving her the other 50? The girl enthusiastically agrees, and while she is getting dressed to go with them, the preacher jumps up on the bed and delivers one of those live-your-own-life sermons with which Shaw, in the nineties, made his first success. Then he is off— in the excitement of his rhetoric, at first forgetting the necklace, which the heiress has to remind him they need.

All three sail away together to an imaginary Balkan country reminiscent of *Arms and the Man*, where they are able to do whatever they like but where their revolt turns out to lead to nothing and eventually to bore them to death. Shaw has evidently put into *Too True to Be Good* a sort of recapitulation of his earlier themes, the shams of bourgeois society: the capitalistic doctor of *The Doctor's Dilemma* is as much a fraud as ever; the pompous British military officer, though retaining an air of authority, has practically ceased even to pretend to be anything other than a fraud and is quite willing to leave the command to a private (drawn from Lawrence of Arabia), if he can only be left in peace with his water-colors; the old-fashioned materialist-atheist who is also the most rigorous of moralists, of the type of Roebuck Ramsden in *Man and Superman*, has lived through into a world where his morality has no power to prevent his son's turning thief, etc. Finally everyone except the preacher sets out for the 'Union of Sensible Republics.'

The preacher is left alone on the shore, abandoned between two worlds. He had come too late for the old and too early for the new. He had had the courage once to steal a necklace but he hadn't carried through his idea. He had given it back to the owner and they had made common cause together: the liberated bourgois girl had gotten 50 per cent of the price, the radicals only 25 apiece. In this last scene, the darkness comes, the clouds gather; the morale of the preacher breaks down. He can only go on explaining and exhorting, whether or not he has anything to say. A keen wind is blowing in, and it may be the breath of life, but it is too fierce for him to bear.

This, Shaw tells us, is a political fable; and now he is to return to politics proper. In *On the Rocks* (1933), he appears to drive him-

self into a corner as he has never before done and then comes
out with a political position which still manages to be somewhat
equivocal.

The first act shows a liberal Prime Minister, hard beset during
a period of depression. Pall Mall and Trafalgar Square are full
of excited crowds. The Prime Minister, on the verge of a breakdown, can think of nothing to do except to call out the police
against them, but he is dissuaded by the Police Commissioner
himself and finally induced to go away for a rest. He has just
been visited by a labor delegation who have impressed him with
the importance of Marxism, and he takes volumes of Marx and
Lenin away with him.

When the curtain goes up on the second act, the Prime Minister has read Marx and Lenin; but the effect upon him is unexpected. He has gained an insight into economic motivation, an
understanding of the technique of making use of it; but he has
not been converted to socialism: he has worked out, on the contrary, an exceedingly clever scheme for preserving the capitalist
state through a program, essentially fascist, of partial nationalization and taxation of unearned incomes. He will conciliate the
various social groups which would normally be antagonistic by
promising a concession to each. The plan seems bidding fair to
succeed when it runs aground on Sir Dexter Rightside, the Liberal Prime Minister's Tory colleague in a coalition National Government. Sir Dexter represents the blind conservatism which sticks
to the *status quo* through sheer obstinacy and inability to imagine
anything else: he threatens to put colored shirts on 'fifty thousand patriotic young Londoners' and to call them into the streets
against the proposed program of the government. The Prime
Minister has to give up his attempt, but he is now forced to face
his situation: 'Do you think I didn't know,' he confesses to his
wife, 'in the days of my great speeches and my roaring popularity,
that I was only whitewashing the slums? I couldn't help knowing
as well as any of those damned Socialists that though the West
End of London was chockful of money and nice people all calling one another by their Christian names, the lives of the millions of people whose labor was keeping the whole show going
were not worth living; but I was able to put it out of my mind

[193]

because I thought it couldn't be helped and I was doing the best that could be done. I know better now! I know that it can be helped, and how it can be helped. And rather than go back to the old whitewashing job, I'd seize you tight around the waist and make a hole in the river with you. . . Why don't I lead the revolt against it all? Because I'm not the man for the job, darling. . . And I shall hate the man who will carry it through for his cruelty and the desolation he will bring on us and our like.'

The shouting of the crowd and the crash of glass is suddenly heard outside. The people have broken into Downing Street. The police begin to club them and ride them down. The people sing, 'England, arise!'

Sir Arthur Chavender's more or less liberal fascism has been defeated by the reactionary fascism of his Tory colleague in the National Government, with whom he is indissolubly united. (There is no question any longer of the superior man: King Magnus has disappeared from the scene.) There is a third point of view, opposed to both, but this, also, sounds rather fascist. Old Hipney, the disillusioned labor veteran, who speaks for the dissatisfied classes, seems to be looking for a Man on Horseback, too: 'Adult suffrage: that was what was to save us all. My God! It delivered us into the hands of our spoilers and oppressors, bound hand and foot by our own folly and ignorance. It took the heart out of old Hipney; and now I'm for any Napoleon or Mussolini or Lenin or Chavender that has the stuff in him to take both the people and the spoilers and oppressors by the scruffs of their silly necks and just sling them into the way they should go with as many kicks as may be needful to make a thorough job of it.' But Chavender declines the job; and the people begin throwing brieks.

The conclusion we are apparently to draw is that parliamentary fascism must fail; and that we may then get either a Lenin or a Mussolini. Is this also a final confession of the failure of Fabianism, which depended on parliament, too?

In any case, at the end of this play, we have come in a sense to the end of Shaw. With the eruption of the uprising, we should be plunged into a situation which could no longer be appropriately handled by the characteristic methods of his comedy. He is still splendid when he is showing the bewilderment of the liberal governing-class prime minister: it is surprising how he is still able to summon his old flickering and piercing wit, his old skill at juggling points of view, to illuminate a new social situation—how quick and skillful he is at describing a new social type: the communist viscount, with his brutal language, which shocks his proletarian allies. But with the shouts and the broken glass, we are made to take account of the fact that Shaw's comedy, for all its greater freedom in dealing with social conditions, is almost as much dependent on a cultivated and stable society as the comedy of Molière, who had his place in the royal dining-room and depended on Louis's favor for the permission to produce his plays. Shaw, as much as Molière, must speak the same language as his audience; he must observe the same conventions of manners. And further than *On the Rocks*—in depicting the realities of the present—we feel that he cannot go.

Then we realize that, after a detour of the better part of half a century, of almost the whole of his artistic career, Shaw has only returned to that Bloody Sunday of 1887 when the Socialists had headed a demonstration and been driven away by the police; and we remember, apropos of Molière, that the most celebrated of British dramatists for a long time found it impossible to get a theater in London for *On the Rocks*.

Shaw's most recent pieces are weaker. *The Simpleton of the Unexpected Isles* (1934) is the only play of the author's which has ever struck me as silly. In it, the Day of Judgment comes to the British Empire, and the privilege of surviving on earth is made to depend upon social utility. But, by setting up a purely theocratic tribunal, Shaw deprives this scene of social point: the principle of selection is so general that it might be applied by the fascists as readily as by the socialists, at the same time that the policy of wholesale extinction seems inspired by an admiration for the repressive tactics of both. The play ends with a salute to the unknown future, which, like the vision of infinity of *Back to Methuselah*, seems perfectly directionless. *The Millionairess* (1936) makes a farce out of the notion that a natural boss, deprived of adventitious authority, will inevitably gravitate again to a position where he can bully and control people, and sounds as if it had been suggested by the later phases of Stalin.

Here it cannot be denied that Bernard Shaw begins to show signs of old age. As the pace of his mind slackens and the texture of his work grows looser, the contradictory impulses and principles which have hitherto provided him with drama begin to show gaping rifts. In his *Preface on Bosses* to *The Millionairess*, he talks about 'beginning a Reformation well to the left of Russia,' but composes the panegyric on Mussolini, with the respectful compliments to Hitler, to which I have already referred.

Yet the openings—the prologue to *The Simpleton*, with its skit on the decay of the British Empire and the knockabout domestic agonies of the first act or two of *The Millionairess*—still explode their comic situations with something of the old energy and wit; and the one-acter, *The Six of Calais*, though it does not crackle quite with the old spark, is not so very far inferior to such an earlier trifle as *How He Lied to Her Husband*. It is interesting to note—what bears out the idea that Shaw is at his best as an artist—that the last thing he is to lose, apparently, is his gift for pure comic invention, which has survived, not much dimmed, though we may tire of it, since the days of *You Never Can Tell*.

And he has also maintained his integrity as a reporter of the processes at work in his time—in regard to which his point of view has never been doctrinaire but always based on observation and feeling. He has not acted a straight role as a socialist; a lot of his writing on public affairs has been nonsense. But his plays down to the very end have been a truthful and continually developing chronicle of a soul in relation to society. Professionally as well as physically—he has just turned eighty-one as I write—he is outliving all the rest of his generation.

Nor can it be said that the confusions of his politics have invalidated his social criticism. Of his educative and stimulative influence it is not necessary today to speak. The very methods we use to check him have partly been learned in his school.

MARXISM AND LITERATURE

1. LET us begin with Marx and Engels. What was the role assigned to literature and art in the system of Dialectical Materialism? This role was much less cut-and-dried than is nowadays often supposed. Marx and Engels conceived the forms of human society in any given country and epoch as growing out of the methods of production which prevailed at that place and time; and out of the relations involved in the social forms arose a 'superstructure' of higher activities such as politics, law, religion, philosophy, literature and art. These activities were not, as is sometimes assumed, wholly explicable in terms of economics. They showed the mold, in ways direct or indirect, of the social configuration below them, but each was working to get away from its roots in the social classes and to constitute a professional group, with its own discipline and its own standards of value, which cut across class lines. These departments 'all react upon one another and upon the economic base. It is not the case that the economic situation is the sole active cause and everything else only a passive effect. But there is a reciprocal interaction within a fundamental economic necessity, which in the last instance always asserts itself' (Engels to Hans Starkenburg, January 25, 1894). So that the art of a great artistic period may reach a point of vitality and vision where it can influence the life of the period down to its very economic foundations. Simply, it must cease to flourish with the social system which made it possible by providing the artist with training and leisure, even though the artist himself may have been working for the destruction of that system.

2. Marx and Engels, unlike some of their followers, never attempted to furnish social-economic formulas by which the validity of works of art might be tested. They had grown up in the sunset of Goethe before the great age of German literature was over, and they had both set out in their youth to be poets; they responded to imaginative work, first of all, on its artistic merits. They could ridicule a trashy writer like Eugène Sue for what they regarded as his *petit bourgeois* remedies for the miseries of contemporary society (*The Holy Family*); they could become bitter about Ferdinand Freiligrath, who had deserted the Communist League and turned nationalist in 1870 (Marx to Engels, August 22, 1870). And Marx could even make similar jibes at Heine when he thought that the latter had stooped to truckling to the authorities or when he read the expressions of piety in his will (Marx to Engels, December 21, 1866 and May 8, 1856). But Marx's daughter tells us that her father loved Heine 'as much as his work and was very indulgent of his political shortcomings. He used to say that the poets were originals, who must be allowed to go their own way, and that one shouldn't apply to them the same standards as to ordinary people.' It was not characteristic of Marx and Engels to judge literature—that is, literature of power and distinction—in terms of its purely political tendencies. In fact, Engels always warned the socialist novelists against the dangers of *Tendenz-Literatur* (Engels to Minna Kautsky, November 26, 1885; and to Margaret Harkness, April 1888). In writing to Minna Kautsky about one of her novels, he tells her that the personalities of her hero and heroine have been dissolved in the principles they represent. 'You evidently,' he says, 'felt the need of publicly taking sides in this book, of proclaiming your opinions to the world. . . But I believe that the tendency should arise from the situation and the action themselves without being explicitly formulated, and that the poet is not under the obligation to furnish the reader with a ready-made historical solution for the future of the conflict which he describes.' When Ferdinand Lassalle sent Marx and Engels his poetic tragedy, *Franz von Sickingen*, and invited them to criticize it, Marx replied that, 'setting aside any purely critical attitude toward the work,' it had on a first reading affected him powerfully—characteristically adding

[198]

that upon persons of a more emotional nature it would doubtless produce an even stronger effect; and Engels wrote that he had read it twice and had been moved by it so profoundly that he had been obliged to lay it aside in order to arrive at any critical perspective. It was only after pulling themselves together and making some purely literary observations that they were able to proceed to discuss, from their special historical point of view, the period with which the drama dealt and to show how Lassalle's own political position had led him to mistake the role of his hero. Aeschylus Marx loved for his grandeur and for the defiance of Zeus by Prometheus; Goethe they both immensely admired: Engels wrote of him as a 'colossal' and 'universal' genius whose career had been marred by an admixture in his character of the philistine and the courtier (*German Socialism in Verse and Prose*); Shakespeare Marx knew by heart and was extremely fond of quoting, but never—despite the long, learned and ridiculous essays which have appeared in the Soviet magazine, *International Literature*—attempted to draw from his plays any general social moral. So far, indeed, was Marx from having worked out a systematic explanation of the relation of art to social arrangements that he could assert, apropos of Greek art, in his *Introduction to the Critique of Political Economy*, that 'certain periods of highest development of art stand in no direct connection with the general development of society, nor with the material basis and the skeleton structure of its organization.'

3. With Marx and Engels there is not yet any tendency to specialize art as a 'weapon.' They were both too much under the influence of the ideal of the many-sided man of the Renaissance, of the 'complete' man, who, like Leonardo, had been painter, mathematician and engineer, or, like Machiavelli, poet, historian and strategist, before the division of labor had had the effect of splitting up human nature and limiting everyone to some single function (Engels' preface to his *Dialectic and Nature*). But with Lenin we come to a Marxist who is specialized himself as an organizer and fighter. Like most Russians, Lenin was sensitive to music; but Gorky tells us that on one occasion, after listening to Beethoven's Appassionata Sonata and exclaiming that he 'would like to

listen to it every day: it is marvelous superhuman music—I always think with pride . . . what marvelous things human beings can do,' he screwed up his eyes and smiled sadly and added: 'But I can't listen to music too often. It affects your nerves, makes you want to say stupid, nice things, and stroke the heads of people who could create such beauty while living in this vile hell. And now you mustn't stroke anyone's head—you might get your hand bitten off.' Yet he was fond of fiction, poetry and the theater, and by no means doctrinaire in his tastes. Krupskaya tells how, on a visit to a Youth Commune, he asked the young people, 'What do you read? Do you read Pushkin?' ' "Oh, no!" someone blurted out. "He was a bourgeois. Mayakovsky for us." Ilyitch smiled. "I think Pushkin is better." ' Gorky says that one day he found Lenin with *War and Peace* lying on the table: ' "Yes, Tolstoy. I wanted to read over the scene of the hunt, then remembered that I had to write a comrade. Absolutely no time for reading." . . . Smiling and screwing up his eyes, he stretched himself deliciously in his armchair and, lowering his voice, added quickly, "What a colossus, eh? What a marvelously developed brain! Here's an artist for you, sir. And do you know something still more amazing? You couldn't find a genuine *muzhik* in literature till this count came upon the scene." ' In his very acute essays on Tolstoy, he deals with him much as Engels deals with Goethe—with tremendous admiration for Tolstoy's genius, but with an analysis of his non-resistance and mysticism in terms not, it is interesting to note, of the psychology of the landed nobility, but of the patriarchal peasantry with whom Tolstoy had identified himself. And Lenin's attitude toward Gorky was much like that of Marx toward Heine. He suggests in one of his letters that Gorky would be helpful as a journalist on the side of the Bolsheviks, but adds that he mustn't be bothered if he is busy writing a book.

4. Trotsky is a literary man as Lenin never was, and he published in 1924 a most remarkable little study called *Literature and Revolution.* In this book he tried to illuminate the problems which were arising for Russian writers with the new society of the Revolution. And he was obliged to come to grips with a ques-

tion with which Marx and Engels had not been much concerned—the question of what Mr. James T. Farrell in his book, *A Note on Literary Criticism,* one of the few sensible recent writings on this subject, calls 'the carry-over value' of literature. Marx had assumed the value of Shakespeare and the Greeks and more or less left it at that. But what, the writers in Russia were now asking, was to be the value of the literature and art of the ages of barbarism and oppression in the dawn of socialist freedom? What in particular was to be the status of the culture of that bourgeois society from which socialism had just emerged and of which it still bore the unforgotten scars? Would there be a new proletarian literature, with new language, new style, new form, to give expression to the emotions and ideas of the new proletarian dictatorship? There had been in Russia a group called the Proletcult, which aimed at monopolizing the control of Soviet literature; but Lenin had discouraged and opposed it, insisting that proletarian culture was not something which could be produced synthetically and by official dictation of policy, but only by natural evolution as a 'development of those reserves of knowledge which society worked for under the oppression of capitalism, of the landlords, of the officials.' Now, in *Literature and Revolution,* Trotsky asserted that 'such terms as "proletarian literature" and "proletarian culture" are dangerous, because they erroneously compress the culture of the future into the narrow limits of the present day.' In a position to observe from his Marxist point of view the effects on a national literature of the dispossession of a dominant class, he was able to see the unexpected ways in which the presentments of life of the novelists, the feelings and images of the poets, the standards themselves of the critics, were turning out to be determined by their attitudes toward the social-economic crisis. But he did not believe in a proletarian culture which would displace the bourgeois one. The bourgeois literature of the French Revolution had ripened under the old regime; but the illiterate proletariat and peasantry of Russia had had no chance to produce a culture, nor would there be time for them to do so in the future, because the proletarian dictatorship was not to last: it was to be only a transition phase and to lead the way to 'a culture which is above classes and which will be the first truly human culture.'

In the meantime, the new socialist literature would grow directly out of that which had already been produced during the domination of the bourgeoisie. Communism, Trotsky said, had as yet no artistic culture; it had only a political culture.

5. All this seems to us reasonable enough. But, reasonable and cultured as Trotsky is, ready as he is to admit that 'one cannot always go by the principles of Marxism in deciding whether to accept or reject a work of art,' that such a work 'should be judged in the first place by its own law—that is, by the law of art,' there is none the less in the whole situation something which is alien to us. We are not accustomed, in our quarter of the world, either to having the government attempt to control literature and art or to having literary and artistic movements try to identify themselves with the government. Yet Russia, since the Revolution, has had a whole series of cultural groups which have attempted to dominate literature either with or without the authority of the government; and Trotsky himself, in his official position, even in combating these tendencies, cannot avoid passing censure and pinning ribbons. Sympathizers with the Soviet regime used to assume that this state of affairs was inseparable from the realization of socialism: that its evils would be easily outgrown and that in any case it was a great thing to have the government take so lively an interest in culture. I believe that this view was mistaken. Under the Tsar, imaginative literature in Russia played a role which was probably different from any role it had ever played in the life of any other nation. Political and social criticism, pursued and driven underground by the censorship, was forced to incorporate itself in the dramatic imagery of fiction. This was certainly one of the principal reasons for the greatness during the nineteenth century of the Russian theater and novel, for the mastery by the Russian writers—from Pushkin's time to Tolstoy's—of the art of implication. In the fifties and sixties, the stories of Turgenev, which seem mild enough to us today, were capable of exciting the most passionate controversies—and even, in the case of *A Sportsman's Sketches*, causing the dismissal of the censor who had passed it— because each was regarded as a political message. Ever since the Revolution, literature and politics in Russia have remained in-

extricable. But after the Revolution the intelligentsia themselves were in power; and it became plain that in the altered situation the identification of literature with politics was liable to terrible abuses. Lenin and Trotsky, Lunacharsky and Gorky, worked sincerely to keep literature free; but they had at the same time, from the years of the Tsardom, a keen sense of the possibility of art as an instrument of propaganda. Lenin took a special interest in the moving pictures from the propaganda point of view; and the first Soviet films, by Eisenstein and Pudovkin, were masterpieces of implication, as the old novels and plays had been. But Lenin died; Trotsky was exiled; Lunacharsky died. The administration of Stalin, unliterary and uncultivated himself, slipped into depending more and more on literature as a means of manipulating a people of whom, before the Revolution, 70 or 80 per cent had been illiterate and who could hardly be expected to be critical of what they read. Gorky seems to have exerted what influence he could in the direction of liberalism: to him was due, no doubt, the liquidation of RAPP, the latest device for the monopoly of culture, and the opening of the Soviet canon to the best contemporary foreign writing and the classics. But though this made possible more freedom of form and a wider range of reading, it could not, under the dictatorship of Stalin, either stimulate or release a living literature. Where no political opposition was possible, there was possible no political criticism; and in Russia political questions involve vitally the fate of society. What reality can there be for the Russians, the most socially-minded writers on earth, in a freedom purely 'esthetic'? Even the fine melodramatic themes of the post-revolutionary cinema and theater, with their real emotion and moral conviction, have been replaced by simple trash not very far removed from Hollywood, or by dramatized exemplifications of the latest 'directive' of Stalin which open the night after the speech that has announced the directive. The recent damning of the music of Shostakovich on the ground that the commissars were unable to hum it seems a withdrawal from the liberal position. And it is probable that the death of Gorky, as well as the imprisonment of Bukharin and Radek, have removed the last brakes from a precipitate descent, in the artistic as well as the political field, into a nightmare of informing and repression. The practice of deliberate falsification of social and political history which began at the time of the Stalin-Trotsky crisis and which has now attained proportions so fantastic that the government does not seem to hesitate to pass the sponge every month or so over everything that the people have previously been told and to present them with a new and contradictory version of their history, their duty, and the characters and careers of their leaders—this practice cannot fail in the end to corrupt every department of intellectual life, till the serious, the humane, the clear-seeing must simply, if they can, remain silent.

6. Thus Marxism in Russia for the moment has run itself into a blind alley—or rather, it has been put down a well. The Soviets seem hardly at the present time to have retained even the Marxist political culture, even in its cruder forms—so that we are relieved from the authority of Russia as we are deprived of her inspiration. To what conclusions shall we come, then, at this time of day about Marxism and literature—basing our views not even necessarily upon texts from the Marxist Fathers, but upon ordinary commonsense? Well, first of all, that we can go even further than Trotsky in one of the dicta I have quoted above and declare that Marxism by itself can tell us nothing whatever about the goodness or badness of a work of art. A man may be an excellent Marxist, but if he lacks imagination and taste he will be unable to make the choice between a good and an inferior book both of which are ideologically unexceptionable. What Marxism *can* do, however, is throw a great deal of light on the origins and social significance of works of art. The study of literature in its relation to society is as old as Herder—and even Vico. Coleridge had flashes of insight into the connection between literary and social phenomena, as when he saw the Greek state in the Greek sentence and the individualism of the English in the short separate statements of Chaucer's Prologue. But the great bourgeois master of this kind of criticism was Taine, with his *race* and *moment* and *milieu*; yet Taine, for all his scientific professions, responded artistically to literary art, and responded so vividly that his summings-up of writers and re-creations of periods sometimes rival or surpass their subjects. Marx and Engels further deepened this study

[204]

of literature in relation to its social background by demonstrating for the first time inescapably the importance of economic systems. But if Marx and Engels and Lenin and Trotsky are worth listening to on the subject of books, it is not merely because they created Marxism, but also because they were capable of literary appreciation.

7. Yet the man who tries to apply Marxist principles without real understanding of literature is liable to go horribly wrong. For one thing, it is usually true in works of the highest order that the purport is not a simple message, but a complex vision of things, which itself is not explicit but implicit; and the reader who does not grasp them artistically, but is merely looking for simple social morals, is certain to be hopelessly confused. Especially will he be confused if the author *does* draw an explicit moral which is the opposite of or has nothing to do with his real purport. Friedrich Engels, in the letter to Margaret Harkness already referred to above, in warning her that the more the novelist allows his political ideas to 'remain hidden, the better it is for the work of art,' says that Balzac, with his reactionary opinions, is worth a thousand of Zola, with all his democratic ones. (Balzac was one of the great literary admirations of both Engels and Marx, the latter of whom had planned to write a book on him.) Engels points out that Balzac himself was, or believed himself to be, a legitimist engaged in deploring the decline of high society; but that actually 'his irony is never more bitter, his satire never more trenchant, than when he is showing us these aristocrats . . . for whom he felt so profound a sympathy,' and that 'the only men of whom he speaks with undissimulated admiration are his most determined political adversaries, the republican heroes of the Cloître-Saint-Merri, the men who at that period (1830-1836) truly represented the popular masses.' Nor does it matter necessarily in a work of art whether the characters are shown engaged in a conflict which illustrates the larger conflicts of society or in one which from that point of view is trivial. In art—it is quite obvious in music, but it is also true in literature—a sort of law of moral interchangeability prevails: we may transpose the actions and the sentiments that move us into terms of whatever we do or are

ourselves. Real genius of moral insight is a motor which will start any engine. When Proust, in his wonderful chapter on the death of the novelist Bergotte, speaks of those moral obligations which impose themselves in spite of everything and which seem to come through to humanity from some source outside its wretched self (obligations 'invisible only to fools—and are they really to them?'), he is describing a kind of duty which he felt only in connection with the literary work which he performed in his dark and fetid room; yet he speaks for every moral, esthetic or intellectual passion which holds the expediencies of the world in contempt. And the hero of Thornton Wilder's *Heaven's My Destination*, the traveling salesman who tries to save souls in the smoking car and writes Bible texts on hotel blotters, is something more than a symptom of Thornton Wilder's religious tendencies: he is the type of all saints who begin absurdly; and Wilder's story would be as true of the socialist Upton Sinclair as of the Christian George Brush. Nor does it necessarily matter, for the moral effect of a work of literature, whether the forces of bravery or virtue with which we identify ourselves are victorious or vanquished in the end. In Hemingway's story *The Undefeated*, the old bull-fighter who figures as the hero is actually humiliated and killed, but his courage has itself been a victory. It is true, as I. Kashkin, the Soviet critic, has said, that Hemingway has written much about decadence, but in order to write tellingly about death you have to have the principle of life, and those that have it will make it felt in spite of everything.

8. The Leftist critic with no literary competence is always trying to measure works of literature by tests which have no validity in that field. And one of his favorite occupations is giving specific directions and working out diagrams for the construction of ideal Marxist books. Such formulas are of course perfectly futile. The rules observed in any given school of art become apparent, not before but after, the actual works of art have been produced. As we were reminded by Burton Rascoe at the time of the Humanist controversy, the esthetic laws involved in Greek tragedy were not formulated by Aristotle until at least half a century after Euripides and Sophocles were dead. And the behavior of the

Marxist critics has been precisely like that of the Humanists. The Humanists knew down to the last comma what they wanted a work of literature to be, but they never—with the possible exception, when pressed, of *The Bridge of San Luis Rey*, about which they had, however, hesitations—were able to find any contemporary work which fitted their specifications. The Marxists did just the same thing. In an article called *The Crisis in Criticism* in the *New Masses* of February 1933, Granville Hicks drew up a list of requirements which the ideal Marxist work of literature must meet. The primary function of such a work, he asserted, must be to 'lead the proletarian reader to recognize his role in the class struggle'—and it must therefore (1) 'directly or indirectly show the effects of the class struggle'; (2) 'the author must be able to make the reader feel that he is participating in the lives described'; and, finally, (3) the author's point of view must 'be that of the vanguard of the proletariat; he should be, or should try to make himself, a member of the proletariat.' This formula, he says, 'gives us . . . a standard by which to recognize the perfect Marxian novel'—and adds 'no novel as yet written perfectly conforms to our demands.' But the doctrine of 'socialist realism' promulgated at the Soviet Writers' Congress of August 1934 was only an attempt on a larger scale to legislate masterpieces into existence—a kind of attempt which always indicates sterility on the part of those who engage in it, and which always actually works, if it has any effect at all, to legislate existing good literature *out of* existence and to discourage the production of any more. The prescribers for the literature of the future usually cherish some great figure of the past whom they regard as having fulfilled their conditions and whom they are always bringing forward to demonstrate the inferiority of the literature of the present. As there has never existed a great writer who really had anything in common with these critics' conception of literature, they are obliged to provide imaginary versions of what their ideal great writers are like. The Humanists had Sophocles and Shakespeare; the socialist realists had Tolstoy. Yet it is certain that if Tolstoy had had to live up to the objectives and prohibitions which the socialist realists proposed he could never have written a chapter; and that if Babbitt and More had been able to enforce against Shakespeare their moral and esthetic injunctions he would never have written a line. The <u>misrepresentation of Sophocles,</u> which has involved even a tampering with his text in the interests not merely of Humanism but of academic classicism in general, has been one of the scandalous absurdities of scholarship. The Communist critical movement in America, which had for its chief spokesman Mr. Hicks, tended to identify their ideal with the work of John Dos Passos. In order to make this possible, it was necessary to invent an imaginary Dos Passos. This ideal Dos Passos was a Communist, who wrote stories about the proletariat, at a time when the real Dos Passos was engaged in bringing out a long novel about the effects of the capitalist system on the American middle class and had announced himself—in the *New Republic* in 1930—politically a 'middle-class liberal.' The ideal Dos Passos was something like Gorky without the mustache—Gorky, in the meantime, having himself undergone some transmogrification at the hands of Soviet publicity—and this myth was maintained until the Communist critics were finally compelled to repudiate it, not because they had acquired new light on Dos Passos, the novelist and dramatist, but because of his attitude toward events in Russia.

9. The object of these formulas for the future, as may be seen from the above quotations from Mr. Hicks, is to make of art an effective instrument in the class struggle. And we must deal with the dogma that 'art is a weapon.' It is true that art may be a weapon; but in the case of some of the greatest works of art, some of those which have the longest carry-over value, it is difficult to see that any important part of this value is due to their direct functioning as weapons. The *Divine Comedy*, in its political aspect, is a weapon for Henry of Luxemburg, whom Dante— with his medieval internationalism and his lack of sympathy for the nationalistic instincts which were impelling the Italians of his time to get away from their Austrian emperors—was so passionately eager to impose on his countrymen. Today we may say with Carducci that we would as soon see the crown of his 'good Frederick' rolling in Olona vale: 'Jove perishes; the poet's hymn remains.' And, though Shakespeare's *Henry IV* and

Henry V are weapons for Elizabethan imperialism, their real center is not Prince Hal but Falstaff; and Falstaff is the father of *Hamlet* and of all Shakespeare's tragic heroes, who, if they illustrate any social moral—the moral, perhaps, that Renaissance princes, supreme in their little worlds, may go to pieces in all kinds of terrible ways for lack of a larger social organism to restrain them—do so evidently without Shakespeare's being aware of it. If these works may be spoken of as weapons at all, they are weapons in the more general struggle of modern European man emerging from the Middle Ages and striving to understand his world and himself—a function for which 'weapon' is hardly the right word. The truth is that there is short-range and long-range literature. Long-range literature attempts to sum up wide areas and long periods of human experience, or to extract from them general laws; short-range literature preaches and pamphleteers with the view to an immediate effect. A good deal of the recent confusion of our writers in the Leftist camp has been due to their not understanding, or being unable to make up their minds, whether they are aiming at long-range or short-range writing.

10. This brings us to the question of what sort of periods are most favorable for works of art. One finds an assumption on the Left that revolutionary or pre-revolutionary periods are apt to produce new and vital forms of literature. This, of course, is very far from the truth in the case of periods of actual revolution. The more highly developed forms of literature require leisure and a certain amount of stability; and during a period of revolution the writer is usually deprived of both. The literature of the French Revolution consisted of the orations of Danton, the journalism of Camille Desmoulins and the few political poems that André Chenier had a chance to write before he was guillotined. The literature of the Russian Revolution was the political writing of Lenin and Trotsky, and Alexander Blok's poem, *The Twelve*, almost the last fruit of his genius before it was nipped by the wind of the storm. As for pre-revolutionary periods in which the new forces are fermenting, they *may* be great periods for literature—as the eighteenth century was in France and the nineteenth century in Russia (though here there was a decadence after 1905).

[209]

But the conditions that make possible the masterpieces are apparently not produced by the impending revolutions, but by the phenomenon of literary technique, already highly developed, in the hands of a writer who has had the support of long-enduring institutions. He may reflect an age of transition, but it will not necessarily be true that his face is set squarely in the direction of the future. The germs of the Renaissance are in Dante and the longing for a better world in Virgil, but neither Dante nor Virgil can in any real sense be described as a revolutionary writer: they sum up or write elegies for ages that are passing. The social organisms that give structure to their thought—the Roman Empire and the Catholic Church—are already showing signs of decay. It is impossible, therefore, to identify the highest creative work in art with the most active moments of creative social change. The writer who is seriously intent on producing long-range works of literature should, from the point of view of his own special personal interests, thank his stars if there is no violent revolution going on in his own country in his time. He may disapprove of the society he is writing about, but if it were disrupted by an actual upheaval he would probably not be able to write.

11. But what about 'proletarian literature' as an accompaniment of the social revolution? In the earlier days of the Communist regime in Russia, one used to hear about Russian authors who, in the effort to eliminate from their writings any vestige of the bourgeois point of view, had reduced their vocabulary and syntax to what they regarded as an A B C of essentials—with the result of becoming more unintelligible to the proletarian audience at whom they were aiming than if they had been Symbolist poets. (Indeed, the futurist poet Mayakovsky has since that time become a part of the Soviet canon.) Later on, as I have said, Soviet culture followed the road that Trotsky recommended: it began building again on the classics and on the bourgeois culture of other countries and on able revolutionary Russian writers who had learned their trade before the Revolution. 'Soviet publishers'— I quote from the Russian edition of *International Literature*, issue 2 of 1936—'are bringing out Hemingway and Proust not merely in order to demonstrate "bourgeois decay." Every genuine

work of art—and such are the productions of Hemingway and Proust—enriches the writer's knowledge of life and heightens his esthetic sensibility and his emotional culture—in a word, it figures, in the broad sense, as a factor of educational value. Liberated socialist humanity inherits all that is beautiful, elevating and sustaining in the culture of previous ages.' The truth is that the talk in Soviet Russia about proletarian literature and art has resulted from the persistence of the same situation which led Tolstoy under the old regime to put on the muzhik's blouse and to go in for carpentry, cobbling and plowing: the difficulty experienced by an educated minority, who were only about 20 per cent of the people, in getting in touch with the illiterate majority. In America the situation is quite different. The percentage of illiterates in this country is only something like 4 per cent; and there is relatively little difficulty of communication between different social groups. Our development away from England, and from the old world generally, in this respect—in the direction of the democratization of our idiom—is demonstrated clearly in H. L. Mencken's *The American Language*; and if it is a question of either the use for high literature of the language of the people or the expression of the dignity and importance of the ordinary man, the country which has produced *Leaves of Grass* and *Huckleberry Finn* has certainly nothing to learn from Russia. We had created during our pioneering period a literature of the common man's escape, not only from feudal Europe, but also from bourgeois society, many years before the Russian masses were beginning to write their names. There has been a section of our recent American literature of the last fifteen years or so—the period of the boom and the depression—which has dealt with our industrial and rural life from the point of view of the factory hand and the poor farmer under conditions which were forcing him to fight for his life, and this has been called proletarian literature; but it has been accompanied by books on the white-collar worker, the storekeeper, the well-to-do merchant, the scientist and the millionaire in situations equally disastrous or degrading. And this whole movement of critical and imaginative writing—though with some stimulus, certainly, from Russia—had come quite naturally out of our literature of the past. It is curious to observe that one of the best of the recent strike novels, *The Land of Plenty* by Robert Cantwell, himself a Westerner and a former mill worker, owes a good deal to Henry James.

12. Yet when all these things have been said, all the questions have not been answered. All that has been said has been said of the past; and Marxism is something new in the world: it is a philosophical system which leads directly to programs of action. Has there ever appeared before in literature such a phenomenon as M. André Malraux, who alternates between attempts, sometimes brilliant, to write long-range fiction on revolutionary themes, and exploits of aviation for the cause of revolution in Spain? Here creative political action and the more complex kind of imaginative writing have united at least to the extent that they have arisen from the same vision of history and have been included in the career of one man. The Marxist vision of Lenin—Vincent Sheean has said it first—has in its completeness and its compelling force a good deal in common with the vision of Dante; but, partly realized by Lenin during his lifetime and still potent for some years after his death, it was a creation, not of literary art, but of actual social engineering. It is society itself, says Trotsky, which under communism becomes the work of art. The first attempts at this art will be inexpert and they will have refractory material to work with; and the philosophy of the Marxist dialectic involves idealistic and mythological elements which have led too often to social religion rather than to social art. Yet the human imagination has already come to conceive the possibility of re-creating human society; and how can we doubt that, as it acquires the power, it must emerge from what will seem by comparison the revolutionary 'underground' of art as we have always known it up to now and deal with the materials of actual life in ways which we cannot now even foresee? This is to speak in terms of centuries, of ages; but, in practicing and prizing literature, we must not be unaware of the first efforts of the human spirit to transcend literature itself.

MOROSE BEN JONSON

WHEN Swinburne published his study of Ben Jonson hardly sixty years ago, he indignantly called attention to the fact that English scholarship, which had shown such devotion to the texts of the Greek and Latin classics, should never, in two centuries and a half, have produced a decent edition of so important an English writer. That complaint can no longer be made—though the definitive edition of Jonson by C. H. Herford and Percy and Evelyn Simpson, brought out by the Oxford University Press, has been slow in appearing and is not yet complete. The first two volumes were published in 1925, and the eighth has only just come out. This, containing Jonson's poems and prose, is the last instalment of the text of Jonson, but it is to be followed by two volumes of commentaries, which ought to be particularly valuable, since no writer is more full of allusions, both topical and learned, than Jonson, and his work has never been properly annotated. There has not appeared, from this point of view and from that of clearing up the text, a serious edition of Jonson since that of William Gifford in 1816. This new one is a model of scholarship, handsomely printed and interestingly illustrated—in some cases, with hitherto unpublished drawings made by Inigo Jones for the décors and costumes of Jonson's masques.

Except, however, for the first two volumes, which assemble biographical materials and contain historical and critical essays on Jonson's various works, the Herford-Simpson edition is not especially to be recommended to the ordinary non-scholarly reader who may want to make the acquaintance of Jonson. It presents the original text with the seventeenth-century punctuation and spelling and with no glossary and no notes except textual ones. The books are, besides, expensive, and the earlier volumes are now hard to get—so the approach to this beetling author remains, as it has always been, rather forbidding and fraught with asperities. The best reprinting of the Gifford edition is also expensive and out of print. The three volumes of selections in the Mermaid Series are full of perplexing misprints, which drop out words or substitute wrong ones, and equipped with inadequate notes that turn up often on the wrong pages. The two volumes in the Everyman's Series include only Jonson's plays, and they are printed in a small dense type that makes them uncomfortable reading; there is a glossary, but it is incomplete. The only breach that I know in the hedge that seems to have sprung up around Jonson, as if his editors had somehow been influenced by their bristling and opaque subject, has been made by Mr. Harry Levin in his *Selected Works of Ben Jonson* (published by Random House). Here, in a clear readable text of his own and with a brilliant introduction, Mr. Levin has got together most of the best of Jonson for a compact and well-printed volume. There is an obstacle, though, even here, for he has furnished no notes and no glossary, and with Jonson, the explanation of a literary reference or the key to a phrase of slang is often absolutely indispensable for the understanding of a passage.

But it is not merely that Jonson's text itself has been a little hard to get at. It is rather that lack of demand has not stimulated popular editions. *Volpone* can still hold an audience—though it took a German adaptation to bring it back into fashion; and *The Alchemist* has been recently done both in New York and in London; but, among a thousand people, say, who have some knowledge and love of Shakespeare, and even some taste for Webster and Marlowe, I doubt whether you could find half a dozen who have any enthusiasm for Jonson or who have seriously read his plays. T. S. Eliot, admitting the long neglect into which Ben Jonson's work had fallen, put up, in *The Sacred Wood*, a strong plea for Jonson as an artist, and thus made a respect for this poet *de rigueur* in literary circles. But one's impression is that what people have read has been, not Jonson, but Eliot's essay. The dramatist himself, a great master for the age that followed his own, is still for ours mostly a celebrated name, whose writings are left unexplored. What I want to do here is to attack the problem of Jonson's unpopularity from what I believe to be a new point of view, and to show that his failure as a drawing attraction, in either the theater or the study, is bound up in a peculiar way with his difficulties as an artist.

It is a fault of Eliot's essay, so expert in its appreciation of the best-woven passages of Jonson's verse, that it minimizes his glaring defects. If you read it without reading Jonson, you will get a most plausible picture of a special kind of great writer, but this picture is not exactly Jonson. What is suppressed is all that Bernard Shaw meant when, telling off the Elizabethan dramatists, he characterized Ben Jonson as a 'brutish pedant'; and, in grappling with Jonson's shortcomings, we cannot perhaps do better than begin by facing squarely those qualities which made it impossible for Shaw—who admired, though he patronized, Shakespeare—to take seriously the comic writer who had, up to Shaw's own appearance, achieved the greatest reputation in English dramatic literature. The point is that Shakespeare, like Shaw, however much they differ in their philosophies, has an immense range, social and moral, in understanding a variety of people. To an intelligent and sensitive man of any school of thought, Shakespeare appears sensitive and intelligent. But Ben Jonson, after Shakespeare, seems neither. Though he attempts a variety of characters, they all boil down to a few motivations, recognizable as the motivations of Jonson himself and rarely transformed into artistic creations. Shakespeare expands himself, breeds his cells as organic beings, till he has so lost himself in the world he has made that we can hardly recompose his personality. Jonson merely splits himself up and sets the pieces—he is to this extent a dramatist—in conflict with one another; but we have merely to put these pieces together to get Jonson, with little left over. In the theater, he aims at several styles, as he tries for a multiplicity of characters, but the variety here, too, is mainly a mere technical matter of metrics and vocabulary, where Shakespeare can summon voices that seem to come from real human throats.

Jonson also lacks natural invention, and his theater has little organic life. His plots are incoherent and clumsy; his juxtapositions of elements are too often like the 'mechanical mixtures' of chemistry that produce no molecular reactions. His chief artifices for making something happen are to introduce his characters in impossible disguises and to have them play incredible practical jokes. Nor has he any sense of movement or proportion: almost everything goes on too long, and while it continues, it does not develop. Nor is his taste in other matters reliable. His puns, as Dryden complained, are sometimes of a stunning stupidity; and when he is dirty, he is, unlike Shakespeare, sometimes disgusting to such a degree that he makes one sympathetic with the Puritans in their efforts to clean up the theater. His reading of Greek and Latin, for all the boasting he does about it, has served him very insufficiently for the refinement and ordering of his work, and usually appears in his plays as either an alien and obstructive element or, when more skilfully managed, as a padding to give the effect of a dignity and weight which he cannot supply himself. He is much better when he lets himself go in a vein that is completely unclassical.

It is surely, then, misleading for Eliot to talk of Jonson's 'polished surface,' to call him a 'great creative mind,' who 'created his own world,' and not to warn you of the crudities and aridities, the uncertainty of artistic intention and the flat-footed dramatic incompetence, that you will run into when you set out to read him. None of his plays, with the exception of *The Alchemist*, really quite comes off as a whole. The three others of the best four of his comedies, though they all suffer from the faults I have mentioned, have elements of genuine humor and passages of admirable writing. But the story of *The Silent Woman* is revolting in its forced barbarity (Jonson's murderous practical jokes have their only analogue in literature in the booby-traps of Rudyard Kipling); *Volpone*, which reaches at moments a kind of heroic magnificence in exploiting its sordid and cruel themes, suffers, also, though somewhat less, from being based upon practical joking, and it is badly let down at the end by an improbable conventional conclusion; and, as for *Bartholomew Fair*, with some terribly funny scenes and a rich pageant of London low-life, there is in it so much too much of everything that the whole thing becomes rather a wallow of which the Pig-Woman and her pigs are all too truly the symbol. Contrast it with Hogarth's *Southwark Fair* (the product, to be sure, of a more disciplined age), equally confused and crowded, but so much better composed, so much sharper and firmer in outline. With *The Alchemist,* Jonson did ring the bell. This comedy is concentrated and well-constructed. There is no element of false morality to blur Jonson's acrid relish of the confidence games of his rogues: the cynicism is carried right through. The verse, which invests with style, which raises to distinction and glitter till it gives a ring almost like poetry, the slang of the underworld and the jargon of its various chicaneries, is an original achievement of Jonson's, which is only sustained in this one play. And, though there are one or two labored devices, the invention is more resourceful and the dialogue more spontaneous than in any of Jonson's other comedies. Yet this play, one of the funniest in English, is not really an example of high comedy as either a play of Molière's or a play of Aristophanes' is. Ben Jonson is not enough of a critic—that is, he has not enough intelligence—for either Molière's kind of interest in character and human relations or Aristophanes' kind of interest in institutions and points of view. *The Alchemist* is a picaresque farce, fundamentally not different from the Marx brothers. And it shows Jonson's poverty of themes that, when he had earlier attempted a tragedy, he should have arrived at a similar story. *Sejanus*, which takes us to the Roman Senate and inside the court of Tiberius, is also a chronicle of the intrigues of rogues who begin by working together but later sell each other out.

This is too offhand a summary of Jonson's work, but I want to get at him in another way.

Ben Jonson seems an obvious example of a psychological type which has been described by Freud and designated by a technical name, *anal erotic*, which has sometimes misled the layman as to what it was meant to imply. Let me introduce it simply by quoting from the account of it in a handbook of psychoanalysis, *The Structure and Meaning of Psychoanalysis* by William Healy, A. F. Bronner and A. M. Bowers. The three main characteristics of this

type are here paraphrased from Freud as follows: '(a) orderli-
ness . . . in an over-accentuated form, pedantry; (b) parsimony,
which may become avarice; (c) obstinacy, which may become defiance and perhaps also include irascibility and vindictiveness.'
Now, Jonson had all these qualities. He was a pedant, whose cult
of the classics had little connection with his special kind of genius.
There is something of the 'compulsive,' in the neurotic sense,
about his constant citing of precedents and his working into the
speeches of his plays passages, sometimes not translated, from the
Greek and Latin authors (though it was common for the Elizabethans to stick in scraps from Seneca or Ovid), as if they were
charms against failure. That he always did fear failure is evident;
and the arrogance, irritability and stubbornness which are also
characteristic of this Freudian type have obviously, in Jonson's
case, their origin in a constant anxiety as to the adequacy of his
powers. The more he defies his audience, vindicates himself
against his critics (though at the same time he puts himself to
special pains to propitiate the vulgar with vulgarity and to impress the learned with learning), in his innumerable prologues,
inductions, interludes between the acts, epilogues, dramatic post-
scripts and apologies added to the printed texts—the more he
protests and explains, declaims at unconscionable length his indifference to and scorn of his detractors, the more we feel that he is
unquiet, not confident. He is offsetting his internal doubts by
demonstrations of self-assertion.

The hoarding and withholding instinct which is the third of the
key traits of this type Jonson also displays to a high degree. This
tendency is supposed to be based on an attitude toward the excretatory processes acquired in early childhood. Such people, according to Freud, have an impulse to collect and accumulate;
they feel that doing so gives them strength and helps them to
resist the pressures that their elders are bringing to bear on them.
Sometimes they simply concentrate on storing up; sometimes they
expend in sudden bursts. They are likely to have a strong interest
in food both from the deglutitionary and the excretatory points
of view; but the getting and laying by of money or of some other
kind of possession which may or may not seem valuable to others
is likely to substitute itself for the infantile preoccupation with

the contents of the alimentary tract. Now, Jonson certainly exemplified this tendency, and he exhibited it in a variety of ways. His learning is a form of hoarding; and allied to it is his habit of collecting words. He liked to get up the special jargons of the various trades and professions and unload them in bulk on the public—sometimes with amusing results, as in the case of the alchemical and astrological patter reeled off by the crooks of *The Alchemist,* and even of the technique of behavior of the courtiers in *Cynthia's Revels,* but more often, as with the list of cosmetics recommended by Wittipol in *The Devil Is an Ass* and, to my taste, with the legal Latin of the divorce scene in *The Silent Woman,* providing some of his most tedious moments. The point is that Ben Jonson depends on the exhibition of stored-away knowledge to compel admiration by itself. And the hoarding and withholding of money is the whole subject of that strange play *Volpone.* Volpone is not an ordinary miser: he is a Venetian 'magnifico,' whose satisfaction in his store of gold is derived not merely from gloating alone but also, and more excitingly, from stimulating others to desire it, to hope to inherit it from him, and then frustrating them with the gratuitous cruelty which has been noted as one of the features of the aggressive side of this Freudian type. The practical jokes in Jonson have usually this sadistic character, and the people who perpetrate them are usually trying either to get something for themselves or to keep someone else from getting something. The many kinds of frauds and sharpers—from pickpockets to promoters—who figure in Jonson's plays as prominently as the practical jokers are occupied with similar aims; and Subtle and Face, in *The Alchemist,* lurk closeted, like Volpone, in a somber house, where they are hoarding their cleverness, too, and plotting their victims' undoing.

I am not qualified to 'analyze' Jonson in the light of this Freudian conception, and I have no interest in trying to fit him into any formulation of it. I am not even sure that the relation between the workings of the alimentary tract and the other phenomena of personality is, as Freud assumes, a relation of cause and effect; but I am sure that Freud has here really seized upon a nexus of human traits that are involved with one another and has isolated a recognizable type, and it seems to me to leap to the eyes that Jonson belongs to this type. I shall fill in the rest of my picture with the special characteristics of Jonson, which are consistent with the textbook description and which in some cases strikingly illustrate it.

Ben Jonson's enjoyment of tavern life and his great reputation for wit have created, among those who do not read him, an entirely erroneous impression of high spirits and joviality; but his portraits show rather the face of a man who habitually worries, who is sensitive and holds himself aloof, not yielding himself to intimate fellowship. In many of his plays there figures an unsociable and embittered personage who sometimes represents virtue and censors the other characters, but is in other cases presented by Jonson as a thoroughly disagreeable person and the butt of deserved persecution. Such, in the second of these categories, are Macilente in *Every Man Out of His Humour*, Morose in *The Silent Woman*, Surly in *The Alchemist* and Wasp in *Bartholomew Fair*. The most conspicuous of these is Morose, and Jonson's treatment of him is particularly significant. The dramatist, on a visit to the country, had encountered a local character who gave him an idea for a play. This was a man who had a morbid aversion to noise. Now, Jonson seems never to have inquired the reason, never to have tried to imagine what the life of such a man would be really like; nor could he ever have been conscious of what it was in himself that impelled him to feel so vivid an interest in him. According to his usual custom, he simply put him on the stage as a 'humour,' an eccentric with an irrational horror of any kind of sound except that of his own voice, who lives in a room with a double wall and the windows 'close shut and caulked' in a street too narrow for traffic, and who, declaring that 'all discourses but mine own' seem to him 'harsh impertinent, and irksome,' makes his servants communicate with him by signs. And the only way that Jonson can find to exploit the possibilities of this neurotic is to make him the agonized victim of a group of ferocious young men, who hunt him in his burrow like a badger, and trick him into marrying a 'silent woman,' who, immediately after the ceremony—while her sponsors raise a hideous racket—opens fire on him with a frenzy of chatter, and turns out in the end to be a boy in disguise. But

[220]

Morose himself is cruel through meanness: he has merited the worst he can suffer. He has wanted to disinherit his nephew, and has consigned him, in a venomous outburst, to the direst humiliation and poverty. Through Morose and through the characters like him, Ben Jonson is tormenting himself for what is negative and recessive in his nature. In *Volpone*, the withholder is punished only after he has had his fling at the delight of tormenting others. Miserliness, unsociability, a self-sufficient and systematic spite—these are among Jonson's dominant themes: all the impulses that grasp and deny. In the final scene of *Cynthia's Revels*, the last play of Jonson's first period, he makes Cynthia rhetorically demand:

> *When hath Diana, like an envious wretch,*
> *That glitters only to his soothed self,*
> *Denying to the world the precious use*
> *Of hoarded wealth, withheld her friendly aid?*

Yet Cynthia is Diana, and Diana is a virgin queen, who has herself forbidden love to her court; and the attitude which she is here repudiating is to supply almost all the subjects for the rest of Jonson's plays, among them all of his best. In these four lines, you have the whole thing in the words that come to his pen: envy, denial, hoarding, withholding. The first of these is very important. (Envy then meant hatred and spite as well as jealousy of what others have, but I am dealing with it here in its modern sense, which is usually the sense of Jonson.) In several of the earlier plays, it has been one of the chief motivations. In those you have had, on the one hand, the worthy and accomplished scholar—Horace of *The Poetaster*, Crites of *Cynthia's Revels*— who is envied by lesser men; and, on the other hand, the poor and exacerbated wit—Macilente in *Every Man Out of His Humour* —who envies lesser men. But both are aspects of the same personality; both are identified with Jonson himself. Whether the injury done the superior man consists of being slandered by fools or by the fools' being better off than he, it is the only fulfilment of the play that he is granted his just revenge, and he scores off his victims with a cruelty almost equal to that of Volpone frustrating his mercenary friends.

With this, there is no love in Jonson's plays to set against these negative values. The references to seduction, frequent though they are, in both his plays and his personal poems, suggest nothing but the coldest of appetites, and often show more gratification at the idea of cuckolding a husband than at that of enjoying a woman. In the plays, two sexual types recur, neither of whom finds any satisfaction in sex. Jonson said of his wife, from whom he separated, that she had been 'a shrew, yet honest'; and the only women in his plays that have even a semblance of life are shrews of the most pitiless breed. The typical wife in Jonson is always ready to doublecross her husband, and she does not want to allow him a moment of self-confidence or tranquillity: whatever the man does must be wrong; yet she may cherish at the same time an illusion that there waits for her somewhere a lover who can give her what she desires and deserves, and the appearance of a tenth-rate courtier may be enough to turn her head. The recurrent male type is a man who is insanely jealous of his wife but, paradoxically, is willing to prostitute her. The rival of the obsessive jealousy is always an obsessive greed either for money, as in the case of Corvino of *Volpone*, or, as in the case of Fitzdottrel of *The Devil Is an Ass*, for some other material advantage which the husband will enjoy by himself: Fitzdottrel likes to dress up and be seen on public occasions, but he never takes his wife with him. We may suspect, reading Jonson today, a connection between the impotence of these husbands to spend any real love on their wives and their fears that they are going to lose them. We may reflect that the self-centered husband might produce the shrewish wife, or that, living with a shrewish wife, a man might grow more self-centered, if he did not, as usually happens with the unfortunate husbands of Jonson's plays, become totaly demoralized. But Jonson had nothing of Shakespeare's grasp of organic human character or situation. It is interesting to contrast these bitches with the heroine of *The Taming of the Shrew*. Katharina's bad temper with men is accompanied by a deep conviction that no man can really want to marry her: it is a defiant assertion of self-respect. And so the jealousy of Othello (if not of Leontes) is explained by his consciousness, as a Moor in Venice, living among cleverer people who feel his color as a bar to close fellowship, of being at a disadvantage with the race to which his wife belongs. Whereas Jonson's two depressing stock figures do not afford very much insight into the causes of the traits they exemplify. Turning up again and again with a monotony of which Shakespeare was incapable, they obviously represent phenomena which Jonson has known at first hand and on which he cannot help dwelling: two more aspects of that negative soul that he is impelled to caricature. Yet sometimes, with his special experience, he can make them reveal themselves—as in the self-torturing Proustian soliloquies of Kiteley in *Every Man in His Humour*—in a way that strips off the skin to show, not what is in the depths, but what is just below the surface.

Jonson's positive ideal of womanhood may be summed up in the well-known lyric that begins, '*Have you seen but a bright lily grow, Before rude hands have touched it?,*' and ends '*O so white! O so soft! O so sweet is she!*' It is something quite remote and unreal which he is unable—when he tries, which is seldom, as in the Celia of *Volpone*—to bring to life in his plays, and, though the poems inspired by it are neat and agreeable enough, they have no human tenderness in them, let alone human passion. The touches in Jonson's poetry that come closest to lyric feeling are invariably evocations of coldness: '*Like melting snow upon a craggy hill . . . Since nature's pride is now a withered daffodil,*' or '*Except Love's fires the virtue have To fright the frost out of the grave,*' (from a poem in which the same stanza begins with the incredibly prosaic couplet: '*As in a ruin, we it call One thing to be blown up or fall . . .*'). And we may cite from the masque called *The Vision of Delight* the lines that remained in the memory of Joyce's Stephen Dedalus: '*I was not wearier where I lay By frozen Tithon's side tonight*' . . . ; as well as the passage from the prose *Discoveries* which Saintsbury selected for praise: 'What a deal of cold business doth a man misspend the better part of life in!—in scattering compliments, tendering visits, gathering and venting news, following feasts and plays, making a little winter-love in a dark corner.' At the end of *Cynthia's Revels*, Cupid tries to shoot Cynthia's courtiers and make them fall in love with one another, but he finds that his bow is powerless: they have been drinking from the fount of Self-Love, in which

Narcissus admired himself, and they are impervious to his shafts. When Diana is told of his presence, she sends him packing at once. Few lovers are united by Jonson. Is there indeed a case in all his work? And in Jonson's latest plays, the heroines undergo a transformation that makes Cynthia seem relatively human. The Lady Pecunia of *The Staple of News*, surrounded by her female retinue, Mortgage, Statute, Band and Wax, is simply a figure in a financial allegory; and so is Mistress Steel, the Magnetic Lady. Both are heiresses, kept close by guardians and sought by baffled suitors. The feminine principle here has been turned by the instinct for hoarding into something metallic, unyielding. The woman has lost all her womanhood: she is literally the hoarded coin. This evidently appeared to Ben Jonson a perfectly natural pleasantry, but it is quite enough to account for the failure, in his time, of these pieces, and for the distaste that we feel for them today.

To these stock characters of Jonson's theater should be added another that evidently derives from the playwright's social situation as well as from his psychology of hoarding. Ben Jonson, from his own account, was the son of a Scotch gentleman who had possessed some little fortune, but who had been thrown into prison, presumably for his Protestant leanings, in the reign of Bloody Mary, and had had his property confiscated. He died before Ben was born, and Ben's mother married a master bricklayer. Young Ben went to Westminster school, under the patronage of one of the masters, whose attention had been attracted by the boy's exceptional abilities, and may have started in at Cambridge on a scholarship; but he was obliged, apparently through poverty, to give up his studies there, and was set to learn the bricklayer's trade, which he loathed and from which he escaped by enlisting to fight in Flanders. Now, one of Jonson's favorite clowns, who varies little from play to play, is a young heir who is an utter numbskull and who, just having come into his money, begins throwing it away by the handful and soon finds himself fleeced by sharpers. This figure, too, in a different way from the envied or the envious man, is obviously the creation of Jonson's own envy, stimulated, no doubt, from two sources—first, the grievance of the man of good birth unjustly deprived of his patrimony, and, second, the sulky resentment of the man who can only withhold against the man who can freely lavish.

Jonson's hardships and uncertainty in his earlier years—when he can never have known anything but poverty—must have spurred him to desperate efforts to ballast and buttress himself. (For, as I have said, I do not necessarily accept the view of Freud that the training of the excretory functions must precede the development of other traits which exhibit resistance through hoarding, though it seems certain that, in personalities like Jonson's, these various traits are related.) He had acquired classical learning where he could not acquire money; and it was to remain for him a reservoir of strength, a basis of social position, to which he was to go on adding all his life. But his habit of saving and holding back—did his Scotch ancestry figure here, too?—had an unfortunate effect on his work, as well as on his personal relations, in that it made it very difficult for him fully to exploit his talents. It is not that the audiences of Jonson's day, the readers who have come to him since, have been unwilling to give themselves to his talents, but that his talents, authentic though they were, have not given themselves to us—or rather, that they were able to give themselves for only a limited period and then only at the expense of much effort. Ben Jonson, at his best, writes brilliantly; he has a genuine dramatic imagination. But it is hard for him to pump up his powers to work that will display their capacities. His addiction to wine—'drink,' Drummond said, 'is one of the elements in which he liveth'—was, I believe, bound up with the problem of getting himself to the point of high-pressure creative activity. He explained the strength of *Volpone* on the basis of its having been written at the time when he had just received a gift of ten dozen of sack; asserted that a passage in *Cataline* had suffered from having been composed when he was drinking watered wine; and apologized for the weakness of his later plays on the ground that he and his 'boys'—by which he meant his drinking companions—had been getting bad wine at their tavern. This shows that he drank while he was writing; and it is possible that liquor, though effective in helping him to keep up his high vein, may also have been to blame for the badness of some of his work. There are at times a peculiar coarseness in the texture of Jonson's writing, a strained falseness in his comic ideas, which, intolerable to a sober mind, may very well have seemed inspired to a constipated writer well primed with sack.

What Jonson was aiming at—from *Cynthia's Revels*, say—was a majesty and splendor of art which should rival the classics he venerated and the work of his more dashing contemporaries, with their rhetoric, color and spirit. But it is hard to be noble and grand with material so negative, so sour, as that which Jonson's experience had given him. To write in blank verse that is also poetry of the imbecile ambitions and the sordid swindles which furnish the whole subject of *The Alchemist* was a feat that even Ben Jonson was never to achieve but once. When he attempts a Roman tragedy, as in *Cataline* or *Sejanus*, his Romans are mostly the envious rogues, the merciless prigs and the treacherous sluts with whom we are familiar in his comedies, and they make a more unpleasant impression for not being humorously treated. When Jonson attempts Renaissance splendor, he always gives it an element of the factitious as well as an element of the vulgar, which, as Mr. Levin says, have the effect of making it look ridiculous. The dreams of Sir Epicure Mammon bring a kind of hard glow to the writing, but his banquets and his beds and his mirrors are imaginary like the gold that is to buy them: they never get on to the stage as does the 'alchemist's' fusty lair. And with *Volpone*, the great difficulty is that the mean motivations of the characters have no intimate connection with the background, the house of a rich Venetian. Volpone is simply another of Jonson's hateful and stingy men, who behaves as if he were envious of others, without being provided by Jonson with any real reason for envy. The magnificence of Jonson's grandees, like the purity of his women, is a value that is always unreal and that can never make a satisfactory counterweight to a poverty and a squalor that are actual and vividly rendered. One has to go to the later French naturalists who were influenced by both Flaubert and Zola to find anything comparable to the poetry which Jonson was able to extract from all the cheap and dirty aspects of London: the 'poor spoonful of dead wine, with flies in't'; the gingerbread made of 'stale bread, rotten eggs, musty ginger and dead honey'; the rogue out of luck,

> at Pie Corner,
> *Taking your meal of steam in, from cooks' stalls,*
> *Where, like the father of hunger, you did walk*
> *Piteously costive, with your pinched horn-nose,*
> *And your complexion of the Roman wash*
> *Stuck full of black and melancholic worms,*
> *Like powder-corns shot at th' artillery-yard;*

the theater pick-ups, 'lean playhouse poultry,' as described by fat Ursula of the pig-roasting booth, 'that has the bony rump sticking out like the ace of spades or the point of a partizan, that every rib of 'em is like the tooth of a saw; or will so grate 'em [their customers] with their hips and shoulders as—take 'em altogether —they were as good lie with a hurdle.' It is the peculiar beauty of *The Alchemist* that the visions of splendor here are all, frankly, complete illusions created out of sordid materials by rogues in the minds of dupes. The poor stupid whore Doll has to impersonate the Queen of Faery and a great lady in romantic circumstances. A more humane writer might have extracted some pathos from this; but Jonson does get an esthetic effect that is quite close to the Flaubertian chagrin.

But, in *Volpone*, where real gold is involved, we are never allowed to see it. The German adaptation of this play made by Stefan Zweig and done here by the Theater Guild, which has also been used as a basis for the current French film, is an improvement on Jonson's original in one very important respect. It shows us what we want we see, what, subconsciously, we have come to demand: the spending, the liberation of Volpone's withheld gold—when Mosca, to everyone's relief, finally flings it about the stage in fistfuls. But Ben Jonson cannot squander his gold, his gold which he has never possessed; he can only squander excrement. Karl Abraham, one of the psychologists quoted in the book referred to above, 'cites, in proof of the close association between sadistic and anal impulses instances in his experiences with neurotics when an explosive bowel evacuation has been a

[227]

substitute for a discharge of anger or rage, or has accompanied it.' Certainly Jonson seems to explode in this fashion. The directness with which he gives way to the impulse is probably another cause of his chronic unpopularity. The climax of *The Poetaster* is the administering of emetic pills, the effects of which take, in this case, the form of a poetic joke. The comic high point of *The Alchemist* comes with the locking of one of the characters in a privy, where he will be overcome by the smell. This whole malodorous side of Jonson was given its fullest and most literal expression in the poem called *The Famous Voyage* which was too much for even Gifford and Swinburne, in which he recounts a nocturnal expedition made by two London blades in a wherry through the roofed-over tunnel of Fleet Ditch, which was the sewer for the public privies above it. A hardly less literal letting-go is the whole play of *Bartholomew Fair*, which followed the more pretentious work (from *Sejanus* through *Catiline*) that we have just been discussing. It is Ben Jonson's least strained and inhibited play, and one of his most successful. He drops verse for colloquial prose; he forgets about classical precedents. He dumps out upon his central group of characters, for the most part pusillanimous examples of the lower middle class, puritan parsons and petty officials, with, of course, a young spendthrift from the country, what must have been a lifetime's accumulation of the billingsgate and gutter practices of the pickpockets, booth-keepers, peddlers, pimps, ballad-singers and professional brawlers of the Elizabethan underworld. This comedy, novel in its day, anticipates both Hogarth and Dickens; but Jonson's impulse to degrade his objects is something not shared by either. Hogarth and Dickens both, for all their appetite for rank vulgarity, are better-humored and more fastidious. The flood of abusive language let loose by the infuriated Pig-Woman, well-written and funny though it is, is outpouring for outpouring's sake: it effects no dramatic move and has in itself no rhetorical development; and the even more filthy travesty of Marlowe's *Hero and Leander* in terms of bankside muck has an ugliness which makes one suspect that Jonson took an ugly delight in defiling a beautiful poem which he could not hope to rival. Yet we cannot but succumb—in certain scenes, at least—to the humor of *Bartholomew Fair*. The tumult of Ursula's booth and her devotion to her roasting pigs, the monumental pocket-picking episode that moves to its foreseen conclusion almost with the inevitability of tragedy—these somehow create more sympathy (always for the characters outside the law) than anything else in Jonson's plays.

And Ben Jonson is somehow a great man of letters, if he is not often a great artist. His very failure to make the best of his gifts had the result of his leaving a body of work full of hints—unrealized ambitions, undeveloped beginnings—which later writers were able to exploit in a way that it was hardly possible for them to do with the work of Shakespeare, which *was* realized, consummate, complete. The most astonishing variety of writers owe quite different kinds of debts to Jonson. It is as if they had found means to deliver, in viable forms of art, the genius that Jonson had had to withhold. Gifford was certainly right in supposing that Milton owed something to such passages as the opening of *Volpone,* in which the hoarder invokes his gold. The whole comedy of Congreve and Wycherley seems to have grown out of the cynical men-about-town, with their bravura-pieces of wit, in *The Silent Woman;* and Swift must have picked up from Jonson, not only the title of *A Tale of a Tub,* but also the style and tone of his series of poems to Stella, which are so much like certain of those in Jonson's series, *A Celebration of Charis,* as well as his general vein of morosely humorous realism, exemplified in *The Lady's Dressing Room* and *A Description of a City Shower.* The comedy of humors eventually led to the one-idea characters of Peacock, which led, later, to those of Aldous Huxley; and it must have contributed to the novels of Dickens, who loved to act Bobadil in *Every Man in His Humour.* Though Tennyson was under the impression that he himself had invented the stanza-form that he made famous in *In Memoriam,* it had already been used by Jonson in his *Elegy* (XXII of *Underwoods*), the tone of which is quite close to Tennyson in his elegiac vein, and in the second of the choruses to *Catiline,* which suggests such weightier use of the meter as one finds in the dedication to Queen Victoria or in the dedication of *Demeter* to Lord Dufferin. And there are touches in Lewis Carroll that seem reminiscent of Jonson: '*I passed by the garden and marked with one eye How the Owl and the Panther were sharing the pie*,' recalls a long nonsense speech in *The Vision of Delight*: '*Yet would I take the stars to be cruel If the crab and the rope-maker ever fight duel*,' etc.; and Sir Politic Would-be of *Volpone*, with his succession of ridiculous inventions, of which he likes to boast, 'Mine own device,' is a forerunner of the White Knight. In the first decades of our own century, that very first-rate comic writer, Ronald Firbank, with how little direct contact one cannot tell, represents the latest development of Ben Jonson's typical methods—eviscerated personalities and monstrous motivations labeled with bizarre names—which, though it shows perhaps a certain decadence, keeps also a good deal of vigor. And James Joyce, who told his friend Frank Budgen that Ben Jonson was one of the only four writers that he had ever read completely through, seems to have had in common with Jonson some of the traits of his psychological type, and may be said to have followed his example —failing, sometimes, from faults like Jonson's—rather, perhaps, than to have exploited to better effect any special aspect of Jonson's work. Joyce, too, hoarded words and learning and attempted to impress his reader by unloading his accumulations; he, too, has his coprophilic side and his husbands who asquiesce, at the same time that they torture themselves, in the sleepings-abroad of their wives; he, too, is defiant and arrogant, self-consciously resistant to pressures, and holds himself apart and aloof.

It would be interesting, from this point of view, to compare Ben Jonson at length with Gogol as well as with Joyce. Undoubtedly Gogol is a case even more narrowly developed than Jonson of the type in question here. He, too, likes to store up words—his note-books were full of the jargons of special trades and milieux; and he voids them in long dense sentences that agglutinate as massive paragraphs. His characters, in *Dead Souls*, are themselves almost always collectors, and they sometimes collect sheer rubbish —like Manilov, who saves all his old pipe-ashes. Gogol loves to write about eating, he has little sensual interest in women. His comedy *The Inspector General*, farcical, at once gross and inhuman, has something in common with Jonson's comedies; and, like Jonson, he is powerless to lift himself—in the unfinished later instalments of *Dead Souls*—out of the satirical comedy of roguery into a sterner and less turbid medium. The virtuous judge and the altruistic landowner of the second part of *Dead Souls* are as obviously maniacs as the misers and boors of the first part—as the senators, conspirators and emperors of Jonson's Roman plays are just as much 'compulsive' one-track minds as the characters of his comedy of 'humours.' So Joyce, with greater genius and wider range than either Jonson or Gogol, cannot seem to function comfortably and freely except when he has given himself, as in his two most ambitious books, the latitude of a comic frame: his protagonists are comic figures, humiliated, persecuted, rueful, and their epics are systematic ironies, in which their heroic pretensions never wholly emerge from the mud. Gogol and Joyce, too, both share with Jonson his ideal of feminine sweetness and purity —seen only in wistful glimpses—that floats somewhere above and divorced from the smelly and dirty earth. With this motif Gogol succeeds least well: the lovely face fleetingly seen in the coach by Chichikov of *Dead Souls*, the maidenly pensionnaire who strikes him dumb at the ball; Jonson, a little better in the lyrics mentioned above; Joyce, with triumphant success in the vision of the wading girl that makes the climax of *A Portrait of the Artist*.

Later years did not mellow Jonson. When he visited Drummond at forty-five, with most of his best work behind him, he was still running down his contemporaries and asserting his own merits as peevishly as in the days when he had written *The Poetaster*; and at a supper given for him by his younger admirers the year before his death, he painfully embarrassed his friends by inordinately praising himself and vilifying his fellow poets. He could never afford to be generous, because he had never achieved what he wanted; and one suspects that, even in the case of such a lesser contemporary as Marston, Jonson's hateful hostility toward him had in it an element of envy of that touch of sublimity and magic which Marston was able to manage and which was quite beyond Jonson's reach. To Drummond he even grumbled about Shakespeare; and his reference to *The Tempest* in *Bartholomew Fair* betrays how much it must have irked him to see his friend, a much older man, find suddenly a new field for his genius in a form so close to that of the masque, in which Jonson had worked for years without ever striking more than an occasional spark from his pedantic made-to-order prettiness. It is therefore all the more a proof of the deep devotion he cherished for the art that they both practiced that he should have put on record so roundly his high opinion of Shakespeare—and not only of Shakespeare, but also of Donne. In his elegy on Shakespeare especially, in estimating him above all their contemporaries and setting him beside the greatest of the ancients, he does justice to all that is noblest in his own aspiring nature, which had to drag so much dead weight, all that is soundest and most acute in his own cramped but virile intellect. The one thing he really loved was literature, and, having served it as well as he could, no touchiness of personal pride could keep him from honoring one who had been fitted to serve it better precisely by the qualification, among others, of possessing, as Jonson said, 'an open and free nature,' so that he 'flowed with that facility that sometimes it was necessary he should be stopped.'

1948

'MR. ROLFE'

THE FIRST DAYS of my first fall at prep school were passed in complete confusion. We were always being shrieked at by bells, which uprooted us from what we were doing and compelled us to report somewhere else. We had to get there while the bell was still ringing, and I used to be swamped by the mob of boys pouring in and out of the classrooms and pushing along the corridors and porches, and finally arrive late in a panic.

One of the places in which I used to land was a room that was larger than the others and that had white classical busts above the blackboards and a dais for the master's desk. This was the room to which I went for Greek, and I realized at the first recitation that what occurred there was of a special nature. The master, who was tall and well-dressed and who loomed taller from sitting on the dais, had an aspect, an accent and a manner unfamiliar to the point of seeming foreign. He was blond, with drooping-lidded blue eyes and a high-domed oval head, which was very inadequately thatched with strands of thin yellow hair, and he wore a yellow drooping mustache of the kind that was supposed then to be English and which reminded me of a character called Mr. Batch who figured in the funny papers. His eyebrows were of the kind that arch away from one another like a pair of quotation marks and had the perpetually lifted look which conventionally indicates distress but also comports with irony, and his mustache concealed his mouth, so that his expression remained enigmatic, and you could never be sure whether he were smiling at you kindly or withering you with mock sweetness.

At any rate, as soon as he entered, he dominated the room to the last row of seats. From the moment he sat down at his desk, rearing his neck and his back very straight and setting out his book before him with a kind of sober directness that was a part of his approach to his subject, he kept the class in a state of tension as if they were witnessing a performance in which—and all too often without knowing their lines—they themselves were to be called upon to take part.

The first characteristics of Mr. Rolfe's which impressed a new boy in his class were the wittiness, pungency and promptitude of his sarcasm and the mercilessness of his demands. He put you on the spot for your assignment as none of the other masters did; he would not allow you to slide over anything, and it seemed that he would not help you; if you failed, he made you feel by some caustic touch a criticism of your classroom personality. He evidently made tacit but definite assumptions about the classroom personalities of us all—I was supposed to be moony and inattentive—which one might feel did one less than justice. He had a way of going around the class in pursuit of the answer to some question—designating us as 'First little gentleman . . . Second little gentleman,' and so forth, and pointing at us with the butt of his pencil—which could put one at a distance and be paralyzing. And there were also his special drawl, which could be musical and yet so mocking, and his queer but distinguished accent. I knew that he was not an Englishman, in spite of his British mustache and though he pronounced words like *bath* and *advanced* with what was called the 'broad *a*.' *Afterwards*, when it came at the end of a sentence, he pronounced *ahfterwúrds*, with the accent on the last syllable. It seemed impossible to appeal to him outside of class or to establish with him the personal relation by which boys seek to protect themselves from masters, and one got to be afraid of being snubbed. If anyone were rash enough to ask him whether Xenophon, which we were to start next term, or the verbs in -μι, which were looming as the next ordeal in the grammar, were as hard as they were rumored to be, he would answer, glancing away: 'Oh, very difficult! almost impossible.'

I had been rather badly trained at my previous school, and I at once resented Mr. Rolfe. I took to brooding outside of class over his sarcasms; and there were days when I was obsessed by his image and some brief derisive remark of which I had been the victim that morning. The Greek class both excited and scared me.

One night I went to see him in his rooms. He had invited us to come to him for help, and I had finally picked up courage to do so. He was engaged with someone else when I came in, and I shyly glanced about the room and then bent over the books on the table. The incident must have been one of those which sharply and suddenly mark the emergence of some new element into consciousness, because whenever I dream of going back to school and calling on Mr. Rolfe, I never find him in his later rooms where I often went to see him, but always in these earlier ones where I could only have gone a few times and in which, when awake, I never place him. These rooms were the rooms of a bachelor but not those of a bachelor schoolmaster: in their relative elegance and luxury, they reminded me rather of the apartment inhabited by a bachelor uncle; and Mr. Rolfe was sitting back on a couch and giving attention to the passages presented to him less like a master after class than like a gentleman receiving at his ease. In the bookrack, with their titles upturned, I saw volumes of Bernard Shaw, and this somewhat startled and shocked me. I had, at fourteen, not yet read Shaw; but I had heard he was a perverse cynic, who considered himself superior to other people and who liked to wound his reader's sensibilities.

Mr. Rolfe, when my turn came to talk to him, answered my questions with his usual aloofness; and I went out of the room convinced that he was a disciple of Bernard Shaw, and that his brilliant performance in the classroom at the expense of us poor Fourth-Formers had something to do with the scandalous plays and the arrogant personality of which I had been hearing such disturbing accounts. I thought that I had conceived an antagonism, bitter and forever intransigent, against Mr. Rolfe and Shaw.

I began to like Greek, however, which I was only just beginning that year. The truth was that, in spite of his sarcasm, Mr. Rolfe shed on everything he dealt with a peculiar imagination and charm, and that this held you even while you resented him. My feeling about Greek was becoming quite different from my feeling about Latin, which I had not been taught especially well and which seemed to me something technical like algebra, with almost no relation to literature or human speech. The Greek words as he pronounced them or wrote them on the board in his clear and beautiful hand took on an esthetic value; and when you came to understand his attitude, the recitation turned into a kind of game, which, though taxing, had its rewards and its amusements.

I came to see that he was not really cruel. Though severe in his conception of his duty toward his students and of their duty toward their work, he was not really the sort of master who takes a joy in humiliating his class. He never failed to acknowledge good work, though he liked to express his approval in Greek; and he told me one day, in his drawl that always sounded ironic, that if I continued as I had been doing I might get to be his favorite pupil. I decided, thinking it over, that he had meant it; but this won me no indulgence or tenderness, and he would curtly correct my vagaries. It was characteristic of Mr. Rolfe, who aimed to do so much more for his pupils than get them through their college examinations, that he should one day have explained to us in passing the theory of the lost *digamma*, which he described as 'a little thing like a tuning fork'; and it was characteristic of me, with my interest in literary *arcana*, that I should then have become fascinated by the letters that had been dropped out of the Greek alphabet. It was suggested to me by Mr. Rolfe that I should do better if I concentrated on those they had retained.

And I came to understand that his rigor was really in the interests of Greek. I have found out from later experience that it requires a rare blend of qualities for a man or a woman to teach Greek well: he must have a real taste for Greek (which seems rarer than a taste for Latin), a real feeling for its luminosity and subtlety, its nobility and naiveté, a lively imaginative picture of the civilization behind it; and he must, at the same time, be capable of insisting on the high degree of intellectual discipline that is needed to keep the class up to the effort demanded by the difficulties of the subject—difficulties which do not consist merely of the more or less automatic application of formulas one has learned, but involve, along with accurate memory, a certain precision of feeling, in which one can be trained by an adept but which cannot be learned by rote. Mr. Rolfe was the perfect

Hellenist. He made you get everything exactly right, and this meant a good deal of drudgery. But one was also always made to feel that there was something worth having there behind the numbered paragraphs and paradigms of Goodwin's Greek grammar, the grim backs and fatiguing notes of the Ginn texts 'for the use of schools'—something exhilarating in the air of the classroom, human, heroic and shining. The prospect of knowing this marvelous thing lent the details excitement—and so it did the daily contest between Mr. Rolfe and you, which eventually became quite jolly. You felt that he was not unkind, that he merely wanted people to learn Greek, that teaching people Greek was an exalted aim to which he had devoted his life, and that he only became really unpleasant with students who did not want to learn it.

I therefore began working hard to keep myself on the right side of his severity. Besides the appetite I had acquired for Greek, I was stimulated also by the fact that I had grown to enjoy his wit. The truth was that I myself had a satirical turn which I was just beginning then to learn to exploit, and that I had never before met in the flesh a real past master of mockery. Hence my resentment, and hence my admiration. I was soon reading Bernard Shaw.

II

The Hill School in 1909 represented a combination of elements which must have made it unique among prep schools. It had been founded by the Reverend Matthew Meigs, a Presbyterian minister from Connecticut, who had settled in Pottstown, Pennsylvania, and started a small school in an old stone house on a hill. In my time it was run by John Meigs, his son, who had extraordinarily enlarged and improved it and made for it a great reputation.

John Meigs, whom we always called 'Professor,' was not really, however, a schoolmaster. He had taken on his father's school and accepted it as a career with reluctance; but once he had done so, he had worked at it tremendously. He had no endowments and no wealthy patrons; and he had at first kept all the accounts, written out all the letters in longhand, and taught twenty-five hours a week as well as personally handled the discipline, the records and the relations with parents. He had created a big school out of small beginnings—just as a boy from a Pennsylvania farm like Henry C. Frick had bought up coke-ovens and created an industry; and, in spite of his New England origins, I have always assimilated John Meigs to the Pennsylvania Dutch of that countryside of the extreme western corner of Montgomery County. A short, stocky man with a wide straight mouth and a square head that was made to seem even more cubelike by a nose flattened out like a boxer's—broken at football, I think—he resembled a successful manufacturer who had made himself something of a man of the world. He had gone to college at Lafayette instead of at Yale or Harvard; and the school had certain qualities of the back Pennsylvania of solid farmhouses and brick-streeted towns rather than of the Eastern seaboard, of Sewickley rather than Philadelphia. Professor had a certain smartness, but it was the smartness of a local man of substance, and not at all like the Episcopalian smartness that one sometimes found in the headmaster of the quite different New England schools. His hair, which was silver and parted in the middle, curled crisply at the corners of his forehead, and he liked to wear a bright red tie, and sometimes a flower in his buttonhole, with a spotless white vest. As he would walk down from the platform after prayers, leading the rest of the school, stepping so firmly and yet jauntily, he was a figure that inspired confidence and in whom one could feel pride.

In the state he was a man of some consequence, quite active in local politics. He had, as one of the masters has told me since, no real interest in education whatever. But he did possess qualities which enabled him to organize a first-rate school. He had certainly a touch of the brutality characteristic of industrial Pennsylvania, but with it went the independence of the man who has built up his own business, and a downright and four-square directness in his dealings with students, parents and faculty. The school was financially sound as I imagine few prep schools have been, and quite free from the tremors and depressions that reflect the inability to raise funds. Nor were there, as far as I was aware, any of those moral leaks which cause favoritism, ill-feeling and inefficiency.

The efficiency of the Hill was perfect—as perfect as Bethlehem Steel. It was a legend at the time that no student who had been graduated from the Hill ever failed to get into college, because the drill we were given was so stiff and the tests we had to pass so difficult that entrance examinations became child's play; and it was true that we mostly landed in the top sections of the college courses. But this system had its disagreeable side. Every moment of our time was disposed of; our whole life was regulated by bells; and—till we reached the Sixth Form, at any rate—we had hardly an hour of leisure. The intention was beneficent, of course; but the remorseless paternalism of the Hill had something of the suffocating repressive effect of the Pennsylvania mill-town in which the company owns the workers' houses, controls their contacts with the outside world, and runs the banks, the schools and the stores. Save for walks in the country and excursions into town, for both of which we had to get permission, we were confined to the Hill grounds, which rose like a segregated plateau in the midst of the little steel town—the narrow and cobbled streets where the greenery showed meager in spring, the slag pits and the blast furnaces that startled new boys and kept them awake at night by blazes that would light up the whole room.

The same ideals in John Meigs, however, which had produced this iron regime had secured for the Hill School some admirable things. He had spared no pains or expense to provide the best equipment obtainable: the staff as well as the plant were as good as they could possibly be. The buildings, the gymnasium, the tennis courts, the swimming pool, the showers, the ballfields somewhat offset the drabness of our surroundings. And the masters, to keep us up to scratch, had to be first-rate, too. Yet, here, I believe, Professor must have been aiming at something beyond efficiency and may have displayed a certain creativeness, for he did get very able men who, though quite different from one another, evidently worked well together and felt a genuine interest in the school. In talking afterwards to boys from other schools, I never found the same enthusiasm for their masters that the Hill graduates had for theirs. Some of them, I came to realize, were quite above the usual prep-school level and would have adorned any university. Alfred Rolfe was one of these. It was

characteristic of Meigs, with his ambition to have the best of everything, that he should have installed, to teach Greek, an accomplished New Englander in the best tradition.

III

For that was what Mr. Rolfe was—a New Englander. And it was
that about him that had seemed to me foreign.

He was moreover a special kind of New Englander: he came
from Concord, Mass.; and this, as I afterwards observed, was quite
distinct from being a Bostonian (and Mr. Rolfe had gone to
Amherst, not Harvard). He had that quality of homeliness and
freshness that one finds in a Concordian like Thoreau, combined,
as it was in Thoreau, with a sharp mind and a fine sensibility.
The Yankee accent and rustic expressions with which he sometimes roughened his speech were a feature he knew how to make
use of to set off his natural elegance, just as his very large feet
and hands were somehow made to play a part in the grace with
which he went about his business, and as the touches of gruffness
and brusqueness that had the sea captains of New England behind them gave his urbanity a greater authority. All this side of
him, in fact, was the rocklike base on which the flowers of Hel-
lenism flourished: the sophistication of his comic sense, his exquisite literary taste, and the benignant incandescence of his
mind. Alfred Rolfe has been my only personal contact with the
Concord of the great period, and I feel that if I had not known
him, I should never really have known what it was, and what a
high civilization it represented. For there was nothing about
Mr. Rolfe either of the schoolmaster or of the provincial. He
had in his early years studied in Germany, but he cared little
for travel or cities, and now spent every school year in Pottstown
and every summer in Concord; yet he seemed to enjoy, just as
Emerson did, the freedom of the great social world as well as of
the great world of literature. His brother, Henry Winchester Rolfe,
was also a classical scholar. I later read a book of his on Petrarch
and discovered that my friend Rolfe Humphries, the Latinist and
poet, had been named after him.

The manners that we tended to learn at the Hill were a little on the heavy and flat side; and Mr. Rolfe, for all his dignity, moved among us with a charming ease and what can only be called a kind of blitheness. He was tall but not very well built: besides large feet and hands, he had shoulders that were narrow and sloping. He stooped and thrust forward his head as he walked; and in the skirted black frock-coat and striped trousers which were *de rigueur* for Sunday chapel, he would look like some long-legged great auk as he stalked back to his rooms after service. Yet he was one of the real ornaments of the school, perhaps its principal ornament.

He was an admirable after-dinner speaker and always in demand for banquets. He cultivated the dry, solemn, drawling manner which Mark Twain had made the fashion but which became very New England in his hands. His face, when he was not in conversation, tended to lapse into a Saint Bernard sadness, and he liked to exploit this for comic effect. He was wonderful at 'morning exercises,' where the reading of profane literature had been substituted for passages from the Bible. His fine voice, deep, resonant and rich, was not the voice of a school elocutionist who likes to play-act for his students, but always remained personal and in some special way colloquial: what it was rich in were nuances of humor and perceptions of the values of style. And the rhythms of poetry to Mr. Rolfe seemed something natural and dear: it was as if they represented a dreaminess which, for all his Yankee commonsense, was a part of his everyday life and did not require a condition of trance. The first time that you heard him read aloud a passage of Homer in class, you knew what Homer was as poetry, and no amount of construing and syntactical analysis could blur the effect of that rhythm. We used also to read Browning's plays with him, for fun, between chapel and midday dinner on Sunday, and he would easily disentangle the speeches of such things as A *Blot on the 'Scutcheon* and get out of them their own kind of music. Sometimes at morning exercises he would read from the New England writers, and he would give them a kind of distinction which I had not known was there. In those days we had been brought up on the New Englanders, and by the time we came to read for ourselves we had decided they were childish and a bore. But Mr. Rolfe could put, say, Oliver Wendell Holmes, whom I did not at that time think amusing, in an attractively different light. When he did scenes from *The Autocrat of the Breakfast-Table*, he really made you hear the people in that ideal Boston boardinghouse: you felt that he had boarded there himself, and that the quality of the talk in its way had been good. His rendering of *The Wonderful One-Hoss Shay* was one of his most brilliant performances. When the deacon swore as deacons do with an 'I dew vum' or an 'I tell *yeou*,' the voice of the old man would come through with a sudden dramatic realism that startled us and made us laugh.

He had certainly the sense of audience. When, in the absence of Professor and Mrs. Meigs, he would preside at our meals in the big dining-room, one felt his presence even here as one did during a recitation. While he would be waiting for the boys to assemble, he would stand up with folded arms, joking with the Sixth-Formers beside him; then he would press the buzzer and say the brief grace—'Bless, O Father, thy gifts to our use and us to thy service: for Christ's sake. Amen'—in which, many times though I heard it, the words never seemed merely a rite, but something said and felt. At the end of the meal, when it would sometimes happen that a general silence fell as we waited for the buzzer to release us, he would mutter some amusing remark which would be caught by the whole room and bring a laugh; if the buzzer stuck, as it sometimes did, he would make it a whole little comedy and would send us out quite lighthearted from the then rather close and crowded dining-room and its Pennsylvania Dutch food.

There was a moment, I remember, when Mr. Rolfe had read something that impressed him about the importance of pulling in one's stomach in order to carry oneself correctly, and when he would preach this to us half-humorously as he attempted to practice it himself. As I watched him one day in the dining-room, throwing back his shoulders and drawing in his chin, which was round and rather recessive, I thought of his luxurious lounging on his comfortable couch and armchair. And there was also his gesture which was so much of a betrayal of his effortful and Spartan pose: a wandering of his hand to his necktie and breast, as a woman fingers a necklace, which came from the something poetic—the something almost romantic—in him. I remembered how he had warned us once in class that it was impossible to study properly when sunk in an easy chair; and I realized that in Mr. Rolfe a certain strain of the sybarite co-existed with rectitude and discipline. I recognized it thus very early because I was unmistakably myself on the sybaritic side. I incurably disliked athletics, carried myself very badly and loved to read in bed. And at this moment I became aware, though I did not formulate the perception, that what made Mr. Rolfe interesting and gave him a sort of rarity was his having reached just that point when a tough and well-tried stock first gets the freedom to smile and to play, to work at belles-lettres for their own sake.

At some point in our early stages of Greek Mr. Rolfe had handed us over for a term or two to his assistant; and by the time I got back to him again, I was no longer so much afraid of him. The Greek class still imposed a certain tension, but it stimulated for those students who had literary tastes a genuine interest in Greek. Mr. Rolfe worked us awfully hard, harder than any other master, but we did feel that we were getting Homer and not just boning assignments. We had to scan every line and understand every form, and we had to translate every word into an English not unworthy of the original. It was as serious to give clumsy equivalents as to miss out on a case or a mood, and would bring down on us his tartest derision. He accepted as a standard for the proper tone of a successful Homeric translation the passage by Dr. Hawtrey cited by Matthew Arnold in his essay on translating Homer: 'Clearly the rest I behold of the dark-eyed sons of Achaia'—and made us commit it to memory.

With all his exacting demands, he had many entertaining devices for relieving the dryness of our drudgery. We were encouraged to think of ὀδύρομαι as 'oh, dear! oh, my!'; we were taught that when γάρ begins a sentence it is always pronounced 'yar,' on the principle on which children are told that a guinea pig's eyes will fall out if you hold it up by its tail; and we were made to learn the speeches of the trial of Orontas in Xenophon and act it out in class. At the end, when Orontas was led into the tent and put to death in a mysterious manner, the boy who played him was taken out into the hall and grisly sounds were heard.

Mr. Rolfe shied so naturally away from the tone of the textbook and the classroom that it was difficult for him to remember the wording of the rules as they were given in the book. There is a principle of Homeric versification which was formulated by Goodwin somewhat as follows: 'The penthemimeral caesura gives the line an anapaestic movement, from which it is often recalled by the bucolic diaeresis.' We would be called upon to demonstrate this by rapping it out on our seat-arms with pencils; but Mr. Rolfe, when he cited the rule, would resist the language of the grammar, by stumbling over the second part and turning the 'from which it is often recalled' into 'from which it is frequently rescued.' The whole thing got thus a faint comic flavor; and this little involuntary touch has always remained in my mind as an example of his putting in its place of the academic side of his subject.

The impulse to parody was strong in him, though he usually indulged it quite casually. When Tennyson's *Enoch Arden* was read once at morning exercises, he suggested that the end of the poem really needed another line:

> *So past the strong heroic soul away.*
> *And when they buried him the little port*
> *Had seldom seen a costlier funeral;*
> And Annie wore her best black bombazine.

I was thus tremendously flattered when he complimented me on a parody of Browning which I had published in the school magazine. And later, when another Hill boy and I had invented, as freshmen at college, an imaginary figure of speech, I was surprised at the amusement it seemed to afford him when we told him about it on a visit. '*Thypsis . . . thypsis,*' he murmured to himself at some later moment of the conversation.

In my last year of school, when I lived above him, I used to go and read in his rooms. It was one of the paradoxes of the Hill, which excelled in literary activity, that Professor, in installing his extraordinary equipment, should almost completely have neglected the library. He must have conceived of books as something to be fed us in calculated doses by the masters in the different departments. He could never have had any interest in making literature generally available, for the two or three small rooms called the library contained almost nothing up to date, and they were full of ancient textbooks and works of reference that had belonged to the Reverend Matthew Meigs and went back to the eighteenth and seventeenth centuries. There were not even good editions of the classics, and I almost put my eyes out my first year at school on a copy of *Vanity Fair* in double columns of microscopic type. (This deficiency was long ago remedied: the library, I am told, is now first-rate.) But at least half a dozen of the masters had considerable private libraries, which they encouraged us to use. And Mr. Rolfe's was among the most interesting, as it was certainly much the handsomest. He went in for well-bound sets, and he kept up with contemporary literature as no other of the masters did. The new volumes of Chesterton and Shaw always appeared on his table, and I sat on his couch and read them. Sometimes he would come in, greet me briefly, put on his pince-nez, sit down in his large armchair and silently correct his papers.

I was still shy with him: for all his humor, he was one of the most remote of the masters. With his conviction of intellectual superiority and a sensitive personal pride, there was one thing that was quite impossible for him—a capacity that makes life easier for schoolmasters: he could not be a good fellow with the boys, he could not meet them on their own level. The masters who lived in the Sixth Form Flat took turns keeping order in the halls, and most of them could do it quite amiably; but it went against the grain with Mr. Rolfe. When one of our bedtime roughhouses became too long and too loud, he would suddenly appear in his bathrobe like the Statue in *Don Giovanni* and freeze us to the marrow. A few cutting words would silence us and send us rather sulky to bed. His rebuke had been so evidently hostile that it made us feel hostile, too. But I who admired him so much was embarrassed by what I felt was the indecency of his having to do this kind of thing at all. I felt that he hated our seeing him in his bathrobe, that he ought never to be seen in a bathrobe; and I pictured him lying in bed, as I so loved to do at home, enjoying some book from the well-stocked bookcase which I had seen through the doorway beside his bed without being able to make out the contents. How he must have loathed and resented being distracted by our scuttlings and shrieks, and obliged to climb two flights of stairs and pit himself against ribald and breathless boys. He liked to live in his rooms like a man at his club.

One day I had a glimpse, my only glimpse, of Mr. Rolfe's pre-school personality. It turned out that some cousins of mine had known him at the end of the eighties when he was studying Greek in Dresden. They had stayed at the same pension with him, and they said that he had been wonderful in those days— so charming and so funny. My mother and aunt came up one week-end, and he produced an old photograph of a group in which he and my cousins figured. They had been playing charades in the pension and had had themselves taken in their costumes. He had said sadly of my pretty dark cousin Bessie, my mother afterwards told me—for I had not been present at the conversation: 'So poor Bessie is dead!' I wondered whether he had ever been in love. He was now such a complete old bachelor that this was almost impossible to imagine. I remembered that when he was clowning in his after-dinner speeches he sometimes made fun of his homeliness.

IV

Against one element of life at the Hill School Mr. Rolfe, by his very tone and presence, provided a constant correction. The Hill had an evangelical side which it required some stubbornness to stand up to. This was mainly, I have always understood, due to the influence of Mrs. Meigs—always known as Mrs. John—a very earnest and capable woman related to the theological Dwights of New Haven. The school had passed through a series of dis-asters—three fires as well as a typhoid epidemic in which a hun-dred students and masters had been ill; and it may be that this had had the effect of stimulating in the Meigses a desperate faith in and dependence on God. But what I was aware of at the time when I was in school was simply that we were worked on sys-tematically by a rotation of visiting evangelists. We had to go not only to chapel, but also—under irresistible pressure—to the meetings of a school Y.M.C.A.; and we were always being called together to listen to special exhortations.

At the bottom of the scale of our speakers was the reformed debauchee and bad egg who testified to the miracle of his salvation. He always had what the stage calls a 'straight man' with him, who gave him his cue and showed him off, with an attitude that fell between that of a man with a trained ape and the 'feeder' of a team of comics. These bums who had been saved used to seem to me still very unpleasant people, who had, before seeing the light, evidently reached such a state of corruption that their new respectability looked precarious, and one listened rather apprehensively to their boasts about their present state of grace as if one feared they might go to pieces as soon as the performance was over.

Then there was a man who had made a specialty of preaching to boys' schools and colleges and whose line was a lachrymose and mealy-mouthed virility. He used to read us Kipling in a way that did much to disgust me with that writer, and announce that he would be accessible in a certain room the next morning and would be glad to discuss with any boy any kind of problem whatever. An imitation of 'Weeping Bob's' speeches has long been current among old Hill men and is one of the things that bind them together. 'Moys,' he used to say in his deep adhesive voice, 'I want to speak to you first of all amout the use of foul and filthy language. Moys: they have a nog up in Alaska that they call the mlue-mlack nog. He is known as the mlue-mlack nog because the insine of his mouth is mlue-mlack. And I want to say to any moy who has the impulse to innulge in foul language that, if he gives way to this impulse and hamitually uses oaths and innecent expressions, the insine of his mouth—spir-it-u-ally speaking—*will mecome mlue-mlack like the mouth of the mlue-mlack nog!*'

A more sophisticated level was represented by a liberal preacher from New York. He was well-dressed in a secular way, and dynamic, free-spoken and pear-shaped. His line was to shock and be witty, to be modern in the interests of the evangelist's God. He was also of course social-minded, and I remember a characteristic touch by which he hoped to make us feel, and to convince himself that he felt, a warm sympathy for the laboring classes:

[247]

'Coming up on the train today, I sat opposite an Italian workman. He was dressed in his work-clothes; he had been sweating; but there was nothing dirty about him except the grime of his work. I caught his breath and it smelled of garlic, but it was a good breath; it was wholesome, not foul.' And then of course there were the two-fisted missionaries who shook us down for funds to Christianize and modernize China.

At the center of all this activity stood a kind of special Hill School myth of sin and regeneration. The legend that was handed on from one class at the Hill to another had it that Professor in his college days had been a very fast young fellow, who was known as 'Cigarette Jack,' and that Mrs. John had snatched him as what used to be called a brand from the burning and had made him into the man we knew. This may very well not have been accurate, but it was what we had come to believe: it was like the miraculous conversion from which a cult or an order dates. It was the archetype of the spiritual drama which we seemed to be expected to enact. The hero of this sacred drama was an able and promising boy, well-fitted to be a leader of men, who at college succumbed to temptation: he gambled, he smoked, he drank; he went with a class of women who were not so much bad as misguided. But he was caught on the edge of the abyss and saved for the life of service. I am afraid that there was a little the impression created that you had to have taken the dip toward perdition or you could not make the plane of the élite. The Sixth Form was searched, as it were, every spring for candidates for this sacrificial role. Mrs. John saw every member separately and probed into the state of his soul in a solemn heart-to-heart talk that usually took place in a room on the top floor of the Meigses' house, which was significantly called 'the Sky Parlor.' I have heard the most grueling accounts of the scenes that sometimes occurred at these interviews; but I myself was not a good prospect, and when it came my turn to go, I found that Mrs. John had forgotten the appointment. She was writing at her desk and was surprised to see me; but she made me sit down and told me gently that the literary type of boy had his temptations, too—the temptation, for example, to become so much absorbed in his intellectual interests that he neglected his relation to his fellows, and she prayed with me a moment and let me go. I walked back to my room relieved and yet feeling a little let down that I had not been considered susceptible to the more exciting kind of temptation.

There was a terrible taboo on sex, which was turned into something frightening. Though I was used, before I came to the Hill, to the adolescent folk-lore and gossip of boys of my own age, my speech and my mind had become so purged by the end of my school career that I was shocked when I heard, after leaving, that Mr. Rolfe had once told the story of the man who had started in church when the Seventh Commandment was read and muttered, 'Oh, now I know where I left my umbrella!'

It was true that the boys from Hill had the reputation of slipping at college, and Mrs. John was attempting to fortify them, but her influence worked, also, the other way. If a boy were not naturally serious-minded (as, I must say, a good many were—in which case they had a decided advantage over boys from most other schools), he might forget about the life of service when the restraints of Hill had been removed; but the pattern of the school myth might have been stamped on his mind so strongly that he would be plunged into despair or disorder by the first drinking party or pick-up. (This is no longer true today: the evangelism has disappeared and the paternalism been very much modified.)

I do not know what Mr. Rolfe thought of all this side of Hill; I do not know even what his religious beliefs were. He might have been a liberal Congregationalist or a conventional Episcopalian. He never talked about religion, and when he presided at chapel, he read the Bible in such a way as to make it seem noble and beautiful just as he did Homer. I particularly remember his giving us the last chapter of *Ecclesiastes*, which did not interest our moralistic evangelists. When he prayed, it was never for salvation, but simply for moral stimulus to enable us to deal with our work or get along with our fellows.

V

My own Presbyterian religious training had involved a certain amount of churchgoing and had more or less familiarized me with the Bible, but I had never known what it was to feel faith as something vital; and from the moment I had begun to think about such things for myself, my reactions toward religion had been negative. Under the constant stimulation of the Hill School, however, I tried hard to keep God in my cosmos. I was unable to accept as real for myself—that is, as having serious claims on me—anything that I could not recognize as a part of my own experience, so I had to try to translate my moments of exalted or expansive feeling into terms of the religious illumination about which I was constantly hearing—just as I imagine the eighteenth-century Deists, who had drawn all the rationalistic conclusions, attempted still to provide a Deity who would be somehow the fountainhead of reason. But the fact irreducibly remained that I didn't have the revelatory experience, that I didn't even want it; that my attitude toward our repertoire of dervishes seemed inevitably to become more humorous, and that what had at first been a certain awed respect for this side of the activity of Hill began to give way to the conviction that it was all in awful taste.

One day in my Sixth Form year, when I was coming back to school on the train, I did at last have a sort of revelation, which was, however, as it were, in reverse. I always had to change in Philadelphia, and, as I usually had to wait for my train, I had got into the habit of killing time in Wanamaker's book department. There I bought one by one all the volumes of Bernard Shaw and even, when there were no more to buy—at the moment I graduated—Archibald Henderson's enormous biography. But I had not yet got to this, and on the occasion of which I speak was reading *Major Barbara*. At the end of the preface about money and religion, I came to the following words: 'At present there is not a single credible established religion in the world.' For a moment I was jolted a little; but I looked out the window at the landscape, rather muddy and sordid with winter, and had to recognize that this was true, that I knew perfectly well it was true, and that I ought to have admitted it before; and the flickering childish faith to which I had been giving artificial respiration expired then and there. I have never thought of religion since save as a delusion entertained by other people which one has to try to allow for and understand. On the train another Hill boy had sat down beside me, and I had reluctantly suspended my reading to have a little conversation with him. He was the simple and candid type. He was built stoutly and went in for football and took the Y.M.C.A. seriously. I derived an ironic pleasure from the reflection that, whereas for him our ridiculous prep-school revivalism would still have the power to plunge him into struggles, earnest labors, sleepless nights, my faith had passed quietly out on the stretch between Norristown and Phoenixville, between two passages of banal conversation in which I had descended affably to the level of my companion. I felt as I had never felt before that such people as he were barbarians.

Professor Meigs had died that autumn—the ordeal of the typhoid epidemic was thought to have weakened his heart; and Mr. Rolfe took over as headmaster. The alumni gave a chapel as memorial, and we were using it by the spring of our commencement. We were to have for our last Sunday service of the year a very famous New York preacher whom we had never heard before. It was as if he were the climax and crown of our whole circus procession of evangelists. But this high point of the theological hierarchy marked for me the nadir of faith. I had heard a great deal about this man. He had long been a public figure. He had been associated with Henry Ward Beecher, and later with Theodore Roosevelt. He was one of those preachers of the turn of the century who had been trying to bring the Christianity of the churches into contact with industrial and social problems; he had published several books on the subject, and even, late in life, turned journalist. I had therefore, I think, been prepared for something a little more stimulating than the figure that appeared in the chapel. He was, to be sure, seventy-seven, but he looked even older—he was the oldest-looking person I had ever seen. He had a beard that was long and stringy and that grew out all around his face. It was the kind of undisciplined beard that we associate with Hebrew prophets, but this old man had none of the fire of the prophet. His eyes under their straggling eyebrows had a grayness almost of blindness, and even his skin was gray. His rather long bottle-ended nose had pores so enormous that you could see them plainly as he passed by the pews up the aisle, supported on either side by one of the adoring Meigs ladies and looking as limp in his long black robe as a Punch-and-Judy puppet from which the showman's hand has been removed. I remembered the scene years later when I saw the Diaghilev ballet do Stravinsky's *L'Oiseau de feu*: the figure of Kashchey the Deathless, the enchanter of the Russian fairy-tales, in his flimsy and hirsute senility, reeling back and forth across the stage as the egg that contains his life is tossed from hand to hand, and finally, when it cracks, collapsing into the arms of his faithful attendants while the captives stream out of his castle—this vision has blended in my memory with the image of that Sunday morning service.

It may be that the religious basis of the school had already been somewhat weakened by the breakdown and death of Professor and by the conduct of public ceremonies by the moderate Mr. Rolfe, whose authority was mainly cultural; it may be that this spokesman of the Church at grips with social problems would have seemed a little less deliquescent if Professor had been there behind him. But the whole thing made an unpleasant impression.

The sermon itself was feeble. The subject was immortality—another link with the imperishable Kashchey, who eventually went to pieces; and this old man, who had prided himself on his modernism, announced in a quavering voice that, though we boys with our lives still before us, might not at this time be disposed to give much serious thought to the life after death, this would come, when we got to be old, to seem 've-ery impo-ortant indeed.' This finished immortality for me—since, if your reason, I told myself, had convinced you in your years of vigor that there existed not a shred of evidence for the survival of the human soul, it was an act of weak-mindedness and cowardice to give in to this primitive myth when you had got to the end of your rope and were about to be extinguished yourself.

I argued the question with a friend of mine, a boy of much intellectual ability, who was related to Mrs. Meigs and whose principles were quite in the tradition of the theology of the Dwights. Some time after our argument, he suddenly renewed it: 'Of course you know,' he said, 'that even if there were no immortality, it would be fatal for the human race to take the belief in it away from people.' I had not yet heard the famous saying about how much difference it makes whether you put truth in the first or the second place; but I knew then, as I left school for college, that the code I was evolving for myself could never have much in common with the official morality of Hill.

VI

Mr. Rolfe ran the school for a time, though I imagine he much preferred teaching. I continued to see him occasionally, and I found that my admiration for him held up as few schoolboy admirations do. I used at first to send him books at Christmas, and when he wrote to thank me for them, he never made the polite pretence of having enjoyed them beyond their merits. He acknowledged Compton Mackenzie's *Youth's Encounter*, about which I had written him a hyperbolic letter, with what I thought was the pointed suggestion that 'μηδὲν ἄγαν is a good motto.' I imagine that my own writings after I got out of college were not of a kind that he particularly approved. When I saw him, he used to kid me in a way that I thought rather old fogyish about the then excellent liberal weekly on which I had a job in the twenties.

The *bête noire* of his later years was progressive education. He used to compose little poems on the subject and was very amusing about it. I had a sort of idea at first that I ought to be on the other side, since my magazine supported John Dewey, but the more I read of Mr. Rolfe's satire, which reached me through the Hill School alumni bulletin, the more I felt that there was something to be said for his position. Wasn't it true that, in order to train children to do anything really well, you had to break them to an exacting discipline as he had done with us in Greek? Without that you couldn't do anything with Greek—you couldn't do anything with anything. How great were the chances that a schoolboy could be counted on to choose what he needed?—my father had made me take Greek, I was too young to know anything about it—or to acquire this discipline through natural bent? Mr. Rolfe may to some extent, of course, have misunderstood and misrepresented what was proposed for progressive education; but when I came later on to see something of the teaching both in progressive institutions and in the ordinary kind, I was appalled by the slackness of the training. Where would our American railroads and ships and buildings and bridges and bathrooms be if the techniques of engineering were taught as the arts and humanities are—so that students are graduated from college, and not merely from progressive colleges, and even take M.A. degrees, without having any idea of the top human achievements in their fields, without, often, being able to express themselves in decent English?

It did not really help to point out that much of our old-fashioned teaching was uninspired. As far as inspiration went, Mr. Rolfe could not teach us an irregular declension without lending its cadences poetry; and one felt that it was doubtful whether progressive education would increase the number of inspired teachers. On the other hand, it probably did tend to make people trust unduly to vague ideas and currents of feeling, to the Rousseauist supposed natural instinct to do well if left to oneself. This trust in the impulses of humanity is perhaps only a transference from the heavens to our hearts of the old idea of Providence; and whatever kind of God Mr. Rolfe believed in, this God, like that of A. E. Housman, had not arranged the world so that anything could be accomplished without somebody in particular doing it and doing it with conscious effort. You had to find out about Homer by digging in the Greek lexicon and grammar: you couldn't find out about it by reading an outline of literature written by somebody else; and he had to teach you Greek: Greek wouldn't teach itself. He did not depend for this purpose on the natural rectitude of our inclinations—either his own or ours—any more than he did on the evangelistic Christ who was supposed to come to your rescue and give you a bracer of salvation, as the victims of dementia praecox are supposed to be roused to normality by the jolt of a shot of insulin.

Mr. Rolfe of course thus represented both the American individualistic tradition which has cultivated the readiness to think and act for oneself without looking to God or the State as something outside oneself, and the older humanistic tradition: the belief in the nobility and beauty of what man as man has accomplished, and the reverence for literature as the record of this. I had been exposed at the Hill to this humanistic spirit at the same time as to the inspirational religion which has always remained linked in my mind with the industrial background of Pottstown;

and the humanism had continued to serve me when the religion had come to seem false. The thing that glowed for me through Xenophon and Homer in those classrooms of thirty years ago has glowed for me ever since.

And at the Hill Mr. Rolfe himself long survived the fading-out of that evangelism. There was a time when I tended to think of him as drying up and growing crabbed at school; but I ran into him one day at Columbia, where he was supervising examinations, and was struck by his kindliness and the attractiveness of his face, which seemed to have grown terribly sad. In the crowd of assembled teachers from a variety of schools and colleges, he still stood out as a distinguished figure who did not seem to belong to that company. An old Hill friend has written me recently of seeing him a few years ago: 'I sat next to him at luncheon. He was then eighty years old and told me that the doctors had said he was in perfect health except for low blood pressure. I told him to drink burgundy or bourbon, and he said that I seemed to speak with authority and experience. He said grace, and when I told him it was a *new* grace, he said he'd be glad to sound the buzzer again and deliver the old grace for dessert.' I wrote to Mr. Rolfe when I heard that he was retiring from Hill. In answering, he explained that he still expected to take a few classes, 'but I shall have plenty of time to write, if I can think of anything to write about. . . I am sorry about Greek,' he said. 'I used to think it would last my day, but it hasn't quite done so'; and he wished me good luck in Greek.

He died last June in Concord, and it is hard to imagine him gone: I had thought of him as a permanent element, a kind of human classic, who persisted through the changes at the Hill and the wars and revolutions of the world. After all, there had always been Mr. Rolfe; and suddenly, as I write this memoir, it seems to me that the stream he was following flowed out of a past that is now remote: from Emerson with his self-dependence, and *The Wonderful One-Hoss Shay* with its satire on the too-perfect Calvinist system; from the days when people went to Germany to hear Wagner and study Greek; from Matthew Arnold, from Bernard Shaw—now almost an old-fashioned classic like Arnold. And I am glad to renew my sense of Alfred Rolfe's contribution to it, as I realize that I myself have been trying to follow and feed it at a time when it has been running low. Its tradition antedates our Christian religion and has in many men's minds survived it, as one may hope it will, also, the political creeds, with their secular evangelism, that are taking the Church's place.

1942

THE HISTORICAL INTERPRETATION
OF LITERATURE *

I WANT to talk about the historical interpretation of literature —that is, about the interpretation of literature in its social, economic and political aspects.

To begin with, it will be worth while to say something about the kind of criticism which seems to be furthest removed from this. There is a kind of comparative criticism which tends to be non-historical. The essays of T. S. Eliot, which have had such an immense influence in our time, are, for example, fundamentally non-historical. Eliot sees, or tries to see, the whole of literature, so far as he is acquainted with it, spread out before him under the aspect of eternity. He then compares the work of different periods and countries, and tries to draw from it general conclusions about what literature ought to be. He understands, of course, that our point of view in connection with literature changes, and he has what seems to me a very sound conception of the whole body of writing of the past as something to which new works are continually being added, and which is not thereby merely increased in bulk but modified as a whole—so that Sophocles is no longer precisely what he was for Aristotle, or Shakespeare what he was for Ben Jonson or for Dryden or for Dr. Johnson, on account of all the later literature that has intervened between them and us. Yet at every point of this continual accretion, the whole field may be surveyed, as it were, spread out before the critic. The critic tries to see it as God might; he calls the books to a Day of Judgment. And, looking at things in this way, he may arrive at

* A lecture delivered at Princeton University, October 23, 1940.

interesting and valuable conclusions which could hardly be reached by approaching them in any other way. Eliot was able to see, for example—what I believe had never been noticed before—that the French Symbolist poetry of the nineteenth century had certain fundamental resemblances to the English poetry of the age of Donne. Another kind of critic would draw certain historical conclusions from these purely esthetic findings, as the Russian D. S. Mirsky did; but Eliot does not draw them.

Another example of this kind of non-historical criticism, in a somewhat different way and on a somewhat different plane, is the work of the late George Saintsbury. Saintsbury was a connoisseur of wines; he wrote an entertaining book on the subject. And his attitude toward literature, too, was that of the connoisseur. He tastes the authors and tells you about the vintages; he distinguishes the qualities of the various wines. His palate was as fine as could be, and he possessed the great qualification that he knew how to take each book on its own terms without expecting it to be some other book and was thus in a position to appreciate a great variety of kinds of writing. He was a man of strong social prejudices and peculiarly intransigent political views, but, so far as it is humanly possible, he kept them out of his literary criticism. The result is one of the most agreeable and most comprehensive commentaries on literature that have ever been written in English. Most scholars who have read as much as Saintsbury do not have Saintsbury's discriminating taste. Here is a critic who has covered the whole ground like any academic historian, yet whose account of it is not merely a chronology but a record of fastidious enjoyment. Since enjoyment is the only thing he is looking for, he does not need to know the causes of things, and the historical background of literature does not interest him very much.

There is, however, another tradition of criticism which dates from the beginning of the eighteenth century. In the year 1725, the Neapolitan philosopher Vico published *La Scienza Nuova*, a revolutionary work on the philosophy of history, in which he asserted for the first time that the social world was certainly the work of man, and attempted what is, so far as I know, the first social interpretation of a work of literature. This is what Vico says about Homer: 'Homer composed the *Iliad* when Greece was young and consequently burning with sublime passions such as pride, anger and vengeance—passions which cannot allow dissimulation and which consort with generosity; so that she then admired Achilles, the hero of force. But, grown old, he composed the *Odyssey*, at a time when the passions of Greece were already somewhat cooled by reflection, which is the mother of prudence—so that she now admired Ulysses, the hero of wisdom. Thus also, in Homer's youth, the Greek people liked cruelty, vituperation, savagery, fierceness, ferocity; whereas, when Homer was old, they were already enjoying the luxuries of Alcinoüs, the delights of Calypso, the pleasures of Circe, the songs of the sirens and the pastimes of the suitors, who went no further in aggression and combat than laying siege to the chaste Penelope—all of which practices would appear incompatible with the spirit of the earlier time. The divine Plato is so struck by this difficulty that, in order to solve it, he tells us that Homer had foreseen in inspired vision these dissolute, sickly and disgusting customs. But in this way he makes Homer out to have been but a foolish instructor for Greek civilization, since, however much he may condemn them, he is displaying for imitation these corrupt and decadent habits which were not to be adopted till long after the foundation of the nations of Greece, and accelerating the natural course which human events would take by spurring the Greeks on to corruption. Thus it is plain that the Homer of the *Iliad* must have preceded by many years the Homer who wrote the *Odyssey*; and it is plain that the former must belong to the northeastern part of Greece, since he celebrates the Trojan War, which took place in his part of the country, whereas the latter belongs to the southeastern part, since he celebrates Ulysses, who reigned there.'

You see that Vico has here explained Homer in terms both of historical period and of geographical origin. The idea that human arts and institutions were to be studied and elucidated as the products of the geographical and climatic conditions in which the people who created them lived, and of the phase of their social development through which they were passing at the moment, made great progress during the eighteenth century. There are

[259]

traces of it even in Dr. Johnson, that most orthodox and classical of critics—as, for example, when he accounts for certain characteristics of Shakespeare by the relative barbarity of the age in which he lived, pointing out, just as Vico had done, that 'nations, like individuals, have their infancy.' And by the eighties of the eighteenth century Herder, in his *Ideas on the Philosophy of History*, was writing of poetry that it was a kind of 'Proteus among the people, which is always changing its form in response to the languages, manners, and habits, to the temperaments and climates, nay even to the accents of different nations.' He said— what could still seem startling even so late as that—that 'language was not a divine communication, but something men had produced themselves.' In the lectures on the philosophy of history that Hegel delivered in Berlin in 1822-23, he discussed the national literatures as expressions of the societies which had produced them—societies which he conceived as great organisms continually transforming themselves under the influence of a succession of dominant ideas.

In the field of literary criticism, this historical point of view came to its first complete flower in the work of the French critic Taine, in the middle of the nineteenth century. The whole school of historian-critics to which Taine belonged—Michelet, Renan, Sainte-Beuve—had been occupied in interpreting books in terms of their historical origins. But Taine was the first of these to attempt to apply such principles systematically and on a large scale in a work devoted exclusively to literature. In the Introduction to his *History of English Literature*, published in 1863, he made his famous pronouncement that works of literature were to be understood as the upshot of three interfusing factors: *the moment, the race and the milieu*. Taine thought he was a scientist and a mechanist, who was examining works of literature from the same point of view as the chemist's in experimenting with chemical compounds. But the difference between the critic and the chemist is that the critic cannot first combine his elements and then watch to see what they will do: he can only examine phenomena which have already taken place. The procedure that Taine actually follows is to pretend to set the stage for the experiment by describing the moment, the race and the milieu, and then to say: 'Such a situation demands such and such a kind of writer.' He now goes on to describe the kind of writer that the situation demands, and the reader finds himself at the end confronted with Shakespeare or Milton or Byron or whoever the great figure is—who turns out to prove the accuracy of Taine's prognosis by precisely living up to this description.

There was thus a certain element of imposture in Taine; but it was the rabbits he pulled out that saved him. If he had really been the mechanist that he thought he was, his work on literature would have had little value. The truth was that Taine loved literature for its own sake—he was at his best himself a brilliant artist—and he had very strong moral convictions which give his writing emotional power. His mind, to be sure, was an analytic one, and his analysis, though terribly oversimplified, does have an explanatory value. Yet his work was what we call creative. Whatever he may say about chemical experiments, it is evident when he writes of a great writer that the moment, the race and the milieu have combined, like the three sounds of the chord in Browning's poem about Abt Vogler, to produce not a fourth sound but a star.

To Taine's set of elements was added, dating from the middle of the century, a new element, the economic, which was introduced into the discussion of historical phenomena mainly by Marx and Engels. The non-Marxist critics themselves were at the time already taking into account the influence of the social classes. In his chapters on the Norman conquest of England, Taine shows that the difference between the literatures produced respectively by the Normans and by the Saxons was partly the difference between a ruling class, on the one hand, and a vanquished and repressed class, on the other. And Michelet, in his volume on the Regency, which was finished the same year that the *History of English Literature* appeared, studies the *Manon Lescaut* of the Abbé Prévost as a document representing the point of view of the small gentry before the French Revolution. But Marx and Engels derived the social classes from the way that people made or got their livings—from what they called the *methods of pro-*

duction; and they tended to regard these economic processes as fundamental to civilization.

The Dialectical Materialism of Marx and Engels was not really so materialistic as it sounds. There was in it a large element of the Hegelian idealism that Marx and Engels thought they had got rid of. At no time did these two famous materialists take so mechanistic a view of things as Taine began by professing; and their theory of the relation of works of literature to what they called the *economic base* was a good deal less simple than Taine's theory of the moment, the race and the milieu. They thought that art, politics, religion, philosophy and literature belonged to what they called the *superstructure* of human activity; but they saw that the practitioners of these various professions tended also to constitute social groups, and that they were always pulling away from the kind of solidarity based on economic classes in order to establish a professional solidarity of their own. Furthermore, the activities of the superstructure could influence one another, and they could influence the economic base. It may be said of Marx and Engels in general that, contrary to the popular impression, they were tentative, confused and modest when it came down to philosophical first principles, where a materialist like Taine was cocksure. Marx once made an attempt to explain why the poems of Homer were so good when the society that produced them was from his point of view—that is, from the point of view of its industrial development—so primitive; and this gave him a good deal of trouble. If we compare his discussion of this problem with Vico's discussion of Homer, we see that the explanation of literature in terms of a philosophy of social history is becoming, instead of simpler and easier, more difficult and more complex.

Marx and Engels were deeply imbued, moreover, with the German admiration for literature, which they had learned from the age of Goethe. It would never have occurred to either of them that *der Dichter* was not one of the noblest and most beneficent of humankind. When Engels writes about Goethe, he presents him as a man equipped for 'practical life,' whose career was frustrated by the 'misery' of the historical situation in Germany in his time, and reproaches him for allowing himself to lapse into the 'cautious, smug and narrow' philistinism of the class from which he came; but Engels regrets this, because it interfered with the development of the 'mocking, defiant, world-despising genius,' 'der geniale Dichter,' 'der gewaltige Poet,' of whom Engels would not even, he says, have asked that he should have been a political liberal if Goethe had not sacrificed to his bourgeois shrinkings his truer esthetic sense. And the great critics who were trained on Marx—Franz Mehring and Bernard Shaw—had all this reverence for the priesthood of literature. Shaw deplores the absence of political philosophy and what he regards as the middle-class snobbery in Shakespeare; but he celebrates Shakespeare's poetry and his dramatic imagination almost as enthusiastically as Swinburne does, describing even those potboiling comedies, *Twelfth Night* and *As You Like It*—the themes of which seem to him most trashy—as 'the Crown Jewels of English dramatic poetry.' Such a critic may do more for a writer by showing him as a real man dealing with a real world at a definite moment of time than the impressionist critic of Swinburne's type who flourished in the same period of the late nineteenth century. The purely impressionist critic approaches the whole of literature as an exhibit of belletristic jewels, and he can only write a rhapsodic catalogue. But when Shaw turned his spotlight on Shakespeare as a figure in the Shavian drama of history, he invested him with a new interest as no other English critic had done.

The insistence that the man of letters should play a political role, the disparagement of works of art in comparison with political action, were thus originally no part of Marxism. They only became associated with it later. This happened by way of Russia, and it was due to special tendencies in that country that date from long before the Revolution or the promulgation of Marxism itself. In Russia there have been very good reasons why the political implications of literature should particularly occupy the critics. The art of Pushkin itself, with its marvelous power of implication, had certainly been partly created by the censorship of Nicholas I, and Pushkin set the tradition for most of the great Russian writers that followed him. Every play, every poem, every story, must be a parable of which the moral is *implied*. If it were stated, the censor would suppress the book as he tried to do with

Pushkin's *Bronze Horseman,* where it was merely a question of the packed implications protruding a little too plainly. Right down through the writings of Chekhov and up almost to the Revolution, the imaginative literature of Russia presents the peculiar paradox of an art that is technically objective and yet charged with social messages. In Russia under the Tsar, it was inevitable that social criticism should lead to political conclusions, because the most urgent need from the point of view of any kind of improvement was to get rid of the tsarist regime. Even the neo-Christian moralist Tolstoy, who pretended to be non-political, was to exert a subversive influence, because his independent preaching was bound to embroil him with the Church, and the Church was an integral part of the tsardom. Tolstoy's pamphlet called *What Is Art?*, in which he throws overboard Shakespeare and a large part of modern literature, including his own novels, in the interest of his intransigent morality, is the example which is most familiar to us of the moralizing Russian criticism; but it was only the most sensational expression of a kind of approach which had been prevalent since Belinsky and Chernyshevsky in the early part of the century. The critics, who were usually journalists writing in exile or in a contraband press, were always tending to demand of the imaginative writers that they should dramatize bolder morals.

Even after the Revolution had destroyed the tsarist government, this state of things did not change. The old habits of censorship persisted in the new socialist society of the Soviets, which was necessarily made up of people who had been stamped by the die of the despotism. We meet here the peculiar phenomenon of a series of literary groups that attempt, one after the other, to obtain official recognition or to make themselves sufficiently powerful to establish themselves as arbiters of literature. Lenin and Trotsky and Lunacharsky had the sense to oppose these attempts: the comrade-dictators of Proletcult or Lev or Rapp would certainly have been just as bad as the Count Benckendorff who made Pushkin miserable, and when the Stalin bureaucracy, after the death of Gorky, got control of this department as of everything else, they instituted a system of repression that made Benckendorff and Nicholas I look like Lorenzo de' Medici. In the meantime, Trotsky, who was Commissar of War but himself a great political writer with an interest in belles-lettres, attempted, in 1924, apropos of one of these movements, to clarify the situation. He wrote a brilliant and valuable book called *Literature and Revolution*, in which he explained the aims of the government, analyzed the work of the Russian writers, and praised or rebuked the latter as they seemed to him in harmony or at odds with the former. Trotsky is intelligent, sympathetic; it is evident that he is really fond of literature and that he knows that a work of art does not fulfill its function in terms of the formulas of party propaganda. But Mayakovsky, the Soviet poet, whom Trotsky had praised with reservations, expressed himself in a famous joke when he was asked what he thought of Trotsky's book—a pun which implied that a Commissar turned critic was inevitably a Commissar still *; and what a foreigner cannot accept in Trotsky is his assumption that it is the duty of the government to take a hand in the direction of literature.

This point of view, indigenous to Russia, has been imported to other countries through the permeation of Communist influence. The Communist press and its literary followers have reflected the control of the Kremlin in all the phases through which it has passed, down to the wholesale imprisonment of Soviet writers which has been taking place since 1935. But it has never been a part of the American system that our Republican or Democratic administration should lay down a political line for the guidance of the national literature. A recent gesture in this direction on the part of Archibald MacLeish, who seems a little carried away by his position as Librarian of Congress, was anything but cordially received by serious American writers. So long as the United States remains happily a non-totalitarian country, we can very well do without this aspect of the historical criticism of literature.

Another element of a different order has, however, since Marx's time been added to the historical study of the origins of works of literature. I mean the psychoanalysis of Freud. This appears as an extension of something which had already got well started before, which had figured even in Johnson's *Lives of the Poets*, and

---

* Первый блин лег наркомом, *The first pancake lies like a narkom* (people's commissar) — a parody of the Russian saying, Первый блин лег комом, *The first pancake lies like a lump*.

of which the great exponent had been Sainte-Beuve: the interpretation of works of literature in the light of the personalities behind them. But the Freudians made this interpretation more exact and more systematic. The great example of the psychoanalysis of an artist is Freud's own essay on Leonardo da Vinci; but this has little critical interest: it is an attempt to construct a case history. One of the best examples I know of the application of Freudian analysis to literature is in Van Wyck Brooks's book, *The Ordeal of Mark Twain,* in which Mr. Brooks uses an incident of Mark Twain's boyhood as a key to his whole career. Mr. Brooks has since repudiated the method he resorted to here, on the ground that no one but an analyst can ever know enough about a writer to make a valid psychoanalytic diagnosis. This is true, and it is true of the method that it has led to bad results where the critic has built a Freudian mechanism out of very slender evidence, and then given us what is really merely a romance exploiting the supposed working of this mechanism, in place of an actual study that sticks close to the facts and the documents of the writer's life and work. But I believe that Van Wyck Brooks really had hold of something important when he fixed upon that childhood incident of which Mark Twain gave so vivid an account to his biographer—that scene at the deathbed of his father when his mother had made him promise that he would not break her heart. If it was not one of those crucial happenings that are supposed to determine the complexes of Freud, it has certainly a typical significance in relation to Mark Twain's whole psychology. The stories that people tell about their childhood are likely to be profoundly symbolic even when they have been partly or wholly made up in the light of later experience. And the attitudes, the compulsions, the emotional 'patterns' that recur in the work of a writer are of great interest to the historical critic.

These attitudes and patterns are embedded in the community and the historical moment, and they may indicate its ideals and its diseases as the cell shows the condition of the tissue. The recent scientific experimentation in the combining of Freudian with Marxist method, and of psychoanalysis with anthropology, has had its parallel development in criticism. And there is thus another element added to our equipment for analyzing literary works, and the problem grows still more complex.

The analyst, however, is of course not concerned with the comparative values of his patients any more than the surgeon is. He cannot tell you why the neurotic Dostoevsky produces work of immense value to his fellows while another man with the same neurotic pattern would become a public menace. Freud himself emphatically states in his study of Leonardo that his method can make no attempt to account for Leonardo's genius. The problems of comparative artistic value still remain after we have given attention to the Freudian psychological factor just as they do after we have given attention to the Marxist economic factor and to the racial and geographical factors. No matter how thoroughly and searchingly we may have scrutinized works of literature from the historical and biographical points of view, we must be ready to attempt to estimate, in some such way as Saintsbury and Eliot do, the relative degrees of success attained by the products of the various periods and the various personalities. We must be able to tell good from bad, the first-rate from the second-rate. We shall not otherwise write literary criticism at all, but merely social or political history as reflected in literary texts, or psychological case histories from past eras, or, to take the historical point of view in its simplest and most academic form, merely chronologies of books that have been published.

And now how, in these matters of literary art, do we tell the good art from the bad? Norman Kemp Smith, the Kantian philosopher, whose courses I was fortunate enough to take at Princeton twenty-five years ago, used to tell us that this recognition was based primarily on an emotional reaction. For purposes of practical criticism this is a safe assumption on which to proceed. It is possible to discriminate in a variety of ways the elements that in any given department go to make a successful work of literature. Different schools have at different times demanded different things of literature: *unity, symmetry, universality, originality, vision, inspiration, strangeness, suggestiveness, improving morality, socialist realism,* etc. But you could have any set of these qualities that any school of writing has called for and still not have a good play, a good novel, a good poem, a good history. If you identify the essence of good literature with any one of these elements or with any combination of them, you simply shift the emotional reaction to the recognition of the element or elements. Or if you add to your other demands the demand that the writer must have *talent*, you simply shift this recognition to the talent. Once people find some grounds of agreement in the coincidence of their emotional reactions to books, they may be able to discuss these elements profitably; but if they do not have this basic agreement, the discussion will make no sense.

But how, you may ask, can we identify this élite who know what they are talking about? Well, it can only be said of them that they are self-appointed and self-perpetuating, and that they will compel you to accept their authority. Impostors may try to put themselves over, but these quacks will not last. The implied position of the people who know about literature (as is also the case in every other art) is simply that they know what they know, and that they are determined to impose their opinions by main force of eloquence or assertion on the people who do not know. This is not a question, of course, of professional workers in literature—such as editors, professors and critics, who very often have no real understanding of the products with which they deal—but of readers of all kinds in all walks of life. There are moments when a first-rate writer, unrecognized or out of fashion with the official chalkers-up for the market, may find his support in the demand for his work of an appreciative cultivated public.

But what is the cause of this emotional reaction which is the critic's divining rod? This question has long been a subject of study by the branch of philosophy called esthetics, and it has recently been made a subject of scientific experimentation. Both these lines of inquiry are likely to be prejudiced in the eyes of the literary critic by the fact that the inquiries are sometimes conducted by persons who are obviously deficient in literary feeling or taste. Yet one should not deny the possibility that something of value might result from the speculations and explorations of men of acute minds who take as their primary data the esthetic emotions of other men.

Almost everybody interested in literature has tried to explain to himself the nature of these emotions that register our approval of artistic works; and I of course have my own explanation.

In my view, all our intellectual activity, in whatever field it takes place, is an attempt to give a meaning to our experience— that is, to make life more practicable; for by understanding things we make it easier to survive and get around among them. The mathematician Euclid, working in a convention of abstractions, shows us relations between the distances of our unwieldy and cluttered-up environment upon which we are able to count. A drama of Sophocles also indicates relations between the various human impulses, which appear so confused and dangerous, and it brings out a certain justice of Fate—that is to say, of the way in which the interaction of these impulses is seen in the long run to work out—upon which we can also depend. The kinship, from this point of view, of the purposes of science and art appears very clearly in the case of the Greeks, because not only do both Euclid and Sophocles satisfy us by making patterns, but they make much the same kind of patterns. Euclid's *Elements* takes simple theorems and by a series of logical operations builds them up to a climax in the square on the hypotenuse. A typical drama of Sophocles develops in a similar way.

Some writers (as well as some scientists) have a different kind of explicit message beyond the reassurance implicit in the mere feat of understanding life or of molding the harmony of artistic form. Not content with such an achievement as that of Sophocles—who has one of his choruses tell us that it is better not to be born, but who, by representing life as noble and based on law, makes its tragedy easier to bear—such writers attempt, like Plato, to think out and recommend a procedure for turning it into something better. But other departments of literature—lyric poetry such as Sappho's, for example—have *less* philosophical content than Sophocles. A lyric gives us nothing but a pattern imposed on the expression of a feeling; but this pattern of metrical quantities and of consonants and vowels that balance has the effect of reducing the feeling, however unruly or painful it may seem when we experience it in the course of our lives, to something orderly, symmetrical and pleasing; and it also relates this feeling to the more impressive scheme, works it into the larger texture, of the body of poetic art. The

[269]

discord has been resolved, the anomaly subjected to discipline. And this control of his emotion by the poet has the effect at second-hand of making it easier for the reader to manage his own emotions. (Why certain sounds and rhythms gratify us more than others, and how they are connected with the themes and ideas that they are chosen as appropriate for conveying, are questions that may be passed on to the scientist.)

And this brings us back again to the historical point of view. The experience of mankind on the earth is always changing as man develops and has to deal with new combinations of elements; and the writer who is to be anything more than an echo of his predecessors must always find expression for something which has never yet been expressed, must master a new set of phenomena which has never yet been mastered. With each such victory of the human intellect, whether in history, in philosophy or in poetry, we experience a deep satisfaction: we have been cured of some ache of disorder, relieved of some oppressive burden of uncomprehended events.

This relief that brings the sense of power, and, with the sense of power, joy, is the positive emotion which tells us that we have encountered a first-rate piece of literature. But stay! you may at this point warn: are not people often solaced and exhilarated by literature of the trashiest kind? They are: crude and limited people do certainly feel some such emotion in connection with work that is limited and crude. The man who is more highly organized and has a wider intellectual range will feel it in connection with work that is finer and more complex. The difference between the emotion of the more highly organized man and the emotion of the less highly organized one is a matter of mere gradation. You sometimes discover books—the novels of John Steinbeck, for example—that seem to mark precisely the borderline between work that is definitely superior and work that is definitely bad. When I was speaking a little while back of the genuine connoisseurs who establish the standards of taste, I meant, of course, the people who can distinguish Grade A and who prefer it to the other grades.

THE WOUND AND THE BOW

Seven Studies in Literature

I bleed by the black stream
For my torn bough!

JAMES JOYCE

DICKENS: THE TWO SCROOGES

To the Students of English 354,
University of Chicago, Summer, 1939

Of ALL THE great English writers, Charles Dickens has received in his own country the scantiest serious attention from either biographers, scholars, or critics. He has become for the English middle class so much one of the articles of their creed — a familiar joke, a favorite dish, a Christmas ritual — that it is difficult for British pundits to see in him the great artist and social critic that he was. Dickens had no university education, and the literary men from Oxford and Cambridge, who have lately been sifting fastidiously so much of the English heritage, have rather snubbingly let him alone. The Bloomsbury that talked about Dostoevsky ignored Dostoevsky's master, Dickens. What happens when the London of Lytton Strachey does take Dickens up is shown in Hugh Kingsmill's book, *The Sentimental Journey*, in which the man who was called by Taine 'the master of all hearts' is made into one of those Victorian scarecrows with ludicrous Freudian flaws — so infantile, pretentious, and hypocritical as to deserve only a perfunctory sneer.

Since Forster's elaborate memoir, which even in the supplemented edition of Ley has never been a real biography, no authoritative book about Dickens has been published. Some of the main facts about his life have till recently been kept from the public, and now that they have finally

3

come out they have usually been presented either by dod-
dering Dickens-fanciers or through the medium of garrulous memoirs. Mr. Ralph Straus and Mr. T. A. Jackson
have recently published studies of Dickens — the one from
the psychological, the other from the Marxist, point of
view — which attempt a more searching treatment; but
though they contain some valuable insights, neither is
really first-rate, for neither handles surely enough or carries to fundamental findings the line which it undertakes.
The typical Dickens expert is an old duffer who, as Mr.
Straus has said, is primarily interested in proving that
Mr. Pickwick stopped at a certain inn and slept in a certain bed.

As for criticism, there has been in English one admirable critic of Dickens, George Gissing, whose prefaces
and whose book on Dickens not only are the best thing on
Dickens in English but stand out as one of the few really
first-rate pieces of literary criticism produced by an Englishman of the end of the century. For the rest, you have
mainly G. K. Chesterton, who turned out in his books on
Dickens some of the best work of which he was capable
and who said some excellent things, but whose writing
here as elsewhere is always melting away into that peculiar
pseudo-poetic booziness which verbalizes with large conceptions and ignores the most obtrusive actualities. Chesterton celebrated the jolly Dickens; and Bernard Shaw offset this picture by praising the later and gloomier Dickens
and insisting on his own debt to the author of Little Dorrit
at a time when it was taken for granted that he must derive from such foreigners as Ibsen and Nietzsche.

Chesterton asserted that time would show that Dickens
was not merely one of the Victorians, but incomparably
the greatest English writer of his time; and Shaw coupled
his name with that of Shakespeare. It is the conviction of
the present writer that both these judgments were justified. Dickens — though he cannot of course pretend to the

rank where Shakespeare has few companions — was nevertheless the greatest dramatic writer that the English had had since Shakespeare, and he created the largest and most varied world. It is the purpose of this essay to show that we may find in Dickens' work today a complexity and a depth to which even Gissing and Shaw have hardly, it seems to me, done justice — an intellectual and artistic interest which makes Dickens loom very large in the whole perspective of the literature of the West.

I

The father of Charles Dickens' father was head butler in the house of John Crewe (later Lord Crewe) of Crewe Hall, Member of Parliament for Chester; and the mother of his father was a servant in the house of The Marquess of Blandford in Grosvenor Square, who was Lord Chamberlain to the Household of George III. This grandmother, after her marriage, became housekeeper at Crewe Hall, and it is assumed that it was through the patronage of her employer that her son John Dickens was given a clerkship in the Navy Pay Office.

John Dickens began at £70 a year and was in time increased to £350. But he had always had the tastes of a gentleman. He was an amiable fellow, with an elegant manner and a flowery vein of talk, who liked to entertain his friends and who could not help creating the impression of a way of life beyond his means. He was always in trouble over bills.

When Charles, who had been born (February 7, 1812) at Portsmouth and had spent most of his childhood out of London at Portsmouth, Portsea and Chatham, who had had a chance to go to the theater and to read the *Arabian Nights* and the eighteenth-century novelists, and had been taught by a tutor from Oxford, came up to London at the age of nine to join his parents, who had been obliged to return there, he was terribly shocked to find them, as a consequence of his father's debts, now living in a little back garret in one of the poorest streets of Camden Town. On February 20, 1824, when Charles was twelve, John Dickens was arrested for debt and taken to the Marshalsea Prison, announcing, as he left the house: 'The sun has set upon me forever!' At home the food began to run low; and they had to pawn the household belongings till all but two rooms were bare. Charles even had to carry his books, one by one, to the pawnshop. It was presently decided that the boy should go to work at six shillings a week for a cousin who manufactured blacking; and through six months, in a rickety old house by the river, full of dirt and infested with rats, he pasted labels on blacking bottles, in the company of riverside boys who called him 'the little gentleman.' He wanted terribly to go on with his schooling, and couldn't grasp what had happened to him. The whole of the rest of the family moved into the Marshalsea with his father; and Charles, who had a lodging near them, went to the jail after work every evening and ate breakfast with them every morning. He was so ashamed of the situation that he would never allow his companion at the blacking warehouse, whose name was Bob Fagin, to go with him to the door of the prison, but would take leave of him and walk up the steps of a strange house and pretend to be going in. He had had a kind of nervous fits in his earlier childhood, and now these began to recur. One day at work he was seized with such an acute spasm that he had to lie down on some straw on the floor, and the boys who worked with him spent half the day applying blacking bottles of hot water to his side.

John Dickens inherited a legacy in May and got out of jail the twenty-eighth; but he let Charles keep on working in the warehouse. The little boys did their pasting next to the window in order to get the light, and people used to stop to look in at them because they had become so quick and skilful at it. This was an added humiliation for Charles; and one day when John Dickens came there, he wondered how his father could bear it. At last — perhaps, Dickens thought, as a result of what he had seen on this visit — John quarreled with Charles's employer, and took the boy out of the warehouse and sent him to school.

These experiences produced in Charles Dickens a trauma from which he suffered all his life. It has been charged by some of Dickens' critics that he indulged himself excessively in self-pity in connection with these hardships of his childhood; it has been pointed out that, after all, he had only worked in the blacking warehouse six months. But one must realize that during those months he was in a state of complete despair. For the adult in desperate straits, it is almost always possible to imagine, if not to contrive, some way out; for the child, from whom love and freedom have inexplicably been taken away, no relief or release can be projected. Dickens' seizures in his blacking-bottle days were obviously neurotic symptoms; and the psychologists have lately been telling us that lasting depressions and terrors may be caused by such cuttings-short of the natural development of childhood. For an imaginative and active boy of twelve, six months of despair are quite enough. 'No words can express,' Dickens wrote of his first introduction to the warehouse, in a document he gave to Forster, 'the secret agony of my soul as I sunk into this companionship; compared these every day associates with those of my happier childhood; and felt my early hopes of growing up to be a learned and distinguished man crushed in my breast. The deep remembrance of the sense I had of being utterly neglected and hopeless; of the shame I felt in my position; of the misery it was to my young heart to believe that, day by day, what I had learned, and thought, and delighted in, and raised my fancy and my emulation up by, was passing away from me, never to be brought back any more; cannot be written. My whole nature was so penetrated with the grief and humiliation of such considerations, that even now, famous and caressed and happy, I often forget in my dreams that I have a dear wife and children; even that I am a man; and wander desolately back to that time of my life.'

He never understood how his father could have abandoned him to such a situation. 'I know my father,' he once told Forster, 'to be as kind-hearted and generous a man as ever lived in the world. Everything that I can remember of his conduct to his wife, or children, or friends, in sickness or affliction is beyond all praise. By me, as a sick child, he has watched night and day, unweariedly and patiently, many nights and days. He never undertook any business, charge or trust that he did not zealously, conscientiously, punctually, honorably discharge. His industry has always been untiring. He was proud of me, in his way, and had a great admiration of [my] comic singing. But, in the case of his temper, and the straitness of his means, he appeared to have lost utterly at this time the idea of educating me at all, and to have utterly put from him the notion that I had any claim upon him, in that regard, whatever.' And Charles never forgave his mother for having wanted to keep him working in the warehouse even after his father had decided to take him out. 'I never afterwards forgot,' he wrote of her attitude at this time. 'I never shall forget, I never can forget.'

Of those months he had never been able to bring himself to speak till, just before conceiving *David Copperfield*, he wrote the fragment of autobiography he sent to Forster; and, even after he had incorporated this material in an altered form in the novel, even his wife and children were never to learn about the realities of his childhood till they read about it after his death in Forster's *Life*. But the work of Dickens' whole career was an attempt to digest these early shocks and hardships, to explain them to himself, to justify himself in relation to them, to give an intelligible and tolerable picture of a world in which such things could occur.

Behind the misfortune which had humiliated Charles was the misfortune which had humiliated his father. John Dickens was a good and affectionate man, who had done the best he was able within the limits of his personality and who had not deserved to be broken. But behind these undeserved misfortunes were sources of humiliation perhaps more disturbing still. The father of Charles Dickens' mother, also a £350-a-year clerk in the Navy Pay Office, with the title of Conductor of Money, had systematically, by returning false balances, embezzled funds to the amount of £5689 3s. 3d. over a period of seven years; and when the fraud was discovered, had fled. And the background of domestic service was for an Englishman of the nineteenth century probably felt as more disgraceful than embezzlement. Certainly the facts about Dickens' ancestry were kept hidden by Dickens himself and have, so far as I know, only been fully revealed in the memoir by Miss Gladys Storey, based on interviews with Mrs. Perugini, Dickens' last surviving daughter, which was published in England in the summer of 1939.

But all these circumstances are worth knowing and bearing in mind, because they help us to understand what Dickens was trying to say. He was less given to false moral attitudes or to fear of respectable opinion than most of the great Victorians; but just as through the offices of his friends and admirers his personal life has been screened from the public even up to our own day, in a way that would have been thought unjustified in the case of a Keats or a Byron of the earlier nineteenth century, so the meaning of Dickens' work has been obscured by that element of the conventional which Dickens himself never quite outgrew. It is necessary to see him as a man in order to appreciate him as an artist — to exorcise the spell which has bewitched him into a stuffy piece of household furni-

ture and to give him his proper rank as the poet of that
portièred and upholstered world who saw clearest through
the coverings and the curtains.

II

If one approaches his first novel, *Pickwick Papers,* with
these facts of Dickens' biography in mind, one is struck by
certain features of the book which one may not have noticed before.

Here the subject has been set for Dickens. He was supposed to provide some sort of text for a series of comic
sporting plates by Seymour — something in the vein of
Surtees' *Jorrocks.* As soon, however, as Dickens' scheme
gives him a chance to get away from the sporting plates
and to indulge his own preoccupations, the work takes a
different turn.

There are in *Pickwick Papers,* especially in the early
part, a whole set of interpolated short stories which make
a contrast with the narrative proper. These stories are
mostly pretty bad and deserve from the literary point of
view no more attention than they usually get; but, even
allowing here also for an element of the conventional and
popular, of the still-thriving school of Gothic horror, we
are surprised to find rising to the surface already the
themes which were to dominate his later work.

The first of these interludes in *Pickwick* deals with the
death of a pantomime clown, reduced through drink to
the direst misery, who, in the delirium of his fever, imagines that he is about to be murdered by the wife whom he
has been beating. In the second story, a worthless husband
also beats his wife and sets an example of bad conduct to
his son; the boy commits a robbery, gets caught and convicted — in prison remains obdurate to his mother's attempts to soften his sullen heart; she dies, he repents, it is
too late; he is transported, returns after seventeen years

and finds no one to love or greet him; he stumbles at last upon his father, now a sodden old man in the workhouse; a scene of hatred and violence ensues; the father, filled with terror, strikes the son across the face with a stick, the son seizes the father by the throat, and the old man bursts a blood-vessel and falls dead. The third story is a document by a madman, which, like the delirium of the dying clown, gives Dickens an opportunity to exploit that vein of hysterical fancy which was to find fuller scope in *Barnaby Rudge* and which was there to figure for him the life of the imagination itself. The narrator has lived in the knowledge that he is to be the victim of hereditary insanity. At last he feels that he is going mad, but at the same moment he inherits money: men fawn upon him and praise him now, but he secretly rejoices in the sense that he is not one of them, that he is fooling them. He marries a girl, who loves another but who has been sold to him by her father and brothers; seeing his wife languish away and coming to understand the situation, fearing also lest she may hand on the family curse, he tries to kill her in her sleep with a razor; she wakes up but dies of the shock. When one of her brothers comes to reproach him, the madman throws him down and chokes him; runs amuck and is finally caught.

But it is in *The Old Man's Tale About the Queer Client* (Chapter XXI) that Dickens' obsessions appear most plainly. Here at the threshold of Dickens' work we are confronted with the Marshalsea Prison. A prisoner for debt, a 'healthy, strong-made man, who could have borne almost any fatigue of active exertion,' wastes away in his confinement and sees his wife and child die of grief and want. He swears to revenge their deaths on the man who has put him there. We have another long passage of delirium, at the end of which the prisoner comes to, to learn that he has inherited his father's money. At a seaside resort where he has been living, he sees a man drowning one evening: the father of the drowning man stands by and begs the ex-prisoner to save his son. But when the wronged man recognizes his father-in-law, the scoundrel who sent him to prison and who allowed his own daughter and grandson to die, he retaliates by letting the boy drown; then, not content with this, he buys up, at 'treble and quadruple their nominal value,' a number of loans which have been made to the old man. These loans have been arranged on the understanding that they are renewable up to a certain date; but the wronged man, taking advantage of the fact that the agreement has never been put on paper, proceeds to call them in at a time when his father-in-law has 'sustained many losses.' The old man is dispossessed of all his property and finally runs away in order to escape prison; but his persecutor tracks him down to a 'wretched lodging' — note well: 'in Camden Town' — and there finally reveals himself and announces his implacable intention of sending his persecutor to jail. The old man falls dead from shock, and the revenger disappears.

In the meantime, the same theme has been getting under way in the main current of the comic novel. Mr. Pickwick has been framed by Dodson and Fogg, and very soon — another wronged man — he will land in the debtors' prison, where a good many of the other characters will join him and where the whole book will deepen with a new dimension of seriousness. The hilarity of the scene in court, in which Mr. Pickwick is convicted of trifling with Mrs. Bardell's affections — a scene openly borrowed from *Jorrocks* but wonderfully transformed by Dickens, and as brilliant as the story of the fiendish revenge on the fiendish father-in-law is bathetic — may disguise from the reader the significance which this episode had for Dickens. Here Dickens is one of the greatest of humorists: it is a laughter which is never vulgar but which discloses the vulgarity of the revered — a laughter of human ecstasy that rises like the phœnix from the cinders to which the dismal denizens of the tribunals have attempted to reduce decent human beings. It represents, like the laughter of Aristophanes, a real escape from institutions.

I shall make no attempt to discuss at length the humor of the early Dickens. This is the aspect of his work that is best known, the only aspect that some people know. In praise of Dickens' humor, there is hardly anything new to say. The only point I want to make is that the humor of Dickens does differ from such humor as that of Aristophanes in being unable forever to inhabit an empyrean of blithe intellectual play, of charming fancies and biting good sense. Dickens' laughter is an exhilaration which already shows a trace of the hysterical. It leaps free of the prison of life; but gloom and soreness must always drag it back. Before he has finished *Pickwick* and even while he is getting him out of jail and preparing to unite the lovers, the prison will close in again on Dickens. While he is still on the last instalments of *Pickwick,* he will begin writing *Oliver Twist* — the story of a disinherited boy, consigned to a workhouse which is virtually a jail and getting away only to fall into the hands of a gang of burglars, pickpockets and prostitutes.

And now we must identify the attitudes with which Dickens' origins and his early experiences had caused him to meet mankind. The ideal of *Pickwick Papers* is a kindly retired business man, piloted through a tough and treacherous world by a shrewd servant of watchful fidelity, who perfectly knows his place: Mr. Pickwick and Sam Weller. But this picture, though real enough to its creator, soon gives way to the figure of a parentless and helpless child — a figure of which the pathos will itself be eclipsed by the horror of the last night in the condemned cell of a betrayer of others to the gallows, and by the headlong descent into hell of a brute who clubs his girl to death and who, treed like a cat by the pursuing mob, hangs himself in trying to escape.

III

Edmund Yates described Dickens' expression as 'blunt' and 'pleasant,' but 'rather defiant.'

For the man of spirit whose childhood has been crushed by the cruelty of organized society, one of two attitudes is natural: that of the criminal or that of the rebel. Charles Dickens, in imagination, was to play the rôles of both, and to continue up to his death to put into them all that was most passionate in his feeling.

His interest in prisons and prisoners is evident from the very beginning. In his first book, *Sketches by Boz*, he tells how he used to gaze at Newgate with 'mingled feelings of awe and respect'; and he sketches an imaginary picture of a condemned man's last night alive, which he is soon to elaborate in *Oliver Twist*. Almost the only passage in *American Notes* which shows any real readiness on Dickens' part to enter into the minds and feelings of the people among whom he is traveling is the fantasy in which he imagines the effects of a sentence of solitary confinement in a Philadelphia jail. He visited prisons wherever he went, and he later found this cruel system imitated in the jail at Lausanne. Dickens was very much gratified when the system was finally abandoned as the result of the prisoners' going mad just as he had predicted they would. He also wrote a great deal about executions. One of the vividest things in *Pictures from Italy* is a description of a guillotining; and one of the most impressive episodes in *Barnaby Rudge* is the narration — developed on a formidable scale — of the hanging of the leaders of the riots. In 1846, Dickens wrote letters to the press in protest against capital punishment for murderers, on the ground among other grounds that this created sympathy for the culprits; in 1849, after attending some executions in Lon-

don with Forster, he started by writing to *The Times* an
agitation which had the effect of getting public hangings
abolished. Even in 1867, in the course of his second visit
to America, 'I have been tempted out,' Dickens wrote
Forster, 'at three in the morning to visit one of the large
police station-houses, and was so fascinated by the study
of a horrible photograph-book of thieves' portraits that I
couldn't put it down.'

His interest in the fate of prisoners thus went a good
deal farther than simple memories of the debtors' prison
or notes of a court reporter. He identified himself readily
with the thief, and even more readily with the murderer.
The man of powerful will who finds himself opposed to
society must, if he cannot upset it or if his impulse to do
so is blocked, feel a compulsion to commit what society
regards as one of the capital crimes against itself. With
the antisocial heroes of Dostoevsky, this crime is usually
murder or rape; with Dickens, it is usually murder. His
obsession with murderers is attested by his topical pieces
for *Household Words;* by his remarkable letter to Forster
on the performance of the French actor Lemaître in a play
in which he impersonated a murderer; by his expedition,
on his second visit to America, to the Cambridge Medical
School for the purpose of going over the ground where
Professor Webster had committed a murder in his labora-
tory and had continued to meet his courses with parts of
the body under the lid of his lecture-table. In Dickens'
novels, this theme recurs with a probing of the psychology
of the murderer which becomes ever more convincing and
intimate. Leaving the murderers of the later Dickens till
we come to his later books, we may, however, point out
here that the crime and flight of Jonas Chuzzlewit already
show a striking development beyond the cruder crime and
flight of Sikes. The fantasies and fears of Jonas are really,
as Taine remarked, the picture of a mind on the edge of
insanity. What is valid and impressive in this episode is

the insight into the consciousness of a man who has put himself outside human fellowship — the moment, for example, after the murder when Jonas is 'not only fearful *for* himself but *of* himself' and half-expects, when he returns to his bedroom, to find himself asleep in the bed.

At times the two themes — the criminal and the rebel — are combined in a peculiar way. *Barnaby Rudge* — which from the point of view of Dickens' comedy and character-drawing is the least satisfactory of his early books — is, up to *Martin Chuzzlewit*, the most interesting from the point of view of his deeper artistic intentions. It is the only one of these earlier novels which is not more or less picaresque and, correspondingly, more or less of an improvisation (though there is a certain amount of organization discernible in that other somber book, *Oliver Twist*); it was the only novel up to that time which Dickens had been planning and reflecting on for a long time before he wrote it: it is first mentioned in 1837, but was not written till 1841. Its immediate predecessor, *The Old Curiosity Shop*, had been simply an impromptu yarn, spun out — when Dickens discovered that the original scheme of *Master Humphreys Clock* was not going over with his readers — from what was to have been merely a short story; but *Barnaby Rudge* was a deliberate attempt to find expression for the emotions and ideas that possessed him.

The ostensible subject of the novel is the anti-Catholic insurrection known as the 'Gordon riots' which took place in London in 1780. But what is obviously in Dickens' mind is the Chartist agitation for universal suffrage and working-class representation in Parliament which, as a result of the industrial depression of those years, came to a crisis in 1840. In Manchester the cotton mills were idle, and the streets were full of threatening jobless men. In the summer of 1840 there was a strike of the whole North of England, which the authorities found it possible to put down only by firing into the working-class crowds; this was followed the next year by a brickmakers' strike, which ended in bloody riots. Now the immediate occasion for the Gordon riots had been a protest against a bill which was to remove from the English Catholics such penalties and disabilities as the sentence of life imprisonment for priests who should educate children as Catholics and the disqualifications of Catholics from inheriting property; but the real causes behind the demonstration have always remained rather obscure. It seems to indicate an indignation more violent than it is possible to account for by mere anti-Catholic feeling that churches and houses should have been burnt wholesale, all the prisons of London broken open, and even the Bank of England attacked, and that the authorities should for several days have done so little to restrain the rioters; and it has been supposed that public impatience at the prolongation of the American War, with a general desire to get rid of George III, if not of the monarchy itself, must have contributed to the fury behind the uprising.

This obscurity, at any rate, allowed Dickens to handle the whole episode in an equivocal way. On the surface he reprobates Lord George Gordon and the rioters for their fanatical or brutal intolerance; but implicitly he is exploiting to the limit certain legitimate grievances of the people: the neglect of the lower classes by a cynical eighteenth-century aristocracy, and especially the penal laws which made innumerable minor offenses punishable by death. The really important theme of the book — as Dickens shows in his preface, when he is discussing one of the actual occurrences on which the story is based — is the hanging under the Shop-lifting Act of a woman who has been dropped by her aristocratic lover and who has forged notes to provide for her child. This theme lies concealed, but it makes itself felt from beginning to end of the book. And as *Pickwick*, from the moment it gets really under way, heads by instinct and, as it were, unconsciously straight for the Fleet prison, so *Barnaby Rudge* is deliberately directed toward Newgate, where, as in *Pickwick* again, a group of characters will be brought together; and the principal climax of the story will be the orgiastic burning of the prison. This incident not only has nothing to do with the climax of the plot, it goes in spirit quite against the attitude which Dickens has begun by announcing. The satisfaction he obviously feels in demolishing the sinister old prison, which, rebuilt, had oppressed him in childhood, completely obliterates the effect of his right-minded references in his preface to 'those shameful tumults,' which 'reflect indelible disgrace upon the time in which they occurred, and all who had act or part in them.' In the end, the rioters are shot down and their supposed instigators hanged; but here Dickens' *parti pris* emerges plainly: 'Those who suffered as rioters were, for the most part, the weakest, meanest and most miserable among them.' The son of the woman hanged for stealing, who has been one of the most violent of the mob and whose fashionable father will do nothing to save him, goes to the scaffold with courage and dignity, cursing his father and 'that black tree, of which I am the ripened fruit.'

Dickens has here, under the stimulus of the Chartist agitation, tried to give his own emotions an outlet through an historical novel of insurrection; but the historical episode, the contemporary moral, and the author's emotional pattern do not always coincide very well. Indeed, perhaps the best thing in the book is the creation that most runs away with the general scheme that Dickens has attempted. Dennis the hangman, although too macabre to be one of Dickens' most popular characters, is really one of his best comic inventions, and has more interesting symbolic implications than Barnaby Rudge himself. Dennis is a professional executioner, who has taken an active part in the revolt, apparently from simple motives of sadism. Knowing the unpopularity of the hangman, he makes

an effort to keep his identity a secret; but he has found
this rather difficult to do, because he sincerely loves his
profession and cannot restrain himself from talking about
it. When the mob invades Newgate, which Dennis knows
so well, he directs the liberation of the prisoners; but in
the end he slips away to the condemned cells, locks them
against the mob and stands guard over the clamoring in-
mates, cracking them harshly over the knuckles when they
reach their hands out over the doors. The condemned are
his vested interest, which he cannot allow the rebels to
touch. But the momentum of the mob forces the issue,
breaks through and turns the criminals loose. When we
next encounter Dennis, he is a stool pigeon, turning his
former companions in to the police. But he is unable to
buy immunity in this way; and he is finally hanged himself. Thus this hangman has a complex value: he is primarily a sadist who likes to kill. Yet he figures as a vio-
lator as well as a protector of prisons. In his rôle of in-
surgent, he attacks authority; in his rôle of hangman,
makes it odious. Either way he represents on Dickens'
part a blow at those institutions which the writer is pretending to endorse. There is not, except in a minor way,
any other symbol of authority in the book.

The formula of *Barnaby Rudge* is more or less reproduced in the other two novels of Dickens that deal with
revolutionary subjects — which, though they belong to
later periods of Dickens' work, it is appropriate to consider
here. In *Hard Times* (1854), he manages in much the
same way to deal sympathetically with the working-class
protest against intolerable industrial conditions at the
same time that he lets himself out from supporting the
trade-union movement. In order to be able to do this, he
is obliged to resort to a special and rather implausible device. Stephen Blackpool, the honest old textile worker,
who is made to argue the cause of the workers before the
vulgar manufacturer Bounderby, refuses to join the union

because he has promised the woman he loves that he will do nothing to get himself into trouble. He thus finds himself in the singular position of being both a victim of the blacklist and a scab. The trade-union leadership is represented only — although with a comic fidelity, recognizable even today, to a certain type of labor organizer — by an unscrupulous spellbinder whose single aim is to get hold of the workers' pennies. Old Stephen, wandering away to look for a job somewhere else, falls into a disused coal-pit which has already cost the lives of many miners, and thus becomes a martyr simultaneously to the employers and to the trade-union movement. In *A Tale of Two Cities* (1859), the moral of history is not juggled as it is in *Barnaby Rudge,* but the conflict is made to seem of less immediate reality by locating it out of England. The French people, in Dickens' picture, have been given ample provocation for breaking loose in the French Revolution; but once in revolt, they are fiends and vandals. The vengeful Madame Defarge is a creature whom — as Dickens implies — one would not find in England, and she is worsted by an Englishwoman. The immediate motive behind *A Tale of Two Cities* is no doubt, as has been suggested and as is intimated at the beginning of the last chapter, the English fear of the Second Empire after Napoleon III's Italian campaign of 1859: Dickens' impulse to write the book closely followed the attempt by Orsini to assassinate Napoleon III in the January of '58. But there is in this book as in the other two — though less angrily expressed — a threat. If the British upper classes, Dickens seems to say, will not deal with the problem of providing for the health and education of the people, they will fall victims to the brutal mob. This mob Dickens both sympathizes with and fears.

Through the whole of his early period, Dickens appears to have regarded himself as a respectable middle-class man.

DICKENS: THE TWO SCROOGES 21

If Sam Weller, for all his outspokenness, never oversteps
his rôle of valet, Kit in *The Old Curiosity Shop* is a model
of deference toward his betters who becomes even a little
disgusting.

When Dickens first visited America, in 1842, he seems
to have had hopes of finding here something in the nature of that classless society which the foreign 'fellow
travelers' of yesterday went to seek in the Soviet Union;
but, for reasons both bad and good, Dickens was driven
back by what he did find into the attitude of an English
gentleman, who resented the American lack of ceremony,
was annoyed by the American publicity, and was pretty
well put to rout by the discomfort, the poverty and the
tobacco-juice which he had braved on his trip to the West.
Maladjusted to the hierarchy at home, he did not fit in
in the United States even so well as he did in England:
some of the Americans patronized him, and others were
much too familiar. The mixed attitude — here seen at its
most favorable to us — which was produced when his British ideas intervened to rein in the sympathy which he
tended to feel for American innovations, is well indicated
by the passage in *American Notes* in which he discusses
the factory-girls of Lowell. These girls have pianos in
their boarding-houses and subscribe to circulating libraries,
and they publish a periodical. 'How very preposterous!'
the writer imagines an English reader exclaiming. 'These
things are above their station.' But what is their station?
asks Dickens. 'It is their station to work,' he answers. 'And
they *do* work. . . . For myself, I know no station in
which, the occupation of today cheerfully done and the
occupation of tomorrow cheerfully looked to, any one of
these pursuits is not most humanizing and laudable. I
know no station which is rendered more endurable to the
person in it, or more safe to the person out of it, by having
ignorance for its associates. I know no station which has
a right to monopolize the means of mutual instruction, im-

provement and rational entertainment; or which has even continued to be a station very long after seeking to do so.' But he remarks that 'it is pleasant to find that many of [the] Tales [in the library] are of the Mills, and of those who work in them; that they inculcate habits of self-denial and contentment, and teach good doctrines of enlarged benevolence.' The main theme of *Nicholas Nickleby* is the efforts of Nicholas and his sister to vindicate their position as gentlefolk.

But there is also another reason why these political novels of Dickens are unclear and unsatisfactory. Fundamentally, he was not interested in politics. As a reporter, he had seen a good deal of Parliament, and he had formed a contemptuous opinion of it which was never to change to the end of his life. The Eatanswill elections in *Pickwick* remain the type of political activity for Dickens; the seating of Mr. Veneering in Parliament in the last of his finished novels is hardly different. The point of view is stated satirically in Chapter XII of *Bleak House,* in which a governing-class group at a country house are made to discuss the fate of the country in terms of the political activities of Lord Coodle, Sir Thomas Doodle, the Duke of Foodle, the Right Honorable William Buffy, M.P., with his associates and opponents Cuffy, Duffy, Fuffy, etc., while their constituents are taken for granted as a certain large number of supernumeraries, who are to be occasionally addressed, and relied upon for shouts and choruses, as on the theatrical stage.' A little later (September 30, 1855), he expresses himself explicitly in the course of a letter to Forster: 'I really am serious in thinking — and I have given as painful consideration to the subject as a man with children to live and suffer after him can honestly give to it — that representative government is become altogether a failure with us, that the English gentilities and subserviences render the people unfit for it, and that the whole thing has broken down since that great seven-teenth-century time, and has no hope in it.'

In his novels from beginning to end, Dickens is making the same point always: that to the English governing classes the people they govern are not real. It is one of the great purposes of Dickens to show you these human ac-tualities who figure for Parliament as strategical counters and for Political Economy as statistics; who can as a rule appear only even in histories in a generalized or idealized form. What does a workhouse under the Poor Laws look like? What does it feel like, taste like, smell like? How does the holder of a post in the government look? How does he talk? what does he talk about? how will he treat you? What is the aspect of the British middle class at each of the various stages of its progress? What are the good ones like and what are the bad ones like? How do they affect you, not merely to meet at dinner, but to travel with, to work under, to live with? All these things Dickens can tell us. It has been one of the principal functions of the modern novel and drama to establish this kind of record; but few writers have been able to do it with any range at all extensive. None has surpassed Dickens.

No doubt this concrete way of looking at society may have serious limitations. Dickens was sometimes actually stupid about politics. His lack of interest in political tactics led him, it has sometimes been claimed, to mistake the actual significance of the legislation he was so prompt to criticize. Mr. T. A. Jackson has pointed out a characteris-tic example of Dickens' inattention to politics in his report of his first trip to America. Visiting Washington in 1842, he registers an impression of Congress very similar to his impressions of Parliament ('I may be of a cold and in-sensible temperament, amounting in iciness, in such mat-ters'); and he indulges in one of his gushings of sentiment over 'an aged, gray-haired man, a lasting honor to the land that gave him birth, who has done good service to his country, as his forefathers did, and who will be remembered scores upon scores of years after the worms bred in its corruption are so many grains of dust — it was but a week since this old man had stood for days upon his trial before this very body, charged with having dared to assert the infamy of that traffic which has for its accursed merchandise men and women, and their unborn children. Now this aged gray-haired man, Mr. Jackson reminds us, was none other than John Quincy Adams, who, far from being on his trial, was actually on the verge of winning in his long fight against a House resolution which had excluded petitions against slavery, and who was deliberately provoking his adversaries for purposes of propaganda. Dickens did not know that the antislavery cause, far from being hopeless, was achieving its first step toward victory. (So on his second visit to America — when, however, he was ill and exhausted — his interest in the impeachment of Andrew Johnson seems to have been limited to 'a misgiving lest the great excitement . . . will damage our receipts' from his readings.) Yet his picture of the United States in 1842, at a period of brave boastings and often squalid or meager realities, has a unique and permanent value. Macaulay complained that Dickens did not understand the Manchester school of utilitarian economics which he criticized in *Hard Times*. But Dickens' criticism does not pretend to be theoretical: all he is undertaking to do is to tell us how practising believers in Manchester utilitarianism behave and how their families are likely to fare with them. His picture is strikingly collaborated by the autobiography of John Stuart Mill, who was brought up at the fountainhead of the school, in the shadow of Bentham himself. In Mill, choked with learning from his childhood, overtrained on the logical side of the mind, and collapsing into illogical despair when the lack began to make itself felt of the elements his education had neglected, the tragic moral of the system of Gradgrind is pointed with a sensational obviousness which would be regarded as exaggeration in Dickens.

This very distrust of politics, however, is a part of the rebellious aspect of Dickens. Dickens is almost invariably *against* institutions: in spite of his allegiance to Church and State, in spite of the lip-service he occasionally pays them, whenever he comes to deal with Parliament and its laws, the courts and the public officials, the creeds of Protestant dissenters and of Church of England alike, he makes them either ridiculous or cruel, or both at the same time.

IV

In the work of Dickens' middle period — after the murder in *Martin Chuzzlewit* — the rebel bulks larger than the criminal.

Of all the great Victorian writers, he was probably the most antagonistic to the Victorian Age itself. He had grown up under the Regency and George IV; had been twenty-five at the accession of Victoria. His early novels are freshened by breezes from an England of coaching and village taverns, where the countryside lay just outside London; of an England where jokes and songs and hot brandy were always in order, where every city clerk aimed to dress finely and drink freely, to give an impression of open-handedness and gallantry. The young Dickens of the earliest preserved letters, who invites his friends to partake of 'the rosy,' sounds not unlike Dick Swiveller. When Little Nell and her grandfather on their wanderings spend a night in an iron foundry, it only has the effect of a sort of Nibelungen interlude, rather like one of those surprise grottoes that you float through when you take the little boat that threads the tunnel of the 'Old Mill' in an amusement park — a luridly lighted glimpse on the same level, in Dickens' novel, with the waxworks, the perform-

ing dogs, the dwarfs and giants, the village church. From
this point it is impossible, as it was impossible for Dickens,
to foresee the full-length industrial town depicted in *Hard
Times.* In that age the industrial-commercial civilization
had not yet got to be the norm; it seemed a disease which
had broken out in spots but which a sincere and cheerful
treatment would cure. The typical reformers of the period
had been Shelley and Robert Owen, the latter so logical a
crank, a philanthropist so much all of a piece, that he
seems to have been invented by Dickens — who insisted
that his Cheeryble brothers, the philanthropic merchants
of *Nicholas Nickleby,* had been taken from living originals.

But when Dickens begins to write novels again after
his return from his American trip, a new kind of character appears in them, who, starting as an amusing buffoon,
grows steadily more unpleasant and more formidable. On
the threshold of *Martin Chuzzlewit* (1843-45: the dates
of its appearance in monthly numbers), you find Pecksniff, the provincial architect; on the threshold of *Dombey
and Son* (1846-48), you find Dombey, the big London
merchant; and before you have got very far with the
idyllic *David Copperfield* (1849-50), you find Murdstone,
of Murdstone and Grimby, wine merchants. All these figures stand for the same thing. Dickens had at first imagined that he was pillorying abstract faults in the manner
of the comedy of humors: Selfishness in *Chuzzlewit,*
Pride in *Dombey.* But the truth was that he had already
begun an indictment against a specific society: the self-
important and moralizing middle class who had been making such rapid progress in England and coming down like
a damper on the bright fires of English life — that is, on
the spontaneity and gaiety, the frankness and independence, the instinctive human virtues, which Dickens admired and trusted. The new age had brought a new kind
of virtues to cover up the flourishing vices of cold avarice

and harsh exploitation; and Dickens detested these virtues.

The curmudgeons of the early Dickens — Ralph Nickleby and Arthur Gride, Anthony and Jonas Chuzzlewit (for *Martin Chuzzlewit* just marks the transition from the early to the middle Dickens) — are old-fashioned moneylenders and misers of a type that must have been serving for decades in the melodramas of the English stage. In Dickens their whole-hearted and outspoken meanness gives them a certain cynical charm. They are the bad uncles in the Christmas pantomime who set off the jolly clowns and the good fairy, and who, as everybody knows from the beginning, are doomed to be exposed and extinguished. But Mr. Pecksniff, in the same novel with the Chuzzlewits, already represents something different. It is to be characteristic of Pecksniff, as it is of Dombey and Murdstone, that he does evil while pretending to do good. As intent on the main chance as Jonas himself, he pretends to be a kindly father, an affectionate relative, a pious churchgoer; he is the pillar of a cathedral town. Yet Pecksniff is still something of a pantomime comic whom it will be easy enough to unmask. Mr. Dombey is a more difficult problem. His virtues, as far as they go, are real: though he is stupid enough to let his business get into the hands of Carker, he does lead an exemplary life of a kind in the interests of the tradition of his house. He makes his wife and his children miserable in his devotion to his mercantile ideal, but that ideal is at least for him serious. With Murdstone the ideal has turned sour: the respectable London merchant now represents something sinister. Murdstone is not funny like Pecksniff; he is not merely a buffoon who masquerades: he is a hypocrite who believes in himself. And where Dombey is made to recognize his error and turn kindly and humble in the end, Mr. Murdstone and his grim sister are allowed to persist in their course of working mischief as a matter of duty.

In such a world of mercenary ruthlessness, always justi-

fied by rigorous morality, it is natural that the exploiter
of others should wish to dissociate himself from the exploited, and to delegate the face-to-face encounters to
someone else who is paid to take the odium. Karl Marx,
at that time living in London, was demonstrating through
these middle years of the century that this system, with its
falsifying of human relations and its wholesale encourage-
ment of cant, was an inherent and irremediable feature of
the economic structure itself. In Dickens, the Mr. Spenlow of *David Copperfield,* who is always blaming his mean
exactions on his supposedly implacable partner, Mr. Jor-
kins, develops into the Casby of *Little Dorrit,* the benignant and white-haired patriarch who turns over the rack-
renting of Bleeding Heart Yard to his bull-terrier of an
agent, Pancks, while he basks in the admiration of his
tenants; and in *Our Mutual Friend,* into Fledgeby, the
moneylender who makes his way into society while the
harmless old Jew Riah is compelled to play the cruel
creditor.

With Dickens' mounting dislike and distrust of the top
layers of that middle-class society with which he had begun by identifying himself, his ideal of middle-class virtue
was driven down to the lower layers. In his earlier novels,
this ideal had been embodied in such patrons and bene-
factors as Mr. Pickwick, the retired business man; the sub-
stantial and warmhearted Mr. Brownlow, who rescued
Oliver Twist; and the charming old gentleman, Mr. Garland, who took Kit Nubbles into his service. In *David
Copperfield* the lawyer Wickfield, who plays a rôle in relation to the hero somewhat similar to those of Brownlow
and Garland, becomes demoralized by too much port and
falls a victim to Uriah Heep, the upstart Pecksniff of a
lower social level. The ideal — the domestic unit which
preserves the sound values of England — is located by
Dickens through this period in the small middle-class
household: Ruth Pinch and her brother in *Martin Chuz-*

zlewit; the bright hearths and holiday dinners of the *Christmas Books;* the modest home to which Florence Dombey descends from the great house near Portland Place, in happy wedlock with the nephew of Sol Gills, the ships'-instrument-maker.

It is at the end of *Dombey and Son,* when the house of Dombey goes bankrupt, that Dickens for the first time expresses himself explicitly on the age that has come to remain:

'The world was very busy now, in sooth, and had a deal to say. It was an innocently credulous and a much ill-used world. It was a world in which there was no other sort of bankruptcy whatever. There were no conspicuous people in it, trading far and wide on rotten banks of religion, patriotism, virtue, honor. There was no amount worth mentioning of mere paper in circulation, on which anybody lived pretty handsomely, promising to pay great sums of goodness with no effects. There were no short-comings anywhere, in anything but money. The world was very angry indeed; and the people especially who, in a worse world, might have been supposed to be bankrupt traders themselves in shows and pretences, were observed to be mightily indignant.'

And now — working always through the observed inter-relations between highly individualized human beings rather than through political or economic analysis — Dickens sets out to trace an anatomy of that society. *Dombey* has been the first attempt; *Bleak House* (1852-53) is to realize this intention to perfection; *Hard Times,* on a smaller scale, is to conduct the same kind of inquiry.

For this purpose Dickens invents a new literary *genre* (unless the whole mass of Balzac is to be taken as something of the sort): the novel of the social group. The young Dickens had summed up, developed and finally outgrown the two traditions in English fiction he had

found: the picaresque tradition of Defoe, Fielding and
Smollett, and the sentimental tradition of Goldsmith and
Sterne. People like George Henry Lewes have complained
of Dickens' little reading; but no artist has ever absorbed
his predecessors — he had read most of them in his early
boyhood — more completely than Dickens did. There is
something of all these writers in Dickens and, using them,
he has gone beyond them all. In the historical novel *Barnaby Rudge* — a detour in Dickens' fiction — he had got
out of Scott all that Scott had to give him. He was to
profit in *Hard Times* by Mrs. Gaskell's industrial studies.
But in the meantime it was Dickens' business to create
a new tradition himself.

His novels even through *Martin Chuzzlewit* had had a
good deal of the looseness of the picaresque school of *Gil
Blas,* where the episodes get their only unity from being
hung on the same hero, as well as the multiple parallel
plots, purely mechanical combinations, that he had acquired from the old plays — though he seems to have been
trying more intensively for a unity of atmosphere and
feeling. But now he is to organize his stories as wholes, to
plan all the characters as symbols, and to invest all the details with significance. *Dombey and Son* derives a new
kind of coherence from the fact that the whole novel is
made to center around the big London business house:
you have the family of the man who owns it, the manager
and his family, the clerks, the men dependent on the ships
that export its goods, down to Sol Gills and Captain Cut-
tle (so *Hard Times* is to get its coherence from the organism of an industrial town).

In *Bleak House,* the masterpiece of this middle period,
Dickens discovers a new use of plot, which makes possible
a tighter organization. (And we must remember that he is
always working against the difficulties, of which he often
complains, of writing for monthly instalments, where
everything has to be planned beforehand and it is impos-

sible, as he says, to 'try back' and change anything, once
it has been printed.) He creates the detective story which
is also a social fable. It is a *genre* which has lapsed since
Dickens. The detective story — though Dickens' friend
Wilkie Collins preserved a certain amount of social satire
— has dropped out the Dickensian social content; and the
continuators of the social novel have dropped the detective
story. These continuators — Shaw, Galsworthy, Wells —
have of course gone further than Dickens in the realistic
presentation of emotion; but from the point of view of
dramatizing social issues, they have hardly improved upon
Bleak House. In Shaw's case, the Marxist analysis, with
which Dickens was not equipped, has helped him to the
tighter organization which Dickens got from his complex
plot. But in the meantime it is one of Dickens' victories in
his rapid development as an artist that he should succeed
in transforming his melodramatic intrigues of stolen in-
heritances, lost heirs and ruined maidens — with their
denunciatory confrontations that always evoke the sound
of fiddling in the orchestra — into devices of artistic dignity. Henceforth the solution of the mystery is to be also
the moral of the story and the last word of Dickens' social
'message.'

Bleak House begins in the London fog, and the whole
book is permeated with fog and rain. In *Dombey* the railway locomotive — first when Mr. Dombey takes his trip to
Leamington, and later when it pulls into the station just
at the moment of Dombey's arrival and runs over the
fugitive Carker as he steps back to avoid his master —
figures as a symbol of that progress of commerce which
Dombey himself represents; in *Hard Times* the uncov-
ered coal-pit into which Stephen Blackpool falls is a symbol for the abyss of the industrial system, which swallows
up lives in its darkness. In *Bleak House* the fog stands for
Chancery, and Chancery stands for the whole web of
clotted antiquated institutions in which England stifles

and decays. All the principal elements in the story — the young people, the proud Lady Dedlock, the philanthropic gentleman John Jarndyce, and Tom-all-Alone's, the rotting London slum — are involved in the exasperating Chancery suit, which, with the fog-bank of precedent looming behind it like the Great Boyg in *Peer Gynt*, obscures and impedes at every point the attempts of men and women to live natural lives. Old Krook, with his legal junkshop, is Dickens' symbol for the Lord Chancellor himself; the cat that sits on his shoulder watches like the Chancery lawyers the caged birds in Miss Flite's lodging; Krook's death by spontaneous combustion is Dickens' prophecy of the fate of Chancery and all that it represents.

I go over the old ground of the symbolism, up to this point perfectly obvious, of a book which must be still, by the general public, one of the most read of Dickens' novels, because the people who like to talk about the symbols of Kafka and Mann and Joyce have been discouraged from looking for anything of the kind in Dickens, and usually have not read him, at least with mature minds. But even when we think we do know Dickens, we may be surprised to return to him and find in him a symbolism of a more complicated reference and a deeper implication than these metaphors that hang as emblems over the door. The Russians themselves, in this respect, appear to have learned from Dickens.

Thus it is not at first that we recognize all the meaning of the people that thrive or survive in the dense atmosphere of *Bleak House* — an atmosphere so opaque that the somnolent ease at the top cannot see down to the filth at the bottom. And it is an atmosphere where nobody sees clearly what kind of race of beings is flourishing between the bottom and the top. Among the middle ranks of this society we find persons who appear with the pretension of representing Law or Art, Social Elegance, Philanthropy, or Religion — Mr. Kenge and Mr. Vholes, Harold

Skimpole, Mr. Turveydrop, Mrs. Pardiggle and Mrs. Jellyby, and Mr. and Mrs. Chadband — side by side with such a sordid nest of goblins as the family of the money-lender Smallweed. But presently we see that all these people are as single-mindedly intent on selfish interests as Grandfather Smallweed himself. This gallery is one of the best things in Dickens. The Smallweeds themselves are artistically an improvement on the similar characters in the early Dickens: they represent, not a theatrical convention, but a real study of the stunted and degraded products of the underworld of commercial London. And the two opposite types of philanthropist: the moony Mrs. Jellyby, who miserably neglects her children in order to dream of doing good in Africa, and Mrs. Pardiggle, who bullies both her children and the poor in order to give herself a feeling of power; Harold Skimpole, with the graceful fancy and the talk about music and art that ripples a shimmering veil over his systematic sponging; and Turveydrop, the Master of Deportment, that parody of the magnificence of the Regency, behind his rouge and his padded coat and his gallantry as cold and as inconsiderate as the Chadbands behind their gaseous preachments. Friedrich Engels, visiting London in the early forties, had written of the people in the streets that they seemed to 'crowd by one another as if they had nothing in common, nothing to do with one another, and as if their only agreement were the tacit one that each shall keep to his own side of the pavement, in order not to delay the opposing streams of the crowd, while it never occurs to anyone to honor his fellow with so much as a glance. The brutal indifference, the unfeeling isolation of each in his private interest, becomes the more repellent the more these individuals are herded together within a limited space.' This is the world that Dickens is describing.

Here he makes but one important exception: Mr. Rouncewell, the ironmaster. Mr. Rouncewell is an ambitious son of the housekeeper at Chesney Wold, Sir Leicester Dedlock's country house, who has made himself a place in the world which Sir Leicester regards as beyond his station. One of the remarkable scenes of the novel is that in which Rouncewell comes back, quietly compels Sir Leicester to receive him like a gentleman and asks him to release one of the maids from his service so that she may marry Rouncewell's son, a young man whom he has christened Watt. When Lady Dedlock refuses to release the maid, Rouncewell respectfully abandons the project, but goes away and has the insolence to run against Sir Leicester's candidate in the next parliamentary election. (This theme of the intervention of the industrial revolution in the relations between master and servant has already appeared in *Dombey and Son* in the admirable interview between Dombey and Polly Toodles, whom he is employing as a wetnurse for his motherless child. Polly's husband, who is present, is a locomotive stoker and already represents something anomalous in the hierarchy of British society. When the Dombeys, who cannot accept her real name, suggest calling Polly 'Richards,' she replies that if she is to be called out of her name, she ought to be paid extra. Later, when Dombey makes his railway journey, he runs into Polly's husband, who is working on the engine. Toodles speaks to him and engages him in conversation, and Dombey resents this, feeling that Toodles is somehow intruding outside his own class.)

But in general the magnanimous, the simple of heart, the amiable, the loving and the honest are frustrated, subdued, or destroyed. At the bottom of the whole gloomy edifice is the body of Lady Dedlock's lover and Esther Summerson's father, Captain Hawdon, the reckless soldier, adored by his men, beloved by women, the image of the old life-loving England, whose epitaph Dickens is now writing. Captain Hawdon has failed in that world, has perished as a friendless and penniless man, and has been buried in the pauper's graveyard in one of the foulest quarters of London, but the loyalties felt for him by the living will endure and prove so strong after his death that they will pull that world apart. Esther Summerson has been frightened and made submissive by being treated as the respectable middle class thought it proper to treat an illegitimate child, by one of those Puritanical females whom Dickens so roundly detests. Richard Carstone has been demoralized and ruined; Miss Flite has been driven insane. George Rouncewell, the brother of the ironmaster, who has escaped from Sir Leicester's service to become a soldier instead of a manufacturer and who is treated by Dickens with the sympathy which he usually feels for his military and nautical characters, the men who are doing the hard work of the Empire, is helpless in the hands of moneylenders and lawyers. Caddy Jellyby and her husband, young Turveydrop, who have struggled for a decent life in a poverty partly imposed by the necessity of keeping up old Turveydrop's pretenses, can only produce, in that society where nature is so mutilated and thwarted, a sickly defective child. Mr. Jarndyce himself, the wise and generous, who plays in *Bleak House* a rôle very similar to that of Captain Shotover in Bernard Shaw's *Heartbreak House* (which evidently owes a good deal to *Bleak House*), is an eccentric at odds with his environment, who, in his efforts to help the unfortunate, falls a prey to the harpies of philanthropy.

With this indifference and egoism of the middle class, the social structure must buckle in the end. The infection from the poverty of Tom-all-Alone's will ravage the mansions of country gentlemen. Lady Dedlock will inevitably be dragged down from her niche of aristocratic idleness to the graveyard in the slum where her lover lies. The idea that the highest and the lowest in that English society of shocking contrasts are inextricably tied together has already appeared in the early Dickens — in Ralph Nickleby

and Smike, for example, and in Sir John Chester and
Hugh — as a sort of submerged motif which is never given
its full expression. Here it has been chosen deliberately
and is handled with immense skill so as to provide the
main moral of the fable. And bound up with it is another
motif which has already emerged sharply in Dickens.
Dickens has evidently in the course of his astonishing rise,
found himself up against the blank and chilling loftiness
— what the French call *la morgue anglaise* — of the English upper classes: as we shall see, he developed a pride of
his own, with which he fought it to his dying day. Pride
was to have been the theme of *Dombey*: the pride of Edith
Dombey outdoes the pride of Dombey and levels him to
the ground. But in *Bleak House*, the pride of Lady Dedlock, who has married Sir Leicester Dedlock for position,
ultimately rebounds on herself. Her behavior toward the
French maid Hortense is the cause of her own debasement. For where it is a question of pride, a high-tempered
girl from the South of France can outplay Lady Dedlock:
Hortense will not stop at the murder which is the logical
upshot of the course of action dictated by her wounded
feelings. Dickens is criticizing here one of the most un-
assailable moral props of the English hierarchical system.

Between *Dombey and Son* and *Bleak House*, Dickens
published *David Copperfield*. It is a departure from the
series of his social novels. Setting out to write the autobiography of which the fragments appear in Forster's *Life*,
Dickens soon changed his mind and transposed this material into fiction. In the first half of *David Copperfield*, at
any rate, Dickens strikes an enchanting vein which he had
never quite found before and which he was never to find
again. It is the poem of an idealized version of the loves
and fears and wonders of childhood; and the confrontation
of Betsey Trotwood with the Murdstones is one of Dickens' most successful stagings of the struggle between the

human and the anti-human, because it takes place on the plane of comedy rather than on that of melodrama. But *Copperfield* is not one of Dickens' deepest books: it is something in the nature of a holiday. David is too candid and simple to represent Dickens himself; and though the blacking warehouse episode is utilized, all the other bitter circumstances of Dickens' youth were dropped out when he abandoned the autobiography.

v

With *Little Dorrit* (1855-57), Dickens' next novel after *Bleak House* and *Hard Times,* we enter a new phase of his work. To understand it, we must go back to his life.

Dickens at forty had won everything that a writer could expect to obtain through his writings: his genius was universally recognized; he was fêted wherever he went; his books were immensely popular; and they had made him sufficiently rich to have anything that money can procure. He had partly made up for the education he had missed by traveling and living on the Continent and by learning to speak Italian and French. (Dickens' commentary on the continental countries is usually not remarkably penetrating; but he did profit very much from his travels abroad in his criticism of things in England. Perhaps no other of the great Victorian writers had so much the consciousness that the phenomena he was describing were of a character distinctively English.) Yet from the time of his first summer at Boulogne in 1853, he had shown signs of profound discontent and unappeasable restlessness; he suffered severely from insomnia and, for the first time in his life, apparently, worried seriously about his work. He began to fear that his vein was drying up.

I believe that Forster's diagnosis — though it may not go to the root of the trouble — must here be accepted as correct. There were, he intimates, two things wrong with Dickens: a marriage which exasperated and cramped him

and from which he had not been able to find relief, and a
social maladjustment which his success had never straightened out.

The opportunities of the young Dickens to meet eligible
young women had evidently been rather limited. That he
was impatient to get married, nevertheless, is proved by
his announcing his serious intentions to three girls in close
succession. The second of these was Maria Beadnell, the
original of Dora in *David Copperfield* and, one supposes,
of Dolly Varden, too, with whom he fell furiously in love,
when he was eighteen and she nineteen. Her father
worked in a bank and regarded Charles Dickens, the
stenographer, as a young man of shabby background and
doubtful prospects; Maria, who seems to have been rather
frivolous and silly, was persuaded to drop her suitor —
with the result for him which may be read in the letters,
painful in their wounded pride and their backfiring of a
thwarted will, which he wrote her after the break. This
was one of the great humiliations of Dickens' early life
he was at that time twenty-one) and, even after he
had liquidated it in a sense by depicting the futilities
of David's marriage with Dora, the disappointment still
seems to have troubled him and Maria to have remained
at the back of his mind as the Ideal of which he had been
cheated.

He lost very little time, however, in getting himself a
wife. Two years after his rejection by Maria Beadnell, he
was engaged to the daughter of George Hogarth, a Scotchman, who, as the law agent of Walter Scott and from having been mentioned in the *Noctes Ambrosianae,* was invested with the prestige of having figured on the fringes
of the Edinburgh literary world. He asked Dickens to
write for the newspaper which he was editing at that time
in London, and invited the young man to his house.
There Dickens found two attractive daughters, and he
married the elder, Catherine, who was twenty. But the

other daughter, Mary, though too young for him to marry — she was only fifteen when he met her — had a strange hold on Dickens' emotions. When, after living with the Dickenses for a year after their marriage, she suddenly died in Dickens' arms, he was so overcome by grief that he stopped writing *Pickwick* for two months and insisted in an obsessed and morbid way on his desire to be buried beside her: 'I can't think there ever was love like I bear her. . . . I have never had her ring off my finger day or night, except for an instant at a time, to wash my hands, since she died. I have never had her sweetness and excellence absent from my mind so long.' In *The Old Curiosity Shop,* he apotheosized her as Little Nell. What basis this emotion may have had in the fashionable romanticism of the period or in some peculiar psychological pattern of Dickens', it is impossible on the evidence to say. But this passion for an innocent young girl is to recur in Dickens' life; and in the meantime his feeling for Mary Hogarth seems to indicate pretty clearly that even during the early years of his marriage he did not identify the Ideal with Catherine.

Catherine had big blue eyes, a rather receding chin and a sleepy and languorous look. Beyond this, it is rather difficult to get a definite impression of her. Dickens' terrible gallery of shrews who browbeat their amiable husbands suggests that she may have been a scold; but surely Dickens himself was no Joe Gargery or Gabriel Varden. We do not know much about Dickens' marriage. We know that, with the exception of his sister-in-law Georgina, Dickens grew to loathe the Hogarths, who evidently lived on him to a considerable extent; and we must assume that poor Catherine, in both intellect and energy, was a good deal inferior to her husband. He lived with her, however, twenty years, and, although it becomes clear toward the end that they were no longer particularly welcome, he gave her during that time ten children.

And if Dickens was lonely in his household, he was
lonely in society, also. He had, as Forster indicates, attained a pinnacle of affluence and fame which made him
one of the most admired and most sought-after persons in
Europe without his really ever having created for himself
a social position in England, that society *par excellence*
where everybody had to have a definite one and where
there was no rank reserved for the artist. He had gone
straight, at the very first throw, from the poor tenement,
the prison, the press table, to a position of imperial supremacy over the imaginations of practically the whole
literate world; but in his personal associations, he cultivated the companionship of inferiors rather than — save,
perhaps, for Carlyle — of intellectual equals. His behavior
toward Society, in the capitalized sense, was rebarbative to
the verge of truculence; he refused to learn its patter and
its manners; and his satire on the fashionable world comes
to figure more and more prominently in his novels. Dickens is one of the very small group of British intellectuals
to whom the opportunity has been offered to be taken up
by the governing class and who have actually declined
that honor.

His attitude — which in the period we have been discussing was still that of the middle-class 'Radical' opposing
feudal precedent and privilege: Mr. Rouncewell, the iron-
master, backed against Sir Leicester Dedlock — is illustrated by the curious story of his relations with Queen
Victoria. In 1857, Dickens got up a benefit for the family
of Douglas Jerrold, in which he and his daughters acted.
The Queen was asked to be one of the sponsors; and, since
she was obliged to refuse any such request for fear of being obliged to grant them all, she invited Dickens to put
on the play at the palace. He replied that he 'did not feel
easy as to the social position of my daughters, etc., at a
Court under those circumstances,' and suggested that the
Queen might attend a performance which should be given

for her alone. She accepted, and sent backstage between the acts asking Dickens to come and speak to her. 'I replied that I was in my Farce dress, and must beg to be excused. Whereupon she sent again, saying that the dress "could not be so ridiculous as that," and repeating the request. I sent my duty in reply, but again hoped Her Majesty would have the kindness to excuse my presenting myself in a costume and appearance that were not my own. I was mighty glad to think, when I woke this morning, that I had carried the point.' The next year he was approached on behalf of the Queen, who wanted to hear him read the *Christmas Carol;* but he expressed his 'hope that she would indulge me by making one of some audience or other — for I thought an audience necessary to the effect.' It was only in the last year of his life — and then only on what seems to have been the pretext on the Queen's part that she wanted to look at some photographs of the battle-fields of the Civil War which Dickens had brought back from America — that an interview was finally arranged. Here the record of Dickens' lecture manager, George Dolby, supplements the account given by Forster. Dickens told Dolby that 'Her Majesty had received him most graciously, and that, as Court etiquette requires that no one, in an ordinary interview with the sovereign, should be seated, Her Majesty had remained the whole time leaning over the head of a sofa. There was a little shyness on both sides at the commencement, but this wore away as the conversation proceeded.' When Victoria regretted that it had not been possible for her ever to hear Dickens read, he replied that he had made his farewell to the platform; when she said that she understood this, but intimated that it would be gracious on Dickens' part so far to forget his resolve as to give her the pleasure of hearing him, he insisted that this would be impossible. Not impossible, perhaps, said the Queen, but inconsistent, no doubt — and she knew that he was the most consistent of men. Yet they parted on very good terms: she invited him to her next levee and his daughter to the drawing-room that followed. If there is some stickling for his dignity on Dickens' part here, there is evidently also some scruple on the Queen's.

To be caught between two social classes in a society of strict stratifications — like being caught between two civilizations, as James was, or between two racial groups, like Proust — is an excellent thing for a novelist from the point of view of his art, because it enables him to dramatize contrasts and to study interrelations which the dweller in one world cannot know. Perhaps something of the sort was true even of Shakespeare, between the provincial bourgeoisie and the Court. Dostoevsky, who had a good deal in common with Dickens and whose career somewhat parallels his, is a conspicuous example of a writer who owes his dramatic scope at least partly to a social maladjustment. The elder Dostoevsky was a doctor and his family origins were obscure, so that his social position was poor in a Russia still predominantly feudal; yet he bought a country estate and sent his sons to a school for the children of the nobility. But the family went to pieces after the mother's death: the father took to drink and was murdered by his serfs for his cruelty. Dostoevsky was left with almost nothing, and he slipped down into that foul and stagnant underworld of the Raskólnikovs and Stavrógins of his novels. Dickens' case had been equally anomalous: he had grown up in an uncomfortable position between the upper and the lower middle classes, with a dip into the proletariat and a glimpse of the aristocracy through their trusted upper servants. But this position, which had been useful to him as a writer, was to leave him rather isolated in English society. In a sense, there was no place for him to go and belong; he had to have people come to him.

And in the long run all that he had achieved could not make up for what he lacked. *Little Dorrit* and *Great Expectations* (1860-61), which follows it after *A Tale of*

Two Cities, are full of the disillusion and discomfort of this period of Dickens' life. The treatment of social situations and the treatment of individual psychology have both taken turns distinctly new.

Dickens now tackles the Marshalsea again, but on a larger scale and in a more serious way. It is as if he were determined once for all to get the prison out of his system. The figure of his father hitherto has always haunted Dickens' novels, but he has never known quite how to handle it. In Micawber, he made him comic and lovable; in Skimpole, he made him comic and unpleasant — for, after all, the vagaries of Micawber always left somebody out of pocket, and there is another aspect of Micawber — the Skimpole aspect he presented to his creditors. But what kind of person, really, had John Dickens been in himself? How had the father of Charles Dickens come to be what he was? Even after it had become possible for Charles to provide for his father, the old man continued to be a problem up to his death in 1851. He got himself arrested again, as the result of running up a wine bill; and he would try to get money out of his son's publishers without the knowledge of Charles. Yet Dickens said to Forster, after his father's death: 'The longer I live, the better man I think him'; and *Little Dorrit* is something in the nature of a justification of John.

Mr. Dorrit is 'a very amiable and very helpless middle-aged gentleman . . . a shy, retiring man, well-looking, though in an effeminate style, with a mild voice, curling hair, and irresolute hands — rings upon the fingers in those days — which nervously wandered to his trembling lip a hundred times in the first half-hour of his acquaintance with the jail.' The arrival of the Dorrit family in prison and their gradual habituation to it are done with a restraint and sobriety never displayed by Dickens up to now. The incident in which Mr. Dorrit, after getting used to accepting tips in his rôle of the Father of the Marshalsea, suddenly becomes insulted when he is offered copper half-pence by a workman, has a delicacy which makes up in these later books for the ebb of Dickens' bursting exuberance. If it is complained that the comic characters in these novels, the specifically 'Dickens characters,' are sometimes mechanical and boring, this is partly, perhaps, for the reason that they stick out in an unnatural relief from a surface that is more quietly realistic. And there are moments when one feels that Dickens might be willing to abandon the 'Dickens character' altogether if it were not what the public expected of him. In any case, the story of Dorrit is a closer and more thoughtful study than any that has gone before of what bad institutions make of men.

But there is also in *Little Dorrit* something different from social criticism. Dickens is no longer satisfied to anatomize the organism of society. The main symbol here is the prison (in this connection, Mr. Jackson's chapter is the best thing that has been written on *Little Dorrit*); but this symbol is developed in a way that takes it beyond the satirical application of the symbol of the fog in *Bleak House* and gives it a significance more subjective. In the opening chapter, we are introduced, not to the debtors' prison, but to an ordinary jail for criminals, which, in the case of Rigaud and Cavalletto, will not make the bad man any better or the good man any worse. A little later, we are shown an English business man who has come back from many years in China and who finds himself in a London — the shut-up London of Sunday evening — more frightening, because more oppressive, than the thieves' London of *Oliver Twist*. ' "Heaven forgive me," said he, "and those who trained me. How I have hated this day!" There was the dreary Sunday of his childhood, when he sat with his hands before him, scared out of his senses by a horrible tract which commenced business with the poor child by asking him, in its title, why he was going to Perdition?' At last he gets himself to the point of going to see his mother, whom he finds as lacking in affection and as gloomy as he could have expected. She lives in a dark and funereal house with the old offices on the bottom floor, one of the strongholds of that harsh Calvinism plus hard business which made one of the mainstays of the Victorian Age; she lies paralyzed on 'a black bier-like sofa,' punishing herself and everyone else for some guilt of which he cannot discover the nature. The Clennam house is a jail, and they are in prison, too. So are the people in Bleeding Heart Yard, small tenement-dwelling shopkeepers and artisans, rack-rented by the patriarchal Casby; so is Merdle, the great swindler-financier, imprisoned, like Kreuger or Insull, in the vast scaffolding of fraud he has contrived, who wanders about in his expensive house — itself, for all its crimson and gold, as suffocating and dark as the Clennams' — afraid of his servants, unloved by his wife, almost unknown by his guests, till on the eve of the collapse of the edifice he quietly opens his veins in his bath.

At last, after twenty-five years of jail, Mr. Dorrit inherits a fortune and is able to get out of the Marshalsea. He is rich enough to go into Society; but all the Dorrits, with the exception of the youngest, known as 'Little Dorrit,' who has been born in the Marshalsea itself and has never made any pretensions, have been demoralized or distorted by the effort to remain genteel while tied to the ignominy of the prison. They cannot behave like the people outside. And yet that outside world is itself insecure. It is dominated by Mr. Merdle, who comes, as the story goes on, to be universally believed and admired — is taken up by the governing class, sent to Parliament, courted by lords. The Dorrits, accepted by Society, still find themselves in prison. The moral is driven home when old Dorrit, at a fashionable dinner, loses control of his wits and slips back into his character at the Marshalsea: ' "Born here," he repeated, shedding tears. "Bred here. Ladies and gentlemen, my daughter. Child of an unfortunate father,

but — ha — always a gentleman. Poor, no doubt, but —
hum — proud." ' He asks the company for 'Testimonials,'
which had been what he had used to call his tips. (Dr.
Manette, in *A Tale of Two Cities*, repeats this pattern
with his amnesic relapses into the shoemaking he has
learned in prison.) Arthur Clennam, ruined by the failure
of Merdle, finally goes to the Marshalsea himself; and
there at last he and Little Dorrit arrive at an understanding. The implication is that, prison for prison, a simple in-
carceration is an excellent school of character compared to
the dungeons of Puritan theology, of modern business, of
money-ruled Society, or of the poor people of Bleeding
Heart Yard who are swindled and bled by all of these.

The whole book is much gloomier than *Bleak House*,
where the fog is external to the characters and represents
something removable, the obfuscatory elements of the
past. The murk of *Little Dorrit* permeates the souls of the
people, and we see more of their souls than in *Bleak
House*. Arthur Clennam, with his broodings on his unlov-
ing mother, who turns out not to be his real mother (a
poor doomed child of natural impulse, like Lady Dedlock's
lover), is both more real and more depressing than Lady
Dedlock. Old Dorrit has been spoiled beyond repair: he
can never be rehabilitated like Micawber. There is not
even a villain like Tulkinghorn to throw the odium on a
predatory class: the official villain Blandois has no organic
connection with the story save as a caricature of social
pretense. (Though the illustrations suggest that he may
have been intended as a sort of cartoon of Napoleon III,
whose régime Dickens loathed — in which case the tie-up
between Blandois and the Clennams may figure a close
relationship between the shady financial interests disguised by the flashy façade of the Second Empire and the
respectable business interests of British merchants, so inhuman behind their mask of morality. Blandois is crushed
in the end by the collapse of the Clennams' house, as peo-

ple were already predicting that Napoleon would be by
that of his own.) The rôle of the Court of Chancery is
more or less played by the Circumlocution Office and the
governing-class family of Barnacles — perhaps the most
brilliant thing of its kind in Dickens: that great satire on
all aristocratic bureaucracies, and indeed on all bureaucracies, with its repertoire of the variations possible within
the bureaucratic type and its desolating picture of the emotions of a man being passed on from one door to another.
But the Circumlocution Office, after all, only influences
the action in a negative way.

The important thing to note in *Little Dorrit* — which
was originally to have been called *Nobody's Fault* — is that
the fable is here presented from the point of view of im-
prisoning states of mind as much as from that of oppressive
institutions. This is illustrated in a startling way by *The
History of a Self-Tormentor,* which we find toward the
end of the book. Here Dickens, with a remarkable pre-
Freudian insight, gives a sort of case history of a woman
imprisoned in a neurosis which has condemned her to the
delusion that she can never be loved. There is still, to be
sure, the social implication that her orphaned childhood
and her sense of being slighted have been imposed on her
by the Victorian attitude toward her illegitimate birth. But
her handicap is now simply a thought-pattern, and from
that thought-pattern she is never to be liberated.

Dickens' personal difficulties make themselves felt like
an ache at the back of *Little Dorrit* — in which he represents his hero as reflecting: 'Who has not thought for a
moment, sometimes? — that it might be better to flow away
monotonously, like the river, and to compound for its insensibility to happiness with its insensibility to pain.' The
strain of his situation with his wife had become particularly acute the year that the book was begun. Dickens had
been very much excited that February to get a letter from

Maria Beadnell, now married. The readiness and warmth
of his response shows how the old Ideal had lighted up
again. He was on the point of leaving for Paris, and during his absence he looked forward eagerly to seeing her:
he arranged to meet her alone. The drop in the tone of his
letters after this meeting has taken place is blighting to
poor Mrs. Winter. He had found her banal and silly, with
the good looks of her girlhood gone. He put her into his
new novel as Flora Finching, a sort of Dora Spenlow vul-
garized and transmogrified into a kind of Mrs. Nickleby
— that is, into another version of Dickens' unforgiven
mother. It seems clear that the type of woman that Dickens is chiefly glorifying during the years from *Martin
Chuzzlewit* through *Little Dorrit:* the devoted and self-
effacing little mouse, who hardly aspires to be loved, derives from Georgina Hogarth, his sister-in-law. Georgina,
who had been eight when Dickens was married, had come
to womanhood in the Dickens household. Dickens grew
fond of her, explaining that his affection was due partly
to her resemblance to her dead sister. She gradually took
over the care of the children, whom Dickens complained
of their mother's neglecting; and became the real head of
the household — creating a situation which is reflected in
these heroines of the novels. The virtues of Ruth Pinch
are brought out mainly through her relation to her brother
Tom; Esther Summerson, who keeps house for Mr. Jarndyce but does not suspect that he wants to marry her, is
suspended through most of *Bleak House* in a relation to
him that is semi-filial; Little Dorrit is shown throughout in
a sisterly and filial relation, and Arthur Clennam, before
he figures as a lover, plays simply, like Mr. Jarndyce, the
rôle of a protective and elderly friend. In the love of Little
Dorrit and Clennam, there seems to be little passion, but
a sobriety of resignation, almost a note of sadness: they
'went down,' Dickens says at the end, "into a modest life
of usefulness and happiness,' one of the objects of which

was to be 'to give a mother's care . . . to Fanny's [her
sister's] neglected children no less than to their own.'

These children of Dickens'—he now had nine—were
evidently giving him anxiety. He used to grumble about
their lack of enterprise; and it would appear from Mrs.
Perugini's story, which trails off in a depressing record of
their failures and follies and untimely deaths, that in general they did not turn out well. The ill-bred daughter and
worthless son of Dorrit probably caricature Dickens' fears.
Surely the Dorrits' travels on the Continent caricature the
progress of the Dickenses. Old Dorrit's rise in the world is
no rescue at the end of a fairy tale, as it would have been
in one of the early novels. The point of the story is that
this rise can be only a mockery: the Dorrits will always be
what the Marshalsea has made them.

The theme of *Little Dorrit* is repeated in *Great Expectations* (1860-61). This second of Dickens' novels in which
the hero tells his own story is like an attempt to fill in
some of the things that have been left out of *David Copperfield*. The story is the reverse of the earlier one. David
was a gentleman by birth, who by accident became a wage
slave. Pip is a boy out of the blacksmith's shop, who by accident gets a chance to become a gentleman. He straightway turns into a mean little snob.

The formula of *Bleak House* is repeated, too. The solution of the puzzle is again Dickens' moral, here more bitterly, even hatefully, delivered. Pip owes his mysterious
income to the convict whom, in his childhood, he be-
friended on the marshes. Abel Magwitch himself had been
a wretched tinker's boy, who had 'first become aware of
[himself] a-thieving turnips for a living.' Later he had
been exploited by a gentlemanly rotter turned crook, who
had left Magwitch to take the rap when they had both
fallen into the hands of the law. The poor rascal had been
impressed by the advantage that his companion's social

status — he had been to the public school — had given him in the eyes of the court; and when Magwitch later prospered in New South Wales, he decided to make a gentleman of Pip. Thus Pip finds himself in a position very similar to Lady Dedlock's: the money that chains him to Magwitch will not merely associate him with a poverty and ignorance more abject than that from which he has escaped, but will put him under obligations to an individual who represents to him the dregs of the underworld, a man with a price on his head. Not only this; but the proud lady here — who has known Pip in his first phase and scorns him because she thinks him a common village boy — turns out to be the daughter of Magwitch and of a woman who has been tried for murder and who is now employed in the humble capacity of housekeeper by the lawyer who got her off.

The symbol here is the 'great expectations' which both Pip and Estella entertain: they figure (Mr. T. A. Jackson has here again put his finger on the point) the Victorian mid-century optimism. Estella and Pip have both believed that they could count upon a wealthy patroness, the heiress of a now disused brewery, to make them secure against vulgarity and hardship. But the patroness vanishes like a phantom, and they are left with their leisure-class habits and no incomes to keep them up. They were originally to lose one another, too: the tragedies in Dickens' novels are coming more and more to seem irremediable. Estella was to marry for his money a brutal country squire, and Pip was never to see her again except for one brief meeting in London. Here is the last sentence of the ending that Dickens first wrote: 'I was very glad afterwards to have had the interview; for, in her face, and in her voice, and in her touch, she gave me the assurance that suffering had been stronger than Miss Havisham's teaching, and had given her a heart to understand what my heart used to be.'

This was to have been all, and it was perfect in tone

and touch. But Bulwer Lytton made Dickens change it to the ending we now have, in which Estella's husband gets killed and Pip and she are united. Dickens was still a public entertainer who felt that he couldn't too far disappoint his audience.

In *Little Dorrit* and *Great Expectations*, there is, therefore, a great deal more psychological interest than in Dickens' previous books. We are told what the characters think and feel, and even something about how they change. And here we must enter into the central question of the psychology of Dickens' characters.

The world of the early Dickens is organized according to a dualism which is based — in its artistic derivation — on the values of melodrama: there are bad people and there are good people, there are comics and there are characters played straight. The only complexity of which Dickens is capable is to make one of his noxious characters become wholesome, one of his clowns turn into a serious person. The most conspicuous example of this process is the reform of Mr. Dombey, who, as Taine says, 'turns into the best of fathers and spoils a fine novel.' But the reform of Scrooge in *A Christmas Carol* shows the phenomenon in its purest form.

We have come to take Scrooge so much for granted that he seems practically a piece of Christmas folklore; we no more inquire seriously into the mechanics of his transformation than we do into the transformation of the Beast in the fairy tale into the young prince that marries Beauty. Yet Scrooge represents a principle fundamental to the dynamics of Dickens' world and derived from his own emotional constitution. It was not merely that his passion for the theater had given him a taste for melodramatic contrasts; it was rather that the lack of balance between the opposite impulses of his nature had stimulated an appetite for melodrama. For emotionally Dickens *was* unstable. Allowing for the English restraint, which masks what the Russian expressiveness indulges and perhaps over-expresses, and for the pretenses of English biographers, he seems almost as unstable as Dostoevsky. He was capable of great hardness and cruelty, and not merely toward those whom he had cause to resent: people who patronized or intruded on him. On one occasion, in the presence of other guests, he ordered Forster out of his house over some discussion that had arisen at dinner; he was certainly not gentle with Maria Winter; and his treatment of Catherine suggests, as we shall see, the behavior of a Renaissance monarch summarily consigning to a convent the wife who has served her turn. There is more of emotional reality behind Quilp in *The Old Curiosity Shop* than there is behind Little Nell. If Little Nell sounds bathetic today, Quilp has lost none of his fascination. He is ugly, malevolent, perverse; he delights in making mischief for its own sake; yet he exercises over the members of his household a power which is almost an attraction and which resembles what was known in Dickens' day as 'malicious animal magnetism.' Though Quilp is ceaselessly tormenting his wife and browbeating the boy who works for him, they never attempt to escape: they admire him; in a sense they love him.

So Dickens' daughter, Kate Perugini, who had destroyed a memoir of her father that she had written, because it gave 'only half the truth,' told Miss Gladys Storey, the author of *Dickens and Daughter,* that the spell which Dickens had been able to cast on his daughters was so strong that, after he and their mother had separated, they had refrained from going to see her, though he never spoke to them about it, because they knew that he did not like it, and would even take music lessons in a house just opposite the one where she was living without daring to pay her a call. 'I loved my father,' said Mrs. Perugini, 'better than any man in the world — in a different way of course. . . . I loved him for his faults.' And she added, as she rose and walked to the door: 'my father was a wicked man — a very wicked man.' But from the memoirs of his other daughter Mamie, who also adored her father and seems to have viewed him uncritically, we hear of his colossal Christmas parties, of the vitality, the imaginative exhilaration, which swept all the guests along. It is Scrooge bursting in on the Cratchits. Shall we ask what Scrooge would actually be like if we were to follow him beyond the frame of the story? Unquestionably he would relapse when the merriment was over — if not while it was still going on — into moroseness, vindictiveness, suspicion. He would, that is to say, reveal himself as the victim of a manic-depressive cycle, and a very uncomfortable person.

This dualism runs all through Dickens. There has always to be a good and a bad of everything: each of the books has its counterbalancing values, and pairs of characters sometimes counterbalance each other from the casts of different books. There has to be a good manufacturer, Mr. Rouncewell, and a bad manufacturer, Mr. Bounderby; a bad old Jew, Fagin, and a good old Jew, Riah; an affable lawyer who is really unscrupulous, Vholes, and a kindly lawyer who pretends to be unfeeling, Jaggers; a malicious dwarf, Quilp, and a beneficent dwarf, Miss Mowcher (though Dickens had originally intended her to be bad); an embittered and perverse illegitimate daughter, Miss Wade, the Self-Tormentor, and a sweet and submissive illegitimate daughter, Esther Summerson. Another example of this tendency is Dickens' habit, noted by Mr. Kingsmill, of making the comic side of his novels a kind of parody on the sentimental side. Pecksniff is a satire on that domestic sentiment which wells up so profusely in Dickens himself when it is a question of a story for the Christmas trade; the performances of the Vincent Crummleses provide a burlesque of the stagy plot upon which *Nicholas Nickleby* is based.

Dickens' difficulty in his middle period, and indeed more or less to the end, is to get good and bad together in one character. He had intended in *Dombey and Son* to make Walter Gay turn out badly, but hadn't been able to bring himself to put it through. In *Bleak House,* however, he had had Richard Carstone undergo a progressive demoralization. But the real beginnings of a psychological interest may be said to appear in *Hard Times,* which, though parts of it have the crudity of a cartoon, is the first novel in which Dickens tries to trace with any degree of plausibility the processes by which people become what they are. We are given a certain sympathetic insight into what has happened to the Gradgrind children; and the conversion of Mr. Gradgrind is very much better prepared for than that of Mr. Dombey. In *Great Expectations* we see Pip pass through a whole psychological cycle. At first, he is sympathetic, then by a more or less natural process he turns into something unsympathetic, then he becomes sympathetic again. Here the effects of both poverty and riches are seen from the inside in one person. This is for Dickens a great advance; and it is a development which, if carried far enough, would end by eliminating the familiar Dickens of the lively but limited stage characters, with their tag lines and their unvarying make-ups.

The crisis of Dickens' later life had already come before *Great Expectations.* That 'old unhappy loss or want of something' which he makes David Copperfield feel after his marriage to Dora had driven him into a dream of retreating to the monastery of the Great St. Bernard, where it had been his original idea to have the whole of *Little Dorrit* take place. But he had ended by resorting to another order which, in mimicking the life of men, may remain almost as impenetrably cut off from it as the monks of the St. Bernard themselves. Dickens embarked upon a series of theatricals, which, though undertaken originally as benefits, took on a semi-professional character and came to look more and more like pretexts for Dickens to indulge his appetite for acting.

He had written Forster of 'the so happy and yet so unhappy existence which seeks its realities in unrealities, and finds its dangerous comfort in a perpetual escape from the disappointment of heart around it.' But now the pressure of this disappointment was to drive him into a deeper addiction to that dangerous comfort of unrealities. It was as if he had actually to embody, to act out in his own person, the life of his imagination. He had always loved acting: as a child, he had projected himself with intensity into the characters of the plays he had seen. He had always loved amateur theatricals and charades. He used to say that it relieved him, if only in a game, to throw himself into the personality of someone else. His whole art had been a kind of impersonation, in which he had exploited this or that of his impulses by incorporating it in an imaginary person rather than — up to this point, at any rate — exploring his own personality. The endings of his early novels, in which the villain was smashingly confounded and the young juvenile got the leading woman, had been the conventional dénouements of Drury Lane. Whole scenes of *Barnaby Rudge* had been high-flown declamations in a blank verse which connects Dickens almost as closely with the dramatic tradition of Shakespeare as with the fictional tradition of Fielding. Dickens admitted that he found it difficult, whenever he became particularly serious, to refrain from falling into blank verse; and though his prose, like everything else in his art, underwent a remarkable development, tightening up and becoming cleaner, he never quite got rid of this tendency. The scene in which Edith Dombey turns upon and unmasks Mr. Carker, with its doors arranged for exits and entrances, its suspense engineered through the presence of the servants, its set speeches, its highfalutin language, its hair-raising reversal of rôles, its interruption at the climactic moment by the sudden sound of the bell that announces the outraged husband — this scene, which is one of the worst in Dickens, must be one of the passages in fiction most completely conceived in terms of the stage. In *Bleak House,* he is still theatrical, but he has found out how to make this instinct contribute to the effectiveness of a novel: the theatrical present tense of the episodes which alternate with Esther Summerson's diary does heighten the excitement of the narrative, and the theatrical Lady Dedlock is an improvement on Edith Dombey. Yet in the novels that follow *Bleak House,* this theatricalism recurs as something never either quite eliminated from or quite assimilated by Dickens' more serious art, an element which remains unreal if it is not precisely insincere and on which his stories sometimes run aground. Later, when he was giving his public readings, he wrote a whole series of stories — *Somebody's Luggage, Mrs. Lirriper, Doctor Marigold* — which were primarily designed for public performance and in which excellent character monologues lead up to silly little episodes in the bad sentimental taste of the period which Dickens had done so much to popularize. Dickens had a strain of the ham in him, and, in the desperation of his later life, he gave in to the old ham and let him rip.

That this satisfied the deeper needs of Dickens as little as it does those of his readers seems to be proved by what followed. He met behind the scenes of the theater sometime in '57 or '58 a young girl named Ellen Ternan, the daughter of a well-known actress. When Dickens first saw her, she was hiding behind one of the properties and crying because she had to go on in a costume that offended her sense of modesty. Dickens reassured her. She was eighteen, and she evidently appealed to that compassionate interest in young women which had made him apotheosize Mary Hogarth. He saw her again and became infatuated. He had been complaining to Forster that 'a sense comes always crashing on me now, when I fall into low spirits, as of one happiness I have missed in life, and one friend and companion I have never made; and it must have seemed to him that now he had found her.

He had made an agreement with Catherine in the early days of their marriage that if either should fall in love with anyone else, he should frankly explain to the other. He now told her that he was in love with Miss Ternan and compelled her to call on the girl. Dickens conducted the whole affair with what appears to us the worst possible taste, though I shall show in a moment that there were special reasons why his behavior seemed natural to him. He arranged to have Ellen Ternan take part in his benefit performances, and, whether by design or not, gave her rôles which ran close enough to the real situation to offend Mrs. Dickens. Mr. Wright, who first made this whole episode public in 1934, believes, probably rightly, that Sydney Carton is Dickens' dramatization of the first hopeless phase of his love. In the spring of '58, however, Dickens arranged a separation from Catherine and left her with one of their sons in London while he removed with the rest of the children and Georgina to the new place he had bought at Gadshill. He published a statement in *Household Words* and circulated a singular letter which was not long in getting into print, in which he explained that he and Catherine had nothing whatever in common and should never have got married; defended, without naming her, Ellen Ternan; and denounced, without naming them, as 'two wicked persons' his mother-in-law and his sister-in-law Helen for having intimated that there could be 'on this earth a more virtuous and spotless creature' than Ellen. It was true that he and Ellen had not been lovers; but he now induced Ellen to be his mistress and set her up in an establishment of her own. He wrote her name into his last three novels as Estella Provis, Bella Wilfer, and finally Helena Landless — her full name was Ellen Lawless Ternan.

In order to understand what is likely to seem to us on
Dickens' part a strange and disagreeable exhibitionism, we
must remember his relation to his public. Perhaps no other
kind of writer depends so much on his audience as the
novelist. If the novelist is extremely popular, he may even
substitute his relation to his public for the ordinary human
relations. And for this reason he responds to his sales in a
way which may seem ridiculous to a writer in a different
field; yet to the novelist the rise or the drop in the number
of the people who buy his books may be felt in very much
the same way as the coolness or the passion of a loved one.
In Dickens' case, a falling-off in the popularity of his
monthly instalments would plunge him into anxiety and
depression. He had played up Sam Weller in *Pickwick*
because he saw that the character was going well, and he
sent Martin Chuzzlewit to America because he found that
interest in the story was flagging. And now it had come
to be true in a sense that his only companion in his fictional world was the public who saw him act and read his
novels. When he began, as he did that same spring, to
give regular public readings — which enabled him to live
these novels, as it were, in his own person, and to feel the
direct impact on his audience — the relation became more
intimate still. For Dickens, the public he addressed in this
statement about his marriage was probably closer than the
wife by whom he had had ten children; and now that he
had fallen in love with Ellen, instead of finding in her a
real escape from the eternal masquerade of his fiction, his
first impulse was to transport her to dwell with him in that
imaginary world itself, to make her a character in a novel
or play, and to pay court to her in the presence of his
public.

But the old sense of 'loss or want' does not seem to have
been cured by all this. 'My father was like a madman,'
says Mrs. Perugini, 'when my mother left home. This affair brought out all that was worst — all that was weakest

in him. He did not care a damn what happened to any of us. Nothing could surpass the misery and unhappiness of our home.' And this misery still hung over the household, in spite of Dickens' festive hospitality, even after the separation had been arranged. Poor Mrs. Dickens in her exile was wretched — 'Do you think he is sorry for me?' she asked Kate on one of the only two occasions when she ever heard her mother mention her father — and there was always at the back of their consciousness this sense of something deeply wrong. Kate Dickens, with more independence than Mamie, does not seem much to have liked having Miss Ternan come to Gadshill; and she finally married a brother of Wilkie Collins, without really caring about him, in order to get away from home. After the wedding, which Mrs. Dickens had not attended, Mamie found her father weeping in Kate's bedroom, with his face in her wedding dress: 'But for me,' he said to her, 'Katy would not have left home.'

This episode of Ellen Ternan has been hushed up so systematically, and the information about it is still so meager, that it is difficult to get an impression of Ellen. We do, however, know something about what Dickens thought of her from the heroines in his last books who are derived from her. Estella is frigid and indifferent: it amuses her to torture Pip, who loves her 'against reason, against promise, against peace, against hope, against happiness, against all discouragement that could be'; she marries a man she does not love for his money. Bella Wilfer up to her conversion by Mr. Boffin is equally intent upon money — which was certainly one of the things that Ellen got out of her liaison with Dickens. Both Estella and Bella are petulant, spoiled and proud. They represent, as it were, the qualities of the Edith Dombey-Lady Dedlock great lady combined with the capriciousness of Dora Spenlow — the old elements of Dickens' women simply mixed in a new way. And these novels of Dickens in which Ellen figures show perhaps more real desperation than *Little Dorrit* itself, with its closing note of modest resignation. It seems to be the general opinion that Ellen was neither so fascinating nor so gifted as Dickens thought her. After his death, she married a clergyman, and she confided to Canon Benham that she had loathed her relationship with Dickens and deeply regretted the whole affair. She had borne Dickens a child, which did not live. It may be — though we have no date — that Dickens' short story, *Doctor Marigold* (1865), which became one of his favorite readings, the monologue of a traveling 'cheap jack,' who keeps an audience entertained with his patter while his child is dying in his arms, is a reflection of this event.

In spite of the energy of a *diable au corps* which enabled him to put on his plays and to perform prodigies of walking and mountain-climbing at the same time that he was composing his complicated novels, the creative strain of a lifetime was beginning to tell heavily on Dickens. He had always felt under an obligation to maintain a standard of living conspicuously lavish for a literary man: in his statement about his separation from his wife, he boasts that he has provided for her as generously 'as if Mrs. Dickens were a lady of distinction and I a man of fortune.' And now he was compelled both by the demon that drove him and by the necessity of earning money in order to keep up the three establishments for which he had made himself responsible and to launch his sons and daughters on the world, to work frantically at his public readings. His nervous disorders persisted: he was troubled while he was writing *Great Expectations* with acute pains in the face; and he developed a lameness in his left foot, which, though he blamed it on taking walks in heavy snowstorms, was also evidently due to the burning-out of his nerves. He was maimed by it all the rest of his life. 'Twice last week,' he writes in '66, 'I was seized in a most distressing manner — apparently in the heart; but, I am persuaded, only in the nervous system.'

Three years had passed since *Great Expectations* before Dickens began another novel; he worked at it with what was for him extreme slowness, hesitation and difficulty; and the book shows the weariness, the fears and the definitive disappointments of this period.

This story, *Our Mutual Friend* (1864-65), like all these later books of Dickens, is more interesting to us today than it was to Dickens' public. It is a next number in the Dickens sequence quite worthy of its predecessors, a development out of what has gone before that is in certain ways quite different from the others. It may be said Dickens never really repeats himself: his thought makes a consistent progress, and his art, through the whole thirty-five years of his career, keeps going on to new materials and effects; so that his work has an interest and a meaning as a whole. The difficulty that Dickens found in writing *Our Mutual Friend* does not make itself felt as anything in the nature of an intellectual disintegration. On the contrary, the book compensates for its shortcomings by the display of an intellectual force which, though present in Dickens' work from the first, here appears in a phase of high tension and a condition of fine muscular training. The Dickens of the old eccentric 'Dickens characters' has here, as has often been noted, become pretty mechanical and sterile. It is a pity that the creator of Quilp and of Mrs. Jarley's waxworks should have felt himself under the necessity of fabricating Silas Wegg and the stuffed animals of Mr. Venus. Also, the complex Dickens plot has come to seem rather tiresome and childish. But Dickens has here distilled the mood of his later years, dramatized the tragic discrepancies of his character, delivered his final judgment on the whole Victorian exploit, in a fashion so impressive that we realize how little the distractions of this period had the power to direct him from the prime purpose of his life: the serious exercise of his art.

As the fog is the symbol for *Bleak House* and the prison for *Little Dorrit*, so the dust-pile is the symbol for *Our Mutual Friend*. It dominates even the landscape of London, which has already been presented by Dickens under such a variety of aspects, but which now appears — though with Newgate looming over it as it did in *Barnaby Rudge* — under an aspect that is new: 'A gray dusty withered evening in London city has not a hopeful aspect,' he writes of the day when Bradley Headstone goes to pay his hopeless court to Lizzie Hexam. 'The closed warehouses and offices have an air of death about them, and the national dread of color has an air of mourning. The towers and steeples of the many house-encompassed churches, dark and dingy as the sky that seems descending on them, are no relief to the general gloom; a sun-dial on a church-wall has the look, in its useless black shade, of having failed in its business enterprise and stopped payment for ever; melancholy waifs and strays of housekeepers and porters sweep melancholy waifs and strays of papers and pins into the kennels, and other more melancholy waifs and strays explore them, searching and stooping and poking for everything to sell. The set of humanity outward from the City is as a set of prisoners departing from gaol, and dismal Newgate seems quite as fit a stronghold for the mighty Lord Mayor as his own state-dwelling.'

The actual dust-pile in question has been amassed by a dust-removal contractor, who has made out of it a considerable fortune. The collection of refuse at that time was still in private hands, and was profitable because the bones, rags and cinders, and even the dust itself, were valuable for various kinds of manufacture. The plot of *Our Mutual Friend* has to do with the struggle of a number of persons to get possession of or some share in this money.

(The other principal industry which figures in *Our Mutual Friend* is the robbing of the dead bodies in the Thames.) But the real meaning of the dust-pile is not in doubt: 'My lords and gentlemen and honorable lords,' writes Dickens, when the heap is being carted away, 'when you in the course of your dust-shoveling and cinder-raking have piled up a mountain of pretentious failure, you must off with your honorable coats for the removal of it, and fall to the work with the power of all the queen's horses and all the queen's men, or it will come rushing down and bury us alive.'

Dickens' line in his criticism of society is very clear in *Our Mutual Friend,* and it marks a new position on Dickens' part, as it results from a later phase of the century. Dickens has come at last to despair utterly of the prospering middle class. We have seen how he judged the morality of the merchants. In *Bleak House,* the iron-master is a progressive and self-sustaining figure who is played off against parasites of various sorts; but in *Hard Times,* written immediately afterward, the later development of Rouncewell is dramatized in the exploiter Bounderby, a new kind of Victorian hypocrite, who pretends to be a self-made man. In *Little Dorrit,* the one set of characters who are comparatively healthy and cheerful still represent that middle-class home which has remained Dicken's touchstone of virtue; but even here there is a distinct change in Dickens' attitude. Mr. Meagles, the retired banker, with his wife and his beloved only daughter, become the prey of Henry Gowan, a well-connected young man of no fortune who manages to lead a futile life (the type has been well observed) between the social and artistic worlds without ever making anything of either. But the smugness and insularity, even the vulgarity, of the Meagleses is felt by Dickens as he has never felt it in connection with such people before. After all, in taking in Tattycoram, the foundling, the Meagleses could not help making her feel her position of inferiority. A little more emphasis in this direction by Dickens and the Meagleses might seem to the reader as odious as they recurrently do to her. Tattycoram herself, with her painful alternations between the extremes of affection and resentment, probably reflects the oscillations of Dickens himself at this period.

But the resentment is to get the upper hand. The Meagleses turn up now as the Podsnaps, that horrendous middle-class family, exponents of all the soundest British virtues, who however, are quite at home in a social circle of sordid adventurers and phony *nouveaux riches,* and on whom Dickens visits a satire as brutal as themselves. Gone are the high spirits that made of Pecksniff an exhilarating figure of fun — gone with the Yoho! of the stagecoach on which Tom Pinch traveled to London. The Podsnaps, the Lammles, the Veneerings, the Fledgebys, are unpleasant as are no other characters in Dickens. It comes to us as a disturbing realization that Dickens is now *afraid* of Podsnap (who, with his talk about the paramount importance of not bringing the blush to the young person's cheek, would of course have been the loudest among those who disapproved of Dickens' affair with Miss Ternan). And Fledgeby, the young moneylender of the second generation, with his peachy cheeks and slender figure, who lives in the Albany and dines out — Grandfather Smallweed is a man beside him! It is startling to find that Dickens has here even hit upon a principle which another group of commercial-patriotic rotters were later to exploit on a large scale. One of the ugliest scenes in Dickens is that in which Fledgeby ascribes his own characteristics to the gentle old Jew Riah and makes him the agent of his meanness and sharp-dealing. And not content with making Fledgeby a cur, Dickens himself shows a certain cruelty in having him ultimately thrashed by Lammle under circumstances of peculiar ignominy and then having the little dolls' dressmaker apply plasters with pepper on them to his wounds. This incident betrays a kind of sadism which we never felt in Dickens' early work — when Nicholas Nickleby beat Squeers, for example — but which breaks out now and then in these later books in a disagreeable fashion.

If the middle class has here become a monster, the gentry have taken on an aspect more attractive than we have ever known them to wear as a class in any previous novel of Dickens. If an increase of satiric emphasis turns the Meagleses into the Podsnaps, so a shift from the satirical to the straight turns the frivolous and idle young man of good family, who has hitherto always been exhibited as more or less of a scoundrel — James Harthouse or Henry Gowan — into the sympathetic Eugene Wrayburn. Eugene and his friend Mortimer Lightwood, the little old diner-out named Twemlow, the only gentleman in the Veneerings' circle, and the Reverend Frank Milvey, 'expensively educated and wretchedly paid,' the Christian turned social worker, are the only representatives of the upper strata who are shown as having decent values; and they are all the remnants of an improverished gentry. Outside these, you find the decent values — or what Dickens intends to be such — in an impoverished proletariat and lower middle class: the modest clerk, the old Jew, the dolls' dressmaker, the dust-contractor's foreman, the old woman who minds children for a living. And the chief heroine is not Bella Wilfer, who has to be cured of her middle-class ideals, but Lizzie Hexam, the illiterate daughter of a Thames-side water-rat. Dickens has here, for the first time in his novels, taken his leading woman from the lowest class; and it will be the principal moral of *Our Mutual Friend* that Wrayburn will have the courage to marry Lizzie. The inevitable conjunction of the high with the low is not here to result in a tragedy but to figure as a fortunate affair. Nor does it involve the whole structure of society in the same way as in the earlier novels: the me-

chanics are somewhat different. The point is made that
the Podsnap-Veneering upper scum of the successful middle class remain unaffected by what has happened and do
not seriously affect anyone else. Such people, in Dickens'
view, have by this time become completely dissociated
from anything that is admirable in English life. Simply,
Eugene Wrayburn no longer appears at the Veneerings'
parties. When they sneer at the unseemliness of his marriage, Mr. Twemlow suddenly flares up and declares with
an authority which makes everyone uncomfortable that
Eugene has behaved like a gentleman; and that is the end
of the book.

Dickens has aligned himself in *Our Mutual Friend*
with a new combination of forces. Shrinking from Podsnap and Veneering, he falls back on that aristocracy he
had so savagely attacked in his youth, but to which,
through his origins, he had always been closer than he
had to the commercial classes. After all, Sir John Chester
had had qualities of coolness, grace and ease which, when
they appear in an excellent fellow like Eugene, are infinitely preferable to Podsnap. The Chartist movement in
England had run into the sands in the fifties; but during
the sixties the trade union movement had been making
remarkable progress. Dickens had begun *Our Mutual
Friend* in the autumn of 1863, and the first number appeared the following May. In July definite steps were
taken at a meeting of French and English workers for an
'international working men's alliance,' and the Workers'
International, under the guidance of Karl Marx, was
founded at the end of September. This trend may have
influenced Dickens, for the final implication of his story
is — to state it in the Marxist language — that the de-
classed representatives of the old professional upper classes
may unite with the proletariat against the commercial
middle class.

There is, however, another element that plays an important rôle in the story: the proletarian who has educated himself to be a member of this middle class. Lizzie Hexam has a brother, whom she has induced to get an education and who, as soon as he has qualified himself to teach, drops his family even more callously than Pip did his; and the schoolmaster of Charley Hexam's school, another poor man who has advanced himself, is the villain of *Our Mutual Friend*. We are a long way here from the days when the villains and bad characters in Dickens, the Quilps and the Mrs. Gamps, could be so fascinating through their resourcefulness and vitality that, as G. K. Chesterton says, the reader is sorry at the end when they are finally banished from the scene and hopes that the discredited scoundrel will still open the door and stick his head in and make one more atrocious remark. Such figures are so much all of a piece of evil that they have almost a kind of innocence. But here Bradley Headstone has no innocence: he is perverted, tormented, confused. He represents a type which begins to appear in these latest novels of Dickens and which originally derives perhaps from those early theatrical villains, of the type of the elder Rudge or Monks in *Oliver Twist*, skulking figures with black looks and ravaged faces: a literary convention of which one would suppose it would be impossible to make anything plausible. Yet Dickens does finally succeed in giving these dark figures reality.

In Bradley Headstone's case, it is his very aspirations which have gone bad and turned the stiff and anxious schoolmaster into a murderer. He wants to marry Lizzie Hexam and he is wounded by her preference for Eugene, whose nonchalance and grace infuriate him because he knows he can never achieve them. In order to make himself a place in society, he has had rigorously to repress his passions; and now that they finally break out, it is more horrible than Bill Sikes or Jonas Chuzzlewit, because we understand Bradley as a human being. Bradley is the first murderer in Dickens who exhibits any complexity of character. And he is the first to present himself as a member of respectable Victorian society. There is a dreadful and convincing picture of the double life led by Headstone as he goes about his duties as a schoolmaster after he has decided to murder Eugene. In *Great Expectations,* the Ellen Ternan character, Estella, rejects the love of the hero. In *Our Mutual Friend,* Bella Wilfer rejects Rokesmith in much the same way — though less cruelly, and though she later marries him. But Rokesmith is a colorless character, and the real agonies of frustrated passion appear in *Our Mutual Friend* in the scene between Bradley and Lizzie. This is the kind of thing — the Carker and Edith Dombey kind of thing — that is likely to be bad in Dickens; but here it has a certain reality and a certain unpleasant power. Who can forget the tophatted schoolmaster striking his fist against the stone wall of the church?

The inference is, of course, that Bradley, if he had not been shipwrecked in this way, would have approximated as closely as possible to some sort of Murdstone or Gradgrind. But his death has a tragic symbolism which suggests a different kind of moral. In order to escape detection, he has disguised himself at the time of the murder as a disreputable waterside character who is known to have a grievance against Eugene. When the man finds out what has happened, he makes capital of it by blackmailing Bradley. Headstone finally tackles him on the edge of the deep lock of a canal, drags him into the water, and holds him under until he is drowned; but in doing so, he drowns himself. It is as if the illiterate ruffian whom he would now never be able to shake off has come to represent the brutish part of Bradley's own nature. Having failed to destroy Eugene, he destroys himself with the brute.

VI

In *The Mystery of Edwin Drood,* the motif of Bradley Headstone is, with certain variations, repeated.

This novel, written five years later, Dickens never lived to finish, and it is supposed to have been left an enigma. We must first try to solve the enigma; and to do so we must proceed with a consciousness of the real meaning of Dickens' work. For though it is true that *Edwin Drood* had been enormously written about, it has been always from the point of view of trying to find out what Dickens intended to do with the plot. None of the more serious critics of Dickens has ever been able to take the novel very seriously. They persist in dismissing it as a detective story with good touches and promising characters, but of no interest in the development of Dickens' genius. Bernard Shaw, who is interested in the social side of Dickens, declares that it is 'only a gesture by a man three quarters dead'; and it is true, as Forster remarked, that *The Mystery of Edwin Drood* seems quite free from the social criticism which had grown more biting as Dickens grew older; but what Forster and Shaw do not see is that the psychological interest which had been a feature of Dickens' later period is carried farther in *Edwin Drood.* Like all the books that Dickens wrote under the strain of his later years, it has behind it bitter judgments and desperate emotions. Here as elsewhere the solution of the mystery was to have said something that Dickens wanted to say.

It did not, it is true, become possible to gauge the full significance of the novel until certain key discoveries had been made in regard to the plot itself; but the creation of such a character as John Jasper at this point in Dickens' development should have had its significance for any student of Dickens and should have led to a more careful consideration, in the light of certain hints supplied by Forster, of the psychological possibilities of the character.

It has remained for two American scholars to hit upon the cardinal secrets that explain the personality of Jasper. As both these discoveries have been made since the publication in 1912 of W. Roberston Nicoll's otherwise comprehensive book, *The Problem of Edwin Drood,* they have not received attention there; they are not included by Thomas Wright in the bibliography of *Edwin Drood* in his *Life of Charles Dickens,* published in 1936; and so far as I know, up to the present time, nobody who has written about Dickens has been in a position to combine these ideas. Yet what happens when one puts them together is startling: the old novel acquires a sudden new value. Just as one can revive invisible ink by holding it over a lamp or bring out three dimensions in a photograph by looking at it through certain lenses, so it is possible to recall to life the character of John Jasper as he must have been conceived by Dickens.

The most important revelation about *Edwin Drood* has been made by Mr. Howard Duffield, who published an article called *John Jasper — Strangler* in *The American Bookman* of February, 1930. Mr. Duffield has here shown conclusively that Jasper is supposed to be a member of the Indian sect of Thugs, who made a profession of ingratiating themselves with travelers and then strangling them with a handkerchief and robbing them. This brotherhood, which had been operating for centuries pretty much all over India and which had given the British government a great deal of trouble before it succeeded in putting them down during the thirties, had already attracted attention in the West. Two of the British officers who had been engaged in the suppression of the Thugs had written books about them — one of them in the form of a story, Meadows Taylor's *Confessions of a Thug,* supposed to be narrated by the Thug himself. Eugène Sue had introduced into *The Wandering Jew* a Thug strangler practicing in Europe; and an American novelist, James de Mille,

was publishing a novel called *Cord and Creese,* which
exploited the situation of an Englishman affiliated with
the Thugs, in the same year, 1869, that Dickens began
Edwin Drood. We know that Dickens' friend, Edward
Bulwer Lytton, had already thought of using this theme.
Dickens himself had mentioned the Thugs in 1857 in
connection with a garrotting epidemic in London. The
publication in 1868 of Wilkie Collins' detective story, *The
Moonstone,* in which a band of Hindu devotees commit
a secret murder in England, seems to have inspired Dickens with the idea of outdoing his friend the next year with
a story of a similar kind.

Now, we know from the statement of Sir Luke Fildes,
Dickens' illustrator in *Edwin Drood,* that Dickens intended to have Jasper strangle Drood with the long scarf
which he (Jasper) wears around his neck; and we know
from many circumstances and certain hints that the story
was to have had its roots in the East. Neville and Helena
Landless are supposed to come from Ceylon; and Mr.
Jasper, who smokes opium and sees elephants in his
trances, is described as having 'thick, lustrous, well-ar-
ranged black hair and whiskers' and a voice that sometimes sounds 'womanish' — in short, as something very
much like a Hindu. Furthermore, as Mr. Duffield had
established, John Jasper — and this explains a good deal
that has never been understood — has been trying to fulfill the ritualistic requirements for a sanctified and successful Thug murder. The Thugs were worshipers of Kali,
the Hindu goddess of destruction, and their methods had
been prescribed by the goddess. They had to commit their
crimes with the fold of cloth which was a fragment of
the gown of Kali. Kali's gown was supposed to be black,
Jasper's scarf is black. This cloth had to be worn, as Jasper's scarf is. A secret burial place had to be selected, as
Jasper selects Mrs. Sapsea's tomb, before the murder took
place. The omens had to be observed, as is done by Mr.

Jasper when he makes his nocturnal trip to the top of the cathedral tower; the call of a rook in sight of a river was regarded as a favorable sign, the approving word of the goddess, and that, one finds, is precisely what Jasper hears. The significance of the birds is planted plainly at the beginning of Chapter II, when the Cloisterham rooks are first mentioned: 'Whosoever has observed that sedate and clerical bird, the rook, may perhaps have noticed that when he wings his way homeward toward nightfall, in a sedate and clerical company, two rooks will suddenly detach themselves from the rest, will retrace their flight for some distance, and will there poise and linger; conveying to mere men the fancy that it is of some occult importance to the body politic, that this artful couple should pretend to have renounced connection with it.' The Thug preys exclusively on travelers: Edwin Drood is going on a journey; and when Jasper, in his second opium dream, is heard talking to himself about the murder, it is all in terms of a journey and a fellow traveler. The Thug is to use exaggerated words of endearment, as Jasper does with Drood. He is to persuade his victim to leave his lodging a little after midnight, as Jasper has done with Drood, and to stupefy him with a drug in his food or drink, as Jasper has obviously done, first with Edwin and Neville, and afterwards with Durdles.

Since Jasper is eventually to be caught, he is evidently to have slipped up in the ritual. Mr. Duffield suggests that Jasper's mistake has been to commit the murder without an assistant; but he has overlooked the Thug superstition (recorded by Edward Thornton in *Illustrations of the History and Practices of the Thugs,* published in 1837) that nothing but evil could come of murdering a man with any gold in his possession. Now, Drood, unknown to Jasper, is carrying the gold ring which Grewgious has given him for Rosa; and we have it on Dickens' own testimony to Forster that the body of Edwin Drood is to be

identified by this ring, which has survived the effects of
the quicklime. True, Edwin has also been wearing the
stickpin and the gold watch; but since Jasper knew about
these and took care to leave them in the weir, he may
have made a point of removing them after Edwin was
drugged and before he was murdered.

Supplementing this interesting discovery we find a
paper by Mr. Aubrey Boyd in the series of *Humanistic
Studies* (Volume IX) published by Washington University, in which he shows that Jasper is also a hypnotist.
Dickens had always been interested in hypnotism. Forster
speaks of his first seriously studying it in 1841. He even
found that he himself, with that extraordinarily magnetic
personality which made it possible for him so to fascinate
his audiences and which exerted, as Mrs. Perugini testi-
fies, so irresistible a power over his family, had the ability
to hypnotize people. His first experiment was performed
on his wife in the course of his earlier trip to America. He
had, he wrote Forster, been 'holding forth upon the subject rather luminously, and asserting that I thought I
could exercise the influence, but had never tried.' 'Kate sat
down, laughing, for me to try my hand upon her. . . . In
six minutes, I magnetized her into hysterics, and then into
the magnetic sleep. I tried again next night, and she fell
into the slumber in little more than two minutes. . . . I
can wake her with perfect ease; but I confess (not being
prepared for anything so sudden and complete) I was on
the first occasion rather alarmed.' Later, we hear of his
hypnotizing John Leech in order to relieve his pain during an illness.

In the meantime, he had a strange experience, reported
by Mrs. Perugini, with an Englishwoman he had met in
Genoa in 1844. This lady, who was married to a Swiss
printer, was afflicted with delusions that "took the form
of a phantom which spoke to her, and other illusionary
figures of the most hideous shapes and gory appearance,

which came in a crowd, chattering one to the other as they pursued her, and after a time faded, veiling their loathsome faces as they disappeared into space.' Dickens, who at the time was suffering from a recurrence of the spasms of pain in his side which had afflicted him as a child in the blacking warehouse, hypnotized her once or twice every day and found that he could control the delusions. He seems to have become obsessed with the case: the treatment went on for months. On one occasion, 'he was in such a fever of anxiety to receive a letter from his friend concerning the state of his wife that he watched through a telescope the arrival of the mailbags into port.' He mesmerized her 'in the open country and at wayside inns where . . . they would halt for refreshment or stay the night. He mesmerized her in railway carriages — anywhere, if the moment was opportune. By degrees she became better and more serene in her mind and body.' The delusions were apparently dispelled.

It was obviously on the cards that Dickens would do something with this subject in his novels; and it ought to have given the Drood experts a lead when they encountered a reference to it in the third chapter of *Edwin Drood*. W. Robertson Nicoll, disregarding this key passage, mentions the matter in another connection: he sees that Jasper has 'willed' Crisparkle to go to the weir, where he will find the watch and stickpin of Edwin; but he does not inquire further. It remained for Mr. Boyd, who has some special knowledge of Mesmer and his writings, to recognize that Dickens has introduced the whole repertory of the supposed feats of mesmerism — called also 'animal magnetism' at the time — just as he has reproduced the practices of the Thugs. Mr. Jasper is clearly exercising 'animal magnetism,' in this case the kind known as 'malicious,' on Rosa Budd in the scene in which he accompanies her at the piano; he is exercising it on Edwin and Neville when he causes them to quarrel in his rooms. It was supposed in Dickens' time that this influence could be projected through the agency of mere sound: hence the insistent keynote in the piano scene and the swelling note of the organ that frightens Rosa in the garden. And it was also supposed to penetrate matter: hence Rosa's remark to Helena that she feels as if Jasper could reach her through a wall. It could be made to impregnate objects in such a way as to remain effective after the master of the magnetic fluid was no longer himself on the scene: Jasper has put a spell on the water in which Edwin's watch and stickpin are to be found. And it is possible, though Mr. Boyd does not suggest it, that the transmission of Jasper's influence from a distance may also explain the behavior, of which the implausible character has been noted, of the men who pursue and waylay Landless.

The revealing hint here, however, is the passage in the third chapter, of which Boyd has understood the significance and which has led him to a brilliant conjecture: 'As, in some cases of drunkenness,' writes Dickens, 'and in others of animal magnetism, there are two states of consciousness that never clash, but each of which pursues its separate course as though it were continuous instead of broken (thus, if I hide my watch when I am drunk, I must be drunk again before I can remember where), so Miss Twinkleton has two distinct and separate phases of being.' Dickens had told Forster that the originality of his idea for *Drood*, 'a very strong one, though difficult to work' (Dickens' words in a letter), was to consist (Forster's words in recounting a conversation with Dickens) 'in the review of the murderer's career by himself at the close, when its temptations were to be dwelt upon as if, not he the culprit, but some other man, were the tempted. The last chapters were to be written in the condemned cell, to which his wickedness, all elaborately elicited from him as if told of another, had brought him.'

John Jasper has, then, 'two states of consciousness'; he

is, in short, what we have come to call a dual personality. On the principle that 'if I hide my watch when I am drunk, I must be drunk again before I can remember where,' it will be necessary, in order to extort his confession, to induce in him that state of consciousness, evidently not the one with which he meets the cathedral world, that has caused him to commit the murder. The possibility of opium, suggested by Robertson Nicoll, ought surely to be excluded, since Wilkie Collins, in *The Moonstone*, had just made use of this device: the man who has taken the Moonstone under the influence of laudanum, administered to him without his knowing it, is made to repeat his action under the influence of a second dose. The drunkenness in which Jasper will betray himself will not, then, be produced by a drug. Dickens must go Collins one better. Mr. Boyd has evidently solved the puzzle in guessing that Helena Landless is eventually to hypnotize Jasper. In the scene at the piano, in which Jasper is made to work upon Rosa with the effect of her becoming hysterical, Helena maintains an attitude of defiance and announces that she is not afraid of him. It had already been established by J. Cuming Walters — it was the first of the important discoveries about *Drood* — that Datchery, the mysterious character who comes to Cloisterham to spy on Jasper, is Helena in disguise. We have been told, in Chapter VII, that Helena had several times 'dressed as a boy and shown the daring of a man' in running away from her brutal stepfather; and Dickens' alterations in his text, both the amplifications of the written copy and the later excisions from the proofs, indicate very clearly that he was aiming — in dealing with such details as Helena's wig and her attempts to conceal her feminine hands — to insinuate evidences of her real identity without allowing the reader to find it out too soon. Helena is to get the goods on Jasper, and in the end, having no doubt acquired in India the same secret which he

had been exploiting (there may be also, as so often in
Dickens, some question of a family relationship), she
will put him in a trance and make him speak.

What Mr. Boyd, however, was not in a position to do
was combine this idea with the Thug theme. The Thugs
were all in a sense divided personalities. Colonel James
L. Sleeman, in his book on the subject, emphasizes what
he calls this 'Jekyll-and-Hyde' aspect of their activities.
The Thugs were devoted husbands and loving fathers;
they made a point — again like Mr. Jasper — of holding
positions of honor in the community. And in their own
eyes they were virtuous persons: they were serving the
cult of the goddess. In their case, the Jekyll-and-Hyde
aspect of their careers was exceptional only from the point
of view of persons outside the cult. When caught, they
would proudly confess to the number of lives they had
taken. But in the case of Mr. Jasper, there is a respectable
and cultivated Christian gentleman living in the same
soul and body with a worshiper of the goddess Kali. The
murder has been rehearsed in his opium dreams: he has
evidently gone to the opium den for that purpose. He has
kept himself under the influence of the drug all the time
he has been plotting the murder. But it will not be possible to make him confess by compelling him to take opium.
Helena, with her stronger will, is to accomplish this
through hypnotism.

And now what has all this to do with the Dickens we
already know? Why should he have occupied the last
years of his life in concocting this sinister detective story?

Let us consider his situation at this period. He is still
living between Gadshill and the house of his mistress
Ellen Lawless Ternan, who appears now in *Edwin Drood*,
identified even more plainly than before, under the name
of Helena Landless. The motif of the disagreeable scene
between Bradley Headstone and Lizzie Hexam is repeated

in the even more unpleasant, though theatrical and un-convincing, interview between Jasper and Rosa Budd — Jasper presenting, like Headstone, a ghastly travesty of the respectable Victorian. The Ellen Ternan heroine is here frankly made an actress: Helena Landless is an im-personator so accomplished that she can successfully play a male character in real life; and she is even more formida-ble than Estella because she is to stand up to and unmask Jasper. Her strength is to be contrasted not only with the fatal duplicity of Jasper, but with the weakness of Drood and Neville. All of these three men are to perish, and Rosa is to marry Mr. Tartar, the foursquare young ex-Navy man, bursting with good spirits, agility and a per-haps rather overdone good health.

Dickens had just finished his public appearances and had said his farewell to the platform. The great feature of his last series of readings had been the murder of Nancy by Sikes, a performance which he had previously tried on his friends and from which Forster and others had wished to dissuade him. He was warned by a woman's doctor of his acquaintance that 'if only one woman cries out when you murder the girl, there will be a contagion of hysteria all over the place.' But Dickens obviously derived from thus horrifying his hearers some sort of satisfaction. The scene was perhaps a symbolical representation of his be-havior in banishing his wife. Certainly the murder of Nancy had taken on something of the nature of an ob-sessive hallucination. Dickens' imagination had always been subject to a tendency of this kind. It had been pointed out by Taine that the fantasies and monomanias of his lunatics only exaggerate characteristics which are apparent in Dickens' whole work — the concentration on and reiteration of some isolated aspect or detail of a person or a place, as when Mr. Dick in *David Copperfield* is haunted by King Charles's head. In one of the sketches of *The Uncommercial Traveller*, written during these later years, Dickens tells of having been obsessed by the image of a drowned and bloated corpse that he had seen in the Paris morgue, which for days kept popping up among the people and things he encountered and sometimes compelled him to leave public places, though it eventually drove him back to the morgue. In the case of the woman in Italy whose delusions he attempted to dispel, one gets the impression that these bloody visions were almost as real to him as they were to her. And now, at the time of these readings, he jokes about his 'murderous instincts' and says that he goes about the street feeling as if he were 'wanted' by the police.

He threw himself at any rate into the murder scene with a passion that became quite hysterical, as if reading it had become at this point in his life a real means of self-expression. At Clifton, he wrote Forster, 'we had a contagion of fainting; and yet the place was not hot. I should think we had from a dozen to twenty ladies taken out stiff and rigid, at various times!' At Leeds, whether in order to intensify the effect or to avert the possible objections of the audience, he hired a man to rise from the stalls and protest in the middle of the murder scene against daring to read such a thing before ladies — with the result that the people hissed him and put him out. It was the opinion of Dickens' doctor that the excitement and strain of acting this episode were the immediate cause of Dickens' death. It always took him a long time to calm himself after he had played this scene, and the doctor, who noted his pulse at the end of each selection, saw that it invariably ran higher then than it did after any of the other scenes. When Dolby, the manager of Dickens' tours, tried to persuade him to cut down on the murder, reserving it for the larger towns, Dickens had a paroxysm of rage: 'Bounding up from his chair, and throwing his knife and fork on his plate (which he smashed to atoms), he exclaimed: "Dolby! your infernal caution will be your ruin one of these days!"' Immediately afterwards, he began to weep and told Dolby that he knew he was right. The doctors eventually compelled him to interrupt his tour and take a rest.

His son, Sir Henry Dickens, who speaks in his memoir of his father of the latter's 'heavy moods of deep depression, of intense nervous irritability, when he was silent and oppressed,' tells of an incident that occurred at a Christmas party the winter before Dickens died: 'He had been ailing very much and greatly troubled with his leg, which had been giving him much pain; so he was lying on a sofa one evening after dinner, while the rest of the family were playing games.' Dickens participated in one of these games, in which you had to remember long strings of words, contributed by the players in rotation. When it came around to Dickens, he gave a name which meant nothing to anybody: 'Warren's Blacking, 30, Strand.' He did this, says his son, who knew nothing at that time of this episode in his father's childhood, 'with an odd twinkle and strange inflection in his voice which at once forcibly arrested my attention and left a vivid impression on my mind for some time afterwards. Why, I could not, for the life of me, understand. . . . At that time, when the stroke that killed him was gradually over-powering him, his mind reverted to the struggles and degradation of his childhood, which had caused him such intense agony of mind, and which he had never been able entirely to cast from him.'

Two weeks before his death, he went to a dinner arranged by Lord and Lady Houghton in order that the Prince of Wales and the King of Belgium might meet him. Lady Houghton was a granddaughter of that Lord Crewe in whose house Dickens' grandfather had been butler. She well remembered going as a child to the house-keeper's room to hear his grandmother tell wonderful stories. Dickens' neuritic foot was giving him such trouble at this time that up till almost an hour before dinner he could not be sure of going. He did finally decide to go; but when he got to the Houghton house, he found that he could not mount the stairs, and the Prince and the Belgian king had to come down to meet him.

But now the Dickens who had been cut off from society has discarded the theme of the rebel and is carrying the theme of the criminal, which has haunted him all his life, to its logical development in his fiction. He is to explore the deep entanglement and conflict of the bad and the good in one man. The subject of *Edwin Drood* is the subject of Poe's *William Wilson,* the subject of *Dr. Jekyll and Mr. Hyde,* the subject of *Dorian Gray.* It is also the subject of that greater work than any of these, Doestoevsky's *Crime and Punishment.* Dostoevsky, who owed so much to Dickens and who was probably influenced by the murder in *Chuzzlewit,* had produced in 1866 a masterpiece on the theme at which Dickens is only just arriving in 1869. Raskólnikov — *raskólnik* means dissenter — combines in his single person the two antisocial types of the deliberate criminal and the rebel, which since Hugh in *Barnaby Rudge* have always been kept distinct by Dickens. Dostoevsky, with the courage of his insight, has studied the states of mind which are the results of a secession from society: the contemptuous will to spurn and to crush confused with the impulse toward human brotherhood, the desire to be loved twisted tragically with the desire to destroy and to kill. But the English Dickens with his middle-class audience would not be able to tell such a story even if he dared to imagine it. In order to stage the 'war in the members,' he must contrive a whole machinery of mystification: of drugs, of telepathic powers, of remote oriental cults.

How far he has come and to how strange a goal we recognize when we note that he has now returned to that

Rochester he so loved in his boyhood — the Rochester
where he had made Mr. Pickwick put up at the Bull Inn
and picnic on good wine and cold fowl out of the hampers
of the Wardles' barouche. Gadshill was next door to
Rochester, and the Cloisterham of the novel is Rochester;
but what Dickens finds in Rochester today is the nightmare of John Jasper. There is plenty of brightness in
Edwin Drood and something of the good things of life:
Mrs. Crisparkle's jams, jellies and spices, Mr. Tartar's
shipshape rooms; but this brightness has a quality new
and queer. The vivid colors of *Edwin Drood* make upon
us an impression more disturbing than the dustiness, the
weariness, the dreariness, which set the tone for *Our Mutual Friend*. In this new novel, which is to be his last,
Dickens has found a new intensity. The descriptions of
Cloisterham are among the best written in all his fiction:
they have a nervous concentration and economy — nervous in the old-fashioned sense — that produces a rather
different effect from anything one remembers in the work
of his previous phases. We are far from the prodigal improvisation of the poetical early Dickens: here every de-
scriptive phrase is loaded with implication. It is as if
Dickens' art, which in *Our Mutual Friend* had seemed to
him so sorely fatigued, has now rested and found a revival. Dickens has at last here abandoned the task of
analyzing society — British imperialism in the East is evidently to play some part in the story, but it is impossible
to tell whether or not this is to have any moral significance. (A writer in the Princeton undergraduate publication *The Nassau Literary Magazine* of May, 1882, who
complains of the little interest that has been shown in
Edwin Drood, suggests that the opium traffic may provide
the social issue here.) The novelist, as far as we can see,
is at this point exclusively concerned with a psychological
problem. The duality of high and low, rich and poor, has
evidently here given place to the duality of good and evil.

The remarkable opening pages in which the Victorian choirmaster, with his side-whiskers and tall hat, mixes in his opium-vision the picture of the English cathedral with memories of the East and awakes in the squalid den to stagger out, short of breath, to his services, is, from the psychological point of view, for its time a complex piece of writing. But the characters that are healthy, pure and good — Rosa Budd, for example, with her baby name — seem almost as two-dimensional as colored paper dolls. We have got back to the fairy tale again. Yet this fairy tale contains no Pickwick: its most convincing figure is Jasper; and its most powerful artistic effect is procured by an instillation into the greenery, the cathedral, the winter sun, the sober and tranquil old town, of the suggestion of moral uncertainty, of evil. Even the English rooks, which in *The Old Curiosity Shop* had figured simply as a pleasant feature of the old English countryside in which Nell and her grandfather wandered, have here become the omens of a terror that comes from outside that English world. The Christmas season itself, of which Dickens had been the laureate, which he had celebrated so often with exuberant charity, hopeful prospects and hearty cheer, is now the appointed moment for the murder by an uncle of his nephew.

Mr. Jasper is, like Dickens, an artist: he is a musician, possesses an enchanting voice. He smokes opium, and so, like Dickens, leads a life of the imagination apart from that of common men. Like Dickens, he is a skilful magician, whose power over his fellows may be dangerous. Like Dickens, he is an alien from another world; yet, like Dickens he has made himself respected in the conventional English community. Is he a villain? From the point of view of the cathedral congregation of Cloisterham, who have admired his ability as an artist, he will be seen to have been playing a diabolic rôle. All that sentiment, all those edifying high spirits, which Dickens has been dispensing so long, which he is still making the effort to dispense — has all this now grown as false as those hymns to the glory of the Christian God which are performed by the worshiper of Kali? And yet in another land there exists another point of view from which Jasper is a good and faithful servant. It has been driven by his *alter ego* and acting in the name of his goddess that Jasper has committed his crime.

None the less, he is a damned soul here and now. All this bright and pious foreground of England is to open or fade away, and to show a man condemned to death. But it will not be the innocent Pickwick, the innocent Micawber, the innocent Dorrit, whom we are now to meet in jail: nor yet the wicked Fagin, the wicked Dennis, the wicked elder Rudge. It will here be a man who is both innocent and wicked. The protest against the age has turned into a protest against self. In this last moment, the old hierarchy of England does enjoy a sort of triumph over the weary and debilitated Dickens, for it has made him accept its ruling that he is a creature irretrievably tainted; and the mercantile middle-class England has had its triumph, too. For the Victorian hypocrite — developing from Pecksniff, through Murdstone, through Headstone, to his final incarnation in Jasper — has finally come to present an insoluble moral problem which is identified with Dickens' own. As Headstone makes his own knuckles bleed in striking them against the church and drowns himself in order to drown Riderhood, so Jasper is eventually to destroy himself. When he announces in the language of the Thugs that he 'devotes' himself to the 'destruction' of the murderer, he is preparing his own execution. (He is evidently quite sincere in making this entry in his diary, since he has now sobered up from the opium and resumed his official personality. It is exclusively of this personality that the diary is to be a record.) So Dickens, in putting his nerves to the torture by enacting the murder of Nancy, has actually invoked his own death.

In this last condemned cell of Dickens, the respectable half of the divided John Jasper was to be brought face to face with the other half. But this confrontation — 'difficult to work,' as Dickens had told Forster — was never, in fact, to take place. For Dickens in his moral confusion was never to dramatize himself completely, was not even in this final phase of his art to succeed in coming quite clear. He was to leave *Edwin Drood* half-finished, with the confession just around the corner.

He had put in a long day on *Drood* when (June 9, 1870) he had a stroke while he was eating dinner. He got up from the table in his stunned condition and said he must go to London; then he fell to the floor and never recovered consciousness. He died the next afternoon.

THE KIPLING THAT NOBODY READ

THE ECLIPSE of the reputation of Kipling, which began about 1910, twenty-five years before Kipling's death and when he was still only forty-five, has been of a peculiar kind. Through this period he has remained, from the point of view of sales, an immensely popular writer. The children still read his children's books; the college students still read his poetry; the men and women of his own generation still reread his early work. But he has in a sense been dropped out of modern literature. The more serious-minded young people do *not* read him; the critics do not take him into account. During the later years of his life and even at the time of his death, the logic of his artistic development attracted no intelligent attention. At a time when W. B. Yeats had outgrown his romantic youth and was receiving the reward of an augmented glory for his severer and more concentrated work, Rudyard Kipling, Yeats's coeval, who had also achieved a new concentration through the efforts of a more exacting discipline, saw the glory of his young-manhood fade away. And during the period when the late work of Henry James, who had passed into a similar eclipse, was being retrieved and appreciated, when the integrity and interest of his total achievement was finally being understood, no attempt was made, so far as I know, to take stock of Kipling's work as a whole.[1] The ordinary person said simply that Kipling

[1] Since this was written, Mr. Edward Shanks has published a book on Kipling. Mr. Shanks addresses himself to the task, but does not make very much progress with it.

was 'written out'; the reviewer rarely made any effort to trace the journey from the breeziness of the early short stories to the bitterness of the later ones. The thick, dark and surly little man who had dug himself into Bateman's, Burwash, Sussex, was left to his bristling privacy, and only occasionally evoked a rebuke for the intolerant and vindictive views which, emerging with the suddenness of a snapping turtle, he sometimes gave vent to in public.

But who *was* Kipling? What did he express? What was the history of that remarkable talent which gave him a place, as a craftsman of English prose, among the few genuine masters of his day? How was it that the art of his short stories became continually more skilful and intense, and yet that his career appears broken?

I

The publication of Kipling's posthumous memoirs — *Something of Myself for My Friends Known and Unknown* — has enabled us to see more clearly the causes for the anomalies of Kipling's career.

First of all, he was born in India, the son of an English artist and scholar, who had gone out to teach architectural sculpture at the Fine Arts School in Bombay and who afterwards became curator of the museum at Lahore. This fact is, of course, well known; but its importance must be specially emphasized. It appears that up to the age of six Kipling talked, thought and dreamed, as he says, in Hindustani, and could hardly speak English correctly. A drawing of him made by a schoolmate shows a swarthy boy with lank straight hair, who might almost pass for a Hindu.

The second important influence in Kipling's early life has not hitherto been generally known, though it figures in the first chapter of *The Light That Failed* and furnished the subject of *Baa, Baa, Black Sheep,* one of the most powerful things he ever wrote. This story had always seemed rather unaccountably to stand apart from the rest of Kipling's work by reason of its sympathy with the victims rather than with the inflictors of a severely repressive discipline; and its animus is now explained by a chapter in Kipling's autobiography and by a memoir recently published by his sister. When Rudyard Kipling was six and his sister three and a half, they were farmed out for six years in England with a relative of Kipling's father. John Lockwood Kipling was the son of a Methodist minister, and this woman was a religious domestic tyrant in the worst English tradition of Dickens and Samuel Butler. The boy, who had been petted and deferred to by the native servants in India, was now beaten, bullied with the Bible, pursued with constant suspicions and broken down by cross-examinations. If one of the children spilled a drop of gravy or wept over a letter from their parents in Bombay, they were forbidden to speak to one another for twenty-four hours. Their guardian had a violent temper and enjoyed making terrible scenes, and they had to learn to propitiate her by fawning on her when they saw that an outburst was imminent.

'Looking back,' says Mrs. Fleming, Kipling's sister, 'I think the real tragedy of our early days, apart from Aunty's bad temper and unkindness to my brother, sprang from our inability to understand why our parents had deserted us. We had had no preparation or explanation; it was like a double death, or rather, like an avalanche that had swept away everything happy and familiar. . . . We felt that we had been deserted, "almost as much as on a doorstep," and what was the reason? Of course, Aunty used to say it was because we were so tiresome, and she had taken us out of pity, but in a desperate moment Ruddy appealed to Uncle Harrison, and he said it was only Aunty's fun, and Papa had left us to be taken care of, because India was too hot for little people. But we knew better than that, because we had been to Nassick, so what was the real reason? Mamma was not ill, like the seepy-weepy Ellen Montgomery's mamma in *The Wide, Wide World*. Papa had not had to go to war. They had not even lost their money; if they had, we could have swept crossings or sold flowers, and it would have been rather fun. But there was no excuse; they had gone happily back to our own lovely home, and had not taken us with them. They was no getting out of that, as we often said.

'Harry (Aunty's son), who had all a crow's quickness in finding a wound to pick at, discovered our trouble and teased us unmercifully. He assured us we had been taken in out of charity, and must do exactly as he told us. . . . We were just like workhouse brats, and none of our toys really belonged to us.'

Rudyard had bad eyes, which began to give out altogether, so that he was unable to do his work at school. One month he destroyed his report so that his guardians at home shouldn't see it; and for punishment was made to walk to school with a placard between his shoulders reading 'Liar.' He had finally a severe nervous breakdown, accompanied by partial blindness, and was punished by isolation from his sister. This breakdown, it is important to note, was made horrible by hallucinations. As a mist, which seemed to grow steadily thicker, shut him in from the rest of the world, he would imagine that blowing curtains were specters or that a coat on a nail was an enormous black bird ready to swoop down upon him.

His mother came back at last, saw how bad things were — when she went up to kiss him good-night, he instinctively put up his hand to ward off the expected blow — and took the children away. But the effects of those years were lasting. Mrs. Fleming tells us that her revulsion against Aunty's son Harry conditioned her reactions toward people who resembled him through all the rest of her life, and says that when, thirty years later, she set out in Southsea one day to see if the 'House of Desolation' were still standing, her heart failed her, and she hurried back: 'I dared not face it.' Rudyard himself told her that he had had a similar experience. 'I think we both dreaded a kind of spiritual imprisonment that would affect our dreams. Less than four years ago [she is writing in 1939], I asked him whether he knew if the house still stood. "I don't know, but if so, I should like to burn it down and plough the place with salt."'

Kipling asserts that this ordeal had 'drained me of any capacity for real, personal hate for the rest of my days'; and his sister denies that it produced in him any permanent injurious effects: 'According to their gloomy theories [the theories of the psychoanalysts], my brother should have grown up morbid and misanthropic, narrow-minded, self-centered, shunning the world, and bearing it, and all men, a burning grudge; for certainly between the ages of six and eleven he was thwarted at every turn by Aunty and the odious Harry, and inhibitions were his daily bread.' Yet here is the conclusion of the story which Kipling made out of this experience: 'There! "Told you so,"' says the boy to his sister. 'It's all different now, and we see just as much of mother as if she had never gone.' But, Kipling adds: 'Not altogether, O Punch, for when young lips have drunk deep of the bitter water of Hate, Suspicion, and Despair, all the Love in the world will not wholly take away that knowledge; though it may turn darkened eyes for a while to the light, and teach Faith where no Faith was.'

And actually the whole work of Kipling's life is to be shot through with hatred.

He was next sent to a public school in England. This school, the United Services College, at a place called Westward Ho!, had been founded by Army and Navy officers who could not afford to send their sons to the more expensive schools. The four and a half years that Kipling spent there gave him *Stalky & Co.*; and the relation of the experience to the book provides an interesting psychological study. The book itself, of course, presents a hair-raising picture of the sadism of the English public-school system. The older boys have fags to wait on them, and they sometimes torment these younger boys till they have reduced them almost to imbecility; the masters are constantly caning the boys in scenes that seem almost as bloody as the floggings in old English sea stories; and the boys revenge themselves on the masters with practical jokes as catastrophic as the Whams and Zows of the comic strip.

The originals of two of Kipling's characters — Major-General L. C. Dunsterville and Mr. G. C. Beresford — have published in their later years (*Stalky's Reminiscences* and *Schooldays with Kipling*) accounts rather discrepant with one another of life at the United Services College. Mr. Beresford, who is a highbrow in *Stalky & Co.* and reads Ruskin in the midst of the mêlée, turns out to be a Nationalist Irishman, who is disgusted with his old friend's later imperialism. He insists that the fagging system did not exist at Westward Ho!; that the boys were never caned on their bare shoulders; and that Kipling, so far as he remembers, was never caned at all except by a single exceptional master. Dunsterville, on the other hand, reports that the younger boys were barbarously bullied by the older: held out of high windows by their ankles and dropped down a stair-well in 'hangings' which in one case broke the victim's leg; and that 'in addition to the blows and the kicks that inevitably accompanied the bullying,' he 'suffered a good deal from the canes of the masters, or the ground-ash sticks of the prefects. I must have been perpetually black and blue. That always sounds so dreadful. . . . But the truth of the matter is, any slight blow produces a bruise. . . . And with one or two savage exceptions, I am sure that the blows I received as a result of bullying or legitimate punishment were harmless enough.

. . .' 'Kicks and blows,' he goes on, 'I minded little, but the moral effect was depressing. Like a hunted animal I had to keep all my senses perpetually on the alert to escape from the toils of the hunter — good training in a way, but likely to injure permanently a not very robust temperament. I was robust enough, I am glad to say, and possibly benefited by the treatment.'

Kipling was, of course, not robust; and the school evidently aggravated the injury which had been done him during his captivity at Southsea. He admits, in *Something of Myself*, that the fagging system was not compulsory; but he asserts that the discipline was brutal, that the students were wretchedly fed, and that he himself, addicted to books and too blind to participate in games, endured a good deal of baiting. The important thing is that he suffered. If we compare the three accounts of Westward Ho! — *Stalky & Co.* with the reminiscences of the two others — the emphasis of Kipling's becomes plain. It is significant that the single master whom Beresford mentions as persecuting the boys should have been inquisitorial and morbidly suspicious — that is, that he should have treated Kipling in the same way that he had already been treated by the *Baa, Baa, Black Sheep* people. And it is also significant that this master does not figure in *Stalky & Co.*, but only appears later in one of the more scrupulous stories which Kipling afterward wrote about the school. The stimulus of unjust suspicion, which did not leave any lasting bitterness with Beresford, had evidently the effect upon Kipling of throwing him back into the state of mind which had been created by the earlier relationship — just as the kickings and canings that Dunsterville nonchalantly shook off sunk deep into the spirit of Kipling. For a boy who has been habitually beaten during the second six years of his life, any subsequent physical punishment, however occasional or light, may result in the reawakening of the terror and hatred of childhood. It thrust him back into the nightmare again, and eventually made a delirium of the memory of Westward Ho!. *Stalky & Co.* — from the artistic point of view, certainly the worst of Kipling's books: crude in writing, trashy in feeling, implausible in a series of contrivances which resemble moving-picture 'gags' — is in the nature of an hysterical outpouring of emotions kept over from school-days, and it probably owes a part of its popularity to the fact that it provides the young with hilarious and violent fantasies on the theme of what they would do to the school bully and their masters if the laws of probability were suspended.

We shall deal presently with the social significance which Kipling, at a later period, was to read back into Westward Ho!. In the meantime, we must follow his adventures when he leaves it in July, 1882, not yet quite seventeen, but remarkably mature for his age and with a set of grown-up whiskers. He went back to his family in India, and there he remained for seven years. The Hindu child, who had lain dormant in England, came to life when he reached Bombay, and he found himself reacting to the old stimuli by beginning to talk Hindustani without understanding what he was saying. *Seven Years Hard* is his heading for his chapter on this phase of his life. His family — as we gather from his address on *Independence* — were by no means well-to-do; and he started right in on a newspaper in Lahore as sole assistant to the editor, and worked his head off for a chief he detested. It was one of the duties of the English journalist in India to play down the periodical epidemics. Kipling himself survived dysentery and fever, and kept on working through his severest illnesses. One hot night in 1886, when he felt, as he says, that he 'had come to the edge of all endurance' and had gone home to his empty house with the sensation that there was nothing left in him but 'the horror of a great darkness, that I must have been fighting for some days,' he read a novel by Walter Besant about a young man who

had wanted to be a writer and who had eventually succeeded in his aim. Kipling decided he would save some
money and get away to London. He wrote short stories
called *Plain Tales from the Hills,* which were run to fill
up space in the paper, and he brought out a book of verse.
His superiors disapproved of his flippancy, and when he
finally succeeded in leaving India, the managing director
of the paper, who had considered him overpaid, told the
young man that he could take it from him that he would
never be worth anything more than four hundred rupees
a month.

The Kipling of these early years is a lively and sympathetic figure. A newspaper man who has access to everything, the son of a scholar who has studied the natives, he
sees the community, like Asmodeus, with all the roofs removed. He is interested in the British of all classes and
ranks — the bored English ladies, the vagabond adventurers, the officers and the soldiers both. 'Having no position to consider,' he writes, 'and my trade enforcing it, I
could move at will in the fourth dimension. I came to
realize the bare horrors of the private's life, and the unnecessary torments he endured. . . . Lord Roberts, at
that time Commander-in-chief of India, who knew my
people, was interested in the men, and — I had by then
written one or two stories about soldiers — the proudest
moment of my young life was when I rode up Simla Mall
beside him on his usual explosive red Arab, while he asked
me what the men thought about their accommodations,
entertainment-rooms, and the like. I told him, and he
thanked me as gravely as though I had been a full Colonel.' He is already tending to think about people in terms
of social and racial categories; but his interest in them at
this time is also personal: 'All the queer outside world
would drop into our workshop sooner or later! say a Captain just cashiered for horrible drunkenness, who reported
his fall with a wry, appealing face, and then — disap-

peared. Or a man old enough to be my father, on the edge
of tears because he had been overpassed for Honors in the
Gazette. . . . One met men going up and down the ladder in every shape of misery and success.' And he gives us
in his soldier stories, along with the triumphs of discipline
and the exploits of the native wars, the hunger of Private
Ortheris for London when the horror of exile seizes him;
the vanities and vices of Mulvaney which prevent him
from rising in the service (*The Courting of Dinah Shadd,*
admired by Henry James, is one of the stories of Kipling
which sticks closest to unregenerate humanity); even the
lunatic obsessions and the crack-up of the rotter gentleman ranker in *Love-o'-Women.*

The natives Kipling probably understood as few Englishmen did in his time; certainly he presented them in
literature as nobody had ever done. That Hindu other self
of his childhood takes us through into its other world. The
voices of alien traditions — in the monologues of *In Black
and White* — talk an English which translates their own
idiom; and we hear of great lovers and revengers who live
by an alien code; young men who have been educated in
England and, half-dissociated from native life, find themselves impotent between two civilizations; fierce Afghan
tribesmen of the mountains, humble people who have
been broken to the mines; loyal Sikhs and untamed mu-
tineers. It is true that there is always the implication that
the British are bringing to India modern improvements
and sounder standards of behavior. But Kipling is obviously enjoying for its own sake the presentation of the
native point of view, and the whole Anglo-Indian situation is studied with a certain objectivity.

He is even able to handle without horror the mixture of
the black and the white. 'The "railway folk,"' says Mr.
E. Kay Robinson, who worked with him on the paper in
Lahore, 'that queer colony of white, half white and three-
quarters black, which remains an uncared-for and discred-

itable excrescence upon British rule in India, seemed to
have unburdened their souls to Kipling of all their grievances, their poor pride, and their hopes. Some of the best
of Kipling's work is drawn from the lives of these people;
although to the ordinary Anglo-Indian, whose social caste
restrictions are almost more inexorable than those of the
Hindu whom he affects to despise on that account, they
are as a sealed book.' And one of the most sympathetic of
these early stories — the once famous *Without Benefit of
Clergy* — is a picture of an Anglo-Indian union: an English official who lives with a Mahomedan girl. Though
Kipling deals rarely in fortunate lovers, these lovers enjoy
their happiness for a time. To their joy, the mother gives
birth to a son, who turns into a small gold-colored little
god,' and they like to sit on the roof and eat almonds and
watch the kites. But then the baby dies of the fever, and
the young wife dies of the cholera; and the husband is
called away to fight the famine and the epidemic. Even
the house where they have lived is destroyed, and the husband is glad that no one else will ever be able to live there.
This idyl, unhallowed and fleeting, is something that the
artist in Kipling has felt, and put down for its sweetness
and pathos.

Through all these years of school and of newspaper
work, with their warping and thwarting influences, Kipling worked staunchly at mastering his craft. For he had
been subjected to yet another influence which has not
been mentioned yet. His father was a painter and sculptor,
and two of his mother's sisters were married to artists —
one to Edward Poynter, the Academician, and the other
to the pre-Raphaelite, Burne-Jones. Besides India and the
United Services College, there had been the pre-Raphaelite movement. In England, Kipling's vacation had always
been spent in London with the Burne-Joneses. Mr. Beresford says that Kipling's attitude at school had been that of
the aesthete who disdains athletics and has no aptitude for

mechanical matters, that he was already preoccupied with writing, and that his literary proficiency and cultivation were amazingly developed for his age. He had had from his childhood the example of men who loved the arts for their own sake and who were particularly concerned about craftsmanship (it is also of interest that his father's family had distinguished themselves in the eighteenth century as founders of bronze bells). Kipling evidently owes his superiority as a craftsman to most of even the ablest English writers of fiction of the end of the century and the early nineteen hundreds, to this inspiration and training. Just as the ballad of *Danny Deever* derives directly from the ballad of *Sister Helen,* so the ideal of an artistic workmanship which shall revert to earlier standards of soundness has the stamp of William Morris and his circle. In 1878, when Rudyard was twelve years old, his father had taken him to the Paris Exhibition and insisted that he learn to read French. The boy had then conceived an admiration for the civilization of the French which evidently contributed later to his interest in perfecting the short story in English.

With all this, his earlier experience in the 'House of Desolation' had equipped him, he says, with a training not unsuitable for a writer of fiction, in that it had 'demanded constant wariness, the habit of observation, and attendance on moods and tempers; the noting of discrepancies between speech and action; a certain reserve of demeanor; and automatic suspicion of sudden favors.'

With such a combination of elements, what might one not expect? It is not surprising to learn that the young Kipling contemplated, after his return to England, writing a colonial *Comédie Humaine.* 'Bit by bit, my original notion,' he writes, 'grew into a vast, vague conspectus — Army and Navy List, if you like — of the whole sweep and meaning of things and efforts and origins throughout the Empire.' Henry James, who wrote an appreciative preface for a collection of Kipling's early stories, said afterwards that he had thought at that time that it might perhaps be true that Kipling 'contained the seeds of an English Balzac.'

II

What became of this English Balzac? Why did the author of the brilliant short stories never develop into an important novelist?

Let us return to *Baa, Baa, Black Sheep* and the situation with which it deals. Kipling says that his Burne-Jones aunt was never able to understand why he had never told anyone in the family about how badly he and his sister were being treated, and he tries to explain this on the principle that children tell little more than animals, for what comes to them they accept as eternally established,' and says that 'badly-treated children have a clear notion of what they are likely to get if they betray the secrets of a prison-house before they are clear of it.' But *is* this inevitably true? Even young children do sometimes run away. And, in any case, Kipling's reaction to this experience seems an abnormally docile one. After all, Dickens made David Copperfield bite Mr. Murdstone's hand and escape; and he makes war on Mr. Murdstone through the whole of his literary career. But though the anguish of these years had given Kipling a certain sympathy with the neglected and persecuted, and caused him to write this one moving short story, it left him — whether as the result of the experience itself or because he was already so conditioned — with a fundamental submissiveness to authority.

Let us examine the two books in which Kipling deals, respectively, with his schooldays and with his youth in India: *Stalky & Co.* and *Kim*. These works are the products of the author's thirties, and *Kim*, at any rate, represents Kipling's most serious attempt to allow himself to grow to the stature of a first-rate creative artist. Each of these books begins with an antagonism which in the work of a greater writer would have developed into a fundamental conflict; but in neither *Stalky* nor *Kim* is the conflict ever permitted to mount to a real crisis. Nor can it even be said to be resolved: it simply ceases to figure as a conflict. In *Stalky*, we are at first made to sympathize with the baiting of the masters by the schoolboys as their rebellion against a system which is an offense against human dignity: but then we are immediately shown that all the ragging and flogging are justified by their usefulness as a training for the military caste which is to govern the British Empire. The boys are finally made to recognize that their headmaster not only knows how to dish it out but is also able to take it, and the book culminates in the ridiculous scene — which may perhaps have its foundation in fact but is certainly flushed by a hectic imagination — in which the Head, in the inflexible justice, undertakes personally to cane the whole school while the boys stand by cheering him wildly.

There is a real subject in *Stalky & Co.*, but Kipling has not had the intelligence to deal with it. He cannot see around his characters and criticize them, he is not even able properly to dramatize; he simply allows the emotions of the weaker side, the side that is getting the worst of it, to go over to the side of the stronger. You can watch the process all too clearly in the episode in which Stalky and his companions turn the tables on the cads from the crammers' school. These cads have been maltreating a fag, and a clergyman who is represented by Kipling as one of the more sensible and decent of the masters suggests to Stalky & Co. that they teach the bullies a lesson. The former proceed to clean up on the latter in a scene which goes on for pages, to the reckless violation of proportion and taste. The oppressors, true enough, are taught a lesson, but the cruelty with which we have already been made disgusted has now passed over to the castigators' side, and there is a disagreeable implication that, though it is caddish for the cads to be cruel, it is all right for the sons of English gentlemen to be cruel to the cads.

Kim is more ambitious and much better. It is Kipling's only successful long story: an enchanting, almost a first-rate book, the work in which more perhaps than in any other he gave the sympathies of the imagination free rein to remember and to explore, and which has in consequence more complexity and density than any of his other works. Yet the conflict from which the interest arises, though it is very much better presented, here also comes to nothing: the two forces never really engage. Kim is the son of an Irish soldier and an Irish nursemaid, who has grown up as an orphan in India, immersed in and assimilated to the native life, so that he thinks, like the young Kipling, in Hindustani. The story deals with the gradual dawning of his consciousness that he is really a Sahib. As a child he has been in the habit of making a little money by carrying messages for a native agent of the British secret service, and the boy turns out to be so bright and so adept at acting the rôle of a native that the authorities decide to train him. He is sent to an English school but does not willingly submit to the English system. Every vacation he dresses as a native and disappears into the sea of native life. The Ideal of this side of his existence is represented by a Thibetan lama, a wandering Buddhist pilgrim, whom he accompanies in the character of a disciple.

Now what the reader tends to expect is that Kim will come eventually to realize that he is delivering into bondage to the British invaders those whom he has always considered his own people, and that a struggle between allegiances will result. Kipling has established for the reader — and established with considerable dramatic effect — the contrast between the East, with its mysticism and its sensuality, its extremes of saintliness and roguery, and

the English, with their superior organization, their confidence in modern method, their instinct to brush away
like cobwebs the native myths and beliefs. We have been
shown two entirely different worlds existing side by side,
with neither really understanding the other, and we have
watched the oscillations of Kim, as he passes to and fro
between them. But the parallel lines never meet; the
alternating attractions felt by Kim never give rise to a
genuine struggle. And the climax itself is double: the adventures of the Lama and of Kim simply arrive at different consummations, without any final victory or synthesis
ever being allowed to take place. Instead, there are a pair
of victories, which occur on separate planes and do not
influence one another: the Lama attains to a condition of
trance which releases him from what the Buddhists call
the Wheel of Things at the same moment that the young
Anglo-Indian achieves promotion in the British secret
service.

The salvation of the Lama has been earned by peni-
tence for a moment of passion: he had been tempted to
kill a man who had torn his sacred chart and struck him,
a Russian agent working against the British. But the pretenses of Kim to a spiritual vocation, whatever spell has
been exerted over him by the Lama, are dispelled when
the moment for action comes, when the Irishman is challenged to a fight: Kim knocks the Russian down and
bangs his head against a boulder. 'I am Kim. I am Kim.
And what is Kim?' his soul repeats again and again, in his
exhaustion and collapse after this episode. He feels that
his soul is 'out of gear with its surroundings — a cog-wheel
unconnected with any machinery, just like the idle cog-
wheel of a cheap Beheea sugar-crusher laid by in a corner.' But he now gets this unattached soul to find a function in the working of the crusher — note the mechanical
metaphor: dissociating himself from the hierarchy represented by the Abbot-Lama, he commits himself to a rôle

in the hierarchy of a practical organization. (So the wolf-reared Mowgli of the *Jungle Books,* the prototype of Kim, ends up rather flatly as a ranger in the British Forestry Service.) Nor does Kipling allow himself to doubt that his hero has chosen the better part. Kim must now exploit his knowledge of native life for the purpose of preventing and putting down any native resistance to the British; but it never seems to occur to his creator that this constitutes a betrayal of the Lama. A sympathy with the weaker party in a relationship based on force has again given way without a qualm to a glorification of the stronger. As the bullying masters of *Stalky & Co.* turn into beneficent Chirons, so even the overbearing officer who figures on his first appearance in *Kim* as a symbol of British stupidity turns out to be none other than Strickland, the wily police superintendent, who has here been acting a part. (It should also be noted that the question of whether or not Kim shall allow himself to sleep with a native woman has here become very important, and that his final emergence as a Sahib is partly determined by his decision in the negative. This is no longer the Kipling of *Without Benefit of Clergy.*)

The Lama's victory is not of this world: the sacred river for which he has been seeking, and which he identifies in his final revelation with a brook near which his trance has occurred, has no objective existence, it is not on the British maps. Yet the anguish of the Lama's repentance — a scene, so far as I remember, elsewhere unmatched in Kipling — is one of the most effective things in the book; and we are to meet this Lama again in strange and unexpected forms still haunting that practical world which Kipling, like Kim, has chosen. The great eulogist of the builder and the man of action was no more able to leave the Lama behind than Kim had been able to reconcile himself to playing the game of English life without him.

III

The fiction of Kipling, then, does not dramatize any fundamental conflict because Kipling would never face one. This is probably one of the causes of his lack of success with long novels. You can make an effective short story, as Kipling so often does, about somebody's scoring off somebody else; but this is not enough for a great novelist, who must show us large social forces, or uncontrollable lines of destiny, or antagonistic impulses of the human spirit, struggling with one another. With Kipling, the right and the wrong of any opposition of forces is usually quite plain at the start; and there is not even the suspense which makes possible the excitement of melodrama. There is never any doubt as to the outcome. The Wrong is made a guy from the beginning, and the high point of the story comes when the Right gives it a kick in the pants. Where both sides are sympathetically presented, the battle is not allowed to occur.

But this only drives us back on another question: how was it that the early Kipling, with his sensitive understanding of the mixed population of India, became transformed into the later Kipling, who consolidated and codified his snobberies instead of progressively eliminating them as most good artists do, and who, like Kim, elected as his lifework the defense of the British Empire? The two books we have been discussing indicate the end of a period in the course of which Kipling had arrived at a decision. Stalky came out in 1899, and Kim in 1901. The decade of the nineties had been critical for Kipling; and in order to understand the new phase of his work which had begun by the beginning of the century, we must follow his adventures in the United States, which he visited in 1889, where he lived from 1892 to 1896, and to which he tried to return in 1899. Kipling's relations with Amer-

ica are certainly the most important factor in his experience during these years of his later twenties and early
thirties; yet they are the link which has been dropped out
of his story in most of the accounts of his life and which
even his posthumous memoirs, revelatory in respect to his
earlier years, markedly fail to supply.

The young man who arrived in London in the fall of
1889 was very far from being the truculent British patriot
whom we knew in the nineteen hundreds. He had not
even gone straight back to England, but had first taken a
trip around the world, visiting Canada and the United
States. Nor did he remain long in the mother-country
when he got there. His whole attitude was that of the
colonial who has sweated and suffered at the outposts of
Empire, making the acquaintance of more creeds and customs than the philosophy of London dreamt of, and who
feels a slight touch of scorn toward the smugness of the
people at home, unaware of how big, varied and active the
world around them is. His 'original notion,' he says, had
been to try 'to tell the Empire something of the world outside England — not directly but by implication': 'What
can they know of England who only England know?' He
rounded out his knowledge of the colonies by traveling in
New Zealand, Australia, South Africa and Southern India. In the January of 1892, he married an American wife.
    Kipling's experience of the United States was in certain
ways like that of Dickens. Neither of them fitted very
well into the English system at home, and both seem to
have been seeking in the new English-speaking nation a
place where they could be more at ease. Both winced at
the crudeness of the West; both were contemptuously
shocked by the boasting — the Pacific Coast in Kipling's
day was what the Mississippi had been in Dickens'. Both,
escaping from the chilliness of England, resented the fa-
miliarity of the States. Yet Kipling, on the occasion of his

first visit, which he records in *From Sea to Sea,* is obviously rejoiced by the naturalness of social relations in America. He tells of 'a very trim maiden' from New Hampshire, with 'a delightful mother and an equally delightful father, a heavy-eyed, slow-voiced man of finance,' whom he met in the Yellowstone. 'Now an English maiden who had stumbled on a dust-grimed, lime-washed, sun-peeled collarless wanderer come from and going to goodness knows where, would, her mother inciting her and her father brandishing his umbrella, have regarded him as a dissolute adventurer. Not so those delightful people from New Hampshire. They were good enough to treat me — it sounds almost incredible — as a human being, possibly respectable, probably not in immediate need of financial assistance. Papa talked pleasantly and to the point. The little maiden strove valiantly with the accent of her birth and that of her reading, and mamma smiled benignly in the background. Balance this with a story of a young English idiot I met knocking about inside his high collars, attended by a valet. He condescended to tell me that "you can't be too careful who you talk to in these parts," and stalked on, fearing, I suppose, every minute for his social chastity. Now that man was a barbarian (I took occasion to tell him so), for he comported himself after the manner of the headhunters of Assam, who are at perpetual feud one with another.'

He declares his faith in the Americans in a conversation with an Englishman 'who laughed at them.' '"I admit everything," said I. "Their Government's provisional; their law's the notion of the moment; their railways are made of hairpins and matchsticks, and most of their good luck lives in their woods and mines and rivers and not in their brains; but, for all that, they be the biggest, finest, and best people on the surface of the globe! Just you wait a hundred years and see how they'll behave when they've had the screw put on them and have forgotten a few of the patriarchal teachings of the late Mr. George Washington. Wait till the Anglo-American-German-Jew — the Man of the Future — is properly equipped. He'll have just the least little kink in his hair now and again; he'll carry the English lungs above the Teuton feet that can walk forever; and he will wave long, thin, bony Yankee hands with the big blue veins on the wrist, from one end of the earth to the other. He'll be the finest writer, poet, and dramatist, 'specially dramatist, that the world as it recollects itself has ever seen. By virtue of his Jew blood — just a little, little drop — he'll be a musician and a painter, too. At present there is too much balcony and too little Romeo in the life-plays of his fellow-citizens. Later on, when the proportion is adjusted and he sees the possibilities of his land, he will produce things that will make the effete East stare. He will also be a complex and highly composite administrator. There is nothing known to man that he will not be, and his country will sway the world with one foot as a man tilts a see-saw plank!"

' "But this is worse than the Eagle at its worst. Do you seriously believe all that?" said the Englishman.

' "If I believe anything seriously, all this I most firmly believe. You wait and see. Sixty million people, chiefly of English instincts, who are trained from youth to believe that nothing is impossible, don't slink through the centuries like Russian peasantry. They are bound to leave their mark somewhere, and don't you forget it." '

'I love this People . . .' he wrote. 'My heart has gone out to them beyond all other peoples.' And he reiterated his faith, in the poem called *An American*, in which 'The American spirit speaks':

> Enslaved, illogical, elate,
>   He greets th' embarrassed Gods, nor fears
> To shake the iron hand of Fate
>   Or match with Destiny for beers.

So, imperturbable he rules,
Unkempt, disreputable, vast —
And, in the teeth of all the schools,
I — I shall save him at the last!

Kipling took his wife to America, and they lived for a time on the estate of her family in Brattleboro, Vermont; then Kipling built a large house: his books were already making him rich. They lived in the United States four years; two daughters were born to them there. Kipling was ready to embrace America, or those aspects of America which excited him; he began using American subjects for his stories: the railroads in .007, the Gloucester fishermen in *Captains Courageous*. He enormously admired Mark Twain, whose acquaintance he had made on his first visit. Yet the effect of contact with the United States was eventually to drive Kipling, as it had Dickens, back behind his British defenses. A disagreeable episode occurred which, undignified and even comic though it seems, is worth studying because it provided the real test of Kipling's fitness to flourish in America, and not merely the test of this, but, at a critical time in his life, of the basic courage and humanity of his character.

The story has been told since Kipling's death in a book called *Rudyard Kipling's Vermont Feud* by Mr. Frederick F. Van de Water. A brother of Mrs. Kipling's, Kipling's friend Wolcott Balestier, had been in the publishing business with Heinemann in London, and Mrs. Kipling had lived much in England and was by way of being an Anglophile. Thus the impulse on Kipling's part to assimilate himself to the Americans was neutralized in some degree by Mrs. Kipling's desire to be English. Kipling, who was accustomed to India, had his own instinctive rudeness. In Vermont, he and Mrs. Kipling tended to stick to the attitudes of the traditional governing-class English maintaining their caste in the colonies: they drove a tandem with a tophatted English coachman, dressed every night for dinner, kept their New England neighbors at a distance.

But Mrs. Kipling had a farmer brother who — the family were partly French — was as Americanized as possible. He was a drinker, a spendthrift and a great local card, famous alike for his ribaldry, his sleigh-racing and his gestures of generosity of a magnificence almost feudal. Mr. Van de Water tells us that, at the time he knew Beatty Balestier, he had the swagger of Cyrano de Bergerac and a leathery face like 'an ailing eagle.' His farm and family suffered. The Kiplings lent him money, and he is said to have paid it back; but they disapproved of his disorderly existence. They seem to have persisted in treating him with some lack of consideration or tact. Beatty was, in any case, the kind of man — unbalanced in character but independent in spirit — who is embittered by obligations and furiously resents interference. Kipling went to Beatty one day and offered to support his wife and child for a year if Beatty would leave town and get a job. He was surprised at the explosion he provoked. This was followed by a dispute about some land across the road from the Kiplings' house. The land belonged to Beatty and he sold it for a dollar to the Kiplings, who were afraid that someone would some day build on it — on the friendly understanding, as he claimed, that he could continue to use it for mowing. When the transfer had been effected, Mrs. Kipling set out to landscape-garden it. The result was that Beatty stopped speaking to them and refused to receive Kipling when he came to call.

This went on for about a year, at the end of which a crisis occurred. Kipling was indiscreet enough to remark to one of the neighbors that he had had 'to carry Beatty for the last year — to hold him up by the seat of his breeches.' This soon reached his brother-in-law's ears. One day Beatty, driving his team and drunk, met Kipling riding his bicycle. He blocked the road, making Kipling fall off, and shouted angrily: 'See here! I want to talk to you!' Kipling answered, 'If you have anything to say, say it to my lawyers.' 'By Jesus, this is no case for lawyers!' retorted Beatty, loosing a tirade of profanity and abuse. He threatened Kipling, according to Kipling, to kill him; according to Beatty, merely to beat him up if he did not make a public retraction.

Kipling had always deplored the lawlessness of America; in his account of his first trip through the West, his disgust and trepidation over the shootings of the frontier are expressed in almost every chapter. And he now became seriously alarmed. He proceeded to have Beatty arrested on charges of 'assault with indecent and opprobrious names and epithets and threatening to kill.' He did not realize that that kind of thing was not done in the United States, where such quarrels were settled man to man, and he could not foresee the consequences. Beatty, who loved scandal, was delighted. He allowed the case to come into court and watched Kipling, who hated publicity, make himself ridiculous in public. The Kiplings at last fled abroad — it was August, 1896 — before the case could come before the Grand Jury.

'So far as I was concerned,' says Kipling of his relations with Americans in general, 'I felt the atmosphere was to some extent hostile.' It was a moment of antagonism to ward England. In the summer of 1895, Venezuela had appealed to the United States for protection against the English in a dispute over the boundaries of British Guiana, and President Cleveland had invoked the Monroe Doctrine and demanded in strong language that England submit the question to arbitration. The Jameson raid on the Transvaal Republic early in 1896, an unauthorized and defeated attempt by an agent of the British South Africa Company to provoke a rising against the Boers, had intensified the feeling against England. Kipling was brought face to face with the issue by an encounter with another American who seemed almost as unrestrained as Beatty Balestier. When Kipling met Theodore Roosevelt, then Assistant Secretary of the Navy, the latter 'thanked God in a loud voice that he had not one drop of British blood in him,' that his ancestry was pure Dutch, and declared that American fear of the British would provide him with funds for a new navy. John Hay had told Kipling that it was hatred of the English that held the United States together.

But during the years that immediately followed the Kiplings' return to England, American relations with England improved. The United States took over the Philippines in 1898 as a result of the Spanish War, and annexed the Hawaiian Islands; and the imperialistic England of Joseph Chamberlain, in fear of Germany, which had favored the Spanish, became extremely sympathetic with the policy of the United States. At the beginning of 1899, then, Rudyard Kipling set forth on an attempt to retrieve his position in America, where he had abandoned the big Brattleboro house. He first composed the celebrated set of verses in which he exhorted the United States to collaborate with the British Empire in 'taking up the White Man's burden' of 'your new-caught, sullen peoples, half-devil and half-child,' who were to be benefited and disciplined in spite of themselves, though at a bitter expense to their captors; and had the poem published on both sides of the Atlantic early in February, at the moment of his sailing for America. But what confronted him on his landing was an announcement in the New York papers that Beatty Balestier was bringing a $50,000 countersuit against him for 'malicious persecution, false arrest and defamation of character'; and the report that Beatty himself either had arrived in New York or was just about to arrive. It was simply another of Beatty's gestures: no suit

was ever brought; but it prevented the Kiplings from returning to Vermont. Rudyard had caught cold on the
boat, and he now came down with double pneumonia and
seemed in danger of not pulling through. His two little
girls had pneumonia, too, and one of them died while he
was ill. When he recovered, he had to hear of her death.
He went back to England in June, as soon as he was able
to travel, and never tried to live in the United States
again.

'It will be long and long,' he wrote in a letter supposed
to date from 1900, 'before I could bring myself to look at
the land of which she [his daughter] was so much a part.'
And his cousin Angela Thirkell writes that, 'Much of the
beloved Cousin Ruddy of our childhood died with Jose-
phine and I feel that I have never seen him as a real person since that year.'

The fear and hatred awakened in Kipling by those fatal
six years of his childhood had been revived by the discipline of Westward Ho! The menaces of Beatty Balestier,
behind which must have loomed for Kipling all that was
wild, uncontrollable, brutal in the life of the United
States, seem to have prodded again the old inflammation.
The schoolboy, rendered helpless in a fight by his bad eyes
and his small stature, was up against the bully again, and
fear drove him to appeal to the authorities. How else can
we account for the fact that the relations of Kipling with
Beatty were ever allowed to get to this point? The truth
was, as Beatty himself later confessed to Mr. Van de
Water, that Rudyard had become involved in a family
quarrel between himself and his sister; and one's impulse
is to say that Kipling ought to have been able to find some
way of extricating himself and making contact with the
rather childlike friendliness that seems to have lurked behind the rodomontade of Beatty. But the terrible seriousness of the issue which the incident had raised for Kipling

is shown by his statement at the hearing that he 'would not retract a word under threat of death from any living man.'

IV

It was the fight he had fought at school, and he would not capitulate to Beatty Balestier. But he surrendered at last to the 'Proosian Bates.' He invoked the protection of the British system and at the same time prostrated himself before the power of British conquest, which was feared in the United States and which even at that moment in South Africa — the Transvaal Republic declared war on Great Britain in the October of the year of his return — was chastising truculent farmers.

It is at the time of his first flight from America and during the years before his attempt to return — 1897-99 — that Kipling goes back to his school-days and depicts them in the peculiar colors that we find in *Stalky & Co.* How little inevitable these colors were we learn from Mr. Beresford's memoir. The head master of Westward Ho!, it appears, though really known as the 'Proosian Bates,' was by no means the intent Spartan trainer for the bloody and risky work of the Empire into which Kipling thought it proper to transform him. The fact was that Mr. Cormell Price had been literary rather than military, a friend of Edward Burne-Jones and an earnest anti-Imperialist. He and Burne-Jones had actually organized, at the time of the Russo-Turkish War, a Workers' Neutrality Demonstration against British intervention. But Kipling must now have a head master who will symbolize all the authority of the British educational system, and a school that will represent all that he has heard or imagined — see his highlighting of the fagging system — about the older and more official public schools. The colonial who has criticized the motherland now sets out systematically to glorify her; and it is the proof of his timidity and weakness that he should loudly overdo this glorification.

And now, having declared his allegiance, he is free to hate the enemies of England. His whole point of view has shifted. The bitter animus so deeply implanted by those six years of oppression of his childhood has now become almost entirely dissociated from the objects by which it was originally aroused. It has turned into a generalized hatred of those nations, groups and tendencies, precisely, which stand toward the dominating authority in the relationship of challengers or victims.

The ideal of the 'Anglo-American-German Jew,' which at the time of Kipling's first trip to America represented for him the future of civilization, now immediately goes by the board. His whole tone toward the Americans changes. In *An Error in the Fourth Dimension* — in *The Day's Work*, published in 1898 — he makes a rich Anglicized American, the son of a railroad king, deciding for no very good reason that he must immediately go to London, flag and stop an English express train. The railroad first brings charges against him, then decides that he must be insane. They cannot understand his temerity, and he cannot understand their consternation at having the British routine interrupted. Kipling no longer admires the boldness of Americans: this story is a hateful caricature, so one-sided that the real comedy is sacrificed. *The Captive* followed in 1902. Here a man from Ohio named Laughton O. Zigler sells to the Boers, during their war with the British, a new explosive and a new machine-gun he has invented. He is captured by the English, who grin at him and ask him why he 'wasn't in the Filipeens suppressing our war!' Later he runs into a man from Kentucky, who refuses to shake his hand and tells him that 'he's gone back on the White Man in six places at once — two hemispheres and four continents — America, England, Canada,

Australia, New Zealand, and South Africa. . . . Go on and prosper . . . and you'll fetch up by fighting for niggers, as the North did.' As a result of these taunts, and of the respect which has been inspired in him by the spectacle of the splendid behavior of the British, Mr. Zigler gives them the formula for his explosive, insists upon remaining their prisoner, and resolves to settle permanently in South Africa. A still later story, *An Habitation Enforced*, in a collection published in 1909, tells of the victory of the English countryside over an American business man and his wife, who have been aimlessly traveling about Europe. The American wife discovers that her own ancestors came originally from the very locality where they have settled, and they are finally — it is the climax of the story — accepted by the English: 'That wretched Sangres man has twice our money. Can you see Marm Conant slapping him between the shoulders? Not by a jugful! The poor beast doesn't exist!' The Americans succumb, deeply gratified. The husband had had a breakdown from overwork, but his equanimity is quite re-established. In short, Kipling's attitude toward Americans has now been almost reversed since the day of his first visit to the States when he had written, 'I love this People.' He now approves of them only when they are prepared to pay their tribute to Mother England and to identify her interests with theirs.

Later still, during the first years of the World War when Americans were figuring as neutrals, his bitterness became absolutely murderous — as in *Sea Constables: A Tale of '15*. And so had his feeling against the Germans even before the war had begun. In *The Edge of the Evening* (1913), Laughton O. Zigler of Ohio turns up again, this time in England, as occupant of a Georgian mansion inherited by one of the British officers who captured him in South Africa. 'Bein' rich suits me. So does your country, sir. My own country? You heard what that Detroit man said at dinner. "A government of the alien, by the alien, for the alien." Mother's right, too. Lincoln killed us. From the highest motives — but he killed us.' What his mother had said was that Lincoln had 'wasted the heritage of his land by blood and fire, and had surrendered the remnant to aliens': ' "My brother, suh," she said, "fell at Gettysburg in order that Armenians should colonize New England today." ' (*Something of Myself* confirms the assumption that these were Kipling's own views.) One night a foreign plane makes a forced landing on the estate. Two men get out of the plane, and one of them shoots at his lordship. Zigler lays him out with a golf-club while another of the Englishmen present collars the other man and breaks his neck (it is all right for an American to be lawless, or even for the right sort of Englishman, if he is merely laying low the alien who is the natural enemy of both). They put the dead German spies in the plane and send it up and out over the Channel.

Kipling is now, in fact, implacably opposed to every race and nation which has rebelled against or competed with the Empire, and to every movement and individual — such as the liberals and Fabians — in England who has criticized the imperial policies. His attitude toward the Irish, for example, illustrates the same simple-minded principle as his attitude toward the Americans. So long as the Irish are loyal to England, Kipling shows the liveliest appreciation of Irish recklessness and the Irish sense of mischief: Mulvaney is Irish, McTurk is Irish, Kim is Irish. But the moment they display these same qualities in agitation against the English, they become infamous assassins and traitors. Those peoples who have never given trouble — the Canadians, the New Zealanders, the Australians — though Kipling has never found them interesting enough to write about on any considerable scale, he credits with the most admirable virtues.

And as a basis for all these exclusions, he has laid down a more fundamental principle for the hatred and fear of his fellows: the anti-democratic principle. We are familiar with the case of the gifted man who has found himself at a disadvantage in relation to his social superiors and who makes himself the champion of all who have suffered in a similar way. What is not so familiar is the inverse of this: the case of the individual who at the period when he has most needed freedom to develop superior abilities has found himself cramped and tormented by the stupidity of social inferiors, and who has in consequence acquired a distrust of the whole idea of popular government. Rudyard Kipling was probably an example of this. The ferocious antagonism to democracy which finally overtakes him must have been fed by the fear of that household at Southsea which tried to choke his genius at its birth. His sister says that through all this period he was in the habit of keeping up their spirit by reminding himself and her that their guardian was 'of such low caste as not to matter . . . She was a *Kuch-nay*, a Nothing-at-all, and that se-cret name was a great comfort to us, and useful, too, when Harry practised his talent for eavesdropping.' Some very unyielding resistance was evidently built up at this time against the standards and opinions of people whom he regarded as lower-class.

The volume called *Traffics and Discoveries*, published in 1904, marks the complete metamorphosis of Kipling. The collection that preceded, *The Day's Work*, though these tendencies had already begun to appear in it, still preserves certain human values: the English officials in the Indian stories — *The Tomb of His Ancestors* and *William the Conqueror* — still display some sympathetic inter-est in the natives. But the Kipling of the South African stories is venomous, morbid, distorted.

When the Boer War finally breaks, Kipling is at once on the spot, with almost all the correct reactions. He is now at the zenith of his reputation, and he receives every official courtesy. And though he may criticize the handling

of a campaign, he never questions the rightness of its object. He has the impulse to get close to the troops, edits a
paper for the soldiers; but his attitude toward the Tommy
has changed. He had already been entertained and enlightened by Lord Dufferin, the British Viceroy in India.
Hitherto, he tells us in his memoirs, he 'had seen the ad-
ministrative machinery from beneath, all stripped and
overheated. This was the first time I had listened to one
who had handled it from above.' Another passage from
Something of Myself shows how his emphasis has altered:
'I happened to fall unreservedly, in darkness, over a man
near the train, and filled my palms with gravel. He explained in an even voice that he was "fractured 'ip, sir.
'Ope you ain't 'urt yourself, sir?" I never got at this unknown Philip Sidney's name. They were wonderful even
in the hour of death — these men and boys — lodgekeepers
and ex-butlers of the Reserve and raw town-lads of
twenty.' Here he is trying to pay a tribute; yet it is obvious that the Kipling who was proud to be questioned
in India by Lord Roberts as if he were a colonel has triumphed over the Kipling who answered him as a spokesman for the unfortunate soldiers. Today he is becoming
primarily a man whom a soldier addresses as 'sir,' as a soldier is becoming for Kipling a man whose capacity for
heroism is indicated by remaining respectful with a fractured hip. The cockney Ortheris of *Soldiers Three* and
the officer who had insulted him at drill had waived the
Courts Martial manual and fought it out man to man; but
by the time of the Boer War the virtue of Kipling's officers
and soldiers consists primarily in knowing their stations.

Kipling had written at the beginning of the war, a
poem called *The Absent-Minded Beggar*, which was an
appeal for contributions to a fund for the families of the
troops in South Africa; but this poem is essentially a
money-raising poem: it had nothing like the spontaneous
feeling of,

I went into a public-'ouse to get a pint o' beer;
The publican 'e up an' sez, 'We serve no red-coats here.'

The Barrack-Room Ballads were good in their kind: they gave the Tommy a voice, to which people stopped and listened. Kipling was interested in the soldier for his own sake, and made some effort to present his life as it seemed to the soldier himself. The poem called *Loot*, for example, which worries Mr. Edward Shanks because it appears to celebrate a reprehensible practice, is in reality perfectly legitimate because it simply describes one of the features of the soldier's experience in India. There is no moral one way or the other. The ballads of *The Five Nations*, on the other hand, the fruits of Kipling's experience in South Africa, are about ninety per cent mere rhymed journalism, decorating the readymade morality of a patriotic partisan. Compare one of the most successful of the earlier series with one of the most ambitious of the later.

> The Injian Ocean sets an' smiles
>   So sof', so bright, so bloomin' blue;
> There aren't a wave for miles an' miles
>   Excep' the jiggle from the screw:
> The ship is swep', the day is done,
>   The bugle's gone for smoke and play;
> An' black agin' the settin' sun
>   The Lascar sings, '*Hum deckty hai!*'

> *For to admire an' for to see,*
>   *For to be'old this world so wide —*
> *It never done no good to me,*
>   *But I can't drop it if I tried!*

Contrast this with *The Return* (from South Africa)

> Peace is declared, an' I return
>   To 'Ackneystadt, but not the same;

Things 'ave transpired which made me learn
    The size and meanin' of the game.
I did no more than others did,
    I don't know where the change began;
I started as an average kid,
    I finished as a thinkin' man.

If England was what England seems
    An' not the England of our dreams,
But only putty, brass an' paint,
    'Ow quick we'd drop 'er! But she ain't!

Before my gappin' mouth could speak
    I 'eard it in my comrade's tone;
I saw it on my neighbor's cheek
    Before I felt it flush my own.
An' last it come to me — not pride,
    Nor yet conceit, but on the 'ole
(If such a term may be applied),
    The makin's of a bloomin' soul.

This is hollow, synthetic, sickening. '*Having no position to consider and my trade enforcing it, I could move at will in the fourth dimension.*' He *has* a position to consider today, he eats at the captain's table, travels in special trains; and he is losing the freedom of that fourth dimension. There is a significant glimpse of the Kipling of the South African imperialist period in the diary of Arnold Bennett: 'I was responding to Pauline Smith's curiosity about the personalities of authors when Mrs. Smith began to talk about Kipling. She said he was greatly disliked in South Africa. Regarded as conceited and unapproachable. The officers of the Union Castle ships dreaded him, and prayed not to find themselves on the same ship as him. It seems that on one ship he had got all the information possible out of the officers, and had then, at the end of the voyage, reported them at headquarters for flirting with passengers — all except the chief engineer, an old Scotchman with whom he had been friendly. With this exception they were all called up to headquarters and reprimanded, and now they would have nothing to do with passengers.'

As for the Indians, they are now to be judged rigorously on the basis of their loyalty to the English in Africa. There are included in *Traffics and Discoveries* two jingoistic Sunday School stories which are certainly among the falsest and most foolish of Kipling's mature productions. In *The Comprehension of Private Copper,* he vents his contempt on an Anglicized Indian, the son of a settler in the Transvaal, who has sided with the Boers against the English; *A Sahibs' War,* on the other hand, presents an exemplary Sikh, who accompanies a British officer to South Africa, serves him with the devotion of a dog, and continues to practice after his leader's death the public-school principles of sportsmanship he has learned from him, in the face of the temptation to a cruel revenge against the treachery of the Boers. As for the Boers themselves, Kipling adopts toward them a systematic sneer. The assumption appears to be that to ambush the British is not cricket. Though the Dutch are unquestionably white men, Kipling manages somehow to imply that they have proved renegades to white solidarity by allying themselves with the black natives.

One is surprised to learn from *Something of Myself* that over a period of seven years after the war (1900-07), Kipling spent almost half his time in South Africa, going there for five or six months of every year. He seems to have so little to show for it: a few short stories, and most of these far from his best. He had made the acquaintance of Cecil Rhodes, and must simply have sat at his feet. The Kiplings lived in a house just off the Rhodes estate; and Kipling devotes long pages to the animals in Rhodes's private zoo and to architectural details of Rhodes's houses.

Even writing in 1935, he sounds like nothing so much as a high-paid publicity agent. It turns out that the Polonius-precepts in the celebrated verses called *If——* were inspired by Kipling's conception of the character of Dr. Jameson, the leader of the Jameson raid.

It may be worth mentioning here in connection with Kipling's submission to official authority that he has been described by a close friend, Viscount Castlerosse, as having abdicated his authority also in other important relations. 'They [the Kiplings],' he says, 'were among the few happy pairs I have ever met; but as far as Kipling was concerned, his married life was one of complete surrender. To him Carrie, as he called her, was more than a wife. She was a mistress in the literal sense, a governess and a matron. In a lesser woman I should have used the term "nurse." Kipling handed himself over bodily, financially and spiritually to his spouse. He had no banking account. All the money which he earned was handed over to her, and she, in turn, would dole him out so much pocket money. He could not call his time or even his stomach his own. . . .

'Sometimes in the evening, enlivened by wine and company, he would take a glass more than he was accustomed to, and then those great big eyes of his would shine brightly behind his strong spectacles, and Rud would take to talking faster and his views would become even more emphatic. If Mrs. Kipling was with him, she would quickly note the change and, sure enough, in a decisive voice she would issue the word of command: "Rud, it is time you went to bed," and Rud always discovered that it was about time he went to bed.

'I myself during the long years never once saw any signs of murmuring or of even incipient mutiny.'

In any case, Kipling has committed one of the most serious sins against his calling which are possible for an imaginative writer. He has resisted his own sense of life and discarded his own moral intelligence in favor of the point of view of a dominant political party. To Lord Roberts and Joseph Chamberlain he has sacrificed the living world of his own earlier artistic creations and of the heterogeneous human beings for whom they were offered as symbols. Here the constaint of making the correct pro-imperialist point is squeezing out all the kind of interest which is proper to a work of fiction. Compare a story of the middle Kipling with a story of Stephen Crane or Joseph Conrad, who were dealing with somewhat similar subjects. Both Conrad and Crane are pursuing their independent researches into the moral life of man. Where the spy who is the hero of *Under Western Eyes* is a tormented and touching figure, confused in his allegiances by the circumstances of his birth, a secret agent in Kipling must invariably be either a stout fellow, because his ruses are to the advantage of the British, or a sinister lying dog, because he is serving the enemy. Where the killing of *The Blue Hotel* is made to implicate everybody connected with it in a common human guilt, a killing in a story by Kipling must absolutely be shown to be either a dastardly or a virtuous act.

To contrast Kipling with Conrad or Crane is to enable us to get down at last to what is probably the basic explanation of the failure of Kipling's nerve. He lacked faith in the artist's vocation. We have heard a good deal in modern literature about the artist in conflict with the bourgeois world. Flaubert made war on the bourgeois; Rimbaud abandoned poetry as piffling in order to realize the adventure of commerce; Thomas Mann took as his theme the emotions of weakness and defeat of the artist overshadowed by the business man. But Kipling neither faced the fight like Flaubert, nor faced the problem in his life like Rimbaud, nor faced the problem in his art like Mann. Something in him, something vulgar in the middle-class British way, something perhaps connected with the Methodist ministers who were his grandfathers on both sides, a tradition which understood preaching and could understand craftsmanship, but had a good deal of respect for the powers that governed the material world and never thought of putting the artist on a par with them — something of this sort at a given point prevented Kipling from playing through his part, and betrayed him into dedicating his talents to the praise of the practical man. Instead of *becoming* a man of action like Rimbaud, a course which shows a boldness of logic, he fell into the ignominious rôle of the artist who prostrates his art before the achievements of soldiers and merchants, and who is always declaring the supremacy of the 'doer' over the man of ideas.

The results of this are very curious and well worth studying from the artistic point of view — because Kipling, it must always be remembered, was a man of really remarkable abilities. Certain of the symptoms of his case have been indicated by George Moore and Dixon Scott, whose discussions of him in *Avowals* and *Men of Letters* are among the few first-rate pieces of criticism that I remember to have seen on the subject. George Moore quotes a passage from *Kim*, a description of evening in India, and praises it for 'the perfection of the writing, of the strong masculine rhythm of every sentence, and of the accuracy of every observation'; but then goes on to point out that 'Mr. Kipling has seen much more than he has felt,' that 'when we come to analyze the lines we find a touch of local color not only in every sentence, but in each part between each semicolon.' So Scott diagnoses admirably the mechanical ingenuity of plot that distinguishes the middle Kipling. 'Switch,' he says, 'this imperatively map-making, pattern-making method upon . . . the element of human nature, and what is the inevitable result? Inevitably, there is the same sudden stiffening and formulation. The char-

acters spring to attention like soldiers on parade; they re-
spond briskly to a sudden description; they wear a fixed
set of idiosyncrasies like a uniform. A mind like this *must*
use types and set counters; it feels dissatisfied, ineffective,
unsafe, unless it can reduce the fluid waverings of character, its flitting caprices and twilit desires, to some tangible
system. The characters of such a man will not only be
definite; they will be definitions.' And he goes on to show
how Kipling's use of dialect makes a screen for his relin-
quishment of his grip on the real organism of human personality: 'For dialect, in spite of all its air of ragged lawlessness, is wholly impersonal, typical, fixed, the code of
a caste, not the voice of an individual. It is when the novelist sets his characters talking the King's English that he
really puts his capacity for reproducing the unconventional and capricious on its trial. Mr. Kipling's plain conversations are markedly unreal. But honest craftsmanship
and an ear for strong rhythms have provided him with
many suits of dialects. And with these he dresses the talk
till it seems to surge with character.'

The packed detail, the automatic plot, the surfaces lac-
quered with dialect, the ever-tightening tension of form,
are all a part of Kipling's effort to impose his scheme by
main force. The strangest result of this effort is to be
seen in a change in the subject matter itself. Kipling actually tends at this time to abandon human beings altogether. In that letter of Henry James in which he speaks
of his former hope that Kipling might grow into an English Balzac, he goes on: 'But I have given that up in proportion as he has come steadily from the less simple in
subject to the more simple — from the Anglo-Indians to
the natives, from the natives to the Tommies, from the
Tommies to the quadrupeds, from the quadrupeds to the
fish, and from the fish to the engines and screws.' This
increasing addiction of Kipling to animals, insects and

machines is evidently to be explained by his need to find characters which will yield themselves unresistingly to being presented as parts of a system. In the *Jungle Books,* the animal characters are each one all of a piece, though in their ensemble they still provide a variety, and they are dominated by a 'Law of the Jungle,' which lays down their duties and rights. The animals have organized the Jungle, and the Jungle is presided over by Mowgli in his function of forest ranger, so that it falls into its subsidiary place in the larger organization of the Empire.

Yet the *Jungle Books* (written in Vermont) are not artistically off the track; the element of obvious allegory is not out of place in such fairy tales. It is when Kipling takes to contriving these animal allegories for grown-ups that he brings up the reader's gorge. What is proved in regard to human beings by the fable called *A Walking Delegate,* in which a pastureful of self-respecting horses turn and rend a yellow loafer from Kansas, who is attempting to incite them to rebellion against their master, Man? A labor leader and the men he is trying to organize are after all, not horses but men. Does Kipling mean to imply that the ordinary workingman stands in the same relation to the employing and governing classes as that in which the horse stands to its owner? And what is proved by *The Mother Hive,* in which an invasion of wax-moths that ruin the stock of the swarm represents the infiltration of socialism? (Compare these with that more humane fable of 1893, *The Children of the Zodiac,* which deals with gods become men.) And, though the discipline of a military unit or of the crew of a ship or a plane may provide a certain human interest, it makes us a little uncomfortable to find Kipling taking up locomotives and representing '.007' instead of the engineer who drives it as the hero of the American railroad; and descending even to the mechanical parts, the rivets and planks of a ship, whose

drama consists solely of being knocked into place by the
elements so that it may function as a co-ordinated whole.

We may lose interest, like Henry James, in the animal
or mechanical characters of Kipling's middle period; but
we must admit that these novel productions have their
own peculiar merit. It is the paradox of Kipling's career
that he should have extended the conquests of his craftsmanship in proportion to the shrinking of the range of his
dramatic imagination. As his responses to human beings
became duller, his sensitivity to his medium increased.

In both tendencies he was, of course, quite faithful to
certain aspects of the life of his age. It was a period, those
early nineteen hundreds, of brilliant technological improvement and of generally stunted intelligence. And
Kipling now appeared as the poet both of the new mechanical methods and of the ideals of the people who
spread them. To re-read these stories today is to feel again
a little of the thrill of the plushy transcontinental Pull-
mans and the spic-and-span transatlantic liners that carried us around in our youth, and to meet again the bright
and bustling people, talking about the polo field and the
stock market, smart Paris and lovely California, the latest
musical comedy and Kipling, in the smoking-rooms or
among the steamer-chairs.

Kipling reflected this mechanical progress by evolving
a new prose technique. We have often since Kipling's day
been harangued by the Futurists and others about the
need for artistic innovations appropriate to the life of the
machine age; but it is doubtful whether any rhapsodist of
motor-cars or photographer of dynamos and valves has
been so successful at this as Kipling was at the time he
wrote *The Day's Work*. These stories of his get their effects with the energy and accuracy of engines, by means
of words that, hard, short and close-fitting, give the impression of ball-bearings and cogs. Beside them, the spout-

ings of the machine fans look like the old-fashioned rhetoric they are. For these latter could merely whoop and roar in a manner essentially romantic over the bigness, the power, the speed of the machines, whereas Kipling exemplified in his form itself the mechanical efficiency and discipline, and he managed to convey with precision both the grimness and the exhilaration which characterized the triumph of the machine.

He also brought to perfection the literary use of the language of the specialized industrial world. He must have been the principal artisan in the creation of that peculiar modern *genre* in which we are made to see some comedy or tragedy through the cheapening or obscuring medium of technical vocabulary or professional slang. He did not, of course, invent the dialect monologue; but it is improbable that we should have had, for example, either the baseball stories of Ring Lardner or the Cyclops episode in *Ulysses* if Kipling had never written.

This is partly no doubt pure virtuosity. Mr. Beresford says that Kipling was by nature as unmechanical as possible, could do nothing with his hands except write; and I have heard an amusing story of his astonishment and admiration at the mechanical proficiency of an American friend who had simply put a castor back on a chair. He had never worked at any of the processes he described, had had to get them all up through the methods of the attentive reporter. But it is virtuosity on a much higher level than that of the imitation literature so often admired in that era. Where Stevenson turns out paler *pastiches* of veins which have already been exploited, Kipling really finds new rhythms, new colors and textures of words, for things that have not yet been brought into literature. For the most part a second-rate writer of verse, because though he can imitate the language of poetry as he can imitate all the other languages, he cannot compensate for the falsity of his feeling by his sharp observation and his expert technique, he is extraordinary as a worker in prose. It is impossible still for a prose writer to read, for example, the first part of *The Bridge-Builders* without marveling at the author's mastery. How he has caught the very look and feel of the materials that go to make bridges and of the various aspects of the waters they have to dominate! And the maneuvers of modern armies against the dusty South African landscapes, and the tempo of American trains, and the relation of the Scotch engineer to the patched-up machines of his ship. The Kipling who put on record all these things was an original and accomplished artist.

For the rest, he writes stories for children. One is surprised in going back over Kipling's work to find that, dating from the time of his settling with his family in Vermont, he published no less than nine children's books: the two *Jungle Books, Captains Courageous, Just So Stories, Stalky & Co., Puck of Pook's Hill, Rewards and Fairies, A History of England, Land and Sea Tales for Scouts and Scouts Masters.* It is as if the natural human feelings progressively forced out of his work by the rigors of organization for its own sake were seeking relief in a reversion to childhood, when one has not yet become responsible for the way that the world is run, where it is enough to enjoy and to wonder at what we do not yet understand. And, on the other hand, the simplified morality to which Kipling has now committed himself is easier to make acceptable to one's readers and oneself if one approaches it from the point of view of the child. (The truth is that much of his work of this period which aims at the intelligence of grown people might almost equally well be subtitled *For Scouts and Scouts Masters.*) These stories, excellent at their best, are most successful when they are *most* irresponsible — as in the *Just So Stories;*

least so, as in *Captains Courageous*, when they lean most heavily on the schoolboy morality.

The most ambitious of them — the two series about Puck of Pook's Hill (1906 and 1910) — have, I know, been much admired by certain critics, including the sensitive Dixon Scott; but my own taste rejects them on rereading them as it did when I read them first at the age for which they were presumably intended. Kipling tells us that the stories in *Rewards and Fairies* were designed to carry a meaning for adults as well as to interest children. But their technical sophistication puts them slightly above the heads of children at the same time that their sugared exploitation of Kipling's Anglo-Spartan code of conduct makes them slightly repugnant to grown-ups.

They are, to be sure, the most embroidered productions of Kipling's most elaborate period. The recovery of obsolete arts and crafts, the re-creation of obsolete idioms, are new pretexts for virtuosity. Kipling's genius for words has been stimulated by the discovery of the English earth and sea; he spreads on the rich grassiness of the English country, the dense fogginess of the English coast, the layers upon layers of tradition that cause the English character to seem to him deep-rooted, deep-colored, deep-meaning. He has applied all his delicacy and strength to this effort to get the mother-country into prose; but his England is never so real as was his India; and the effect, for all the sinewy writing, is somehow fundamentally decadent. The Normans and the Saxons and the Elizabethans, the great cathedral-builders and sailors and divines, perpetrating impossible 'gags,' striking postures that verge on the 'ham,' seem almost to anticipate Hollywood. The theme of the rôle and the ordeal of the artist which figures in *Rewards and Fairies* suffers from being treated in the vein of *Stalky & Co*. In the story called *The Wrong Thing*, he embarks on a promising subject: the discrepancy between the aim of the artist who is straining to top the standards of his craft, and the quite irrelevant kinds of interest that the powers that employ him may take in him; but he turns it into a farce and ruins it.

Kipling's England is perhaps the most synthetic of all his creations of this period, when he depends so much on tools and materials as distinguished from sympathy and insight. Scott says that these stories are opalescent; and this is true, but they show the defects of opals that have been artificially made and whose variegated glimmerings and shiftings do not seem to convey anything mysterious.

v

Yet, in locating the Ideal in the Empire, Kipling was not without his moments of uneasiness. If the Empire is really founded on self-discipline, the fear of God, the code of *noblesse oblige,* if it really involves a moral system, then we are justified in identifying it with 'the Law'; but suppose that it is not really so dedicated.

> If England was what England seems,
> An' not the England of our dreams,
> But only putty, brass an' paint,
> 'Ow quick we'd drop 'er! *But she ain't!*

Yet *Recessional,* perhaps the best set of verses that Kipling ever wrote, is a warning that springs from a doubt; and the story called *The Man Who Would Be King* is surely a parable of what might happen to the English if they should forfeit their moral authority. Two low-class English adventurers put themselves over on the natives of a remote region beyond Afghanistan, organize under a single rule a whole set of mountain tribes; but the man who has made himself king is destroyed by the natives that have adored him the instant they come to realize that he is not a god, as they had supposed, but a man. The Wesleyan preacher in Kipling knows that the valiant dust of man can build only on dust if it builds not in the name of God; and he is prepared to pound the pulpit and call down the Almighty's anger when parliamentarians or ministers or generals debauch their office or hold it light. Kipling always refused official honors in order to keep himself free; and his truculence had its valuable aspect in that it aided him to resist the briberies of his period of glory and fortune. In the volume of his collected addresses, which he calls *A Book of Words*, there are some sincere and inspiriting sermons. 'Now I do not ask you not to be carried away by the first rush of the great game of life. That is expecting you to be more than human,' he told the students at McGill University in the fall of 1907, when the height of his popularity was past. 'But I *do* ask you, after the first heat of the game, that you draw breath and watch your fellows for a while. Sooner or later, you will see some man to whom the idea of wealth as mere wealth does not appeal, whom the methods of amassing that wealth do not interest, and who will not accept money if you offer it to him at a certain price. At first you will be inclined to laugh at this man and to think that he is not "smart" in his ideas. I suggest that you watch him closely, for he will presently demonstrate to you that money dominates everybody except the man who does not want money. You may meet that man on your farm, in your village, or in your legislature. But be sure that, whenever or wherever you meet him, as soon as it comes to a direct issue between you, his little finger will be thicker than your loins. You will go in fear of him: he will not go in fear of you. You will do what he wants: he will not do what you want. You will find that you have no weapon in your armoury with which you can attack him; no argument with which you can appeal to him. Whatever you gain, he will gain more.'

If Kipling *had* taken a bribe, it was not that of reputation or cash; it was rather the big moral bribe that a political system can offer: the promise of mental security. And even here a peculiar integrity — as it were, an integrity of *temperament* that came to exist in dissociation from the intellect — survived the collapse of the system and saved Kipling in the end from his pretenses. How this happened is the last chapter of his story.

There was, as I say, a Wesleyan preacher in Kipling. The Old Testament served him as an armory of grim instances and menacing visions to drive home the imperial code; or, on occasions when the imperial masters failed to live up to this code, of scorching rhetorical language (though with more of malignancy than of grandeur) for the chastisement of a generation of vipers. But Kipling had no real religion. He exploited, in his poems and his fiction, the mythology of a number of religions.

We may be inclined to feel, in reading Kipling — and to some extent we shall be right — that the various symbols and gods which figure in his stories and poems are mere properties which the writer finds useful for his purposes of rhetoric or romance. Yet we cannot but suspect in *Kim* and in the stories of metempsychosis that Kipling has been seriously influenced by the Buddhism which he had imbibed with his first language in his boyhood. Mr. Beresford corroborates this: he says that the Kipling of *Westward Ho!* talked Buddhism and reincarnation. And it is certainly with Buddhism that we first find associated a mystical side of Kipling's mind which, in this last phase, is to emerge into the foreground.

We left the Lama of *Kim* attaining the Buddhist ecstasy and escaping from the Wheel of Things at the same moment that Kim gets promotion and finally becomes a spoke in the wheel of British administration. But the world-beyond of the Lama is to seep back into Kipling's work in queer and incongruous forms. Among the strained political fables of the collection called *Traffics and Discoveries*, which is the beginning of the more somber later Kipling, there is a story of a wireless operator who is possessed by the soul of Keats. It may be that Kipling's Southsea experience, in driving him back into his imagination for defense against the horror of reality, had had the effect both of intensifying his fancies and of dissociating them from ordinary life — so that the ascent out of the Wheel of Things and the visitations of an alien soul became ways of representing this. The effort of the grown-up Kipling to embrace by the imagination, to master by a disciplined art, what he regarded as the practical realities is to be subject to sudden recoils. In the Kipling of the middle period, there is a suppressed but vital element which thrusts periodically a lunatic head out of a window of the well-bricked façade.

This element is connected with the Lama, but it is also connected with something else more familiar to the Western world: the visitations and alienations of what is now known as neurotic personality. Here again Kipling was true to his age. While the locomotives and airplanes and steamers were beating records and binding continents, the human engine was going wrong. The age of mechanical technique was also the age of the nerve sanitarium. In the stories of the early Kipling, the intervention of the supernatural has, as a rule, within the frame of the story itself, very little psychological interest; but already in 'They' and *The Brushwood Boy* the dream and the hallucination are taking on a more emphatic significance. With *The House Surgeon* and *In the Same Boat*, they are in process of emerging from the fairy tale: they become recognizable as psychiatric symptoms. The depression described in *The House Surgeon* has been transferred, by the artifice of the story, to persons unconcerned in the tragedy through the influence from a distance of someone else; but the woman with whom the terror originates is suffering morbidly from feelings of guilt, and the sensations are evidently based on the first-hand experience of the author.

'And it was just then that I was aware of a little gray shadow, as it might have been a snowflake seen against the light, floating at an immense distance in the background of my brain. It annoyed me, and I shook my head to get rid of it. Then my brain telegraphed that it was the forerunner of a swift-striding gloom which there was yet time to escape if I would force my thoughts away from it, as a man leaping for life forces his body forward and away from the fall of a wall. But the gloom overtook me before I could take in the meaning of the message. I moved toward the bed, every nerve already aching with the foreknowledge of the pain that was to be dealt it, and sat down, while my amazed and angry soul dropped, gulf by gulf, into that horror of great darkness which is spoken of in the Bible, and which, as the auctioneers say, must be experienced to be appreciated.

'Despair upon despair, misery upon misery, fear after fear, each causing their distinct and separate woe, packed in upon me for an unrecorded length of time, until at last they blurred together, and I heard a click in my brain like the click in the ear when one descends in a diving bell, and I knew that the pressures were equalized within and without, and that, for the moment, the worst was at an end. But I knew also that at any moment the darkness might come down anew; and while I dwelt on this speculation precisely as a man torments a raging tooth with his tongue, it ebbed away into the little gray shadow on the brain of its first coming, and once more I heard my brain, which knew what would recur, telegraph to every quarter for help, release or diversion.'

And although the periodical irrational panics of the couple of *In the Same Boat* are explained as the result of pre-natal shocks, the description of the man and woman themselves, with their 'nerve doctors,' their desperate drug-taking, their shaky and futile journeys in flight from their neurotic fears, their peculiar neurotic relationship, constitutes an accurate account of a phenomenon of contemporary life which, at the time that Kipling was writing, had hardly been described in fiction.

Observe that in both these stories, as in the stories of war neurosis that will follow, the people who suffer thus are quite innocent, their agony is entirely unearned. I believe that the only cases in which the obsessive horror is connected with any kind of guilt are those in which a man is hounded to death by the vision of a woman he has wronged. This theme recurs regularly with Kipling from the time of *The Phantom Rickshaw,* one of the very first of his short stories, through the remarkable *Mrs. Bathurst* of his middle period, and up to the strange and poisoned *Dayspring Mishandled,* which was one of the last things he wrote. We cannot speculate with very much assurance on the relation of this theme of betrayal to the other recurring themes of Kipling's work. We do not know enough about his life to be able to assign it to an assumption on the part of the six-year-old Kipling that he must somehow have sinned against the mother who had abandoned him so inexplicably at Southsea; or to relate it to the strange situation of Dick Heldar in *The Light That Failed,* who vainly adores, and goes blind in adoring, the inexplicably obdurate Maisie. All we can say is that the theme of the anguish which is suffered without being deserved has the appearance of having been derived from a morbid permanent feeling of injury inflicted by his experience at Southsea.

Certainly the fear of darkness passing into the fear of blindness which runs all through his work from *The Light That Failed to 'They'* is traceable directly to his breakdown and to the frightening failure of his eyes. This was a pattern he seems to have repeated. Illnesses were critical for Kipling. It was after his illness in India that he set out to contend with a society which must have seemed to him indifferent and brutal by making himself a writer; and it was after his illness in New York that he decided to turn his back on America and to accept all the values that that retreat implied. It was after the breakdown in which Kim had brooded on his true identity that he emerged as a fullblown British agent. From the darkness and the physical weakness, the Kipling of the middle period has come forth with tightened nerves, resolved to meet a state of things in which horses are always being whipped or having their heads blown off, in which schoolboys are bullied and flogged, in which soldiers are imprisoned in barracks and fed to the bayonets and guns, by identifying himself with horses — as in the story called *A Walking Delegate* — that gang together to kick and maul another horse, with schoolboys — as in *The Moral Reformers* of *Stalky* — that gloat in torturing other schoolboys, with soldiers that get the sharpest satisfaction from stabbing and pot-shotting other soldiers. He has set himself with all the stiff ribs of a metal-armatured art to stand up to this world outside that gets its authority from its power to crush and kill: the world of the Southsea house that has turned into the world of the Empire; to compete with it on its own terms. And yet the darkness and the illness return. It is a key to the whole work of Kipling that the great celebrant of physical courage should prove in the long run to convey his most moving and convincing effects in describing moral panic. Kipling's bullyings and killings are contemptible: they are the fantasies of the physically helpless. The only authentic heroism to be found in the fiction of Kipling is the heroism of moral fortitude on the edge of a nervous collapse.

And in the later decades of Kipling's life the blackness and the panic close down; the abyss becomes more menacing. It is the Crab, both devil and destiny, which in the story called *The Children of the Zodiac* lies always in wait for the poet and finally comes to devour him. The nurse-like watchfulness of Mrs. Kipling and Kipling's fear of stepping out of her régime, which appeared to his friend an impediment to the development of his genius, were no doubt, on the contrary, in his extreme instability, a condition of his being able to function at all — just as the violence of his determination to find the answer to the problems of society and a defense against the forces that plagued him in the program of an imperialist government was evidently directly related to the violence of desperation of his need.

But now both of these shelters he had built himself — the roof of his family life, the confidence of his political idealism — were suddenly to be broken down.

In 1914-18, the British Empire collided with a competitor. All England went to war, including Kipling's only son. The boy, not yet out of his teens, was killed in an attack before Loos in September, 1915, and his body was never found. John Kipling had at first been reported missing, and his father waited for months in the hope of getting a letter from Germany announcing that he had been taken prisoner.

These war years left Kipling defenseless. It had been easy to be grimly romantic on the subject of the warfare in India when Kipling had never seen fighting; it had even been possible, as a reporter at the front, to Meissonier the campaign in South Africa in the bright colors of the new nineteenth centry. But the long systematic waste of the trench warfare of the struggle against Germany discouraged the artistic exploitation of the cruelties and gallantries of battle. The strain of the suspense and the horror taxed intolerably those attitudes of Kipling's which had been in the first instance provoked by a strain and which had only at the cost of a strain been kept up.

From even before the war, the conduct of British policy

had been far from pleasing to Kipling. He saw clearly the
careerism and the venality of the modern politician; and
he was bitterly opposed on principle to the proposals of
the radicals and liberals. In May, 1914, when civil war
with Ulster was threatening, he delivered at Tunbridge
Wells and allowed to be circulated as a penny leaflet a
speech against the Home Rule Bill of a virulence almost
hysterical. The attempt to free Ireland he excoriates as on
a level with the Marconi scandals. 'The Home Rule Bill,'
he declares, 'broke the pledged faith of generations; it offi-
cially recognized sedition, privy conspiracy and rebellion;
it subsidized the secret forces of boycott, intimidation and
murder; and it created an independent stronghold in
which all these forces could work together, as they have
always and openly boasted that they would, for the destruction of Great Britain.'

This was to remain Kipling's temper in public questions. The victory of the Bolsheviks in Russia of course
made the picture blacker: one sixth of the area of the
globe, he said, had 'passed bodily out of civilization.'

> Our world has passed away,
> In wantonness o'erthrown.
> There is nothing left to-day
> But steel and fire and stone!

he wrote when the war began. And when Kipling was
sickened and broken with steel and fire and stone, there
was little for his spirit to lean on.

Little but the practice of his craft, which now reflects
only the twisted fragments of Kipling's exploded cosmos.

These latest stories of Kipling's have attracted meager
attention for reasons that are easily comprehensible. The
disappearance in the middle Kipling of the interest in
human beings for their own sake and the deliberate cul-

tivation of the excommunicatory imperialist hatreds had
already had the effect of discouraging the appetite of the
general public; and when the human element reappeared
in a new tormented form in Kipling's later stories, the
elliptical and complex technique which the writer had by
that time developed put the general reader off. On the
other hand, the highbrows ignored him, because, in the
era of Lawrence and Joyce, when the world was disgusted
with soldiering and when the imperialisms were apparently deflated, they could take no interest in the point of
view. In their conviction that Kipling could never hold
water, they had not even enough curiositv to wonder
what had happened to an author who must have enchanted them in their childhood. And in a sense they
were, of course, correct. Kipling *had* terribly shrunk; he
seemed a man who had had a stroke and was only half
himself — whereas Yeats was playing out superbly the last
act of a personal drama which he had sustained unem-
barrassed by public events, and Henry James was now
seen in retrospect to have accomplished, in his long career,
a prodigy of disinterested devotion to an art and a criticism
of life. Where there was so much wreckage around, political, social and moral, the figure of the disinterested
artist commanded especial respect.

Yet the Kipling who limped out of the wreckage,
shrunken and wry though he looks, has in a sense had his
development as an artist. Some of these stories are the
most intense in feeling as they are among the most concentrated in form that Kipling ever wrote; to a writer, they
are perhaps the most interesting. The subjects are sometimes hard to swallow, and the stories themselves —
through a tasteless device which unfortunately grew on
Kipling as he got older — are each preceded and followed
by poems which elaborate or elucidate their themes in the
author's synthetic verse and which dull the effect of
the excellent prose. But here Kipling's peculiar method,

trained with deadly intention, scores some of its cleanest hits.

Let us, however, first consider the subjects of these final collections of stories (*A Diversity of Creatures, Debits and Credits,* and *Limits and Renewals*). The fragments of the disintegrated Kipling fall roughly into five classes: tales of hatred, farces based on practical jokes, studies of neurotic cases, tales of fellowship in religion, and tales of personal bereavement.

The tales of hatred — hatred of Americans and the Germans: *Sea Constables* and *Mary Postgate* — become murderous at the time of the war (though they give place to other kinds of themes later). The hatred of democracy — in the satire called *As Easy as A.B.C.* (which appeared in 1912) — is carried to lengths that would be Swiftian if Kipling had subjected the whole human race to the death ray of his abstract contempt, but which — as Edward Shanks points out — is rendered rather suspect by the exemption from the annihilating irony of a group of disciplined officials. The morals of these stories are odious and the plots mostly contrived and preposterous; yet they acquire a certain dignity from the desperation of bitterness that animates them.

Then there are the practical jokes — a category which includes the comic accidents: practical jokes engineered by the author. These have always been a feature of Kipling. His addiction to this form of humor seems to have derived originally from the boobytraps and baitings of *Westward Ho!*; later, changing sides, he identified them rather with the lickings-into-shape inflicted by regimental raggings. The victims of these pulverizing hoaxes fall into two classes: petty tyrants, who humiliate and bully, and who always have to be cads; and political idealists and godless intellectuals, who have to be nincompoops. Kipling likes nothing better than to hurl one of these latter into a hive of bees or, as in one of his early stories, to silence his opinions by a sunstroke. A first principle of Kipling's world is revenge: the humiliated must become the humiliator. One might expect this kind of thing to disappear in the work of the latest Kipling; but the formula becomes instead much more frequent, and it comes to play a special rôle. The practical joke with its extravagant laughter is a violent if hollow explosion for the relief of nervous strain; and the severity of this strain may be gauged by the prodigious dimensions of the hoaxes in which Kipling now labors to concentrate the complex calculation of an Ibsen and the methodical ferocity of a Chinese executioner.

In some of these stories, the comic disaster is exploited as a therapeutic device. There are six stories of war neurosis in Kipling's last two collections. The situation of the shattered veteran provided him with an opportunity for studying further a subject which had haunted him all his life: the condition of people who seem to themselves on the borderline of madness. Here the sufferers are still perfectly guiltless. In one case, an appearance of guilt, in another, a conviction of guilt, turn out to be actually unjustified. But the picture is now more realistically filled out than it was by the pre-natal occurrences which were the best Kipling could do for motivation for the neurotics of *In the Same Boat*. The war supplies real causes for derangement; and Kipling sees that such short-circuits may be mended by going back to the occasion that gave rise to the obsession and disentangling the crossed wires. But his principal prescriptions for saving people from the effects of the horror and the strain of the war are such apropos comic accidents and well-aimed benevolent frauds as, in reality, are rarely possible and which would be of doubtful efficacity if they were. In one story, the fantasy of the sick man turns out to be based on a reading in hospital of a novel by Mrs. Ewing (as the soldiers in *The Janeites* find solace in the novels of Jane Austen) —

which also gives the veteran, when he recovers, a beneficent interest in life: that of planting wayside gardens.
Another ex-soldier is saved by a dog.

Kipling's homeless religious sense resorts to strange fel-
lowships and faiths to bolster up his broken men. He had
been made a Freemason in India, and Freemasonry had
figured in *Kim* and had seemed to crop up in the guise of
Mithraism in the Roman stories of *Puck of Pook's Hill.*
Now he invents, for a new series of stories, a circle of
philanthropic Masons who meet in the back room of a
tobacconist's and who try to help men that have been
wrecked by the war. A new ideal — but a new ideal conceived by a tired and humbled man — of a brotherhood
which shall not be delimited by the exclusions of a fighting unit or caste begins to appear in these stories. Mithraism figures again in *The Church That Was at Antioch:*
the young Roman officer turned Mithraist says of his
mother, 'She follows the old school, of course — the home-
worships and the strict Latin Trinity. . . . But one wants
more than that'; and he ends by getting murdered by the
Jews in revenge for his protection of the Apostle Paul. In
another story, *The Manner of Men,* Saint Paul appears
again and rescues a neurotic sea-captain: 'Serve Caesar,'
says Paul. 'You are not canvas I can cut to advantage at
present. But if you serve Caesar you will be obeying at
least some sort of law. . . . If you take refuge under
Caesar at sea, you may have time to think. Then I may
meet you again, and we can go on with our talks. But that
is as the God wills. What concerns you *now,*' he concludes, in a tone that recalls at the same time the Buch-
manite and the psychoanalyst, 'is that, by taking service,
you will be free from the fear that has ridden you all your
life.'

The Paul of these final stories, so different from his
early heroes, may evidently tell us something about Kipling's changed conception of himself. Paul had preached

the Word to the Gentiles as Kipling had preached the Law to the colonials and the Americans; Paul, like Kipling, is ill-favored and undersized, 'a little shrimp of a man,' who has 'the woman's trick of taking the tone and color of whoever he talked to' and who is scarred from old floggings and from his encounters with the beasts of the arena. Paul, like Kipling, is brash and tense; he is dedicated to a mission which has saved him from fear. But observe that, though he advises the shaky captain to take service with Caesar for a time, he has himself gone on to something higher.

This, then, is quite another Kipling. His prophets have an altered message: Kipling is losing his hatred. His captains have been afraid all their lives. His soldiers are no longer so cocky, so keen to kill inferior peoples, so intent on the purposes of the Empire. And officers and soldiers are now closer, as they were in the earliest stories: they are now simply civilians back in mufti, between whom the bond of having been in the war is stronger than the class differences of peace-time. And they are the remnants of a colossal disaster. I shall quote one of the pieces in verse with which Kipling supplements these stories, because, indifferent though it is as poetry, it strikingly illustrates this change:

> I have a dream — a dreadful dream —
> A dream that is never done,
> I watch a man go out of his mind,
> And he is My Mother's Son.
>
> They pushed him into a Mental Home,
> And that is like the grave:
> For they do not let you sleep upstairs,
> And you're not allowed to shave.
>
> And it was *not* disease or crime
> Which got him landed there,

But because they laid on My Mother's Son
    More than a man could bear.

What with noise, and fear of death,
    Waking, and wounds and cold,
They filled the Cup for My Mother's Son
    Fuller than it could hold.

They broke his body and his mind
    And yet they made him live,
And they asked more of My Mother's Son
    Than any man could give.

For, just because he had not died
    Nor been discharged nor sick:
They dragged it out with My Mother's Son
    Longer than he could stick. . . .

And no one knows when he'll get well —
    So, there he'll have to be:
And, 'spite of the beard in the looking-glass,
    I know that man is me!

The theme of inescapable illness dominates the whole later Kipling. In some cases, the diseases are physical, but there is always the implication of a psychological aspect. In *A Madonna of the Trenches* and *The Wish House* — gruesome ghost stories of love and death that make *The End of the Passage* and *The Mark of the Beast* look like harmless bogey tales for children — cancer serves as a symbol for rejected or frustrated love. And it is not clear in *Dayspring Mishandled* whether the detestable literary man Castorley is being poisoned by his wife and the doctor or by the consciousness of the wrong he has committed. The strangest of all these stories is *Unprofessional*, in which cancer, spasms of insanity, the aftermath of the war, and the influence of the something beyond human life combine in a clinical fantasy on the beneficent possibilities of science. Here the white mice and the London woman convulsed with suicidal seizures, sets toward death periodically imparted by mysterious cosmic tides, are Kipling's uncanniest image for the workings of nervous disorders.

The old great man is back again in the 'House of Desolation' at Southsea, tormented unjustly, ill, deserted by those he loves, and with the haunted darkness descending on that world which his determined effort had once enabled him to see so distinctly. In one of the latest of his stories, *Proofs of Holy Writ*, he makes Shakespeare speak to Ben Jonson of a man whom Shakespeare describes as 'going down darkling to his tomb 'twixt cliffs of ice and iron' — phrases hardly characteristic of Shakespeare but extremely appropriate to Kipling.

It is striking that some of the most authentic of Kipling's early stories should deal with children forsaken by their parents and the most poignant of his later ones with parents bereaved of their children. The theme of the abandoned parent seems to reflect in reversal the theme of the abandoned child. The former theme has already appeared in *'They'* (written after the death of Kipling's daughter), associated with the themes of blindness and the deprivation of love; and even before that, in *Without Benefit of Clergy*.

Certainly two of these last stories of Kipling's are among the most moving he wrote. There is a passage in *Mary Postgate* like the plucking of a tightened string that is just about to break. The plain and dull English female 'companion' is to burn up the belongings of a young soldier — like most of Kipling's children, an orphan — to whom she has stood in a maternal rôle and who has just been killed in a plane. Kipling tells in one of his typical inventories of the items, mainly relics of boyhood sports, that Mary has to destroy; and then: 'The shrubbery was filling with twilight by the time she had completed her arrangements and sprinkled the sacrificial oil. As she lit the match that would burn her heart to ashes, she heard a groan or a grunt behind the dense Portugal laurels.' *The match that would burn her heart to ashes*: they are the first words that we have yet encountered, the only words that we shall have encountered, that are not matter-of-fact; and here the observation of Kipling, of which George Moore complained that it was too systematic and too technical, making it *Portugal laurels* where another writer would have simply written *shrubbery* — here this hardness of concrete detail is suddenly given new value by a phrase on another plane.

So in that other remarkable story, *The Gardener*, Kipling's method of preparing a finale by concealing essential information in an apparently casual narrative produces an effect of tremendous power. This method, which Kipling has developed with so much ingenuity and precision, serves in some of his stories to spring surprises that are merely mechanical; but it has always had its special appropriateness to those aspects of the English character with which Kipling has been particularly concerned in that it masks emotion and purpose under a pretense of coldness and indifference; and here it is handled in a masterly fashion to dramatize another example of the impassive Englishwoman. The implications of *Mary Postgate* prevent us from accepting it fully: we know too well that the revengeful cruelty which impels the heroine of the story to let the shattered German aviator die is shared by the author himself. But *The Gardener* may conquer us completely. I am not sure that it is not really the best story that Kipling ever wrote. Like the rest of even the best of Kipling, it is not quite on the highest level. He must still have his fairy-tale properties; and we may be disposed to protest at his taste when we find that the Puck of Pook's Hill element is supplied by the apparition of Jesus. But if we have been following Kipling's development, we recognize that this fact is significant. The rôle that Christ has formerly played in Kipling — as in the poem called *Cold Iron* — has been that of a *pukka Sahib* who knows how to take his punishment. This is the first time, so far as I remember, that Kipling's Christ has shown pity — as Kipling pities now rather than boasts about the self-disciplined and much-enduring British. And the symbol at once bares the secret and liberates the locked-up emotion with a sudden and shocking force. The self-repression and the hopeless grief of the unmarried mother in *The Gardener* speak for the real Kipling. Here he has found for them intense expression in the concentrated forms of his art.

The big talk of the work of the world, of the mission to command of the British, even the hatefulness of fear and disappointment, have largely faded away for Kipling. He composes as a memorial to his son and to the system in devotion to which the half-American boy has died a history of the Irish Guards in the war, in which Lieutenant John Kipling is hardly mentioned. But, meticulously assembling, by the method by which he once seemed to build so solidly, the scattered memories of his son's battalion, he seems merely to be striving, by wisps and scraps, to re-create the terrible days that preceded the death of his child. Even the victory over the Germans can never make that right.

UNCOMFORTABLE CASANOVA

WHY has Jacques Casanova attracted so little attention in English? So far as I know there is nothing very serious except Havelock Ellis's essay, and that does not go far into the subject. Mr. S. Guy Endore's book, though a good piece of work in its way, is only a popular biography. Yet the Chevalier de Seingalt was a most remarkable man, who had some of the qualities of greatness. The Prince de Ligne listed his name with those of Louis XV, Frederick the Great, Beaumarchais, d'Alembert and Hume as among the most interesting men he had known, and the great sharper really belongs in that company.

When we begin reading Casanova's *Memoirs,* we think him amusing but cheap. Yet we end by being genuinely impressed by him.

He was a type who was very familiar in the America of the boom of the twenties. In our time he might have had the career of a Rothstein or a Nicky Arnstein or a Dapper Don Tourbillon, but he would have far transcended the sphere of such men and he would have felt for them the uneasy scorn that he felt for St. Germain and Cagliostro. For Casanova was only half of the underworld — he lived half in darkness, half in light. But the sound and superior part of him was always insecure because it was based on knavery: hence his succession of misadventures and the final unsatisfactoriness of his life. Casanova was an uncomfortable man — he could never make his life come right. And it makes us uncomfortable to read about him.

There is a sound kind of coarseness, which is not incompatible with the finest work or the most scrupulously ordered life: the coarseness of animality or of the hand-to-hand struggle with existence, which may nourish such work and such a life. And there is a bad kind of coarseness which spoils everything, even where a man is equipped with genuinely superior gifts. The coarseness of Casanova was the bad kind. He came out of the Venetian actors' world, and was never sure whether his mother, a shoemaker's daughter, had had him by a down-at-heels nobleman who had gone on the stage and married her or by the manager of the theater where she acted. From some heritage of moral squalor Casanova could never emerge, and he was ravaged by it all his life more vitally than by any of the diseases that were his mere superficial exasperations.

But the superior qualities of such a man have continually to keep themselves sharp against the dangers that always confront him, the dangers that he can never get away from because they are part of himself. The drama of Casanova's career creates a tension which is both exciting and trying because his highly developed intelligence, his genius as an actor on the stage of life, are always poised on the brink of a pit where taste, morals, the social order, the order of the world of the intellect, may all be lost in the slime. Yet even when he has slipped to the bottom, he keeps his faculties clear; and so he commands our respect.

We have had an immense amount of controversy as to whether Casanova told the truth in connection with this or that incident, and a good many inaccuracies have been proved on him. But whether he falsified the facts unconsciously or deliberately makes very little difference. In his own way Casanova was truthful; it may even be said that one of his most admirable traits — not as a man but as a writer — was precisely a fidelity to truth. He may have in-

vented some of the adventures in the *Memoirs*, but his
story follows reality for all that. Someone has said that if
the *Memoirs* is a novel, Casanova is the greatest novelist
who ever lived. Though he was personally extremely vain,
he certainly spares himself as little as any autobiographer
on record. It is not true, as the popular legend seems to
have it, that he represents himself as triumphing easily
over innumerable complacent women. On the contrary,
he will sometimes devote the better part of a volume to a
detailed description of some siege in which he ignomini-
ously failed. The ultimate aim of Casanova is not so much
to glorify himself as to tell us an astonishing story that
illustrates how people behave, the way in which life works
out.

When other writers borrow from Casanova, they are
likely to sentimentalize or romanticize him where Casanova's great virtue is his mercilessness with romantic and
sentimental conventions. I remember an attempt at a
popular play based on the Henriette episode. Henriette
in the *Memoirs* is a young French girl who has run away
from home in men's clothes and whom the youthful Casanova meets in his travels. She is the first French girl he
has known, the first *jeune fille spirituelle*; and his love
affair with her has a freshness and seriousness, almost a
kind of ecstasy, that none has ever had for him before
and that none is ever to have again. He happens to have
money at the time and is able to buy her a whole ward-
robe of pretty clothes. They go to Parma together, and
there they live in style. Casanova gets a box at the opera;
they take the air in the public gardens with the royalties —
till she is recognized by one of the courtiers and is compelled to go back to her family. Casanova's account of
this episode is one of the most attractive love affairs in
literature. When he and Henriette have finally had to
part, at Geneva, he finds that she has written with her
diamond on the window of their room at the inn: 'You

will forget Henriette, too.' Now the contemporary play I
speak of exploited this charming story and then followed
it with a conventional sequel made up out of the whole
cloth, in which Casanova many years later was made to
come back to the inn to find Henriette grown old and with
a son who turns out to be his.

But what happens in the *Memoirs* is quite different.
Casanova does come back to the inn, middle-aged, down
on his luck and with a depressing venereal disease. He *has*
forgotten about staying there with Henriette, and he does
not even recognize their room till he notices the writing
on the window: 'Remembering in a flash the moment
when Henriette had written those words thirteen years
before, I felt the hair stand up on my head. . . . Overcome, I dropped into a chair. . . . Comparing the self I
was now with the self I had been then, I had to recognize
that I was less worthy to possess her. I still knew how to
love, but I realized I had no longer the delicacy that I had
had in those earlier days, nor the feelings which really
justify the transports of the senses, nor the same tender
ways, nor finally a certain probity which extends itself
even to one's weaknesses; but what frightened me was to
have to acknowledge that I no longer possessed the same
vigor.'

Years afterwards, while he is traveling in Provence, his
coach breaks down in the middle of the night and some
people who live near the road take him in. The mistress
of the house hides her face in the hood she has worn out-
of-doors — then as soon as they have got into the house,
she announces that she has sprained her ankle and is
obliged to take to her bed, so that Casanova is only permitted to wait upon her in her room and talk to her
through the bed-curtains. He does not find out till after
he has left that the countess is Henriette, who has by this
time grown so fat that she cannot bear to have him see
her. But he has been traveling with a tough little Venetian

girl of bisexual capabilities, and the countess carries on a flirtation with her and finally makes her sleep with her. This is all life has left of their romance.

The real theme of Casanova is the many things a life may hold — the many rôles a man may play and the changes brought by time. I have never read a book — either autobiography or fiction — which seems to give you a life so completely. I know of no book which shows so strikingly the rhythmic recurrences which character produces in personal destiny. Casanova's adventures are always different but always the same thing. He arrives in some new place, he puts himself over, he achieves brilliant social successes or performs dashing deeds, his best qualities and gifts have full scope, then he overplays his hand or misses his step or something discreditable is discovered about him, and he has to make his getaway. There was something about him, one supposes, that in the long run made people find him intolerable. And his love affairs have their pattern, too: when the responsibilities involved in them become onerous, he marries the ladies off if he can; if not, he gently lets the affair lapse.

The first part of the story is funny and gay — it has a Venetian carnival liveliness; the last part, although it is told with the eighteenth-century rapidity and dryness, is almost unbearably sad. It is probable that Casanova was never able to bring himself to finish it. The manuscript as we have it does not cover the whole of the period indicated by Casanova in his title: it stops just as he is returning to Venice, but gets him no farther than Trieste. He had been banished by the Inquisition and was allowed to return to his native city only at the price of acting as a spy for them. It was the most humiliating episode in his life; and he has remarked by the way several times that he is not sure he will have the courage to go through with his original project of writing his life up to the year 1797. He may also have been guilty of a Freudian oversight in

dropping out two chapters near the end. They were missing in the Brockhaus manuscript, but were found later
by Arthur Symons at Dux; and they turn out to contain
the dismal climax of Casanova's adventure with two girls
upon whom he had been trying to work by an old and
well-tried technique of his. He had discovered that you
could go a long way with girls if you took them to masquerades in pairs; but on this occasion the girls did not
fall, and Casanova before the evening was over got merci-
lessly razzed by the masqueraders.

Yet in his final asylum at Dux, where his patron left
him alone for long periods and where he was constantly
bedeviled by the servants, where he sometimes contemplated suicide, he did get down most of the story; and it
is one of the most remarkable presentations in literature
of a man's individual life as it seems to him in the living.
All the appetites are there — fine dinners, attractive
women, amusements; and the exhilaration of travel, of
fighting for one's personal pride, of the winning of wealth
and consideration, of winning one's personal liberty.
There is in Casanova's account of his escape from the
Leads prison in Venice, whether he fabricated the story
or not, something more than a mere tale of adventure: he
has made of it a thrilling expression of the hatred of the
human spirit for jails, of the will to be free that breaks
away in contempt of the remonstrances of reason (in the
person of the appalled old count who refuses to join the
others and keeps telling them why they cannot succeed).

There is even the appetite of the intellect. the great
raconteur loved the conversation of men like d'Alembert
and Voltaire; and the master gambler was an amateur
mathematician. And when one can have no more brilliant
dinners and make love to no more women, when one has
no longer appreciative companions to listen to one's stories
and can no longer travel and try one's luck — one can at
least summon one's intellectual resources, work at prob-

lems, write one's memoirs; one can still test one's nerve and strength by setting down an account of life as one has found it, with all its anticlimax and scandal, one's own impossible character and all. The writing of the *Memoirs* represented a real victory of the mind and the spirit. Scoundrels like Casanova do not usually put themselves on record, and when they do they are usually at pains to profess the morality of respectable people. There is a certain amount of this, as we shall see in a moment, in Casanova's autobiography, too; but when all Casanova's obeisances to the established authorities have been made, life itself in his story turns out to be an outlaw like him. He confesses in his preface that he considers it a creditable deed to fleece a fool; and in reading him, we get to a point where we ourselves almost feel impatience when Casanova's prospective victims fail to succumb to his confidence games. He said that he feared the *Memoirs* were *'par trop cynique'* ever to be published. And he was apparently partly right: the original manuscript still lies locked up in Brockhaus's vaults in Leipzig, and no one knows what the editors may have omitted.

The *Memoirs*, then, required the courage of an individual point of view — and they required a capacity for feeling. Has any novelist or poet ever rendered better than Casanova the passing glory of the personal life? — the gaiety, the spontaneity, the generosity of youth: the ups and downs of middle age when our character begins to get us and we are forced to come to terms with it; the dreadful blanks of later years, when what is gone is gone. All that a life of this kind can contain Casanova put into his story. And how much of the world! — the eighteenth century as you get it in no other book; society from top to bottom; Europe from England to Russia; a more brilliant variety of characters than you can find in any eighteenth-century novel.

But the interests of such a man are limited. Casanova knew better than anyone how the world and how one's personal vicissitudes went. But he had very little imagination for the larger life of society. He saw the corruption of the old régime in France and commented on it after the Revolution, but he had never been among those who wanted to see the old régime go. On the contrary — like a Rothstein — he was content with the world as he found it. Though the Inquisition had nearly done for him, he never ceased to treat it with respect and was willing in his last bad days to turn informer and report to these censors — though rather inefficiently, it appears — on naked models in the Venetian art-schools and indecent and ungodly books in the libraries. Though he had at other times called himself a 'philosopher' and in his speculative writings had vaguely foreshadowed Darwinism, he had never criticized Church or State. He accepted all the current worldly values — the hierarchies, institutions, dominations. He never questioned, never protested, defended his honor according to the code, but never brought up in connection with anything the principle of a larger issue. Casanova's originality was largely confined to a sort of personal effrontery which, having persisted all through his life in spite of his repeated attempts to reform it, had ended by acquiring in his *Memoirs* a certain intellectual dignity when he had found finally that all his struggles to make himself a place in society were vain and that this was the only companion that was left him in his solitude at Dux.

A man of superior intelligence as he knew himself to be, he had always aimed at the good things of the world as the rich and powerful judged good things. What he really wanted, to be sure, was something different from what they wanted. He does not seem to have cared about social position or financial security for their own sakes: what he enjoyed was the adventure of playing a rôle, creating a situation; whereas the powerful and the rich only wanted

to follow their routine. But his drama was usually conceived in terms of their values. It was the cheap side of
him, the lackey in him, which did not look beyond the
habits of his masters.

And this is a part of the explanation of the fact that
Casanova has attracted comparatively so little serious attention. In English of course it is his scandalous reputation which has made him practically taboo — so that he
has remained largely unknown to the English-reading
public save for volumes of erotic excerpts in libraries of
classic pornography. But in general it may be said that
what is good in Casanova makes serious readers too uneasy and what is inferior disgusts them too much for him
to become an accepted classic. There are a whole host of
people on the Continent studying Casanova; but Casano-
vists seem almost in the category of stamp and coin collectors and people who devote their lives to looking for
buried Spanish treasure. They are mostly preoccupied
with verifying dates and tracking down identities. Casanova, fascinating though he is, does not lead to anything
bigger than himself.

Compare him with Rousseau, for example. Rousseau
was a much less attractive man, and his *Confessions* are
infinitely less readable than Casanova's *Memoirs*. At his
best, to my taste at any rate, he is still pretty flavorless and
Swiss. Yet the Geneva clockmaker's son in a situation not
unlike Casanova's — he, too, had been a vagabond, a thief,
a hanger-on of the great, had suffered as a battered-about
apprentice and a servant in rich men's houses — made an
issue of his maladjustment. Casanova could show considerable strength of character in compelling the great to
treat him as an equal — as when he forced Count Branicki
to fight a duel and afterwards became his friend; but it
never seems to have occurred to the actor's son to say,
after he had come one of his croppers masquerading as a

man of quality: 'I am better at being a great lord than you people are yourselves — for I have the personality and the imagination and the brains to create such a gorgeous great lord as your silly conventional society never dreamed of — hence I am superior to you and hence do not need to compete with you!' Whereas Rousseau finally came to the conclusion that the times must be out of joint when Rousseau found himself out of place. From the moment of his sudden revelation, on the way to see Diderot at Vincennes, that man was by nature good and that it was institutions alone which had corrupted him, that all his own miseries had been due, not to his aberrations and shortcomings, but to the sins of the society that had bred him — from this moment he stuck to his point at the price of resigning from society, of exiling himself even from those circles in which the other eighteenth-century philosophers had found so agreeable a welcome and so sympathetic a hearing.

You may say that it was Rousseau's neurotic character which prevented him from getting on with people and that he took it out in scolding society; and you may say that Casanova was at least as near to an accurate account of the situation when he attributed his own misfortunes to his faults. But the fact was that Rousseau had been led to a general truth by his individual case and, in spite of his ignominious adventures, had the courage and dignity of one who knew it. He belonged to the class of thinkers who, in opposing the prevalent philosophy of their time, find that they have behind them a great pressure of unformulated general feeling and who themselves prevail as the spokesmen of the age that follows theirs.

Casanova once came with a lady of quality to pay a visit to Rousseau in his retirement. The callers found him lacking in affability and failed to get very much out of him though Casanova admitted that Rousseau had talked intelligently. Madame d'Urfé thought him boorish, and they laughed about him after they had left.

Casanova, ignoring his many humiliations, was still trying to crash the gate at a time when Rousseau, for all his clumsiness, had got hold of the lever of the Revolution.

JUSTICE TO EDITH WHARTON

Before Edith Wharton died, the more commonplace work of her later years had had the effect of dulling the reputation of her earlier and more serious work. It seemed to me that the notices elicited by her death did her, in general, something less than justice; and I want to try to throw into relief the achievements which did make her important during a period — say, 1905-1917 — when there were few American writers worth reading. This essay is therefore no very complete study, but rather in the nature of an impression by a reader who was growing up at that time.

Mrs. Wharton's earliest fiction I never found particularly attractive. The influences of Paul Bourget and Henry James seem to have presided at the birth of her talent; and I remember these books as dealing with the artificial moral problems of Bourget and developing them with the tenuity of analysis which is what is least satisfactory in James. The stories tended to take place either in a social void or against a background of Italy or France which had somewhat the character of expensive upholstery. It was only with *The House of Mirth*, published in 1905, that Edith Wharton emerged as an historian of the American society of her time. For a period of fifteen years or more, she produced works of considerable interest both for its realism and its intensity.

One has heard various accounts of her literary beginnings. She tells us in her autobiography that a novel which she had composed at eleven and which began, 'Oh, how do you do, Mrs. Brown? . . . If only I had known you were going to call, I should have tidied up the drawing room' — had been returned by her mother with the chilling comment, 'Drawing-rooms are always tidy.' And it is said that a book of verse which she had written and had had secretly printed was discovered and destroyed by her parents, well-to-do New Yorkers of merchant stock, who thought it unladylike for a young woman to write. It seems to be an authentic fact, though Mrs. Wharton does not mention it in her memoirs, that she first seriously began to write fiction after her marriage during the period of a nervous breakdown, at the suggestion of Dr. S. Weir Mitchell, who himself combined the practice of literature with his pioneer work in the field of female neuroses. Thereafter she seems to have depended on her writing to get her through some difficult years, a situation that became more and more painful. Her husband, as she tells us, had some mental disease which was steadily growing worse from the very first years of their marriage, and he inhabited a social world of the rich which was sealed tight to intellectual interests. Through her writing, she came gradually into relation with the international literary world and made herself a partially independent career.

Her work was, then, the desperate product of a pressure of maladjustments; and it very soon took a direction totally different from that of Henry James, as a lesser disciple of whom she is sometimes pointlessly listed. James's interests were predominantly esthetic: he is never a passionate social prophet; and only rarely — as in *The Ivory Tower,* which seems in turn to have derived from Mrs. Wharton — does he satirize plutocratic America. But a passionate social prophet is precisely what Edith Wharton became. At her strongest and most characteristic, she is a brilliant example of the writer who relieves an emotional strain by denouncing his generation.

It is true that she combines with indignation against a

specific phase of American society a general sense of inexorable doom for human beings. She was much haunted
by the myth of the Eumenides; and she had developed
her own deadly version of the working of the Aeschylean
necessity — a version as automatic and rapid, as decisive
and as undimmed by sentiment, as the mechanical and
financial processes which during her lifetime were transforming New York. In these books, she was as pessimistic
as Hardy or Maupassant. You find the pure expression of
her hopelessness in her volume of poems, *Artemis to
Actaeon*, published in 1909, which, for all its hard accent
and its ponderous tone, its 'impenetrables' and 'incom-
municables' and 'incommensurables,' its 'immemorial al-
titudes august,' was not entirely without interest or merit.
'Death, can it be the years shall naught avail?' she asks in
one of the sonnets called *Experience*: ' "Not so," Death
answered. "They shall purchase sleep." ' But in the poem
called *Moonrise over Tyringham*, she seems to be emerging from a period of strain into a relatively tranquil stoicism. She is apostrophizing the first hour of night:

> Be thou the image of a thought that fares
> Forth from itself, and flings its ray ahead,
> Leaping the barriers of ephemeral cares,
> To where our lives are but the ages' tread,
>
> And let this year be, not the last of youth,
> But first — like thee! — of some new train of hours,
> If more remote from hope, yet nearer truth,
> And kin to the unpetitionable powers.

But the catastrophe in Edith Wharton's novels is almost
invariably the upshot of a conflict between the individual
and the social group. Her tragic heroines and heroes are
the victims of the group pressure of convention; they are
passionate or imaginative spirits, hungry for emotional and
intellectual experience, who find themselves locked into

a small closed system, and either destroy themselves by
beating their heads against their prison or suffer a living
death in resigning themselves to it. Out of these themes
she got a sharp pathos all her own. The language and
some of the machinery of *The House of Mirth* seem old-
fashioned and rather melodramatic today; but the book
had some originality and power, with its chronicle of a
social parasite on the fringes of the very rich, dragging out
a stupefying routine of week-ends, yachting trips and dinners, and finding a window open only twice, at the beginning and at the end of the book, on a world where all
the values are not money values.

The Fruit of the Tree, which followed it in 1907, although its characters are concerned with larger issues, is
less successful than *The House of Mirth,* because it is
confused between two different kinds of themes. There
is a more or less trumped-up moral problem *à la* Bourget
about a 'mercy killing' by a high-minded trained nurse,
who happened to have an 'affinity,' as they used to say at
that period, with the husband of the patient. But there is
also the story of an industrial reformer, which is on the
whole quite ably handled — especially in the opening
scenes, in which the hero, assistant manager of a textile
mill, is aroused by an industrial accident to try to remove
the conditions which have caused it and finds himself up
against one of those tight family groups that often dominate American factory towns, sitting ensconced in their
red-satin drawing-rooms on massively upholstered sofas,
amid heavy bronze chandeliers and mantels surrounded
by obelisk clocks; and in its picture of his marriage with
the mill-owning widow and the gradual drugging of his
purpose under the influence of a house on Long Island
of a quality more gracious and engaging but on an equally
overpowering scale.

Edith Wharton had come to have a great hand with all
kinds of American furnishings and with their concomitant

landscape-gardening. Her first book had been a work on interior decorating; and now in her novels she adopts the practice of inventorying the contents of her characters' homes. Only Clyde Fitch, I think, in those early nineteen-hundreds made play to the same degree with the miscellaneous material objects with which Americans were surrounding themselves, articles which had just been manufactured and which people were being induced to buy. I suppose that no other writer of comedies of any other place or time has depended so much on stage sets and, especially, on stage properties: the radiators that bang in *Girls*, the artificial orange in *The Truth*, the things that are dropped under the table by the ladies in the second act of *The Climbers*. But in the case of Edith Wharton, the *décors* become the agents of tragedy. The characters of Clyde Fitch are embarrassed or tripped up by these articles; but the people of Edith Wharton are pursued by them as by spirits of doom and ultimately crushed by their accumulation. These pieces have not been always made newly: sometimes they are *objets d'art*, which have been expensively imported from Europe. But the effect is very much the same: they are something extraneous to the people and, no matter how old they may be, they seem to glitter and clank with the coin that has gone to buy them. A great many of Mrs. Wharton's descriptions are, of course, satiric or caustic; but when she wants to produce an impression of real magnificence, and even when she is writing about Europe, the thing still seems rather inorganic. She was not only one of the great pioneers, but also the poet, of interior decoration.

In *The Custom of the Country* (1913), Mrs. Wharton's next novel about the rich — *The Reef* is a relapse into 'psychological problems' — she piles up the new luxury of the era to an altitude of ironic grandeur, like the glass mountain in the *Arabian Nights*, which the current of her imagination manages to make incandescent. The first scene sets the key for the whole book: 'Mrs. Spragg and her visitor were enthroned in two heavy gilt armchairs in one of the private drawing-rooms of the Hotel Stentorian. The Spragg rooms were known as one of the Looey suites, and the drawing-room walls, above their wainscoting of highly varnished mahogany, were hung with salmon-pink damask and adorned with oval portraits of Marie Antoinette and the Princess de Lamballe. In the center of the florid carpet a gilt table with a top of Mexican onyx sustained a palm in a gilt basket tied with a pink bow. But for this ornament, and a copy of *The Hound of the Baskervilles* which lay beside it, the room showed no traces of human use, and Mrs. Spragg herself wore as complete an air of detachment as if she had been a wax figure in a show-window.' In the last pages — it is an admirable passage — Undine Spragg's little boy is seen wandering alone amid the splendors of the Paris *hôtel* which has crowned his mother's progress from the Stentorian: 'the white fur rugs and brocade chairs' which 'seemed maliciously on the watch for smears and ink-spots,' 'his mother's wonderful lacy bedroom, all pale silks and velvets, artful mirrors and veiled lamps, and the boudoir as big as a drawing-room, with pictures he would have liked to know about, and tables and cabinets holding things he was afraid to touch,' the library, with its 'rows and rows of books, bound in dim browns and golds, and old faded reds as rich as velvet: they all looked as if they might have had stories in them as splendid as their bindings. But the bookcases were closed with gilt trellising, and when Paul reached up to open one, a servant told him that Mr. Moffatt's secretary kept them locked because the books were too valuable to be taken down.'

It is a vein which Sinclair Lewis has worked since — as in the opening pages of *Babbitt*, where Babbitt is shown entangled with his gadgets; and in other respects *The Custom of the Country* opens up the way for Lewis, who dedicated *Main Street* to Edith Wharton. Mrs. Wharton has already arrived at a method of doing crude and harsh people with a draftsmanship crude and harsh. Undine Spragg, the social-climbing divorcée, though a good deal less humanly credible than Lily Bart of *The House of Mirth,* is quite a successful caricature of a type who was to go even farther. She is the prototype in fiction of the 'gold-digger,' of the international cocktail bitch. Here the pathos has been largely subordinated to an implacable animosity toward the heroine; but there is one episode both bitter and poignant, in which a discarded husband of Undine's, who has been driven by her demands to work in Wall Street and left by her up to his neck in debt, goes home to Washington Square through 'the heat, the noise, the smells of disheveled midsummer' New York, climbs to the room at the top of the house where he has kept his books and other things from college, and shoots himself there.

The other side of this world of wealth, which annihilates every impulse toward excellence, is a poverty which also annihilates. The writer of one of the notices on Mrs. Wharton's death was mistaken in assuming that *Ethan Frome* was a single uncharacteristic excursion outside the top social strata. It is true that she knew the top strata better than she knew anything else; but both in *The House of Mirth* and *The Fruit of the Tree,* she is always aware of the pit of misery which is implied by the wastefulness of the plutocracy, and the horror or the fear of this pit is one of the forces that determine the action. There is a Puritan in Edith Wharton, and this Puritan is always insisting that we must face the unpleasant and the ugly. Not to do so is one of the worst sins in her morality; sybarites like Mr. Langhope in *The Fruit of the Tree,* amusing himself with a dilettante archaeology on his income from a badly-managed factory, like the fatuous

mother of *Twilight Sleep,* who feels so safe with her fa-
cial massage and her Yogi, while her family goes to pieces
under her nose, are among the characters whom she treats
with most scorn. And the three novels I have touched on
above were paralleled by another series — *Ethan Frome,
Bunner Sisters* and *Summer* — which dealt with *milieux*
of a different kind.

Ethan Frome is still much read and well-known; but
Bunner Sisters has been undeservedly neglected. It is the
last piece in the volume called *Xingu* (1916), a short
novel about the length of *Ethan Frome.* This story of two
small shopkeepers on Stuyvesant Square and a drug-addict
clockmaker from Hoboken, involved in a relationship like
a triple noose which will gradually choke them all, is one
of the most terrible things that Edith Wharton ever wrote;
and the last page, in which the surviving sister, her lifelong companion gone and her poor little business lost, sets
out to look for a job, seems to mark the grimmest moment
of Edith Wharton's darkest years. Here is not even the
grandeur of the heroic New England hills: ' "Ain't you
going to leave the *ad*-dress?" the young woman called out
after her. Ann Eliza went out into the thronged street.
The great city, under the fair spring sky, seemed to throb
with the air of innumerable beginnings. She walked on,
looking for another shop window with a sign in it.'

Summer (1917), however, returns to the Massachusetts
of *Ethan Frome,* and, though neither so harrowing nor so
vivid, is by no means an inferior work. Making hats in a
millinery shop was the abyss from which Lily Bart re-
coiled; the heroine of *Summer* recoils from the nethermost
American social stratum, the degenerate 'mountain people. Let down by the refined young man who works in the
public library and wants to become an architect, in a way
that anticipates the situation in Dreiser's *American Tragedy,* she finds that she cannot go back to her own people
and allows herself to be made an honest woman by the

rather admirable old failure of a lawyer who had brought her down from the mountain in her childhood. It is the first sign on Mrs. Wharton's part of a relenting in the cruelty of her endings. 'Come to my age,' says Charity Royall's protector, 'a man knows the things that matter and the things that don't; that's about the only good turn life does us.' Her blinding bitterness is already subsiding.

But in the meantime, before *Summer* was written, she had escaped from the hopeless situation created by her husband's insanity. The doctors had told her he was hopeless; but she had had difficulty in inducing his family to allow her to leave him with an attendant. The tragedy of *Bunner Sisters* is probably a transposition of this; and the relief of the tension in *Summer* is evidently the result of her new freedom. She was at last finally detached from her marriage; and she took up her permanent resident in France. The war came, and she threw herself into its activities.

And now the intensity dies from her work as the American background fades. One can see this already in *Summer*, and *The Age of Innocence* (1930) is really Edith Wharton's valedictory. The theme is closely related to those of *The House of Mirth* and *Ethan Frome*: the frustration of a potential pair of lovers by social or domestic obstructions. But setting it back in the generation of her parents, she is able to contemplate it now without quite the same rancor, to soften it with a poetic mist of distance. And yet even here the old impulse of protest still makes itself felt as the main motive. If we compare *The Age of Innocence* with Henry James's *Europeans,* whose central situation it reproduces, the pupil's divergence from the master is seen in the most striking way. In both cases, a Europeanized American woman — Baroness Münster, Countess Olenska — returns to the United States to intrude upon and disturb the existence of a conservative provincial society; in both cases, she attracts and almost captivates an intelligent man of the community who turns out, in the long run, to be unable to muster the courage to take her, and who allows her to go back to Europe. Henry James makes of this a balanced comedy of the conflict between the Bostonian and the cosmopolitan points of view (so he reproached her with not having developed the theme of Undine Spragg's marriage with a French nobleman in terms of French and American manners, as he had done with a similar one in *The Reverberator*); but in Edith Wharton's version one still feels an active resentment against the pusillanimity of the provincial group and also, as in other of her books, a special complaint against the timid American male who has let the lady down.

Up through *The Age of Innocence,* and recurring at all points of her range from *The House of Mirth* to *Ethan Frome,* the typical masculine figure in Edith Wharton's fiction is a man set apart from his neighbors by education, intellect and feeling, but lacking the force or the courage either to impose himself or to get away. She generalizes about this type in the form in which she knew it best in her autobiographical volume: 'They combined a cultivated taste with marked social gifts,' she says; but 'their weakness was that, save in a few cases, they made so little use of their ability': they were content to 'live in dilettanish leisure,' rendering none of 'the public services that a more enlightened social system would have exacted of them.' But she had described a very common phenomenon of the America of after the Civil War. Lawrence Selden, the city lawyer, who sits comfortably in his bachelor apartment with his flowerbox of mignonette and his first edition of La Bruyere and allows Lily Bart to drown, is the same person as Lawyer Royall of *Summer,* with his lofty orations and his drunken lapses. One could have found him during the big-business era in almost any American city or town: the man of superior abilities who had the impulse toward self-improvement and independence, but who had been more or less rendered helpless by the surf of headlong money-making and spending which carried him along with its breakers or left him stranded on the New England hills — in either case thwarted and stunted by the mediocre level of the community. In Edith Wharton's novels these men are usually captured and dominated by women of conventional morals and middle-class ideals; when an exceptional woman comes along who is thirsting for something different and better, the man is unable to give it to her. This special situation Mrs. Wharton, with some conscious historical criticism but chiefly impelled by a feminine animus, has dramatized with much vividness and intelligence. There are no first-rate men in these novels.

The Age of Innocence is already rather faded. But now a surprising lapse occurs. (It is true that she is nearly sixty.)

When we look back on Mrs. Wharton's career, it seems that everything that is valuable in her work lies within a quite sharply delimited area — between *The House of Mirth* and *The Age of Innocence*. It is sometimes true of women writers — less often, I believe, of men — that a manifestation of something like genius may be stimulated by some exceptional emotional strain, but will disappear when the stimulus has passed. With a man, his professional, his artisan's life is likely to persist and evolve as a partially independent organism through the vicissitudes of his emotional experience. Henry James in a virtual vacuum continued to possess and develop his *métier* up to his very last years. But Mrs. Wharton had no *métier* in this sense. With her emergence from her life in the United States, her settling down in the congenial society of Paris, she seems at last to become comfortably adjusted; and with her adjustment, the real intellectual force which she has exerted through a decade and a half evaporates almost completely. She no longer maims or massacres her characters. Her grimness melts rapidly into benignity. She takes an interest in young people's problems, in the solicitude of parents for children; she smooths over the misunderstandings of lovers; she sees how things may work out very well. She even loses the style she has mastered. Beginning with a language rather ponderous and stiff, the worst features of the style of Henry James and a stream of clichés from old novels and plays, she finally — about the time of *Ethan Frome* — worked out a prose of flexible steel, bright as electric light and striking out sparks of wit and color, which has the quality and pace of New York and is one of its distinctive artistic products. But now not merely does she cease to be brilliant, she becomes almost commonplace.

The Glimpses of the Moon, which followed *The Age of Innocence,* is, as someone has said, scarcely distinguishable from the ordinary serial in a women's magazine; and indeed it is in the women's magazines that Mrs. Wharton's novels now begin first to appear. *A Son at the Front* is a little better, because it had been begun in 1918 and had her war experience in it, with some of her characteristic cutting satire at the expense of the belligerents behind the lines. It is not bad as a picture of the emotions of a middle-aged civilian during the war — though not so good as Arnold Bennett's *The Pretty Lady*.

Old New York was a much feebler second boiling from the tea-leaves of *The Age of Innocence.* I have read only one of Mrs. Wharton's novels written since *Old New York: Twilight Sleep* is not so bad as her worst, but suffers seriously as a picture of New York during the middle nineteen-twenties from the author's long absence abroad. Mrs. Wharton is no longer up on her American interior-decorating — though there are some characteristic passages of landscape-gardening: '"Seventy-five thousand bulbs this year!" she thought as the motor swept by the sculptured gateway, just giving and withdrawing a flash of turf sheeted with amber and lilac, in a setting of twisted and scalloped evergreens.'

The two other books that I have read since then — *The Writing of Fiction* (which does, however, contain an excellent essay on Proust) and the volume of memoirs called *A Backward Glance* — I found rather disappointing. The backward glance is an exceedingly fleeting one which dwells very little on anything except the figure of Henry James, of whom Mrs. Wharton has left a portrait entertaining but slightly catty and curiously superficial. About herself she tells us nothing much of interest; and she makes amends to her New York antecedents for her satire of *The Age of Innocence* by presenting them in tinted miniatures, prettily remote and unreal. It is the last irony of *The Age of Innocence* that Newland Archer should become reconciled to 'old New York.' 'After all,' he eventually came to tell himself, 'there was good in the old ways.' Something like this seems to have happened to Edith Wharton. Even in *A Backward Glance,* she confesses that 'the weakness of the social structure' of her parents' generation had been 'a blind dread of innovation'; but her later works show a dismay and a shrinking before what seemed to her the social and moral chaos of an age which was battering down the old edifice that she herself had once depicted as a prison. Perhaps, after all, the old mismated couples who had stayed married in deference to the decencies were better than the new divorced who were not aware of any duties at all.

The only thing that does survive in *A Backward Glance* is some trace of the tremendous blue-stocking that Mrs. Wharton was in her prime. The deep reverence for the heroes of art and thought — though she always believed that Paul Bourget was one of them — of the woman who in earlier days had written a long blank-verse poem about

Vesalius, still makes itself felt in these memoirs. Her culture was rather heavy and grand — a preponderance of Goethe and Schiller, Racine and La Bruyère — but it was remarkably solid for an American woman and intimately related to her life. And she was one of the few Americans of her day who cared enough about serious literature to take the risks of trying to make some contribution to it. Professor Charles Eliot Norton — who had, as she dryly remarks, so admirably translated Dante — once warned her that 'no great work of the imagination' had 'ever been based on illicit passion.' Though she herself in her later years was reduced to contemptuous complaints that the writers of the new generations had 'abandoned creative art for pathology,' she did have the right to insist that she had 'fought hard' in her earlier days 'to turn the wooden dolls' of conventional fiction 'into struggling, suffering human beings.' She had been one of the few such human beings in the America of the early nineteen hundreds who found an articulate voice and set down a durable record.

The above was written in 1937. An unfinished novel by Edith Wharton was published in 1938. This story, *The Buccaneers,* deserves a word of postscript. The latter part of it, even allowing for the fact that it was never carried beyond a first draft, seems banal and a little trashy. Here as elsewhere the mellowness of Mrs. Wharton's last years has dulled the sharp outlines of her fiction: there are passages in *The Buccaneers* which read like an old-fashioned story for girls. But the first section has a certain brilliance. The figures of the children of the *nouveaux riches* at Saratoga during the seventies, when the post-Civil-War fortunes were rolling up, come back rather diminished in memory but in lively and charming colors, like the slides of those old magic lanterns that are mentioned as one of their forms of entertainment. And we learn from Mrs. Wharton's scenario for the unfinished part of the tale that it was to have had rather an interesting development. She has here more or less reversed the values of the embittered *Custom of the Country:* instead of playing off the culture and tradition of Europe against the vulgar Americans who are insensible to them, she dramatizes the climbing young ladies as an air-clearing and revivifying force. In the last pages she lived to write she made it plain that the hard-boiled commercial elements on the rise in both civilizations were to come to understand one another perfectly. But there is also an Anglo-Italian woman, the child of Italian revolutionaries and a cousin of Dante Gabriel Rossetti, who has been reduced to working as a governess and who has helped to engineer the success of the American girls in London. The best of these girls has been married to a dreary English duke, who represents everything least human in the English aristocratic system. Laura Testvalley was to forfeit her own hopes of capturing an amateur esthete of the older generation of the nobility in order to allow the young American to elope with an enterprising young Englishman; and thus to have let herself in for the fate of spending the rest of her days in the poverty and dulness of her home, where the old revolution had died. As the light of Edith Wharton's art grows dim and at last goes out, she leaves us, to linger on our retina, the large dark eyes of the clever spinster, the serious and attentive governess, who trades in worldly values but manages to rebuff these values; who, in following a destiny of solitude and discipline, contends for the rights of the heart; and who, child of a political movement played out, yet passes on something of its impetus to the emergence of the society of the future.

HEMINGWAY: GAUGE OF MORALE

ERNEST HEMINGWAY's *In Our Time* was an odd and original book. It had the appearance of a miscellany of stories and fragments; but actually the parts hung together and produced a definite effect. There were two distinct series of pieces which alternated with one another: one a set of brief and brutal sketches of police shootings, bullfight crises, hangings of criminals, and incidents of the war; and the other a set of short stories dealing in its principal sequence with the growing-up of an American boy against a landscape of idyllic Michigan, but interspersed also with glimpses of American soldiers returning home. It seems to have been Hemingway's intention — *'In Our Time'* — that the war should set the key for the whole. The cold-bloodedness of the battles and executions strikes a discord with the sensitiveness and candor of the boy at home in the States; and presently the boy turns up in Europe in one of the intermediate vignettes as a soldier in the Italian army, hit in the spine by machine-gun fire and trying to talk to a dying Italian: *'Senta,* Rinaldi. *Senta,'* he says, 'you and me, we've made a separate peace.'

But there is a more fundamental relationship between the pieces of the two series. The shooting of Nick in the war does not really connect two different worlds: has he not found in the butchery abroad the same world that he knew back in Michigan? Was not life in the Michigan woods equally destructive and cruel? He had gone once with his father, the doctor, when he had performed a

Caesarean operation on an Indian squaw with a jackknife and no anaesthetic and had sewed her up with fishing leaders, while the Indian hadn't been able to bear it and had cut his throat in his bunk. Another time, when the doctor had saved the life of a squaw, her Indian had picked a quarrel with him rather than pay him in work. And Nick himself had sent his girl about her business when he had found out how terrible her mother was. Even fishing in Big Two-Hearted River — away and free in the woods — he had been conscious in a curious way of the cruelty inflicted on the fish, even of the silent agonies endured by the live bait, the grasshoppers kicking on the hook.

Not that life isn't enjoyable. Talking and drinking with one's friends is great fun; fishing in Big Two-Hearted River is a tranquil exhilaration. But the brutality of life is always there, and it is somehow bound up with the enjoyment. Bullfights are especially enjoyable. It is even exhilarating to build a simply priceless barricade and pot the enemy as they are trying to get over it. The condition of life is pain; and the joys of the most innocent surface are somehow tied to its stifled pangs.

The resolution of this dissonance in art made the beauty of Hemingway's stories. He had in the process tuned a marvelous prose. Out of the colloquial American speech, with its simple declarative sentences and its strings of Nordic monosyllables, he got effects of the utmost subtlety. F. M. Ford has found the perfect simile for the impression produced by this writing: 'Hemingway's words strike you, each one, as if they were pebbles fetched fresh from a brook. They live and shine, each in its place. So one of his pages has the effect of a brook-bottom into which you look down through the flowing water. The words form a tesellation, each in order beside the other.'

Looking back, we can see how this style was already being refined and developed at a time — fifty years before

—when it was regarded in most literary quarters as hopelessly non-literary and vulgar. Had there not been the
nineteenth chapter of *Huckleberry Finn?* — 'Two or three
nights went by; I reckon I might say they swum by; they
slid along so quick and smooth and lovely. Here is the way
we put in the time. It was a monstrous big river down
there — sometimes a mile and a half wide,' and so forth.
These pages, when we happen to meet them in Carl Van
Doren's anthology of world literature, stand up in a striking way beside a passage of description from Turgenev;
and the pages which Hemingway was later to write about
American wood and water are equivalents to the tran-
scriptions by Turgenev — the *Sportsman's Notebook* is
much admired by Hemingway — of Russian forests and
fields. Each has brought to an immense and wild country
the freshness of a new speech and a sensibility not yet
conventionalized by literary associations. Yet it *is* the
European sensibility which has come to Big Two-Hearted
River, where the Indians are now obsolescent; in those
solitudes it feels for the first time the cold current, the hot
morning sun, sees the pine stumps, smells the sweet fern.
And along with the mottled trout, with its 'clear water-
over-gravel color,' the boy from the American Middle
West fishes up a nice little masterpiece.

In the meantime there had been also Ring Lardner,
Sherwood Anderson, Gertrude Stein, using this American
language for irony, lyric poetry or psychological insight.
Hemingway seems to have learned from them all. But he
is now able to charge this naïve accent with a new complexity of emotion, a new shade of emotion: a malaise.
The wholesale shattering of human beings in which he
has taken part has given the boy a touch of panic.

II

The next fishing trip is strikingly different. Perhaps the
first had been an idealization. Is it possible to attain to

such sensuous bliss merely through going alone into the woods: smoking, fishing, and eating, with no thought about anyone else or about anything one has ever done or will ever be obliged to do? At any rate, today, in *The Sun Also Rises,* all the things that are wrong with human life are there on the holiday, too — though one tries to keep them back out of the foreground and to occupy one's mind with the trout, caught now in a stream of the Pyrenees, and with the kidding of the friend from the States. The feeling of insecurity has deepened. The young American now appears in a seriously damaged condition: he has somehow been incapacitated sexually through wounds received in the war. He is in love with one of those international sirens who flourished in the cafés of the post-war period and whose ruthless and uncontrollable infidelities, in such a circle as that depicted by Hemingway, have made any sort of security impossible for the relations between women and men. The lovers of such a woman turn upon and rend one another because they are powerless to make themselves felt by *her.*

The casualties of the bullfight at Pamplona, to which these young people have gone for the *fiesta,* only reflect the blows and betrayals of demoralized human beings out of hand. What is the tiresome lover with whom the lady has just been off on a casual escapade, and who is unable to understand that he has been discarded, but the man who, on his way to the bull ring, has been accidentally gored by the bull? The young American who tells the story is the only character who keeps up standards of conduct, and he is prevented by his disability from dominating and directing the woman, who otherwise, it is intimated, might love him. Here the membrane of the style has been stretched taut to convey the vibrations of these qualms. The dry sunlight and the green summer landscapes have been invested with a sinister quality which must be new in literature. One enjoys the sun and the green as one enjoys suckling pigs and Spanish wine, but the uneasiness and apprehension are undruggable.

Yet one can catch hold of a code in all the drunkenness and the social chaos. 'Perhaps as you went along you did learn something,' Jake, the hero, reflects at one point. 'I did not care what it was all about. All I wanted to know was how to live in it. Maybe if you found out how to live in it you learned from that what it was all about.' 'Everybody behaves badly. Give them the proper chance,' he says later to Lady Brett.

' "You wouldn't behave badly." Brett looked at me.' In the end, she sends for Jake, who finds her alone in a hotel. She has left her regular lover for a young bullfighter, and this boy has for the first time inspired her with a respect which has restrained her from 'ruining' him: 'You know it makes one feel rather good deciding not to be a bitch.' We suffer and we make suffer, and everybody loses out in the long run; but in the meantime we can lose with honor.

This code still markedly figures, still supplies a dependable moral backbone, in Hemingway's next book of short stories, *Men Without Women*. Here Hemingway has mastered his method of economy in apparent casualness and relevance in apparent indirection, and has turned his sense of what happens and the way in which it happens into something as hard and clear as a crystal but as disturbing as a great lyric. Yet it is usually some principle of courage, of honor, of pity — that is, some principle of sportsmanship in its largest human sense — upon which the drama hinges. The old bullfighter in *The Undefeated* is defeated in everything except the spirit which will not accept defeat. You get the bull or he gets you: if you die, you can die game; there are certain things you cannot do. The burlesque show manager in *A Pursuit Race* refrains from waking his advance publicity agent when he overtakes him and realizes that the man has just lost a long struggle against whatever anguish it is that has driven him to drink and dope. 'They got a cure for that,' the manager had said to him before he went to sleep; ' "No," William Campbell said, "they haven't got a cure for anything.' " The burned major in *A Simple Enquiry* — that strange picture of the bedrock stoicism compatible with the abasement of war — has the decency not to dismiss the orderly who has rejected his proposition. The brutalized Alpine peasant who has been in the habit of hanging a lantern in the jaws of the stiffened corpse of his wife, stood in the corner of the woodshed till the spring will make it possible to bury her, is ashamed to drink with the sexton after the latter has found out what he has done. And there is a little sketch of Roman soldiers just after the Crucifixion: 'You see me slip the old spear into him? — You'll get into trouble doing that some day. — It was the least I could do for him. I'll tell you he looked pretty good to me in there today.'

This Hemingway of the middle twenties — *The Sun Also Rises* came out in '26 — expressed the romantic disillusion and set the favorite pose for the period. It was the moment of gallantry in heartbreak, grim and nonchalant banter, and heroic dissipation. The great watchword was 'Have a drink'; and in the bars of New York and Paris the young people were getting to talk like Hemingway.

III

The novel, *A Farewell to Arms*, which followed *Men Without Women*, is in a sense not so serious an affair. Beautifully written and quite moving of course it is. Probably no other book has caught so well the strangeness of life in the army for an American in Europe during the war. The new places to which one was sent of which one had never heard, and the things that turned out to be in them; the ordinary people of foreign countries as one saw them when one was quartered among them or obliged to perform some common work with them; the pleasures of which one managed to cheat the war, intensified by the uncertainty and horror — and the uncertainty, nevertheless, almost become a constant, the horror almost taken for granted; the love affairs, always subject to being suddenly broken up and yet carried on while they lasted in a spirit of irresponsible freedom which derived from one's having forfeited control of all one's other actions — this Hemingway got into his book, written long enough after the events for them to present themselves under an aspect fully idyllic.

But *A Farewell to Arms* is a tragedy, and the lovers are shown as innocent victims with no relation to the forces that torment them. They themselves are not tormented within by that dissonance between personal satisfaction and the suffering one shares with others which it has been Hemingway's triumph to handle. *A Farewell to Arms*, as the author once said, is a *Romeo and Juliet*. And when Catherine and her lover emerge from the stream of action — the account of the Caporetto retreat is Hemingway's best sustained piece of narrative — when they escape from the alien necessities of which their romance has been merely an accident, which have been writing their story for them, then we see that they are not in themselves convincing as human personalities. And we are confronted with the paradox that Hemingway, who possesses so remarkable a mimetic gift in getting the tone of social and national types and in making his people talk appropriately, has not shown any very solid sense of character, or, indeed, any real interest in it. The people in his short stories are satisfactory because he has only to hit them off: the point of the story does not lie in personalities, but in the emotion to which a situation gives rise. This is true even in *The Sun Also Rises*, where the characters are sketched with wonderful cleverness. But in *A Farewell to Arms*, as soon as we are brought into real intimacy with the lovers, as soon as the author is obliged to see them through a searching personal experience, we find merely an idealized relationship, the abstractions of a lyric emotion.

With *Death in the Afternoon*, three years later, a new development for Hemingway commences. He writes a book not merely in the first person, but in the first person in his own character as Hemingway, and the results are unexpected and disconcerting. *Death in the Afternoon* has its value as an exposition of bullfighting; and Hemingway is able to use the subject as a text for an explicit statement of his conception of man eternally pitting himself — he thinks the bullfight a ritual of this — against animal force and the odds of death. But the book is partly infected by a queer kind of maudlin emotion, which sounds at once neurotic and drunken. He overdoes his glorification of the bravery and martyrdom of the bullfighter. No doubt the professional expert at risking his life single-handed is impressive in contrast to the flatness and unreality of much of the business of the modern world; but this admirable miniaturist in prose has already made the point perhaps more tellingly in the little prose poem called *Banal Story*. Now he offsets the virility of the bullfighters by anecdotes of the male homosexuals that frequent the Paris cafés, at the same time that he puts his chief celebration of the voluptuous excitement of the spectacle into the mouth of an imaginary old lady. The whole thing becomes a little hysterical.

The master of that precise and clean style now indulges in purple patches which go on spreading for pages. I am not one of those who admire the last chapter of *Death in the Afternoon*, with its rich, all too rich, unrollings of memories of good times in Spain, and with its what seem to me irrelevant reminiscences of the soliloquy of Mrs. Bloom in *Ulysses*. Also, there are interludes of kidding of a kind which Hemingway handles with skill when he assigns them to characters in his stories, but in connection with which he seems to become incapable of exercising good sense or good taste as soon as he undertakes them in his own person (the burlesque *Torrents of Spring* was an early omen of this). In short, we are compelled to recognize that, as soon as Hemingway drops the burning-glass of the disciplined and objective art with which he has learned to concentrate in a story the light of the emotions that flood in on him, he straightway becomes befuddled, slops over.

This befuddlement is later to go further, but in the meantime he publishes another volume of stories — *Winner Take Nothing* — which is almost up to its predecessor. In this collection he deals much more effectively than in *Death in the Afternoon* with that theme of contemporary decadence which is implied in his panegyric of the bull-fighter. The first of these stories, *After the Storm,* is another of his variations — and one of the finest — on the theme of keeping up a code of decency among the hazards and pains of life. A fisherman goes out to plunder a wreck: he dives down to break in through a porthole, but inside he sees a woman with rings on her hands and her hair floating loose in the water, and he thinks about the passengers and crew being suddenly plunged to their deaths (he has almost been killed himself in a drunken fight the night before). He sees the cloud of sea birds screaming around, and he finds that he is unable to break the glass with his wrench and that he loses the anchor grapple with which he next tries to attack it. So he finally goes away and leaves the job to the Greeks, who blow the boat open and clean her out.

But in general the emotions of insecurity here obtrude themselves and dominate the book. Two of the stories deal with the hysteria of soldiers falling off the brink of their nerves under the strain of the experiences of the war, which here no longer presents an idyllic aspect; another deals with a group of patients in a hospital, at the same time crippled and hopeless; still another (a five-page masterpiece) with a waiter, who, both on his own and on his customers' account, is reluctant to go home at night, because he feels the importance of a 'clean well-lighted cafe' as a refuge from the 'nothing' that people fear. *God Rest You Merry, Gentlemen* repeats the theme of castration of *The Sun Also Rises;* and four of the stories are concerned more or less with male or female homosexuality. In the last story, *Fathers and Sons,* Hemingway reverts to the Michigan woods, as if to take the curse off the rest: young Nick had once enjoyed a nice Indian girl with plump legs and hard little breasts on the needles of the hemlock woods.

These stories and the interludes in *Death in the Afternoon* must have been written during the years that followed the stock-market crash. They are full of the apprehension of losing control of oneself which is aroused by the getting out of hand of a social-economic system, as well as of the fear of impotence which seems to accompany the loss of social mastery. And there is in such a story as *A Clean Well-Lighted Place* the feeling of having got to the end of everything, of having given up heroic attitudes and wanting only the illusion of peace.

IV

And now, in proportion as the characters in his stories run out of fortitude and bravado, he passes into a phase where he is occupied with building up his public personality. He has already now become a legend, as Mencken was in the twenties; he is the Hemingway of the handsome photographs with the sportsmen's tan and the outdoor grin, with the ominous resemblance to Clark Gable, who poses with giant marlin which he has just hauled in off Key West. And unluckily — but for an American inevitably — the opportunity soon presents itself to exploit this personality for profit: he turns up delivering Hem-

ingway monologues in well-paying and trashy magazines;
and the Hemingway of these loose disquisitions, arrogant,
belligerent and boastful, is certainly the worst-invented
character to be found in the author's work. If he is obnoxious, the effect is somewhat mitigated by the fact that he
is intrinsically incredible.

There would be no point in mentioning this journalism
at all, if it did not seem somewhat to have contributed to
the writing of certain unsatisfactory books. *Green Hills of
Africa* (1935) owes its failure to falling between the two
genres of personal exhibitionism and fiction. 'The writer
has attempted,' says Hemingway, 'to write an absolutely
true book to see whether the shape of a country and the
pattern of a month's action can, if truly presented, compete with a work of the imagination.' He does try to present his own rôle objectively, and there is a genuine Hemingway theme — the connection between success at big-
game hunting and sexual self-respect — involved in his
adventures as he presents them. But the sophisticated technique of the fiction writer comes to look artificial when it
is applied to a series of real happenings; and the necessity
of sticking to what really happened makes impossible the
typical characters and incidents which give point to a work
of fiction. The monologues by the false, the publicity,
Hemingway with which the narrative is interspersed are
almost as bad as the ones that he has been writing for the
magazines. He inveighs with much scorn against the literary life and against the professional literary man of the
cities; and then manages to give the impression that he
himself is a professional literary man of the touchiest and
most self-conscious kind. He delivers a self-confident lecture on the high possibilities of prose writing; and then
produces such a sentence as the following: 'Going down-
hill steeply made these Spanish shooting boots too short
in the toe and there was an old argument, about this
length of boot and whether the bootmaker, whose part I

had taken, unwittingly first, only as interpreter, and finally embraced his theory patriotically as a whole and, I believed, by logic, had overcome it by adding onto the heel.' As soon as Hemingway begins speaking in the first person, he seems to lose his bearings, not merely as a critic of life, but even as a craftsman.

In another and significant way, *Green Hills of Africa* is disappointing. *Death in the Afternoon* did provide a lot of data on bullfighting and build up for us the bull-fighting world; but its successor tells us little about Africa. Hemingway keeps affirming — as if in accents of defiance against those who would engage his attention for social problems — his passionate enthusiasm for the African country and his perfect satisfaction with the hunter's life; but he has produced what must be one of the only books ever written which make Africa and its animals seem dull. Almost the only thing we learn about the animals is that Hemingway wants to kill them. And as for the natives, though there is one fine description of a tribe of marvelous trained runners, the principal impression we get of them is that they were simple and inferior people who enormously admired Hemingway.

It is not only that, as his critics of the Left had been complaining, he shows no interest in political issues, but that his interest in his fellow beings seems actually to be drying up. It is as if he were throwing himself on African hunting as something to live for and believe in, as something through which to realize himself; and as if, expecting of it too much, he had got out of it abnormally little, less than he is willing to admit. The disquiet of the Hemingway of the twenties had been, as I have said, undruggable — that is, in his books themselves, he had tried to express it, not drug it, had given it an appeasement in art; but now there sets in, in the Hemingway of the thirties, what seems to be a deliberate self-drugging. The situation is indicated objectively in *The Gambler, the Nun and the*

Radio, one of the short stories of 1933, in which everything from daily bread to 'a belief in any new form of government' is characterized as 'the opium of the people' by an empty-hearted patient in a hospital.

But at last there did rush into this vacuum the blast of the social issue, which had been roaring in the wind like a forest fire.

Out of a series of short stories that Hemingway had written about a Florida waterside character he decided to make a little epic. The result was *To Have and Have Not,* which seems to me the poorest of all his stories. Certainly some deep agitation is working upon Hemingway the artist. Craftsmanship and style, taste and sense, have all alike gone by the board. The negative attitude toward human beings has here become definitely malignant: the hero is like a wooden-headed Punch, always knocking people on the head (inferiors — Chinamen or Cubans); or, rather, he combines the characteristics of Punch with those of Popeye the Sailor in the animated cartoon in the movies. As the climax to a series of prodigies, this stupendous pirate-smuggler named Harry Morgan succeeds, alone, unarmed, and with only a hook for one hand — though at the cost of a mortal wound — in outwitting and destroying with their own weapons four men carrying revolvers and a machine gun, by whom he has been shanghaied in a launch. The only way in which Hemingway's outlaw suffers by comparison with Popeye is that his creator has not tried to make him plausible by explaining that he does it all on spinach.

The impotence of a decadent society has here been exploited deliberately, but less successfully than in the earlier short stories. Against a background of homosexuality, impotence and masturbation among the wealthy holidaymakers in Florida, Popeye-Morgan is shown gratifying his wife with the same indefatigable dexterity which he has displayed in his other feats; and there is a choral refrain of praise of his *cojones,* which wells up in the last pages of the book when the abandoned Mrs. Popeye regurgitates Molly Bloom's soliloquy.

To be a man in such a world of maggots is noble, but it is not enough. Besides the maggots, there are double-crossing rats, who will get you if they are given the slightest chance. What is most valid in *To Have and Have Not* is the idea — conveyed better, perhaps, in the first of the series of episodes than in the final scenes of massacre and agony — that in an atmosphere (here revolutionary Cuba) in which man has been set against man, in which it is always a question whether your companion is not preparing to cut your throat, the most sturdy and straightforward American will turn suspicious and cruel. Harry Morgan is made to realize as he dies that to fight this bad world alone is hopeless. Again Hemingway, with his barometric accuracy, has rendered a moral atmosphere that was prevalent at the moment he was writing — a moment when social relations were subjected to severe tensions, when they seemed sometimes already disintegrating. But the heroic Hemingway legend has at this point invaded his fiction and, inflaming and inflating his symbols, has produced an implausible hybrid, half Hemingway character, half nature myth.

Hemingway had not himself particularly labored this moral of individualism *versus* solidarity, but the critics of the Left labored it for him and received his least creditable piece of fiction as the delivery of a new revelation. The progress of the Communist faith among our writers since the beginning of the depression has followed a peculiar course. That the aims and beliefs of Marx and Lenin should have come through to the minds of intellectuals who had been educated in the bourgeois tradition as great awakeners of conscience, a great light, was quite natural and entirely desirable. But the conception of the dynamic

Marxist will, the exaltation of the Marxist religion, seized the members of the professional classes like a capricious contagion or hurricane, which shakes one and leaves his neighbor standing, then returns to lay hold on the second after the first has become quiet again. In the moment of seizure, each one of them saw a scroll unrolled from the heavens, on which Marx and Lenin and Stalin, the Bolsheviks of 1917, the Soviets of the Five-Year Plan, and the GPU of the Moscow trials were all a part of the same great purpose. Later the convert, if he were capable of it, would get over his first phase of snow blindness and learn to see real people and conditions, would study the development of Marxism in terms of nations, periods, personalities, instead of logical deductions from abstract propositions or — as in the case of the more naïve or dishonest — of simple incantatory slogans. But for many there was at least a moment when the key to all the mysteries of human history seemed suddenly to have been placed in their hands, when an infallible guide to thought and behavior seemed to have been given them in a few easy formulas.

Hemingway was hit pretty late. He was still in *Death in the Afternoon* telling the 'world-savers,' sensibly enough, that they should 'get to see' the world 'clear and as a whole. Then any part you make will represent the whole, if it's made truly. The thing to do is work and learn to make it.' Later he jibed at the literary radicals, who talked but couldn't take it; and one finds even in *To Have and Have Not* a crack about a 'highly paid Hollywood director, whose brain is in the process of outlasting his liver so that he will end up calling himself a Communist, to save his soul.' Then the challenge of the fight itself — Hemingway never could resist a physical challenge — the natural impulse to dedicate oneself to something bigger than big-game hunting and bullfighting, and the fact that the class war had broken out in a country to which he was romantically attached, seem to have combined to make him align himself with the Communists as well as the Spanish Loyalists at a time when the Marxist philoosphy had been pretty completely shelved by the Kremlin, now reactionary as well as corrupt, and when the Russians were lending the Loyalists only help enough to preserve, as they imagined would be possible, the balance of power against Fascism while they acted at the same time as a police force to beat down the real social revolution.

Hemingway raised money for the Loyalists, reported the battle fronts. He even went so far as to make a speech at a congress of the League of American Writers, an organization rigged by the supporters of the Stalinist régime in Russia and full of precisely the type of literary revolutionists that he had been ridiculing a little while before. Soon the Stalinists had taken him in tow, and he was feverishly denouncing as Fascists other writers who criticized the Kremlin. It has been one of the expedients of the Stalin administration in maintaining its power and covering up its crimes to condemn on trumped-up charges of Fascist conspiracy, and even to kidnap and murder, its political opponents of the Left; and, along with the food and munitions, the Russians had brought to the war in Spain what the Austrian journalist Willi Schlamm called that diversion of doubtful value for the working class: 'Herr Vyshinsky's Grand Guignol.'

The result of this was a play, *The Fifth Column*, which, though it is good reading for the way the characters talk, is an exceedingly silly production. The hero, though an Anglo-American, is an agent of the Communist secret police, engaged in catching Fascist spies in Spain; and his principal exploit in the course of the play is clearning out, with the aid of a single Communist, an artillery post manned by seven Fascists. The scene is like a pushover and getaway from one of the cruder Hollywood Westerns.

It is in the nature of a small boy's fantasy, and would probably be considered extravagant by most writers of books for boys.

The tendency on Hemingway's part to indulge himself in these boyish day-dreams seems to begin to get the better of his realism at the end of *A Farewell to Arms,* where the hero, after many adventures of fighting, escaping, love-making and drinking, rows his lady thirty-five kilometers on a cold and rainy night; and we have seen what it could do for Harry Morgan. Now, as if with the conviction that the cause and the efficiency of the GPU have added several cubits to his stature, he has let this tendency loose; and he has also found in the GPU's grim duty a pretext to give rein to the appetite for describing scenes of killing which has always been a feature of his work. He has progressed from grasshoppers and trout through bulls and lions and kudus to Chinamen and Cubans, and now to Fascists. Hitherto the act of destruction has given rise for him to complex emotions: he has identified himself not merely with the injurer but also with the injured; there has been a masochistic complement to the sadism. But now this paradox which splits our natures, and which has instigated some of Hemingway's best stories, need no longer present perplexities to his mind. The Fascists are dirty bastards, and to kill them is a righteous act. He who had made a separate peace, who had said farewell to arms, has found a reason for taking them up again in a spirit of rabietic fury unpleasantly reminiscent of the spy mania and the sacred anti-German rage which took possession of so many civilians and staff officers under the stimulus of the last war.

Not that the compensatory trauma of the typical Hemingway protagonist is totally absent even here. The main episode is the hero's brief love affair and voluntary breaking off with a beautiful and adoring girl whose acquaintance he has made in Spain. As a member of the Junior

League and a graduate of Vassar, she represents for him — it seems a little hard on her — that leisure-class playworld from which he is trying to get away. But in view of the fact that from the very first scenes he treats her with more or less open contempt, the action is rather lacking in suspense as the sacrifice is rather feeble in moral value. One takes no stock at all in the intimation that Mr. Philip may later be sent to mortify himself in a camp for training Young Pioneers. And in the meantime he has fun killing Fascists.

In *The Fifth Column,* the drugging process has been carried further still: the hero, who has become finally indistinguishable from the false or publicity Hemingway, has here dosed himself not only with whiskey, but with a seductive and desirous woman, for whom he has the most admirable reasons for not taking any responsibility, with sacred rage, with the excitement of a bombardment, and with indulgence in that headiest of sports, for which he has now the same excellent reasons: the bagging of human beings.

v

You may fear, after reading *The Fifth Column,* that Hemingway will never sober up; but as you go on to his short stories of this period, you find that your apprehensions were unfounded. Three of these stories have a great deal more body — they are longer and more complex — than the comparatively meager anecdotes collected in *Winner Take Nothing.* And here are his real artistic successes with the material of his adventures in Africa, which make up for the miscarried *Green Hills: The Short Happy Life of Francis Macomber* and *The Snows of Kilimanjaro,* which disengage, by dramatizing them objectively, the themes he had attempted in the earlier book but that had never really got themselves presented. And here is at least a beginning of a real artistic utilization of Hemingway's experience in Spain: an incident of the war in two pages which outweighs the whole of *The Fifth Column* and all his Spanish dispatches, a glimpse of an old man, 'without politics,' who has so far occupied his life in taking care of eight pigeons, two goats and a cat, but who has now been dislodged and separated from his pets by the advance of the Fascist armies. It is a story which takes its place among the war prints of Callot and Goya, artists whose union of elegance with sharpness has already been recalled by Hemingway in his earlier battle pieces: a story which might have been written about almost any war.

And here — what is very remarkable — is a story, *The Capital of the World,* which finds an objective symbol for, precisely, what is wrong with *The Fifth Column.* A young boy who has come up from the country and waits on table in a pension in Madrid gets accidentally stabbed with a meat knife while playing at bullfighting with the dishwasher. This is the simple anecdote, but Hemingway has built in behind it all the life of the pension and the city: the priesthood, the working-class movement, the grown-up bullfighters who have broken down or missed out. 'The boy Paco,' Hemingway concludes, 'had never known about any of this nor about what all these people would be doing on the next day and on other days to come. He had no idea how they really lived nor how they ended. He did not realize they ended. He died, as the Spanish phrase has it, full of illusions. He had not had time in his life to lose any of them, or even, at the end, to complete an act of contrition.' So he registers in this very fine piece the discrepancy between the fantasies of boyhood and the realities of the grown-up world. Hemingway the artist, who feels things truly and cannot help recording what he feels, has actually said good-bye to these fantasies at a time when the war correspondent is making himself ridiculous by attempting to hang on to them still.

The emotion which principally comes through in *Fran-*

cis *Macomber* and *The Snows of Kilimanjaro* — as it figures also in *The Fifth Column* — is a growing antagonism
to women. Looking back, one can see at this point that the
tendency has been there all along. In *The Doctor and the
Doctor's Wife*, the boy Nick goes out squirrel-hunting
with his father instead of obeying the summons of his
mother; in *Cross Country Snow*, he regretfully says farewell to male companionship on a skiing expedition in
Switzerland, when he is obliged to go back to the States
so that his wife can have her baby. The young man in
Hills Like White Elephants compels his girl to have an
abortion contrary to her wish; another story, *A Canary for
One*, bites almost unbearably but exquisitely on the loneliness to be endured by a wife after she and her husband
shall have separated; the peasant of *An Alpine Idyll*
abuses the corpse of his wife (these last three appear under the general title *Men Without Women*). Brett in *The
Sun Also Rises* is an exclusively destructive force: she
might be a better woman if she were mated with Jake,
the American; but actually he is protected against her and
is in a sense revenging his own sex through being unable
to do anything for her sexually. Even the hero of *A Farewell to Arms* eventually destroys Catherine — after enjoying her abject devotion — by giving her a baby, itself born
dead. The only women with whom Nick Adams' relations
are perfectly satisfactory are the little Indian girls of his
boyhood who are in a position of hopeless social disadvantage and have no power over the behavior of the white
male — so that he can get rid of them the moment he has
done with them. Thus in *The Fifth Column* Mr. Philip
brutally breaks off with Dorothy — he has been rescued
from her demoralizing influence by his enlistment in the
Communist crusade, just as the hero of *The Sun Also
Rises* has been saved by his physical disability — to revert
to a little Moorish whore. Even Harry Morgan, who is
represented as satisfying his wife on the scale of a Paul

Bunyan, deserts her in the end by dying and leaves her racked by the cruelest desire.[1]

And now this instinct to get the woman down presents itself frankly as a fear that the woman will get the man down. The men in both these African stories are married to American bitches of the most soul-destroying sort. The hero of *The Snows of Kilimanjaro* loses his soul and dies of futility on a hunting expedition in Africa, out of which he has failed to get what he had hoped. The story is not quite stripped clean of the trashy moral attitudes which have been coming to disfigure the author's work: the hero, a seriously intentioned and apparently promising writer, goes on a little sloppily over the dear early days in Paris when he was earnest, happy and poor, and blames a little hysterically the rich woman whom he has married and who has debased him. Yet it is one of Hemingway's remarkable stories. There is a wonderful piece of writing at the end when the reader is made to realize that what has seemed to be an escape by plane, with the sick man looking down on Africa, is only the dream of a dying man. The other story, *Francis Macomber*, perfectly realizes its purpose. Here the male saves his soul at the last minute,

[1] There would probably be a chapter to write on the relation between Hemingway and Kipling, and certain assumptions about society which they share. They have much the same split attitude toward women. Kipling anticipates Hemingway in his beliefs that 'he travels the fastest that travels alone' and that 'the female of the species is more deadly than the male;' and Hemingway seems to reflect Kipling in the submissive infra-Anglo-Saxon women that make his heroes such perfect mistresses. The most striking example of this is the amoeba-like little Spanish girl, Maria, in *For Whom the Bell Tolls*. Like the docile native 'wives' of English officials in the early stories of Kipling, she lives only to serve her lord and to merge her identity with him; and this love affair with a woman in a sleeping-bag, lacking completely the kind of give and take that goes on between real men and women, has the all-too-perfect felicity of a youthful erotic dream. One suspects that *Without Benefit of Clergy* was read very early by Hemingway and that it made on him a lasting impression. The pathetic conclusion of this story of Kipling's seems unmistakably to be echoed at the end of *A Farewell to Arms*.

and then is actually shot down by his woman, who does not want him to have a soul. Here Hemingway has at last got what Thurber calls the war between men and women right out into the open and has written a terrific fable of the impossible civilized woman who despises the civilized man for his failure in initiative and nerve and then jealously tries to break him down as soon as he begins to exhibit any. (It ought to be noted, also, that whereas in *Green Hills of Africa* the descriptions tended to weigh down the narrative with their excessive circumstantiality, the landscapes and animals of *Francis Macomber* are alive and unfalteringly proportioned.)

Going back over Hemingway's books today, we can see clearly what an error of the politicos it was to accuse him of an indifference to society. His whole work is a criticism of society: he has responded to every pressure of the moral atmosphere of the time, as it is felt at the roots of human relations, with a sensitivity almost unrivaled. Even his preoccupation with licking the gang in the next block and being known as the best basketball player in high school has its meaning in the present epoch. After all, whatever is done in the world, political as well as athletic, depends on personal courage and strength. With Hemingway, courage and strength are always thought of in physical terms, so that he tends to give the impression that the bullfighter who can take it and dish it out is more of a man than any other kind of man, and that the sole duty of the revolutionary socialist is to get the counter-revolutionary gang before they get him.

But ideas, however correct, will never prevail by themselves: there must be people who are prepared to stand or fall with them, and the ability to act on principle is still subject to the same competitive laws which operate in sporting contests and sexual relations. Hemingway has expressed with genius the terrors of the modern man at the danger of losing control of his world, and he has also, within his scope, provided his own kind of antidote. This antidote, paradoxically, is almost entirely moral. Despite Hemingway's preoccupation with physical contests, his heroes are almost always defeated physically, nervously, practically: their victories are moral ones. He himself, when he trained himself stubbornly in his unconventional unmarketable art in a Paris which had other fashions, gave the prime example of such a victory; and if he has sometimes, under the menace of the general panic, seemed on the point of going to pieces as an artist, he has always pulled himself together the next moment. The principle of the Bourdon gauge, which is used to measure the pressure of liquids, is that a tube which has been curved into a coil will tend to straighten out in proportion as the liquid inside it is subjected to an increasing pressure.

The appearance of *For Whom the Bell Tolls* since this essay was written in 1939 carries the straightening process further. Here Hemingway has largely sloughed off his Stalinism and has reverted to seeing events in terms of individuals pitted against specific odds. His hero, an American teacher of Spanish who has enlisted on the side of the Loyalists, gives his life to what he regards as the cause of human liberation; but he is frustrated in the task that has been assigned him by the confusion of forces at cross-purposes that are throttling the Loyalist campaign. By the time that he comes to die, he has little to sustain him but the memory of his grandfather's record as a soldier in the American Civil War. The psychology of this young man is presented with a certain sobriety and detachment in comparison with Hemingway's other full-length heroes; and the author has here succeeded as in none of his earlier books in externalizing in plausible characters the elements of his own complex personality. With all this, there is an historical point of view which he has learned from his political adventures: he has aimed to reflect in this episode the whole course of the Spanish War and the tangle of tendencies involved in it.

The weaknesses of the book are its diffuseness — a shape that lacks the concision of his short stories, that sometimes sags and sometimes bulges; and a sort of exploitation of the material, an infusion of the operatic, that lends itself all too readily to the movies.

THE DREAM OF H. C. EARWICKER

JAMES JOYCE's *Ulysses* was an attempt to present directly the thoughts and feelings of a group of Dubliners through the whole course of a summer day. *Finnegans Wake* is a complementary attempt to render the dream fantasies and the half-unconscious sensations experienced by a single person in the course of a night's sleep.

This presents a more difficult problem to the reader as well as to the writer. In *Ulysses,* the reader was allowed to perceive the real objective world in which the Blooms and Dedalus lived, and their situation and relationships in that world, so that its distortions or liquefactions under the stress of special psychological states still usually remained intelligible. But in *Finnegans Wake* we are not supplied with any objective data until the next to the last chapter, when the hero — and then only rather dimly — wakes up for a short time toward morning; and we are dealing with states of consciousness which, though they sometimes have something in common with the drunken imaginations of the Night Town scene in *Ulysses* or the free associations of Mrs. Bloom's insomniac reveries, are even more confused and fluid than these; so that it becomes on a first reading the reader's prime preoccupation to puzzle out who the dreamer is and what has been happening to him. And since Joyce has spent seventeen years elaborating and complicating this puzzle, it is hardly to be expected that one reading will suffice to unravel it completely.

Let me try to establish, however, some of the most important facts which provide the realistic foundation for

this immense poem of sleep. The hero of *Finnegans Wake*
is a man of Scandinavian blood, with what is apparently
an adapted Scandinavian name: Humphrey Chimpden
Earwicker, who keeps a pub called The Bristol in Dublin.
He is somewhere between fifty and sixty, blond and
ruddy, with a walrus mustache, very strong but of late
years pretty fat. When embarrassed, he has a tendency to
stutter. He has tried his hand at a number of occupations;
has run for office and has gone through a bankruptcy. He
is married to a woman named Ann, a former salesgirl, who
is more or less illiterate and whose maiden name seems to
have begun with Mac. They are both Protestants in a
community of Catholics, he an Episcopalian and she a
Presbyterian; and by reason both of his religion and of his
queer-sounding foreign name, he feels himself, like Bloom
in *Ulysses,* something of an alien among his neighbors.
The Earwickers have three children — a girl named Isobel,
who has evidently passed adolescence, and two younger
boys, twins: Kevin and Jerry. There are also a maid-of-all-
work called Kate and a man about the place called Tom.

It is a Saturday night in summer, after a disorderly evening in the pub. Somebody — probably Earwicker himself
— has been prevailed upon to sing a song: later, when it
was closing time, he had to put a man outside, who abused
him and threw stones at the window. There has also been
a thunderstorm. Earwicker has been drinking off and on
all day and has perhaps gone to bed a little drunk. At any
rate, his night is troubled. At first he dreams about the
day before, with a bad conscience and a sense of humiliation: then, as the night darkens and he sinks more deeply
into sleep, he has to labor through a nightmare oppression.

He and his wife are sleeping together; but he has no
longer any interest in her as a woman. He is preoccupied
now with his children. His wife is apparently much
younger than he, was only a girl when he married her; so
that it is easy for him to confuse his first feelings for her

with something like an erotic emotion which is now being
aroused by his daughter. And his affection for his favorite
son is even acquiring homosexual associations. Little
Kevin is relatively sedate: named after the ascetic St.
Kevin, he may be destined for the Catholic priesthood.
Jerry (Shem) is more volatile and has given evidences of
a taste for writing; and it is Jerry rather than Kevin
(Shaun) with whom the father has tended to identify
himself.

To tell the story in this way, however, is to present it
the wrong way around. It depends for its dramatic effect
on our not finding out till almost the end — pages 555-590,
in which Earwicker partially wakes up – that the flights
of erotic fantasy and the horrors of guilt of his dream have
been inspired by his feelings for his children. The pub is
on the edge of the Phoenix Park, between it and the River
Liffey and not far from the suburb of Chapelizod, which
is said to have been the birthplace of Iseult. At the very
beginning of the dream, we find Earwicker figuring as
Tristram; and through the whole night he is wooing
Iseult; he carries her off, he marries her. The Freudian
censor has intervened to change *Isobel* into *Iseult la Belle*
— as well as to turn the ana (upper)-Liffey, which figures
in the dream as a woman, into *Anna Livia Plurabelle*.
The idea of incest between father and daughter is developed on page 115; the transition from Isobel to Iseult is
indicated in the 'Icy-la-Belle' of page 246; and the sister
of the twins is designated by her family nickname 'Izzy'
on page 431. But, though the boys have been given their
real names and planted pretty clearly — on pages 26-27 —
it is not until almost the end — on page 556 — that a definite identification of Earwicker's daughter with Iseult is
made. In the same way, it is not until the passage on pages
564-565 that we are led to connect with Earwicker's son
the homosexual motif which has first broken into his
dream with the ominous incident of the father's accosting

a soldier in the park and subsequently being razzed by the police, and which works free toward morning — page 474 — to the idea, not related to actuality, of 'some chubby boy-bold love of an angel.'

In the meantime, the incest taboo and the homosexuality taboo have together — as in the development of Greek tragedy out of the old myths of cannibalism and incest — given rise, during Earwicker's effortful night, to a whole mythology, a whole morality. He is Tristram stealing Iseult, yes; but — at the suggestion of an Adam's mantelpiece in the bedroom where he is sleeping — he is also Adam, who has forfeited by his sin the Paradise of the Phoenix Park; at the suggestion of a copy of Raphael's picture of Michael subduing Satan which hangs on the bedroom wall, he is an archangel wrestling with the Devil. And he has fallen not merely as Adam but also as Humpty Dumpty (he is fat and his first name is Humphrey); as the hero of the ballad of *Finnegan's Wake,* who fell off a scaffold while building a house (but came to life again at the sound of the word 'Whisky'); and as Napoleon (an obelisk dedicated to Wellington is a feature of the Phoenix Park, though there is apparently no Wellington Museum). Since the landmarks of the life of Swift still keep their prestige in Dublin, he is Swift, who loved Stella and Vanessa with the obstructed love of a father and whose mind was finally blotted by madness: Swift's cryptic name for Stella, 'Ppt,' punctuates the whole book.

And Earwicker is also making up in sleep for an habitual feeling of helplessness due to his belonging to a racial and religious minority. He is sometimes the first Danish conqueror of Ireland, who sailed up that very Liffey; sometimes Oliver Cromwell, that other hated heathen invader.

But it is Joyce's further aim to create, through Earwicker's mythopoeic dream, a set of symbols even more general and basic. He has had the idea of making Ear-

wicker, resolved into his elemental components, include
the whole of humanity. The river, with its feminine personality, Anna Livia Plurabelle, comes to represent the
feminine principle itself. At one time or another all the
women who figure in Earwicker's fantasy are merged into
this stream of life which, always renewed, never pausing,
flows through the world built by men. The daughter, still
a little girl, is early identified with a cloud, which will
come down to earth as rain and turn into the rapid young
river; the Anna Livia Plurabelle chapter describes a lively
woman's coming-of-age; in the end, the mature river,
broader and slower now, will move toward her father, the
sea. The corresponding masculine principle is symbolized
by the Hill of Howth, which rises at the mouth of the
Liffey; and the idea of the hill as a citadel and the idea
of the city as a male construction associate themselves with
this: the man is a hill that stands firm while the river runs
away at his feet; he is a fortress, he is Dublin, he is all the
cities of the world.

And if Earwicker is animated in sleep by the principles
of both the sexes, he has also a double existence in the
rôles of both Youth and Old Age. Canalizing his youthful
impulses in a vision of himself as his favorite son, he
dreams himself endowed with a resilience to go out and
try life again; exalted by a purity of idealism which has
not yet been tainted by experience, and yet bubbling with
roguish drolleries, blithely beloved by the girls. On the
other hand, foreshadowing his own decline, he sees the
vision of a chorus of old men, who, drivelingly reminiscent, at the same time gloat and scold at the thought of the
vigorous young Tristram kissing Iseult on the other side
of the bushes, and exclaim in admiration — an expansion
of Earwicker's feelings at the sight of his own sleeping son
— over the form of the sleeping Earwicker (Shaun-Jerry).
The old men are named Matthew Gregory, Marcus Lyons,
Luke Tarpey and Johnny MacDougall; and they are iden-

tified variously with the four apostles, the Four Masters
(early sages of Irish legend), the Four Waves of Irish
mythology, the four courts of Dublin, and the four prov-
inces of Ireland (Johnny MacDougall is evidently Ulster:
he always follows at some distance behind the others).
These fathers are always associated with a gray ass and
sycamore trees, and have perhaps been suggested to Earwicker by four sycamore trees on the Liffey, among which
a neighbor's donkey has been grazing. All of these major
motifs are woven in and out from beginning to end of the
book, and each at a given point receives a complete development: the woman-river in pages 196-216 — the well-
known Anna Livia Plurabelle chapter; the male city-
fortress-hill in pages 532-554 (already published separately
as *Haveth Childers Everywhere*); the Young Man in the
chapters about Shaun, pages 403-473; and the Old Men,
providing a contrast, just before, in 383-399.

There are also a stone and an elm on opposite sides of
the Liffey, which represent the death principle and the
life principle (Ygdrasil). The tree has several graciously
rustling solos (a notable one at the end, beginning on
page 619), and in the Anna Livia Plurabelle chapter she
has a long conversation with the stone, which blends with
the gossip of two old washerwomen drying clothes on the
riverbank. This dialogue is only one of many dialogues
which are really always the same disputation, and in
which one of the parties, like the stone, is always hard-
boiled, immobile and prosaic, while the other is sensitive,
alive, rather light-mindedly chattering or chirping. The
tougher of the two parties in these interchanges is always
browbeating or bullying the other. Sometimes they are
Satan and Saint Michael; sometimes they are transmogrified antitheses derived from Aesop's fables: the Mookse
and the Gripes (the Fox and the Grapes), the Ondt and
the Gracehoper (the Ant and the Grasshopper); but all
these dualisms are evidently connected with the diverse

temperaments of Earwicker's twins (who sometimes appear as Cain and Abel), and represent the diverse elements in the character of Earwicker himself, as these struggle within his own consciousness, the aggressive side sometimes reflecting certain powers in the external world — the force of hostile opinion or the police — which he now fears, now feels he can stand up to. The various pairs, however, shift their balance and melt into one another so readily that it is impossible to give any account of them which will cover all the cases in the book.

Besides all this, just as Joyce in *Ulysses* laid the *Odyssey* under requisition to help provide a structure for his material — material which, once it had begun to gush from the rock of Joyce's sealed personality at the blow of the Aaron's rod of free association, threatened to rise and submerge the artist like the flood which the sorcerer's apprentice let loose by his bedeviled broom; so in the face of an even more formidable danger, he has here brought in the historical theory of the eighteenth-century philosopher, Giambattista Vico, to help him to organize *Finnegans Wake*. It was Vico's idea that civilizations always pass through three definite phases: a phase when people imagine gods, a phase when they make up myths about heroes, and a phase when they see things in terms of real men. It will be noted that the figures mentioned above divide themselves among these three categories of beings. Vico further believed that history moved in cycles and that it was always repeating itself, which — to the frequent exasperation of the reader — *Finnegans Wake* is also made to do. And there is also a good deal more out of Vico, which you can find out about in *Our Exagmination*[1] but which

---

[1] *Our Exagmination Round His Factification for Incamination of Work in Progress*, published by New Directions at Norfolk, Connecticut. This is a collection of papers from *Transition*, the Paris magazine in which *Finnegans Wake* first appeared. The writers have taken their cues from Joyce himself, and he seems to have

seems even more idle and forced than the most forced and idle aspects of the Odysseyan parallel in *Ulysses*. The fact that there is a Vico Road in the Dublin suburb Dalkey — 'The Vico Road goes round and round to meet where terms begin' — gives Joyce a peg in actuality on which to hang all this theory.

There is one important respect in which Joyce may seem to depart from Vico. Vico, so far as is known, did not believe in progress: his cycles did not spiral toward an earthly goal; his hope for salvation was in heaven. But the cycles of *Finnegans Wake* do result in a definite progression. As Earwicker lives through from darkness to light, he does slough off his feeling of guilt. By morning the Devil has been vanquished by Michael; Youth has bounded free of Age; the Phoenix of Vico and the Phoenix Park has risen from its ashes to new flight; Tristram has built a castle (Howth Castle) for his bride; and Iseult, once the object of an outlawed love, now married and growing older, turns naturally and comfortably at last into the lawful wife in the bed beside him, whom Earwicker is making an effort not to jab with his knees; the tumult and turbidity of Saturday night run clear in the peace of Sunday morning; the soul, which has been buried in sleep, is resurrected, refreshed, to life.

Yet if one looks at the book as a whole, one finds that the larger cycle does return upon itself. This will be seen when I discuss the last pages. In the meantime, let me merely point out that we do not find in *Finnegans Wake* any climax of exaltation comparable either to the scene where Stephen Dedalus realizes his artist's vocation or to Molly Bloom's great affirmative. The later book represents an aging phase in the constant human subject with which

chosen this way of providing the public with a key. It is, in fact, rather doubtful whether without the work done by *Transition* it would be possible to get the hang of the book at all. See also Mr. Max Eastman's account of an interview with Joyce on the subject in Part III, Chapter III, of *The Literary Mind*.

the series of Joyce's books has dealt. This subject — which must never be lost sight of, though in this case it is easy to do so — is the nexus of intimate relationships involved in a family situation. We find it first in the *Portrait of an Artist* in the attitude of Dedalus toward his family, and in the delicate but vital displacement in the relations of the young married couple who figure in the short story called *The Dead.* In *Exiles,* another young married couple come back from abroad with a son, and a more serious displacement takes place when the wife meets an old lover. In *Ulysses,* the relations of man and wife, by this time almost middle-aged, have been affected by more serious readjustments, and they are related in a complex way to the relations of the Blooms to their children, of Dedalus to his parents, and of both the Blooms to Dedalus. Now, in *Finnegans Wake,* the husband and wife have reached an age at which, from the emotional point of view, they seem hardly important to one another, and at which the chief source of interest is the attitude of the father toward the children — 'the child we all love to place our hope in,' as Earwicker thinks in the last moments before the rising sun wakes him up. (We have already had intimations of this relationship in the adoptively paternal instincts of Bloom toward the spiritually parentless Dedalus; in Joyce's little lyric poems, poignant to the point of anguish, that deal with his own children; and in the poem called *Ecce Puer,* in which the family cycle appears.)

Here this family situation has been explored more profoundly by Joyce than in any of his previous books. In sleep, the conventions and institutions with which we discipline and give shape to our lives are allowed partly to dissolve and evaporate, so as partly to set free the impulses of the common human plasm out of which human creatures are made; and then the sexual instincts of the man and the woman, the child's instinct and the parent's instinct, the masculine and feminine principles themselves,

come into play in confusing ways, shadow forth disturbing relationships, which yet spring from the prime processes of life. *Finnegans Wake* carries even farther the
kind of insight into such human relations which was already carried far in *Ulysses;* and it advances with an
astounding stride the attempt to find the universally human in ordinary specialized experience which was implied
in the earlier book by the Odyssean parallel. Joyce will
now try to build up inductively the whole of human history and myth from the impulses, conscious and dormant,
the unrealized potentialities, of a single human being,
who is to be a man even more obscure and even less well-
endowed, even less civilized and aspiring, than was Leo-
pold Bloom in *Ulysses.*

Finnegans Wake, in conception as well as in execution,
is one of the boldest books ever written.

II

In order to get anything out of *Finnegans Wake,* you
must grasp a queer literary convention. It has been said
by T. S. Eliot that Joyce is the greatest master of language
in English since Milton. Eliot has also pointed out that
Milton is mainly a writer for the *ear.* Now Joyce through
a large part of his adult life has been almost as blind as
Milton; and he has ended, just as Milton did, by dealing
principally in auditory sensations. There is as little visual-
ization in *Finnegans Wake* as in *Samson Agonistes.* Our
first criticism, therefore, is likely to be that nothing is *seen*
in Earwicker's dream. It is, after all, not uncommon in
dreams to have the illusion of seeing people and places as
clearly as when we are awake; and in the dream literature
with which we are already familiar — *Alice in Wonder-
land, The Temptation of Saint Anthony* — the dreamers
are visited by plain apparitions, not merely by invisible
voices. But we must assume with *Finnegans Wake* that
Earwicker's imagination, like Joyce's is almost entirely

auditory and verbal. We have been partly prepared by *Ulysses*, in which we listen to the thoughts of the characters but do not see them very distinctly.

But there is another and more serious difficulty to be got over. We are continually being distracted from identifying and following Earwicker, the humble proprietor of a public house, who is to encompass the whole microcosm of the dream, by the intrusion of all sorts of elements — foreign languages, literary allusions, historical information — which could not possibly have been in Earwicker's mind. The principle on which Joyce is operating may evidently be stated as follows. If the artist is to render directly all the feelings and fancies of a sleeper, primitive, inarticulate, infinitely imprecise as they are, he must create a literary medium of unexampled richness and freedom. Now it is also Joyce's purpose in *Finnegans Wake* to bring out in Earwicker's consciousness the processes of universal history: the languages, the cycles of society, the typical relationships of legend, are, he is trying to show us, all implicit in every human being. He has, as I have indicated, been careful to hook up his hero realistically with the main themes of his universal fantasia: the Bible stories, the Battle of Waterloo, Tristram and Iseult, and so forth. But since Earwicker's implications *are* shown to be universal, the author has the right to summon all the resources of his superior knowledge in order to supply a vehicle which will carry this experience of sleep. He has the same sort of justification for making the beings in Earwicker's dream speak Russian in fighting the siege of Sebastopol (which has got in by way of a picture hanging in Earwicker's house) as Thomas Hardy has, for example, to describe in his own literary vocabulary a landscape seen by an ignorant person. If it is objected that in *Finnegans Wake* the author is supposed to be not *describing*, but presenting the hero's consciousness directly, Joyce might reply that his procedure had precedent not only in poetry, but also in pre-naturalistic fiction: even the characters of Dickens were allowed to make speeches in blank verse, even the characters of Meredith were allowed to converse in apothegms. Why shouldn't H. C. Earwicker be allowed to dream in a language which draws flexibility and variety from the author's enormous reservoir of colloquial and literary speech, of technical jargons and foreign tongues?

Yet here is where the reader's trouble begins, because here, in spite of the defense just suggested, a convention that seems indispensable has been disconcertingly violated. What Joyce is trying to do is to break out of the Flaubertian naturalism into something that moves more at ease and that commands a wider horizon, something that is not narrowly tied down to the data about a certain man living in a certain year on a certain street of a certain city; and the reaction is of course quite natural: it was inevitable that the symbol and the myth, the traditional material of poetry, should have asserted themselves again against the formulas of scientific precision which had begun to prove so cramping. But here the act of escaping from them shocks, just as it sometimes did in Proust. Proust argues in an impressive way, in the final section of his novel, the case against nineteenth-century naturalism; yet who has not been made uncomfortable at finding that Proust's personal manias have been allowed to affect the structure of his book: that a story which has been presented as happening to real people should not maintain a consistent chronology, that it should never be clear whether the narrator of the story is the same person as the author of the book, and that the author, who ought to know everything, should in some cases leave us in doubt as to the facts about his hero? One had felt, in reading *Ulysses,* a touch of the same uneasiness when the phantasmagoria imagined by Bloom in the drunken Night Town scene was enriched by learned fancies which would seem to be more appropriate to Dedalus. And now in *Finnegans Wake* the balloon of this new kind of poetry pulls harder at its naturalistic anchor. We are in the first place asked to believe that a man like H. C. Earwicker would seize every possible pretext provided by his house and its location to include in a single night's dream a large number of historical and legendary characters. And is it not pretty farfetched to assume that Earwicker's awareness of the life of Swift or the Crimean War is really to be accurately conveyed in terms of the awareness of Joyce, who has acquired a special knowledge of these subjects? Also, what about the references to the literary life in Paris and to the book itself as Work in Progress, which take us right out of the mind of Earwicker and into the mind of Joyce?

There are not, to be sure, very many such winks and nudges as this, though the shadow of Joyce at his thankless task seems sometimes to fall between Earwicker and us. Joyce has evidently set himself limits as to how far he can go in this direction; and he may urge that since Earwicker is universal man, he must contain the implications of Joyce's destiny as he does those of Swift's and Napoleon's, though he has never heard of him as he has of them, and that to give these implications a personal accent is only to sign his canvas. Yet, even granting all this and recognizing the difficulty of the task and accepting without reservation the method Joyce has chosen for his purpose, the result still seems unsatisfactory, the thing has not quite come out right. Instead of the myths' growing out of Earwicker, Earwicker seems swamped in the myths. His personality is certainly created: we get to know him and feel sympathy for him. But he is not so convincing as Bloom was: there has been too much literature poured into him. He has exfoliated into too many arabesques, become hypertrophied by too many elements. And not merely has he to carry this load of myths; he has

also been all wound round by what seems Joyce's growing self-indulgence in an impulse to pure verbal play.

Here another kind of difficulty confronts us. There is
actually a special kind of language which people speak
in dreams and in which they sometimes even compose
poetry. This language consists of words and sentences
which, though they seem to be gibberish or nonsense
from the rational point of view, betray by their telescop-
ings of words, their combinations of incongruous ideas,
the involuntary preoccupations of the sleeper. Lewis Carroll exploited this dream language in *Jabberwocky*, and
it has been studied by Freud and his followers, from
whom Joyce seems to have got the idea of its literary possibilities. At any rate, *Finnegans Wake* is almost entirely
written in it.

The idea was brilliant in itself, and Joyce has in many
cases carried it out brilliantly. He has created a whole
new poetry, a whole new humor and pathos, of sentences
and words that go wrong. The special kind of equivocal
and prismatic effects aimed at by the symbolist poets have
here been achieved by a new method and on psychological principles which give them a new basis in humanity.
But the trouble is, it seems to me, that Joyce has somewhat overdone it. His method of giving words multiple
meanings allows him to go on indefinitely introducing
new ideas; and he has spent no less than seventeen years
embroidering *Finnegans Wake* in this way.

What has happened may be shown by the following
examples. First, a relatively simple one from a passage
about the Tree: 'Amengst menlike trees walking or trees
like angels weeping nobirdy aviar soar anywing to eagle
it!' It is quite clear in the last seven words how an ornitho-
logical turn has been given to 'nobody ever saw anything
to equal it.' Here is a more complex one: Earwicker, pic-

turing himself in the chapter in which he partially wakes
up, is made to designate his hair with the phrase 'beer wig.'
This has as its basis *bar wig*, which has rushed into the
breach as *beer wig* under the pressure of Earwicker's profession as a dispenser of drinks in his pub, of the fact that
his hair is yellow, and of his tendency to imagine that
his queer last name is being caricatured by his neighbors
as 'Earwigger' — a tendency which has led to his dream
being impishly haunted by earwigs. There are thus four
different ideas compressed in these two words. But let us
examine — with the aid of the hints provided by the *Exagmination* — an even more complicated passage. Here is
Earwicker-Joyce's depiction of the madness and eclipse of
Swift: 'Unslow, malswift, pro mean, proh noblesse, Atrahore, melancolores, nears; whose glauque eyes glitt bedimmed to imm; whose fingerings creep o'er skull: till
quench., asterr mist calls estarr and graw, honath Jon
raves homes glowcoma.' This passage, besides the more
or less obvious ones, contains apparently the following
ideas: Laracor, Swift's living in Ireland, combined with
the *atra cura, black care,* that rides behind the horseman
in the first poem of Book Three of Horace's *Odes*; the
Horatian idea that death comes to the mean and the noble
alike; *proh*, the Latin interjection of regret, and *pro*, perhaps referring to Swift's championship of the impoverished Irish; *melancolores, melancholy* plus *black-colored*;
glauque, French *gray-blue*, plus, Greek *glaux, owl* — gray
evening plus Swift's blue eyes, which also had an owlish
appearance; in *glitt bedimmed to imm*, the double consonants evidently represent a deadening of the senses;
creep o'er skull, French *crépuscule, twilight; asterr*, Greek
aster, star, Swift's Stella, whose real name was Esther;
Vanessa's real name was Hester — so Stella calls Hester a
(q)wench; perhaps German *mist, dung, trash,* plays some
part here, too — as well as German *starr, rigid; graw* evidently contains German *grau*, gray; *honath Jon* is *honest*

John and *Jonathan*; *glowcoma* is *glaucoma*, a kind of
blindness, plus the idea of a pale glow of life persisting
in a coma. This passage has some beauty and power; but
isn't it overingenious? Would anyone naturally think of
Horace when he was confronted with 'Atrahore'? And,
even admitting that it may be appropriate to associate
Latin with Swift, how does the German get in? Swift did
not know German nor had he any German associations.[1]

In some cases, this overlaying of meanings has had the
result of rendering quite opaque passages which at an
earlier stage — as we can see by comparing the finished
text with some of the sections as they first appeared — were
no less convincingly dreamlike for being more easily comprehensible. You will find three versions of a passage in
Anna Livia Plurabelle on page 164 of the *Exagmination*;
and on page 213 of the book you will see that Joyce has
worked up still a fourth. My feeling is that he ought to
have stopped somewhere between the second and the
third. Here is Version I of 1925: 'Look, look, the dusk is
growing. What time is it? It must be late. It's ages now
since I or anyone last saw Waterhouse's clock. They took
it asunder, I heard them say. When will they reassemble
it?' And here is Version 4 of 1939: 'Look, look, the dusk
is growing. My branches lofty are taking root. And my
cold cher's gone ashley. Fieluhr? Filou! What age is at?
It saon is late. 'Tis endless now senne eye or erewone last
saw Waterhouse's clogh. They took it asunder, I hurd
thum sigh. When will they reassemble it?' There is a gain

[1] I chose this passage because a partial exposition of it, which I take
to be more or less authoritative, had appeared in the *Exagmination*
(in the paper by Mr. Robert McAlmon). I did not remember to
have read it in its place in *Finnegans Wake*, and was unable to find
it when I looked for it. Since then I have been told by another
reader who has been over and over the book that this sentence about
Swift is not included. This is interesting because it indicates the
operation of a principle of selection. Joyce suffered himself from
glaucoma, and it may be that he eliminated the reference because
he felt that it was too specifically personal.

in poetry, certainly; but in the meantime the question and the answer have almost disappeared. Has it really made Anna Livia any more riverlike to introduce the names of several hundred rivers (*saon* is *Saône* doing duty as *soon,* and *cher* is the *Cher* for French *chair*) — as he also introduces in other sections the names of cities, insects, trees? And why drag in *Erewhon*? In the same way, the talk of the Old Men, which, when it first came out in *Navire d'Argent,* seemed almost equal in beauty to the Anna Livia Plurabelle chapter, has now been so crammed with other things that the voices of the actual speakers have in places been nearly obliterated.

Joyce has always been rather deficient in dramatic and narrative sense. *Ulysses* already dragged; one got lost in it. The moments of critical importance were so run in with the rest that one was likely to miss them on first reading. One had to think about the book, read chapters of it over, in order to see the pattern and to realize how deep the insight went. And *Finnegans Wake* is much worse in this respect. The main outlines of the book are discernible, once we have been tipped off as to what it is all about. It is a help that, in forming our hypothesis, the principle of Occam's razor applies; for it is Joyce's whole design and point that the immense foaming-up of symbols should be reducible to a few simple facts. And it must also be conceded by a foreigner that a good deal which may appear to him mysterious would be plain enough to anyone who knew Dublin and something about Irish history, and that what Joyce has done here is as legitimate as it would be for an American writer to lay the scene of a similar fantasy somewhere on Riverside Drive in New York and to assume that his readers would be able to recognize Grant's Tomb, green buses, Columbia University and the figure of Hendrik Hudson. A foreign reader of *Finnegans Wake* should consult a map of Dublin, and look up the articles on Dublin and Ireland in the *Encyclopædia Britannica*.

Yet it seems to me a serious defect that we do not really understand what is happening till we have almost finished the book. *Then* we can look back and understand the significance of Earwicker's stuttering over the word *father* on page 45; we can see that 'Peder the Greste, altipaltar' on page 344 combines, along with Peter the Great and *agreste, pederast* and *pater;* we can conclude that the allusion on page 373 about 'begetting a wife which begame his niece by pouring her young-things into skintighs' refers back to the little story on pages 21-23, and that this whole theme is a device of the 'dream-work' to get over the incest barrier by disguising Earwicker's own children as the children of a niece.

But in the meantime we have had to make our way through five hundred and fifty-four pages; and there is much that is evidently important that we still do not understand. How, for example, is the story of the 'prankquean' just mentioned related to the motif of the letter scratched up by the chicken from the dump heap; and what is the point about this letter? The theme is developed at prodigious length in the chapter beginning on page 104; and it flickers all through the book. It turns up near the end — pages 623-624 — with new emotional connotations. The idea of letters and postmen plays a prominent part all through. Little Kevin is represented as giving the postman's knock; and Earwicker — though he here seems to be identifying himself with the other son, Jerry — is caught up into a long flight of fantasy in which he imagines himself a postman. The letter comes from Boston, Massachusetts, and seems to have been written by some female relation, perhaps the niece mentioned above. One feels that there is a third woman in the story, and that something important depends on this. Yet a considerable amount of rereading has failed, in the case of the present writer, to clear the matter up.

Finnegans Wake, in the actual reading, seems to me for two thirds of its length not really to bring off what it attempts. Nor do I think it possible to defend the procedure of Joyce on the basis of an analogy with music. It is true that there is a good deal of the musician in Joyce: his phonograph record of *Anna Livia* is as beautiful as a fine tenor solo. But nobody would listen for half an hour to a composer of operas or symphonic poems who went on and on in one mood as monotonously as Joyce has done in parts of *Finnegans Wake,* who scrambled so many motifs in one passage, or who returned to pick up a theme a couple of hours after it had first been stated, when the listeners would inevitably have forgotten it.[1]

[1] This essay was written in the summer of 1939, just after *Finnegans Wake* came out, and I have reprinted it substantially as it first appeared. Since then an article by Mr. John Peale Bishop in *The Southern Review* of summer, 1939, and studies by Mr. Harry Levin in *The Kenyon Review* of Autumn, 1939, and in *New Directions* of 1939, have thrown further light on the subject; and I have also had the advantage of discussions with Mr. Thornton Wilder, who has explored the book more thoroughly than anyone else I have heard of. It is to be hoped that Mr. Wilder will some day publish something about *Finnegans Wake;* and in the meantime those interested in the book should consult the essays mentioned, upon which I have sometimes drawn in revising the present study.

One suggestion of Mr. Bishop's should certainly be noted here. He believes that the riddle of the letter is the riddle of life itself. This letter has been scratched up from a dung-heap and yet it has come from another world; it includes in its very brief length marriage, children and death, and things to eat and drink — all the primary features of life, beyond which the ideas of the illiterate writer evidently do not extend; and Earwicker can never really read it, though the text seems exceedingly simple and though he confronts it again and again.

I ought to amend what is said in this essay on the basis of a first reading by adding that *Finnegans Wake,* like *Ulysses,* gets better the more you go back to it. I do not know of any other books of which it is true as it is of Joyce's that, though parts of them may leave us blank or repel us when we try them the first time, they gradually build themselves up for us as we return to them and think

`I believe that the miscarriage of *Finnegans Wake,* in so far as it does miscarry, is due primarily to two tendencies of Joyce's which were already in evidence in *Ulysses:* the impulse, in the absence of dramatic power, to work up an epic impressiveness by multiplying and complicating detail, by filling in abstract diagrams and laying on intellectual conceits, till the organic effort at which he aims has been spoiled by too much that is synthetic; and a curious shrinking solicitude to conceal from the reader his real subjects. These subjects are always awkward and distressing: they have to do with the kind of feelings which people themselves conceal and which it takes courage in the artist to handle. And the more daring Joyce's subjects become, the more he tends to swathe them about with the fancywork of his literary virtuosity. It is as if it were not merely Earwicker who was frightened by the state of his emotions but as if Joyce were embarrassed, too.

Yet, with all this, *Finnegans Wake* has achieved certain amazing successes. Joyce has caught the psychology of sleep as no one else has ever caught it, laying hold on states of mind which it is difficult for the waking intellect to re-create, and distinguishing with marvelous delicacy between the different levels of dormant consciousness.

---

about them. That this should be true is due probably to some special defect of *rapport* between Joyce and the audience he is addressing, to some disease of his architectural faculty; but he compensates us partly for this by giving us more in the long run than we had realized at first was there, and he eventually produces the illusion that this fiction has a reality like life's, because, behind all the antics, the pedantry, the artificial patterns, something organic and independent of these is always revealing itself; and we end by recomposing a world in our mind as we do from the phenomena of experience. Mr. Max Eastman reports that Joyce once said to him, during a conversation on *Finnegans Wake,* when Mr. Eastman had suggested to Joyce that the demands made on the reader were too heavy and that he perhaps ought to provide a key: 'The demand that I make of my reader is that he should devote his whole life to reading my works.' It is in any case probably true that they will last you a whole lifetime.

There are the relative vividness of events reflected from the day before; the nightmare viscidity and stammering of the heavy slumbers of midnight; the buoyance and self-assertive vitality which gradually emerge from this; the half-waking of the early morning, which lapses back into the rigmaroles of dreams; the awareness, later, of the light outside, with its effect as of the curtain of the eyelids standing between the mind and the day. Through all this, the falling of twilight, the striking of the hours by the clock, the morning fog and its clearing, the bell for early mass, and the rising sun at the window, make themselves felt by the sleeper. With what brilliance they are rendered by Joyce! And the voices that echo in Earwicker's dream — the beings that seize upon him and speak through him: the Tree and the River, the eloquence of Shaun, the mumbling and running-on of the Old Men; the fluttery girl sweetheart, the resigned elderly wife, the nagging and jeering gibberish — close to madness and recalling the apparition of Virag in the Walpurgisnacht scene of *Ulysses,* but here identified with the Devil — which comes like an incubus with the darkness and through which the thickened voices of the Earwicker household occasionally announce themselves startlingly: 'Mawmaw, luk, your beeftay's fizzin' over' or 'Now a muss wash the little face.' Joyce has only to strike the rhythm and the timbre, and we know which of the spirits is with us.

Some of the episodes seem to me wholly successful: the Anna Livia chapter, for example, and the end of *Haveth Childers Everywhere,* which has a splendor and a high-spirited movement of a kind not matched elsewhere in Joyce. The passage in a minor key which precedes this major *crescendo* and describes Earwicker's real habitations — 'most respectable . . . thoroughly respectable . . . partly respectable,' and so forth — is a masterpiece of humorous sordidity (especially 'copious holes emitting mice'); and so is the inventory — on pages 183-184 — of all the useless and rubbishy objects in the house where Shem the Penman lives. The *Ballad of Persse O'Reilly* (*perce-oreille, earwig*) — which blazons the shame of Earwicker — is real dream literature and terribly funny; as is also the revelation — pages 572-573 — of the guilty and intricate sex relationships supposed to prevail in the Earwicker family, under the guise of one of those unintelligible summaries of a saint's legend or a Latin play. The waking-up chapter is charming in the passage — page 565 — in which the mother comforts the restless boy and in the summing-up — page 579 — of the married life of the Ear-wickers; and it is touchingly and thrillingly effective in throwing back on all that has gone before the shy im-poverished family pathos which it is Joyce's special des-tiny to express.

Where he is least happy, I think, is in such episodes as the voyage, 311 ff., the football game, 373 ff, and the siege of Sebastopol, 338 ff. (all in the dense nightmarish part of the book, which to me is, in general, the dullest). Joyce is best when he is idyllic, nostalgic, or going in-sane in an introspective way; he is not good at energetic action. There is never any direct aggressive clash between the pairs of opponents in Joyce, and there is consequently no real violence (except Dedalus' smashing the chandelier in self-defense against the reproach of his dead mother). All that Joyce is able to do when he wants to represent a battle is to concoct an uncouth gush of language. In gen-eral one feels, also, in *Finnegans Wake* the narrow limita-tions of Joyce's interests. He has tried to make it universal by having Earwicker take part in his dream in as many human activities as possible: but Joyce himself has not the key either to politics, to sport or to fighting. The de-partments of activity that come out best are such quiet ones as teaching and preaching.

The finest thing in the book, and one of the finest things Joyce has done, is the passage at the end where

Ann, the wife, is for the first time allowed to speak with
her full and mature voice. I have noted that Joyce's fiction usually deals with the tacit readjustment in the relationships between members of a family, the almost imper-
ceptible moment which marks the beginning of a phase. In
Finnegans Wake, the turning-point fixed is the moment
when the husband and wife know definitely — they
will wake up knowing it — that their own creative sexual
partnership is over. That current no longer holds them
polarized — as man and woman — toward one another; a
new polarization takes place: the father is pulled back toward the children. 'Illas! I wisht I had better glances,' he
thinks he hears Ann-Anna saying (page 626) 'to peer to
you through this baylight's growing. But you're changing,
acoolsha, you're changing from me, I can feel. Or is it me
is? I'm getting mixed. Brightening up and tightening
down. Yes, you're changing, sonhusband, and you're turning, I can feel you, for a daughterwife from the hills again.
Imlamaya. And she is coming. Swimming in my hindmoist.
Diveltaking on me tail. Just a whisk brisk sly spry spink
spank sprint of a thing theresomere, saultering. Saltarella
come to her own. I pity your oldself I was used to. Now a
younger's there.' It is the 'young thin pale soft shy slim
slip of a thing, sauntering by silvamoonlake' (page 202 in
the Anna Livia Plurabelle section) that she herself used
to be, who now seems to her awkward and pert, and the
wife herself is now the lower river running into the sea.
The water is wider here; the pace of the stream is calmer:
the broad day of experience has opened. 'I thought you
were all glittering with the noblest of carriage. You're
only a bumpkin. I thought you the great in all things, in
guilt and in glory. You're but a puny. Home!' She sees
him clearly now: he is neither Sir Tristram nor Lucifer;
and he is done with her and she with him. 'I'm loothing
them that's here and all I lothe. Loonely in me loneness.
For all their faults. I am passing out. O bitter ending! I'll

slip away before they're up. They'll never see me. Nor know. Nor miss me. And it's old and old it's sad and old it's sad and weary I go back to you, my cold father, my cold mad father, my cold mad feary father.' . . . The helpless and heartbreaking voices of the Earwicker children recur: 'Carry me along, taddy, like you done through the toy fair' — for now she is herself the child entrusting herself to the sea, flowing out into the daylight that is to be her annihilation . . . 'a way a lone a last a loved a long the' . . .

The Viconian cycle of existence has come full circle again. The unfinished sentence which ends the book is to find its continuation in the sentence without a beginning with which it opens. The river which runs into the sea must commence as a cloud again; the woman must give up life to the child. The Earwickers will wake to another day, but the night has made them older: the very release of the daylight brings a weariness that looks back to life's source.

In these wonderful closing pages, Joyce has put over all he means with poetry of an originality, a purity and an emotional power, such as to raise *Finnegans Wake,* for all its excesses, to the rank of a great work of literature.

1964. This essay was written in 1939, not long, as I have said, after the book's publication. Though I had read the instalments in *transition,* I had been through the whole book only once and had not become aware of its architecture, as solid and simple and monumental as the surface is complicated. I had not even grasped the full significance of the antithetical roles of Shem and Shaun, Earwicker's twin sons, who are reflected in all the other pairs of opposites: Mutt and Jute, the two washerwomen, the Mookse and the Gripes, the Ondt and the Gracehoper, etc.; nor that the first part of the book is dominated by the sensitive and poetic and mother-protected Shem, that the brothers struggle and merge in the darkness of deepest night, and that, emerging from this struggle, the sensual and practical, the conventional, rather boring Shaun grows into a giant figure who dominates the remaining episodes. The longer one reads the book, the more of it comes to life and the more it communicates emotion, and I should by no means say today as I have above that two-thirds of it is unsuccessful.

I should note also that from one of Joyce's published letters it appears that I was mistaken in supposing that old Johnny MacDougall was Ulster. I do not know whether anyone has suggested that — since the four old men in one of their aspects are supposed to represent the four gospels — one of the reasons for old Johnny's belatedness may be the very much later date than those of the other three gospels which used to be assigned to John.

PHILOCTETES: THE WOUND AND THE BOW

THE *Philoctetes* of Sophocles is far from being his most popular play. The myth itself has not been one of those which have excited the modern imagination. The idea of Philoctetes' long illness and his banishment to the bleak island is dreary or distasteful to the young, who like to identify themselves with men of action — with Heracles or Perseus or Achilles; and for adults the story told by Sophocles fails to set off such emotional charges as are liberated by the crimes of the Atreidai and the tragedies of the siege of Troy. Whatever may have been dashing in the legend has been lost with the other plays and poems that dealt with it. Philoctetes is hardly mentioned in Homer; and we have only an incomplete account of the plays by Aeschylus and Euripides, which hinged on a critical moment of the campaign of the Greeks at Troy and which seem to have exploited the emotions of Greek patriotism. We have only a few scattered lines and phrases from that other play by Sophocles on the subject, the *Philoctetes at Troy,* in which the humiliated hero was presumably to be cured of his ulcer and to proceed to his victory over Paris.

There survives only this one curious drama which presents Philoctetes in exile — a drama which does not supply us at all with what we ordinarily expect of Greek tragedy, since it culminates in no catastrophe, and which indeed resembles rather our modern idea of a comedy (though the record of the lost plays of Sophocles show that there must have been others like it). Its interest depends almost as much on the latent interplay of character, on a gradual psychological conflict, as that of *Le Misanthrope*. And it assigns itself, also, to a category even more special and less generally appealing through the fact (though this, again, was a feature not uncommon with Sophocles) that the conflict is not even allowed to take place between a man and a woman. Nor does it even put before us the spectacle — which may be made exceedingly thrilling — of the individual in conflict with his social group, which we get in such plays devoid of feminine interest as *Coriolanus* and *An Enemy of the People*. Nor is the conflict even a dual one, as most dramatic conflicts are — so that our emotions seesaw up and down between two opposed persons or groups: though Philoctetes and Odysseus struggle for the loyalty of Neoptolemus, he himself emerges more and more distinctly as representing an independent point of view, so that the contrast becomes a triple affair which makes more complicated demands on our sympathies.

A French dramatist of the seventeenth century, Chateaubrun, found the subject so inconceivable that, in trying to concoct an adaptation which would be acceptable to the taste of his time, he provided Philoctetes with a daughter named Sophie with whom Neoptolemus was to fall in love and thus bring the drama back to the reliable and eternal formula of Romeo and Juliet and the organizer who loves the factory-owner's daughter. And if we look for the imprint of the play on literature since the Renaissance, we shall find a very meager record: a chapter of Fénelon's *Télémaque*, a discussion in Lessing's *Laocoön*, a sonnet of Wordsworth's, a little play by André Gide, an adaptation by John Jay Chapman — this is all, so far as I know, that has any claim to interest.

And yet the play itself *is* most interesting, as some of these writers have felt; and it is certainly one of Sophocles'

masterpieces. If we come upon it in the course of reading
him, without having heard it praised, we are surprised to
be so charmed, so moved — to find ourselves in the presence of something that is so much less crude in its subtlety
than either a three-cornered modern comedy like *Candida*
or *La Parisienne* or an underplayed affair of male loyalty
in a story by Ernest Hemingway, to both of which it has
some similarity. It is as if having the three men on the
lonely island has enabled the highly sophisticated Sophocles to get further away from the framework of the old
myths on which he has to depend and whose barbarities,
anomalies and absurdities, tactfully and realistically
though he handles them, seem sometimes almost as much
out of place as they would in a dialogue by Plato. The
people of the *Philoctetes* seem to us more familiar than
they do in most of the other Greek tragedies;[1] and they
take on for us a more intimate meaning. Philoctetes remains in our mind, and his incurable wound and his invincible bow recur to us with a special insistence. But
what is it they mean? How is it possible for Sophocles to
make us accept them so naturally? Why do we enter with
scarcely a stumble into the situation of people who are
preoccupied with a snake-bite that lasts forever and a
weapon that cannot fail?

Let us first take account of the peculiar twist which
Sophocles seems to have given the legend, as it had come
to him from the old epics and the dramatists who had
used it before him.

The main outline of the story ran as follows: The demi-
god Heracles had been given by Apollo a bow that never
missed its mark. When, poisoned by Deianeira's robe, he
had had himself burned on Mount Oeta, he had per-

[1] 'Apropos of the rare occasions when the ancients seem just like us,
it always has seemed to me that a wonderful example was the repentance of the lad in the (*Philoctetes?*) play of Sophocles over his
deceit, and the restoration of the bow.' — Mr. Justice Holmes to Sir
Frederick Pollock, October 2, 1921.

suaded Philoctetes to light the pyre and had rewarded him
by bequeathing to him this weapon. Philoctetes had thus
been formidably equipped when he had later set forth
against Troy with Agamemnon and Menelaus. But on the
way they had to stop off at the tiny island of Chrysè to
sacrifice to the local deity. Philoctetes approched the
shrine first, and he was bitten in the foot by a snake. The
infection became peculiarly virulent; and the groans of
Philoctetes made it impossible to perform the sacrifice,
which would be spoiled by ill-omened sounds; the bite
began to suppurate with so horrible a smell that his companions could not bear to have him near them. They removed him to Lemnos, a neighboring island which was
much larger than Chrysè and inhabited, and sailed away
to Troy without him.

Philoctetes remained there ten years. The mysterious
wound never healed. In the meantime, the Greeks, hard
put to it at Troy after the deaths of Achilles and Ajax and
baffled by the confession of their soothsayer that he was
unable to advise them further, had kidnapped the soothsayer of the Trojans and had forced him to reveal to them
that they could never win till they had sent for Neoptolemus, the son of Achilles, and given him his father's armor,
and till they had brought Philoctetes and his bow.

Both these things were done. Philoctetes was healed at
Troy by the son of the physician Asclepius; and he fought
Paris in single combat and killed him. Philoctetes and
Neoptolemus became the heroes of the taking of Troy.

Both Aeschylus and Euripides wrote plays on this subject long before Sophocles did; and we know something
about them from a comparison of the treatments by the
three different dramatists which was written by Dion
Chrysostom, a rhetorician of the first century A.D. Both
these versions would seem to have been mainly concerned
with the relation of Philoctetes to the success of the Greek
campaign. All three of the plays dealt with the same epi-

sode: the visit of Odysseus to Lemnos for the purpose of getting the bow; and all represented Odysseus as particularly hateful to Philoctetes (because he had been one of those responsible for abandoning him on the island), and obliged to resort to cunning. But the emphasis of Sophocles' treatment appears fundamentally to have differed from that of the other two. In the drama of Aeschylus, we are told, Odysseus was not recognized by Philoctetes, and he seems simply to have stolen the bow. In Euripides, he was disguised by Athena in the likeness of another person, and he pretended that he had been wronged by the Greeks as Philoctetes had been. He had to compete with a delegation of Trojans, who had been sent to get the bow for their side and who arrived at the same time as he; and we do not know precisely what happened. But Dion Chrysostom regarded the play as 'a masterpiece of declamation' and 'a model of ingenious debate,' and Jebb thinks it probable that Odysseus won the contest by an appeal to Philoctetes' patriotism. Since Odysseus was pretending to have been wronged by the Greeks, he could point to his own behavior in suppressing his personal resentments in the interests of saving Greek honor. The moral theme thus established by Aeschylus and Euripides both would have been simply, like the theme of the wrath of Achilles, the conflict between the passions of an individual — in this case, an individual suffering from a genuine wrong — and the demands of duty to a common cause.

This conflict appears also in Sophocles; but it takes on a peculiar aspect. Sophocles, in the plays of his we have, shows himself particularly successful with people whose natures have been poisoned by narrow fanatical hatreds. Even allowing for the tendency of Greek heroes, in legend and history both, to fly into rather childish rages, we still feel on Sophocles' part some sort of special point of view, some sort of special sympathy, for these cases. Such people — Electra and the embittered old Oedipus — suffer as much as they hate: it is because they suffer they hate. They horrify, but they waken pity. Philoctetes is such another: a man obsessed by a grievance, which in his case he is to be kept from forgetting by an agonizing physical ailment; and for Sophocles his pain and hatred have a dignity and an interest. Just as it is by no means plain to Sophocles that in the affair of Antigone *versus* Cleon it is the official point of view of Cleon, representing the interests of his victorious faction, which should have the last word against Antigone, infuriated by a personal wrong; so it is by no means plain to him that the morality of Odysseus, who is lying and stealing for the fatherland, necessarily deserves to prevail over the animus of the stricken Philoctetes.

The contribution of Sophocles to the story is a third person who will sympathize with Philoctetes. This new character is Neoptolemus, the young son of Achilles, who, along with Philoctetes, is indispensable to the victory of the Greeks and who has just been summoned to Troy. Odysseus is made to bring him to Lemnos for the purpose of deceiving Philoctetes and shanghai-ing him aboard the ship.

The play opens with a scene between Odysseus and the boy, in which the former explains the purpose of their trip. Odysseus will remain in hiding in order not to be recognized by Philoctetes, and Neoptolemus will go up to the cave in which Philoctetes lives and win his confidence by pretending that the Greeks have robbed him of his father's armor, so that he, too, has a grievance against them. The youth in his innocence and candor objects when he is told what his rôle is to be, but Odysseus persuades him by reminding him that they can only take Troy through his obedience and that once they have taken Troy, he will be glorified for his bravery and wisdom. 'As soon as we have won,' Odysseus assures him, 'we shall conduct ourselves with perfect honesty. But for one short day of dishonesty, allow me to direct you what to do — and then forever after you will be known as the most righteous of men.' The line of argument adopted by Odysseus is one with which the politics of our time have made us very familiar. 'Isn't it base, then, to tell false-hoods?' Neoptolemus asks. 'Not,' Odysseus replies, 'when a falsehood will bring our salvation.'

Neoptolemus goes to talk to Philoctetes. He finds him in the wretched cave — described by Sophocles with char-acteristic realism: the bed of leaves, the crude wooden bowl, the filthy bandages drying in the sun — where he has been living in rags for ten years, limping out from time to time to shoot wild birds or to get himself wood and water. The boy hears the harrowing story of Philoc-tetes' desertion by the Greeks and listens to his indigna-tion. The ruined captain begs Neoptolemus to take him back to his native land, and the young man pretends to consent. (Here and elsewhere I am telescoping the scenes and simplifying a more complex development.) But just as they are leaving for the ship, the ulcer on Philoctetes' foot sets up an ominous throbbing in preparation for one of its periodical burstings: 'She returns from time to time,' says the invalid, 'as if she were sated with her wander-ings.' In a moment he is stretched on the ground, writhing in abject anguish and begging the young man to cut off his foot. He gives Neoptolemus the bow, telling him to take care of it till the seizure is over. A second spasm, worse than the first, reduces him to imploring the boy to throw him into the crater of the Lemnian volcano: so he himself, he says, had lit the fire which consumed the tor-mented Heracles and had got in return these arms, which he is now handing on to Neoptolemus. The pain abates a little; 'It comes and goes,' says Philoctetes; and he en-treats the young man not to leave him. 'Don't worry about

that. We'll stay.' 'I shan't even make you swear it, my son.
'It would not be right to leave you' (it would not be right,
of course, even from the Greeks' point of view). They
shake hands on it. A third paroxysm twists the cripple;
now he asks Neoptolemus to carry him to the cave, but
shrinks from his grasp and struggles. At last the abscess
bursts, the dark blood begins to flow. Philoctetes, faint and
sweating, falls asleep.

The sailors who have come with Neoptolemus urge him
to make off with the bow. 'No,' the young man replies.
'He cannot hear us; but I am sure that it will not be
enough for us to recapture the bow without him. It is he
who is to have the glory — it was he the god told us to
bring.'

While they are arguing, Philoctetes awakes and thanks
the young man with emotion: 'Agamemnon and Menelaus were not so patient and loyal.' But now they must get
him to the ship, and the boy will have to see him unde-
ceived and endure his bitter reproaches. 'The men will
carry you down,' says Neoptolemus. 'Don't trouble them:
just help me up,' Philoctetes replies. 'It would be too disagreeable for them to take me all the way to the ship.' The
smell of the suppuration has been sickening. The young
man begins to hesitate. The other sees that he is in doubt
about something: 'You're not so overcome with disgust at
my disease that you don't think you can have me on the
ship with you?' —

οὐ δή σε δυσχέρεια τοῦ νοσήματος

ἔπεισεν ὥστε μή μ' ἄγειν ναύτην ἔτι;

The answer is one of the most effective of those swift and
brief speeches of Sophocles which for the first time make
a situation explicit (my attempts to render this dialogue
colloquially do no justice to the feeling and point of the
verse):

ἅπαντα δυσχέρεια, τὴν αὑτοῦ φύσιν

ὅταν λιπών τις δρᾷ τὰ μὴ προσεικότα.

'Everything becomes disgusting when you are false to your
own nature and behave in an unbecoming way.'

He confesses his real intentions; and a painful scene
occurs. Philoctetes denounces the boy in terms that would
be appropriate for Odysseus; he sees himself robbed of his
bow and left to starve on the island. The young man is
deeply worried: 'Why did I ever leave Scyros?' he asks
himself. 'Comrades, what shall I do?'

At this moment, Odysseus, who has been listening,
pops out from his hiding place. With a lash of abuse at
Neoptolemus, he orders him to hand over the arms. The
young man's spirit flares up: when Odysseus invokes the
will of Zeus, he tells him that he is degrading the gods by
lending them his own lies. Philoctetes turns on Odysseus
with an invective which cannot fail to impress the generous Neoptolemus: Why have they come for him now? he
demands. Is he not still just as ill-omened and loathsome
as he had been when they made him an outcast? They
have only come back to get him because the gods have
told them they must.

The young man now defies his mentor and takes his
stand with Philoctetes. Odysseus threatens him: if he
persists, he will have the whole Greek army against him,
and they will see to it that he is punished for his treason.
Neoptolemus declares his intention of taking Philoctetes
home; he gives him back his bow. Odysseus tries to inter-
vene; but Philoctetes has got the bow and aims an arrow
at him. Neoptolemus seizes his hand and restrains him.
Odysseus, always prudent, beats a quiet retreat.

Now the boy tries to persuade the angry man that he
should, nevertheless, rescue the Greeks. 'I have proved my
good faith,' says Neoptolemus; 'you know that I am not
going to coerce you. Why be so wrong-headed? When the

gods afflict us, we are obliged to bear our misfortunes; but must people pity a man who suffers through his own choice? The snake that bit you was an agent of the gods, it was the guardian of the goddess's shrine, and I swear to you by Zeus that the sons of Asclepius will cure you if you let us take you to Troy.' Philoctetes is incredulous, refuses. 'Since you gave me your word,' he says, 'take me home again.' 'The Greeks will attack me and ruin me.' 'I'll defend you.' 'How can you?' 'With my bow.' Neoptolemus is forced to consent.

But now Heracles suddenly appears from the skies and declares to Philoctetes that what the young man says is true, and that it is right for him to go to Troy. He and the son of Achilles shall stand together like lions and shall gloriously carry the day. — The *deus ex machina* here may of course figure a change of heart which has taken place in Philoctetes as the result of his having found a man who recognizes the wrong that has been done him and who is willing to champion his cause in defiance of all the Greek forces. His patron, the chivalrous Heracles, who had himself performed so many generous exploits, asserts his influence over his heir. The long hatred is finally exorcised.

In a fine lyric utterance which ends the play, Philoctetes says farewell to the cavern, where he has lain through so many nights listening to the deep-voiced waves as they crashed against the headland, and wetted by the rain and the spray blown in by the winter gales. A favorable wind has sprung up; and he sails away to Troy.

It is possible to guess at several motivations behind the writing of the *Philoctetes*. The play was produced in 409, when — if the tradition of his longevity be true — Sophocles would have been eighty-seven; and it is supposed to have been followed by the *Oedipus Coloneus*, which is assigned to 405 or 406. The latter deals directly with old age; but it would appear that the *Philoctetes* anticipates this theme in another form. Philoctetes, like the outlawed

Oedipus, is impoverished, humbled, abandoned by his people, exacerbated by hardship and chagrin. He is accursed: Philoctetes' ulcer is an equivalent for the abhorrent sins of Oedipus, parricide and incest together, which have made of the ruler a pariah. And yet somehow both are sacred persons who have acquired superhuman powers, and who are destined to be purged of their guilt. One passage from the earlier play is even strikingly repeated in the later. The conception of the wave-beaten promontory and the sick man lying in his cave assailed by the wind and rain turns up in the *Oedipus Coloneus* (Coloneus was Sophocles' native deme) with a figurative moral value. So the ills of old age assail Oedipus. Here are the lines, in A. E. Housman's translation:

> This man, as me, even so,
> Have the evil days overtaken;
> And like as a cape sea-shaken
> With tempest at earth's last verges
> And shock of all winds that blow,
> His head the seas of woe,
> The thunders of awful surges
> Ruining overflow:
> Blown from the fall of even,
>   Blown from the dayspring forth,
> Blown from the moon in heaven,
>   Blown from night and the North.

But Oedipus has endured as Philoctetes has endured in the teeth of all the cold and the darkness, the screaming winds and the bellowing breakers: the blind old man is here in his own person the headland that stands against the storm.

We may remember a widely current story about the creator of these two figures. It is said that one of Sophocles' sons brought him into court in his advanced old age on the complaint that he was no longer competent to manage his property. The old poet is supposed to have recited a passage from the play which he had been writing: the chorus in praise of Coloneus, with its clear song of nightingales, its wine-dark ivy, its crocus glowing golden and its narcissus moist with dew, where the stainless stream of the Cephisus wanders through the broad-swelling plain and where the gray-leaved olive grows of itself beneath the gaze of the gray-eyed Athena — shining Colonus, breeder of horses and of oarsmen whom the Nereids lead. The scene had been represented on the stage and Sophocles had been made to declare: 'If I am Sophocles, I am not mentally incapable; if I am mentally incapable, I am not Sophocles.' In any case, the story was that the tribunal, composed of his fellow clansmen, applauded and acquitted the poet and censored the litigating son. The ruined and humiliated heroes of Sophocles' later plays are still persons of mysterious virtue, whom their fellows are forced to respect.

There is also a possibility, even a strong probability, that Sophocles intended Philoctetes to be identified with Alcibiades. This brilliant and unique individual, one of the great military leaders of the Athenians, had been accused by political opponents of damaging the sacred statues of Hermes and burlesquing the Eleusinian mysteries, and had been summoned to stand trial at Athens while he was away on his campaign against Sicily. He had at once gone over to the Spartans, commencing that insolent career of shifting allegiances which ended with his returning to the Athenian side. At a moment of extreme danger, he had taken over a part of the Athenian fleet and had defeated the Spartans in two sensational battles in 411 and 410, thus sweeping them out of the Eastern Aegean and enabling the Athenians to dominate the Hellespont. The *Philoctetes* was produced in 409, when the Athenians already wanted him back and were ready to cancel the charges against him and to restore him to citizenship. Alcibiades was a startling example of a bad character who was indispensable. Plutarch says that Aristophanes well describes the Athenian feeling about Alcibiades when he writes: 'They miss him and hate him and long to have him back.' And the malady of Philoctetes my have figured his moral defects: the unruly and unscrupulous nature which, even though he seems to have been innocent of the charges brought against him, had given them a certain plausibility. It must have looked to the Athenians, too, after the victories of Abydos and Cyzicus, as if he possessed an invincible bow. Plutarch says that the men who had served under him at the taking of Cyzicus did actually come to regard themselves as undefeatable and refused to share quarters with other soldiers who had fought in less successful engagements.

Yet behind both the picture of old age and the line in regard to Alcibiades, one feels in the *Philoctetes* a more general and fundamental idea: the conception of superior strength as inseparable from disability.

For the superiority of Philoctetes does not reside merely in the enchanted bow. When Lessing replied to Winckelmann, who had referred to Sophocles' cripple as if he were an example of the conventional idea of impassive classical fortitude, he pointed out that, far from exemplifying impassivity, Philoctetes becomes completely demoralized every time he has one of his seizures, and yet that this only heightens our admiration for the pride which prevents him from escaping at the expense of helping those who have deserted him. 'We despise,' says the objectors, 'any man from whom bodily pain extorts a shriek. Ay, but not always; not for the first time, nor if we see that the sufferer strains every nerve to stifle the expression of his pain; not if we know him otherwise to be a man of firmness; still less if we witness evidences of his firmness in the very midst of his sufferings, and observe that, although

pain may have extorted a shriek, it has extorted nothing
else from him, but that on the contrary he submits to the
prolongation of his pain rather than renounce one iota of
his resolutions, even where such a concession would
promise him the termination of his misery.'

André Gide, in his *Philoctète*, the obstinacy of the invalid hermit takes on a character almost mystical. By persisting in his bleak and lonely life, the Philoctetes of Gide
wins the love of a more childlike Neoptolemus and even
compels the respect of a less hard-boiled Odysseus. He is
practicing a kind of virtue superior not only to the virtue
of the latter, with his code of obedience to the demands of
the group, but also to that of the former, who forgets his
patriotic obligations for those of a personal attachment.
There is something above the gods, says the Philoctetes of
Gide; and it is virtue to devote oneself to this. But what is
it? asks Neoptolemus. I do not know, he answers; oneself!
The misfortune of his exile on the island has enabled him
to perfect himself: 'I have learned to express myself better,' he tells them, 'now that I am no longer with men.
Between hunting and sleeping, I occupy myself with
thinking. My ideas, since I have been alone so that nothing, not even suffering, disturbs them, have taken a subtle
course which sometimes I can hardly follow. I have come
to know more of the secrets of life than my masters had
ever revealed to me. And I took to telling the story of my
sufferings, and if the phrase was very beautiful, I was by
so much consoled; I even sometimes forgot my sadness by
uttering it. I came to understand that words inevitably become more beautiful from the moment they are no longer
put together in response to the demands of others. . . .'
The Philoctetes of Gide is, in fact, a literary man: at once
a moralist and an artist, whose genius becomes purer and
deeper in ratio to his isolation and outlawry. In the end,
he lets the intruders steal the bow after satisfying himself
that Neoptolemus can handle it, and subsides into a bliss-

ful tranquillity, much relieved that there is no longer any
reason for people to seek him out.

With Gide we come close to a further implication,
which even Gide does not fully develop but which must
occur to the modern reader: the idea that genius and disease, like strength and mutilation, may be inextricably
bound up together. It is significant that the only two
writers of our time who have especially interested themselves in Philoctetes — André Gide and John Jay Chapman
— should both be persons who have not only, like the hero
of the play, stood at an angle to the morality of society and
defended their position with stubbornness, but who have
suffered from psychological disorders which have made
them, in Gide's case, ill-regarded by his fellows; in Chapman's case, excessively difficult. Nor is it perhaps accidental that Charles Lamb, with his experience of his sister's
insanity, should in his essay on *The Convalescent* choose
the figure of Philoctetes as a symbol for his own 'nervous
fever.'

And we must even, I believe, grant Sophocles some
special insight into morbid psychology. The tragic themes
of all three of the great dramatists — the madnesses, the
murders and the incests — may seem to us sufficiently morbid. The hero with an incurable wound was even a stock
subject of myth not confined to the Philoctetes legend:
there was also the story of Telephus, also wounded and
also indispensable, about which both Sophocles and Euripides wrote plays. But there is a difference between the
treatment that Sophocles gives to these conventional epic
subjects and the treatments of the other writers. Aeschylus
is more religious and philosophical; Euripides more romantic and sentimental. Sophocles by comparison is clinical.
Arthur Platt, who had a special interest in the scientific
aspect of the classics, says that Sophocles was scrupulously
up-to-date in the physical science of his time. He was himself closely associated by tradition with the cult of the

healer Asclepius, whose son is to cure Philoctetes: Lucian had read a poem which he had dedicated to the doctor-god; and Plutarch reports that Asclepius was supposed to have visited his hearth. He is said also to have been actually a priest of another of the medical cults. Platt speaks particularly of his medical knowledge — which is illustrated by the naturalism and precision of his description of Philoctetes' infected bite.

But there is also in Sophocles a cool observation of the behavior of psychological derangements. The madness of Ajax is a genuine madness, from which he recovers to be horrified at the realization of what he has done. And it was not without good reason that Freud laid Sophocles under contribution for the naming of the Oedipus complex — since Sophocles had not only dramatized the myth that dwelt with the violation of the incest taboo, but had exhibited the suppressed impulse behind it in the speech in which he makes Jocasta attempt to reassure Oedipus by reminding him that it was not uncommon for men to dream about sleeping with their mothers — 'and he who thinks nothing of this gets through his life most easily.' Those who do not get through life so easily are presented by Sophocles with a very firm grasp on the springs of their abnormal conduct. Electra is what we should call nowadays schizophrenic: the woman who weeps over the urn which is supposed to contain her brother's ashes is not 'integrated,' as we say, with the fury who prepares her mother's murder. And certainly the fanaticism of Antigone — 'fixated,' like Electra, on her brother — is intended to be abnormal, too. The banishment by Jebb from Sophocles' text of the passage in which Antigone explains the unique importance of a brother and his juggling of the dialogue in the scene in which she betrays her indifference to the feelings of the man she is supposed to marry are certainly among the curiosities of Victorian scholarship — though he was taking his cue from the complaint of Goethe that

Antigone had been shown by Sophocles as acting from trivial motives and Goethe's hope that her speech about her brother might some day be shown to be spurious. Aristotle had cited this speech of Antigone's as an outstanding example of the principle that if anything peculiar occurs in a play the cause must be shown by the dramatist. It was admitted by Jebb that his rewriting of these passages had no real textual justification; and in one case he violates glaringly the convention of the one-line dialogue. To accept his emendation would involve the assumption that Aristotle did not know what the original text had been and was incapable of criticizing the corrupted version. No: Antigone forgets her fiancé and kills herself for her brother. Her timid sister (like Electra's timid sister) represents the normal feminine point of view. Antigone's point of view is peculiar, as Aristotle says. (The real motivation of the Antigone has been retraced with unmistakable accuracy by Professor Walter R. Agard in *Classical Philology* of July, 1937.)

These insane or obsessed people of Sophocles all display a perverse kind of nobility. I have spoken of the authority of expiation which emanates from the blasted Oedipus. Even the virulence of Electra's revenge conditions the intensity of her tenderness for Orestes. And so the maniacal fury which makes Ajax run amok, the frenzy of Heracles in the Nessus robe, terribly though they transform their victims, can never destroy their virtue of heroes. The poor disgraced Ajax will receive his due of honor after his suicide and will come to stand higher in our sympathies than Menelaus and Agamemnon, those obtuse and brutal captains, who here as in the *Philoctetes* are obviously no favorites of Sophocles'. Heracles in his final moments bids his spirit curb his lips with steel to keep him from crying out, and carry him through his self-destructive duty as a thing that is to be desired.

Some of these maladies are physical in origin, others are

psychological; but they link themselves with one another. The case of Ajax connects psychological disorder as we get it in Electra, for example, with the access of pain and rage that causes Heracles to kill the herald Lichas; the case of Heracles connects a poisoning that produces a murderous fury with an infection that, though it distorts the personality, does not actually render the victim demented: the wound of Philoctetes, whose agony comes in spasms like that of Heracles. All these cases seem intimately related.

It has been the misfortune of Sophocles to figure in academic tradition as the model of those qualities of coolness and restraint which that tradition regards as classical. Those who have never read him — remembering the familiar statue — are likely to conceive something hollow and marmoreal. Actually, as C. M. Bowra says, Sophocles is 'passionate and profound.' Almost everything that we are told about him by the tradition of the ancient world suggests equanimity and amiability and the enjoyment of unusual good fortune. But there is one important exception: the anecdote in Plato's *Republic* in which Sophocles is represented as saying that the release from amorous desire which had come to him in his old age had been like a liberation from an insane and cruel master. He *has* balance and logic, of course: those qualities that the classicists admire; but these qualities only count because they master so much savagery and madness. Somewhere even in the fortunate Sophocles there had been a sick and raving Philoctetes.

And now let us go back to the *Philoctetes* as a parable of human character. I should interpret the fable as follows. The victim of a malodorous disease which renders him abhorrent to society and periodically degrades him and makes him helpless is also the master of a superhuman art which everybody has to respect and which the normal man finds he needs. A practical man like Odysseus, at the same time coarse-grained and clever, imagines that

he can somehow get the bow without having Philoctetes
on his hands or that he can kidnap Philoctetes the bowman without regard for Philoctetes the invalid. But the
young son of Achilles knows better. It is at the moment
when his sympathy for Philoctetes would naturally inhibit
his cheating him — so the supernatural influences in Sophocles are often made with infinite delicacy to shade into
subjective motivations — it is at this moment of his natural
shrinking that it becomes clear to him that the words of
the seer had meant that the bow would be useless without
Philoctetes himself. It is in the nature of things — of this
world where the divine and the human fuse — that they
cannot have the irresistible weapon without its loathsome
owner, who upsets the processes of normal life by his
curses and his cries, and who in any case refuses to work
for men who have exiled him from their fellowship.

It is quite right that Philoctetes should refuse to come
to Troy. Yet it is also decreed that he shall be cured when
he shall have been able to forget his grievance and to devote his divine gifts to the service of his own people. It is
right that he should refuse to submit to the purposes of
Odysseus, whose only idea is to exploit him. How then is
the gulf to be got over between the ineffective plight of
the bowman and his proper use of his bow, between his
ignominy and his destined glory? Only by the intervention
of one who is guileless enough and human enough to treat
him, not as a monster, nor yet as a mere magical property
which is wanted for accomplishing some end, but simply
as another man, whose sufferings elicit his sympathy and
whose courage and pride he admires. When this human
relation has been realized, it seems at first that it is to have
the consequence of frustrating the purpose of the expedition and ruining the Greek campaign. Instead of winning
over the outlaw, Neoptolemus has outlawed himself as
well, at a time when both the boy and the cripple are desperately needed by the Greeks. Yet in taking the risk to

his cause which is involved in the recognition of his common humanity with the sick man, in refusing to break his word, he dissolves Philoctetes' stubbornness, and thus cures him and sets him free, and saves the campaign as well.